The Death of a Confederate

The Death of a Confederate

SELECTIONS FROM THE LETTERS

OF THE ARCHIBALD SMITH FAMILY

OF ROSWELL, GEORGIA, 1864–1956

Edited by Arthur N. Skinner &

James L. Skinner

THE UNIVERSITY OF GEORGIA PRESS

ATHENS & LONDON

©1996 by the
University of Georgia Press
Athens, Georgia 30602
All rights reserved
Designed by Richard Hendel
Set in Bulmer by Books International Inc.
Printed and bound by Thomson-Shore, Inc.
The paper in this book meets the
guidelines for permanence and durability
of the Committee on Production
Guidelines for Book Longevity of the
Council on Library Resources.
Printed in the United States of America
00   99   98   97   96   c   5   4   3   2   1

Library of Congress
Cataloging in Publication Data

The death of a Confederate : selections from the letters of
the Archibald Smith family of Roswell, Georgia,
1864–1956 / edited by Arthur N. Skinner and James L.
Skinner.
p.   cm.
Includes bibliographical references (p.   ) and index.
ISBN 0-8203-1844-2 (alk. paper)
1. Smith, Archibald, 1801–1886—Family—
Correspondence. 2. Smith family—Correspondence.
3. Roswell (Ga.)—Biography. 4. United States—
History—Civil War, 1861–1865—Personal narratives,
Confederate.   5. Georgia—History—Civil War,
1861–1865—Personal narratives, Confederate.
I. Skinner, Arthur N.   II. Skinner, James L.
CT275.S52417A4   1996
973.7'82—dc20 95-52514

British Library Cataloging in Publication Data available

FRONTISPIECE: William Seagrove ("Willie") Smith
(1834–65). Courtesy of the Georgia Department of
Archives and History

For Willie

DE MORTUIS NIL NISI BONUM

Title of a Speech by

William Seagrove Smith,

from the Junior Exhibition,

Oglethorpe University,

March 29, 1854

Preface ix

Genealogical Chart xiii
   The Family of
   William Seagrove Smith

Introduction xv

List of Correspondents xlvii

"A Time of Anxiety and Apprehension"
   January–May 1864 3

"Driven from Our Homes"
   May–November 1864 45

"The Vile Wicked Wretch"
   November–December 1864 141

"The Failure of Our Hopes"
   January–July 1865 161

The Monument
   September 1865– February 1867 199

"The Last Time I Saw Him"
   1869–1956 250

Afterword 268

Bibliography 271

Index 281

Contents

Preface

This book is about the Civil War and its aftermath in the South. Drawn from actual correspondence, the book tells the story of a loyal Confederate planter's family that settled in the wilds of northwest Georgia. It tells how General Sherman's march through that state uprooted the family and swept them along in a relentless tide of tragedy, and it tells how they coped with the chaos that enveloped the South at the end of the Civil War. Central to their story is the loss of their oldest son and how his memory was preserved by the family, was obscured by the passage of time, and was ultimately recovered.

William Seagrove ("Willie") Smith (1834–65) was the oldest son of Archibald and Anne Magill Smith of Camden County, Georgia, who had migrated in 1838, with five other families from the Georgia coast, to found the "colony" of Roswell, Georgia, some twenty miles north of what would later become Atlanta. Maintaining their agricultural ways apart from the other members of what became largely an industrial colony, the Smiths first rented a farm in the Lebanon community north of the others; then, in 1844–45 Archibald Smith built the plantation home in Roswell where the Smiths' papers were found after the Skinner family inherited the home in 1981. We have deposited these papers at the Georgia Department of Archives and History in Atlanta (AC 88-012).

Our purpose in this book is to present selections from those materials that revolve around the death of Willie, a sensitive and intelligent young man who, after attempts at textile manufacturing in Arkansas and teaching in his native St. Marys, Georgia, enlisted on November 19, 1861, as a private in Company A (Captain Screven's Company) of the First (Olmstead's) Regiment of Georgia Infantry, Battalion of the Savannah Volunteer Guards, subsequently known as Company A, Eighteenth Battalion, Georgia Infantry. He was detailed to the Signal Corps in late 1862, remained on duty with it in Savannah until the fall of that city at the end of 1864, and participated in General Hardee's retreat through the Carolinas to Raleigh, North Carolina, where Willie died of disease on July 7, 1865.

Paralleling and complementing Willie Smith's story is that of his younger brother, Archie (1844–1923), who enrolled in the Georgia Military Institute (GMI) in Marietta in 1862 and served as quartermaster sergeant with the GMI cadets as they were pushed back by Sherman's march toward Savannah. The family had hoped that Archie, who they felt was not physically fit for the hardships of warfare, would be safe at the institute. Although circumstance placed him as much in harm's way as it had his older brother, Archie safely endured the war and subsequently fathered the last generation of the Archibald Smiths.

Our annotations are based on papers and Bibles found in the Smith home, on materials on file at the Georgia Department of Archives and History and the Georgia Historical Society, and on books and sources listed in the bibliography. We are particularly indebted to Robert Manson Myers's monumental work, *The Children of Pride*. We gratefully acknowledge the assistance of Elizabeth Reid Murray of Raleigh, North Carolina, for help with local names and places, and of Eloise Y. Thompson of St. Marys, Georgia, in helping with names associated with this early home of the Smiths, as well as the assistance of the capable staffs at the Georgia Department of Archives and History; the Georgia Historical Society; the Woodruff Library of Emory University; the University of Georgia Libraries; the Thomason Library of Presbyterian College; the Bryan Lang Library of Woodbine, Georgia; the Historic Roswell Preservation Commission; the Roswell Historical Society;

The Smith Plantation Home, Roswell, Georgia, as it appeared in 1940

the Bartram Trail Regional Library, Washington, Georgia; and the South Georgia Regional Library, Valdosta. Thanks are due also to John Idol of Hillsborough, North Carolina, and to Jim Skinner of Annapolis, Maryland, for help and encouragement. Ramona Skinner read proof carefully.

The Smiths' letters and recollections were found widely scattered throughout their Roswell home. Many of the letters presented in this volume were found in Willie Smith's trunk, which he shipped to his family as Sherman approached his duty station in Savannah. In publishing these letters, we have, for the sake of the reader, edited them lightly, silently correcting spelling errors and adding punctuation and paragraph breaks where common and visual sense demand them. Willie's mother, Anne Magill Smith, and sisters, Lizzie and Helen, for example, wrote their letters in solid, virtually unpunctuated blocks. After an introduction to the letters, we break into their sequence only to provide what we think are essential bridges to letters that follow.

We have included in this volume most of the extant Smith correspondence dated 1864 and 1865. From 1866 on, we became increasingly selective in order to focus attention on accounts and recollections of William Smith's life and death, on the difficult but loving arrangements that were made for his gravestone, on the Smiths' attempts to reassemble their shattered lives in Roswell following the Civil War, and on some of the significant events in the life of the family through the next generation. In the Smith-Stephens correspondence at the end of the volume, we concentrated on those letters that describe their friendship and their shared love of the South. Throughout all the correspondence we deleted letters or portions of letters that seemed repetitious or that distracted attention from the main flow of events.

As much as possible we have preserved the Smiths' writing, including the frequent cropping of vowels and syllables, as in *drop'd, bless'd, enrol'd, rec'd, servts* [servants], and *oppy* [opportunity]; the characteristic British spellings, as in *pretence, parlour, favourable,* and *shewing;* and even the irregular plural forms, as in *lilys, poppys, berrys,* and *societys.* Such light editing not only preserves much of the original flavor of the correspondence but also reveals individual habits of the correspondents, for example those that the Smiths had of ending their letters with some form of the words *affection* and *affectionately:* Anne Smith used *aff,* Archibald, *affe,* William, *afft,* and Archie, *affct.*

We are compelled to add the fact that we have no blood ties to the Smith family and invite the reader to share our own objective fascination with these people. The last living member of the family, our mother's aunt, Mary Norvell Smith (1890–1981), married Archie's youngest son, Arthur William Smith (1881–1960), a sensitive and artistic Atlanta architect whom we grew up calling "Uncle Arthur."

GENEALOGICAL CHART: *The Family of William Seagrove Smith*

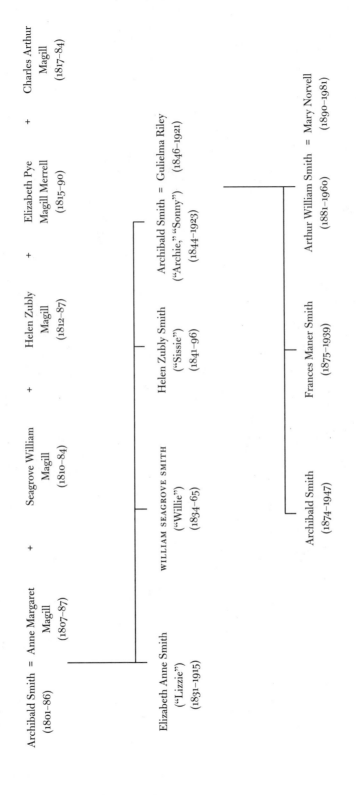

Introduction

Our purpose in this introduction is to provide enough background on the Smith family of Roswell, Georgia, to enable the reader to appreciate their Civil War correspondence, particularly with their eldest son, Willie. We will also survey extant family letters and recollections to the year 1864, when dislocation and war tear the family apart. At this point we will allow the Smiths to speak for themselves, editing their correspondence lightly and providing explanatory notes.

In late December 1838 a planter named Archibald Smith (1801–86) led his family from Camden County on the Georgia-Florida line into the foothills of north Georgia, just over the Chattahoochee River, into an area that had been ceded by the Cherokee Nation only three years before.[1] In the wagons approaching the new village of Roswell were his wife, Anne Magill Smith (1807–87); their daughter, Elizabeth Anne Smith (1831–1915); their son,

William Seagrove Smith (1834–65); and two of Mrs. Smith's sisters: Helen Zubly Magill (1812–87) and Elizabeth Pye Magill (1815–90).[2]

They were leaving two failed plantations: Appenzelle, several miles up the St. Marys River from the Atlantic Ocean and named after the Swiss canton from whence both Archibald Smith and his wife's Zubly ancestors had come; and Jersey Point, north of St. Marys on King's Bay.[3] Smith had tried to grow rice at Appenzelle and cotton at Jersey Point. Contributing to his problems had been a failed effort to educate and to free his slaves.[4] Although the Smiths were slaveholding planters, they were hardly genteel grandees unaccustomed to work, and although they were an old coastal family, they hardly represented "old money."

The family was joining five other planter families from the Georgia coast in an almost utopian experiment that had been inspired by Roswell King (1765–1844), who, in early travels into the north Georgia gold country as a representative for the Bank of Darien, had noted the industrial potential of the water power available from Cedar (Vickery) Creek as it plunged into the Chattahoochee. Roswell's son Barrington (1789–1866) would soon become the leader of this group of families—known as "The Colony"—who were not moving simply to escape the sickly climate of the coast. They wanted to build a community that would combine industry and agriculture. Because they were all Presbyterians, their vision included an ideal religious community as well, and they founded the Roswell Presbyterian Church in 1839, the same year they began the Roswell Manufacturing Company, which soon began producing cotton goods and, by 1846, woolens.

Archibald Smith was to maintain his agricultural ways long after the other families moved into the center of the village and built beautiful Greek Revival homes there. Roswell King and his daughter Eliza Hand built Primrose Cottage. King's son Barrington, after first living in a cabin whose frequent additions earned it the sobriquet of "The Labyrinth" or "The Castle," built the superb Barrington Hall. James Stephens Bulloch (1793–1849) moved his family into Bulloch Hall; the family of John Dunwody (1786–1858) occupied Dunwody Hall (later Mimosa Hall); and the Reverend Nathaniel Alpheus Pratt (1796–1879), called to be the minister at the Presbyterian Church, built Great Oaks.

These homes were finished before Archibald Smith built his farmhouse—not a mansion like the others—a mile north of the center of the village, a symbolic distance that indicated not only his wish to maintain his agricultural ways but also a desire for the privacy that would always characterize his descendants. He had first farmed a plantation to the north in the community

Archibald Smith (1801–86) and Anne Magill Smith (1807–87).
Courtesy of the Georgia Department of Archives and History

Willie Smith with his sister Elizabeth Anne ("Lizzie") Smith (1831–1915).

Archibald ("Archie") Smith (1844–1923), with his sister Helen Zubly ("Sissie") Smith (1841–96). Courtesy of the Georgia Department of Archives and History

of Lebanon before he purchased land lot 413, a forty-acre tract, and completed his plantation home on it in July 1845.

By the time the Smiths had moved into their home, the family had grown with the birth of two more children, Helen Zubly (1841–96) and Archibald (1844–1923), always called Archie or Sonny. The Smiths obviously intended the older son, Willie, to inherit the plantation, for they sent him off for a gentleman's education at Oglethorpe University, then in Milledgeville, from which he was graduated in 1855. His older sister, Lizzie, had received some formal education at the Greensboro (Georgia) Female College, but it seems that the younger children, Helen and Archie, were educated mostly at home, under the tutelage of their aunt Helen Zubly Magill.

Charter members of the Roswell Presbyterian Church, the Smiths were deeply religious and somewhat puritanical. Lizzie played the piano and organ at the church, while Helen Magill taught a children's Sunday school class there. There are frequent references in the family correspondence to their walking the half mile from their home to the church. In some recollections composed around 1910, Archie Smith comments on a major difference between other "Colony people" and his father's family: "They proposed to keep the devil out of the town but most of them were willing for him to have a cat hole in the back door. Father did not know of the cat hole arrangement and tried to keep him out altogether. This made trouble."[5]

Archie also notes a distinction between all planter families in Roswell and those who came later: "What were called the Colony people were as distinct almost from the ordinary settlers of the country as from the Indians, who had lately been removed." Wealth and education seem to be the distinguishing characteristics: "Most of the 'colony people' had handsome houses, plenty of servants, carriages, and a plantation. They were an educated and exclusive society. They had their own church with an educated pastor who was one of them, and a good school, while the others had log cabins and cultivated small patches or worked in the cotton mill built by the colony, and many of them had no education except what they got in the colony Sunday school." Thus is recorded a distinction between the low country planters and the up-country farmers, one that was sharpened by those who came to work in the Roswell mills.

But Archibald Smith concerned himself primarily with agriculture and agricultural experimentation. He farmed almost four hundred acres, largely to the north and northwest of his home, and kept notebooks (now part of the Smith Papers) about his times of planting, use of fertilizers, and the weather. He wrote a letter to the *New England Farmer,* published on January 18, 1851, in which he detailed his observations on agriculture in Georgia.[6] He was, however, also a stockholder in the Roswell Manufacturing Company, and it seems that from it the family derived most of its income during the Civil War. As Anne Smith told Willie in a letter of January 15, 1864, "Economically you know the Factory is our only means of support."[7]

The blend of agriculture and industry so characteristic of early Roswell is mirrored in a marriage that took place in the Smith family. The first assistant hired to help Barrington King with the Roswell Manufacturing Company was Henry Merrell (1816–83) of Utica, New York. In 1841 Merrell married Archibald Smith's sister-in-law Elizabeth Pye Magill (1817–90). The Smiths even seriously considered a manufacturing career for Willie, who went with Merrell to Arkansas in 1856 and lived with him there while he effectively began the industrial revolution in that state.[8]

Willie was the pride and hope of his parents, and they seemed as concerned about his happiness as they were conscious of his need to choose a vocation. After returning from Arkansas in 1856, Willie attempted to teach school in his native St. Marys at the Camden County Academy, which dates from the end of the eighteenth century. In 1840 its commissioners erected a "commodious academy building with four classrooms" west of the Presbyterian Church. When principal H. L. Harvey resigned in July 1856 because the commissioners had disapproved his rule expelling students who failed examinations, Willie Smith, who had been elected to succeed him for the next term, was requested "to come at once and take charge of the Academy." It is unclear how long he remained principal of the academy.[9]

Although Willie's letters detailing his difficulties with teaching do not survive, his mother's replies indicate that the young man believed that his was not a strong enough moral influence on his students. His mother's letter to him of October 21, 1856, tells as much about Willie as it does about Roswell: "Believe me darling you know little yet of the depravity of the human heart. You were always carefully guarded from contact with it & educated as you were here where all the parents had the same great end in view, viz. the religious training of their children. You had no experience of what the children of careless parents are. The people of Roswell are a peculiar people. Few men can be found like Mr. [Barrington] King, so faithful to his God & his family while so absorbed in business & very few like good old Mr. Dunwody & their children.[10] Are those by whom mostly you are measuring others? My dear son you are too desponding."

Willie's father also at this time offered characteristic advice. In a letter dated August 18, 1856, Archibald says, " Aim at a control, not only of your scholars but of all who come in your sphere; but to this end, it will be necessary to live in better company too; let your familiar intercourse be with the

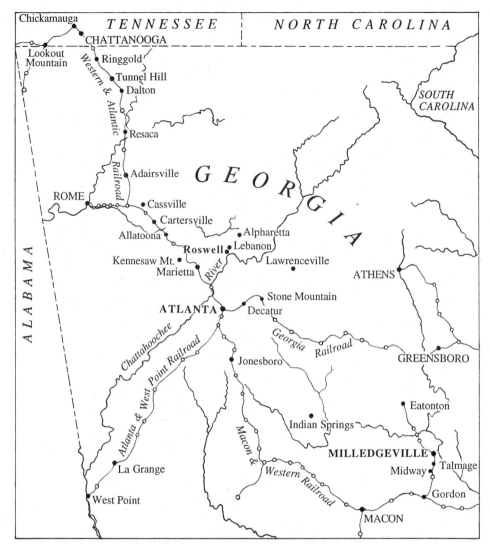

North Georgia, circa 1863

Father, & the Son, thro the Spirit; never rest satisfied unless you have an abiding sense of their presence that they go in & out with you & you with them. . . . Don't blindly follow the wish of the parent to teach this or that. Tell them yes, you will prepare them for it. Aim to teach the art of application, of study. Get up the spirit."

On October 8 of the same year, Archibald wrote, "Your letters are getting too short; if you have a monotonous occupation and run out of common topics, speculate a little with your imagination; this is one of your defects, & you should try to correct it. I have felt the same, and having felt the unpleasantness of it, wish you to do better. . . . The more I see of life, the more I am convinced that one can not have a permanently active mind, without physical powers in tone, and therefore the necessity of attention to develop the bodily as well as the mental powers. I wish you to think of the propriety of introducing calisthenic exercises as a part of the routine of your school in school hours."[11]

Willie also received some worldly advice from his uncle Charles Arthur Magill (1817–84), in an August 20, 1856, letter from Murfreesboro in Pike County, Arkansas, where he was assisting Henry Merrell: "Make up your mind my boy that you are now fully committed, that the great battle of life has with you begun in earnest, & that you will fight it out to the bitter end. Yes, the bitter end. . . . Will, when your school grows so large that you can not attend to it let me know & I will come down & relieve your modesty by taking the girl part of it. I know you would rather teach boys because you can make them do what you tell them, but the girls are as keen & sharp as the gentleman. . . . When I lived in Camden Co., I think I knew every man woman and child in it, but times have very much altered since then."

The few surviving Smith family letters written before the Civil War demonstrate some of the substance and tone that will move throughout the correspondence of that time. The Smiths were very keen on growing flowers and on observing wildflowers, making many references in their correspondence to what was blooming and when, and sending bulbs and roots to relatives and friends. Lizzie, Willie, and Helen Smith all did drawings and watercolors, usually of floral subjects. To this day, flower pictures painted by the Smith women hang in the house. The first extant letter written by Archie Smith is one that he composed when he was twelve years old and sent to Willie in St. Marys. Penned by his aunt Helen Zubly Magill on August 28, 1856, it begins with a question about flowers: "My dear Brother, Can you find out what flowers are when they are pressed? I send you two kinds that I don't think I ever saw before, & I don't think you ever had. We've got two pomegranates on the bush down in the garden."

Later come observations and questions about birds. "Sunday evening a log-cock came & sat on one of the trees on the grass, & stayed there ever so long; & he was picking, & he got a big hole; he could most go in & then I went off & didn't see him any more. Auntie says, she thinks he was there ten minutes but I think he was there 20 minutes, or half an hour. He cut & hammered & chipped ever so long any how. Next morning early, I heard something I thought was one & went after him before sunrise, but I couldn't find him, & next morning I got up before sunrise, & went in the orchards to get some peaches." He then asks if his brother has "seen any Nonpareils yet," referring to a kind of finch or painted bunting of the southern

United States. This question is followed by, "Have you found any flowers there to botanise yet?"

We must assume that Willie set the tone in the family for being an acute observer and lover of nature. When he was in Arkansas in 1856, he kept notes on his observations of birds. He also collected information on mineralogy and geology for the noted geological surveyor David Dale Owen. In 1860 in Arkansas he collected the skin of an unidentified bird that he wanted to name after one of his university professors, James Woodrow, and in 1864 he kept notes about plants that he observed in Lowndes County, Georgia, and in Chatham County, Georgia, near Savannah.[12]

Willie's and his family's characteristic seriousness about religious matters, as well as the kind of people they knew in St. Marys and elsewhere, is also demonstrated by a surviving letter to Willie in St. Marys, dated October 15, 1856, from John Elbert DuBose, a young man who had recently left St. Marys to attend Oglethorpe University:[13] "I have even now but little time to spare, & must not occupy it with excuses." In haste to begin a career in the ministry, he exclaims, "I could get no higher than Soph., & what is worse, they have probationed me so much in Greek, that there is no chance to rise; so I suppose I must content myself with the idea of remaining here three years." But he has already a plan to compensate. "I shall try to make my stay in the Seminary one year shorter."

Then comes a change of subject and mood that seems to be characteristic of the Smiths and those who knew them. "There is nothing here that will interest you, so I must ask of old St. Marys, & those left behind. How are you getting along among the girls? Have any of them captivated you, or are you invulnerable to the darts of my Jennie's eyes? How are the uptown folks? Do you go there often? How is Miss Mary, Nanna, and above all Miss Ria? Speak the candid truth, & tell me if she seems to be better or worse. Tell me all about her: the slightest thing will be of interest. How are the home folks? Miss Julia & the Crichtons?"[14]

Willie Smith returned to Arkansas in April 1859 to serve as an assistant to his uncle Henry Merrell. A letter from Willie to Roswell in November of that year details the annual production of Merrell's industrial village in Pike County. Willie would remain with Merrell through June 1860, when Willie accompanied his uncle and aunt Elizabeth Magill Merrell on an extended trip up the Mississippi and through Illinois, Minnesota, Michigan, New York, Canada, and Connecticut. He then escorted Elizabeth Merrell to Roswell for a visit. That autumn he returned to Arkansas with her and his aunt Helen Zubly Magill. He and Miss Magill returned to Roswell in early

1861 and witnessed Jefferson Davis's inauguration as president of the Confederate States of America in Montgomery, Alabama, on February 18.[15]

Willie's only other surviving letter written before 1863 comes on Christmas Day 1861, following his enlistment in the Savannah Volunteer Guards on November 19.[16] The letter was written to his sister Helen from Fort Screven, a military base near Savannah that was then in Confederate hands. It had been built on Tybee Island, facing the Atlantic Ocean at the mouth of the Savannah River and was named after the Revolutionary War hero General James Screven. Willie was probably there for his basic training, and the subject and tone show the characteristic ambiguity between religious seriousness and sheer fun. "We are having a very quiet time. The *Leesburg*[17] could not get here last evening (a Yankee schooner was at the mouth of Romney Marsh) and so the fellows are out of their Xmass dinner, and their liquor. We were to have a gay time here today. A whole parcel of ladies were to come down and put up a Xmass tree with socks and drawers etc. for the soldiers, and we were all to go up front of the Captain's tent and draw for them, but I suppose the proximity of the Yankees scared them off."

But Willie found compensations for this loss: "I am almost glad that the *Leesburg* was stopped (altho' it has cut me out of my good dinner), for if she had come there would have been so much drunkenness and rowing that the camp would not have been endurable. . . . To celebrate the day I have brushed my hair, pants, and shoes, & put on one of my pretty shirts, & washed my face and hands. The weather is as beautiful as could be. Yesterday and the day before were quite cold. There was ice both nights, but today is warm and bright, and there is a gentle breeze stirring, and the mocking birds are singing. In fact, one of those lovely days that is only seen in low country winters."

The letter concludes with flowers, family, and a picture: "I have packed a couple of wild flowers to send you to brag on, but you speak of Roses and Violets. The Aster grew on the wall of the Ft. I picked it last Sunday. The others I picked this morning for a Xmass present for you. . . . I do not associate with Billy E.[18] much. He lives with the Officers, but he always has a pleasant word when we meet. He spent the evening in my tent last Monday. . . . I wish I could draw a picture of our camp for you. It is in a grove of Palmetto trees, and looks like pictures I have seen of English camps in India."

The Smiths complemented their eye for flowers and pictures with a well-developed ear for music. Willie played the flute; Lizzie played the piano and was the organist at the Presbyterian Church. Brother and sister no doubt played duets in the parlor, as some of the hundreds of titles of sheet music found in the house would attest. Although there is no indication that he studied music seriously, even young Archie tried his hand at the violin.

Because Tybee Island had been occupied by federal forces on November 24, 1861, it seems unlikely that Willie could have been at Fort Screven on Christmas Day, even though his letter is clearly placed and dated. Perhaps Willie's ousted Confederates moved to a position south of the island near the mouth of Romney Marsh, a position that they then renamed Fort Screven. When the Confederates abandoned Tybee, they had set fire to the lighthouse, and Willie may well have been the first of many Smith family members displaced by federal forces.[19]

Willie was soon assigned to duty with the Signal Corps. His duty stations were at Rose Dew and Beaulieu points, which were on the Little Ogeechee and Vernon rivers, about twelve miles south of Savannah. The next extant letter from him, written to his sister Lizzie on March 8, 1863, begins with flowers. "I recd. your letter with the beautiful Nemophilas in it last night and proceed to answer it at once so that this time at least you shall not have cause to complain. I wish indeed that I could be at home to go about with you to hunt for flowers, but I have found by experience that wishing is a very useless occupation. The name of the Jessamine I sent you is Catalonian Jessamine, it is very well worth having as it is a more luxuriant grower than the English."

Then, without a break, follows a reference to war. "We did not think Genl B's proclamation all a notion, but I thought there was a good deal of bombast in it.[20] We have been looking for the enemy every day and now they seem to have begun the attack as this morning there are three iron clads and several other vessels in the Ogeechee and they are firing out there now, altho' no immediate danger to the city is apprehended and strong hopes are felt, that we can defend the approaches." In the next sentence comes a reference to family. "Mary Low and Eliza Stiles with the children left yesterday and Maggie went this morning. Cousin Sarah has gone to Macon to visit Billy and Siddie so Cousin Kate and Carrie are all the ladies left in the house and they say they will stay till the last as they are only two and have no children to be in the way."[21]

And to conclude: "I wish you could see thro' my eyes when I look at the flowers. The Camellias are not more beautiful, but they and the white and pink Azaleas are just perfectly lovely. The white azaleas are incomparably more beautiful than any of our wild ones. In fact they are perfect. Henry Stiles has just been in. He is the same hearty whistling old fellow he always was."[22]

His sister Lizzie's letters are particularly concerned with flowers and requests for palmetto, which she and the other Smith women profitably turn into hats. On April 28, 1863, she begins, "You must hurry up your furlough. The honeysuckles are coming out very fast. I have not yet been after any for I had no idea they were open yet but yesterday I saw a fellow with a great handful of them. They must have come from the new river road or some such place. I am going out this evening to look for some & some lilies." On May 9, she begins,

> I don't know if I have written to tell you what a nice hat I have made of the palmetto which you & A dried for us. Both of us fellows have hats & I have made one for A, too. They are all beautiful. Mine is the admiration of everyone. Mrs Tom King[23] says it is the prettiest hat she ever saw it is a marvel of whiteness & lightness. The feather is a beautiful trimming for it. Sissy has some of the drab feathers & some of those beautiful white ones which you brought from Arkansas & it looks sweet. If you had not braided one for yourself so much nicer I would make one for you too. The hats for society will be very profitable. I have already three engaged & I know of two more people who would engage hats if they knew they could get them. I have no doubt we could sell as many as we could make. Do before you come up find out the different prices of hats. Mrs Ralph King[24] has one coarse & ugly which I hear cost $28 in Savannah & of course the extortioner society wants to get the highest prices for all their things. You really must hurry up & get your furlough. The Azaleas will all be over if you don't.

Father gives advice about finances and more serious matters on May 14. "You have arrived (long ago I think) at that time of life when you ought to be married. At any rate be looking about for a Wife. You may find one with sense enough to willingly live with you without requiring all the luxuries of an ancient establishment before she is willing to try and make your mutual lives more happy. . . . So just set to and make love to the light of your eyes, either personally, or by letter and have every thing ready for the piping times of peace."

Interspersed throughout the 1863 correspondence are concerns about everything from naming a new dog to the servants' health (the Smiths almost never used the term *slave*). But, after a calm beginning about "a great many pretty white honeysuckles at the river," Helen Smith's June 12, 1863, letter to her brother delivers two abrupt surprises. "Uncle Smith[25] is better but very bad indeed. Last night in all the confusion and hurry he was howl-

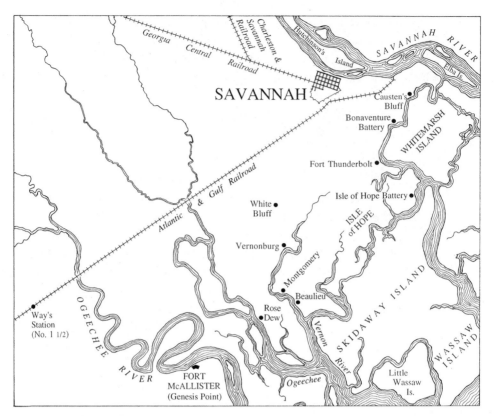

Confederate defenses around Savannah, Georgia, 1863–64.
Willie Smith's stations were generally Beaulieu and Rose Dew.

ing and squalling that he was struck by lightning and somebody must come
and stay with him." The "confusion and hurry" to which Helen refers was
caused by a fire.

I can't write you much because it is time for the letters to be sent and we
have just finished breakfast because the kitchen burnt down last night and
the storeroom and almost every thing. They only saved some beef and
bacon. All the salt and syrup and tallowlard are gone. Fortunately it was
raining hard or the house would have taken fire for it was very hot at the
upstairs windows and sparks were falling on the shed. It was quite early
about 11 and Davy and Moses were both at home and Hanna was here
too.[26] She worked like a horse bringing water. After the roof fell in they
flung water on the meat box and outed it and then fished out the meat with
pitch forks, and the beef barrel was burnt down to the pickle, but the beef
was not injured in the least, but nothing else was saved. The wind carried

The kitchen at the Smith Plantation Home. The original kitchen on this foundation burned June 11, 1863.

the fire away from the house, so I don't think the house could have burned.[27]

Another crisis confronting the Smiths was the military status of young Archie. On April 2, 1862, the Confederate Congress had declared that every able-bodied male between eighteen and thirty-five years of age was subject to conscription into military service. Archie Smith turned eighteen on April 25, 1862; therefore, he and his family became concerned about his status and obligation. Archie had enrolled at the Georgia Military Institute (GMI) before October 1862, but concerns about the school and his service dominate the family correspondence to the end of the war. Like many other cadets, Archie worried constantly that he was not doing his duty at GMI, and by late May 1861 most cadets had left to join the army. A controversy over conscription in early 1862 caused more cadets to leave, not wishing to be branded with the exemption that Governor Joe E. Brown had gained for them. (Brown was outraged in April 1862 when the Confederate Congress passed a conscription law that did not exempt military school cadets, and many GMI Cadets used this act as an excuse to join the army.) On the other hand, increased Confederate casualties in the summer and fall 1862 caused enrollment at the institute to rise. Archie, therefore, was concerned about being branded as a shirker at a place that harbored the sons of some of the wealthiest men in the state as well as the son of Joe Brown himself. By action of the Georgia legislature on May 1, 1863, officers and cadets of the Georgia Military Institute were exempted from Confederate service.[28]

That war seemed distant from Roswell in July 1863, but it would soon come closer. On July 13, Anne wrote Willie, "We are all feeling sad at the fall of Vicksburg,[29] the falling back of Gen. Lee's army &c. The general opinion seems to be that the fall of V. will be the prolongation of the war & now we are in a state of suspense on account of the attack on Charleston.[30] God has not been honoured as he should have been particularly at Vicksburg for when the enemy was so frequently repulsed there the glory & the praise was given to man."

She must speak for her entire family and for many Southerners in her July 20 letter to Willie when she muses, "I think things have never appeared so dark since the commencement of the war. I trembled when I heard of the invasion of Pennsylvania.[31] It seemed to me we had not the same reason to look for God's blessing & tho' no very serious disaster has befallen us in that quarter there has been a fearful waste of life, & while we all have confidence in Gen. Lee believing he is acting in the fear of God, I cannot help fearing he has taken a false step. Our armies are being so diminished that it seems impossible that we can long hold out against the hosts who are arrayed against us."

The war was not close enough to prevent Lizzie and Helen from persuading their mother to make a pilgrimage to the restorative sulphur waters of Indian Springs, a popular resort near Jackson, Georgia, about halfway between Atlanta and Macon. In 1863 it had no fewer than four resort hotels. Archie and cousin Charlotte Cuthbert Barnwell (1842–1922)[32] joined Mrs. Smith and Helen on this vacation, which lasted from late July until mid–August 1863.

While they were at the resort, Helen Zubly Magill, who had remained behind in Roswell, wrote on August 13, reporting on military preparations there: "Have you heard, they are speaking of erecting fortifications here? I do not know exactly where, but somewhere on the Shallow ford road; as they say when the enemy come to Roswell, they will probably come, on the old Indian trail. I cannot see the use of obstructing one, out of so many approaches to a place; nor why they suppose they will come on the old Indian trail, when there are so many roads; and I suppose they could come without a road, if they were very anxious. . . . They have a grand military organization here now: Infantry, Cavalry, & Artillery; the three departments, commanded by three of the Royal family.[33] Have two cannon, and plenty of small arms. I heard last night, they were going to barricade the street, between the Pratts' & Lewis's."[34]

After returning from Indian Springs, Anne Smith wrote to Willie on August 24 about the shadows gathering to the north of Roswell. "We hear to-day that there is fighting going on at Chattanooga, & I suppose it is true, for Sonny writes that a great many troops are going up to reinforce Bragg.[35] Your Father rode out the other day to see the fortifications which are being made. He says they are not to be laughed at. They are a series of works commanding all the approaches to this place & may prove very effectual against such a body of cavalry as would probably come here. . . . We have buried some things, papers, &c under a walnut tree in the garden a little N. W. of the tree. It is well for you to know it. If Bragg does fall back to Atlanta of course the Factories will be destroyed but by keeping quiet we shall probably escape personal injury. At any rate it will not be worth while to try to find a safer place, for no place will be secure unless the Lord interpose in our behalf. Pray with us my darling that we may be delivered out of the hand of our enemies."

At the same time, in Marietta, Archie was worrying about the part that he was not playing. He wrote from GMI on August 28 and 29 that "there is great likelihood of the school suspending. Things seems to be going to the dogs generally. Major Richardson is going away and there seems to be another breakup in the wind. There are only four in my class and I think two of them are likely to go, and things are likely to get worse. Major Richardson was the salt of the place and now he is going. I don't know what we will do if we recite to old Eve. We won't learn any thing and old Capers is away almost all of the time, & I don't see what I will do unless I go into service."[36]

He frets, "If they don't get some better professors here when Major R. goes away I think it might be best for me to go to the North Carolina institute,[37] and if you think it worth while and will let me know at once, I will ask the Major something about it before he goes. Enough about leaving the G.M.I., but while I stay here I wish Father would give me so much a month or a week to spend for something to eat, for we don't get enough some time and what we do get is worse and worse."

His mother did not think much of the plan to go to North Carolina. She wrote to Willie on August 31, "The plan of going to the N. C. Institute, I think, is not feasible, for the Geo. Cadets were only exempted by Geo. Brown's special exertions & they may not have the same privilege in N. C. & he might at once come under the conscription. My idea is that he had best hold on in Marietta as long as the school holds together. Let me know what you think—even if he learns nothing here, the exemption is worth the expense tho' the Institute is shamefully managed. There are over 200 boys at \$200 for the 5 months & yet there are not professors enough to hear the recitations—dear Son I do not like to trouble you with all these cares & anxieties but I at the same time love to lean upon you & feel thankful that I can rely on your judgment."

By September the Smiths were thinking seriously of evacuating their Roswell home and of refugeeing to property that Archibald Smith owned in Clinch County, near the Florida line. Anne Smith writes to Willie on September 7 that they planned "to go to Clinch " and to "prepare to make a crop there next year & have a log house put up for us if the retreat is made. . . . Whatever we leave here would be destroyed. A great many bad & unsafe Negroes have been bought by the Kings. A number of them have run away at different times, & Miss Rees's house was broken open & her things destroyed, supposed by them." The next day Willie's father wrote, "There is so much prospect that Savannah will be disturbed this winter by the Yankees that I think it best not to send my Negroes there, but as soon as the crop here is gathered to send them to Clinch to occupy some of our land there."

Speaking of her own preparations, Willie's mother writes on September 14, "I feel so tired my Dear Son that I cannot write much of a letter. I have just come from the garret where I have been trying to make some packing arrangements in case we are driven off." Her husband has told her that "We cannot pretend to save any thing but necessary clothing & some bedding, for if the Yankees get the better of us there will be such a rush that it will be difficult to take any thing." If the family could, they would pack and send the piano at once, "for we should never be able to replace it."

Referring to the federal occupation of Chattanooga, Tennessee, just across the Georgia line, she adds, "We hear of large reinforcements going up & that Gen. Johnston is at Kingston to which place our troops have fallen back.[38] This is allowing the enemy to approach very near us but there seems to be great confidence felt that we shall prevail against them." The leader of the community, Barrington King, expressed this confidence. "Mr King says he does not intend to move until the Yankees actually set fire to his house, but when that comes he may not find it an easy matter to get away, tho' he has plenty of carriages & horses & plenty of money to replace their comforts even if every thing in his house is destroyed."

In the same letter, Anne Smith mentions having heard from Captain Thomas Edward King. Tom King had helped his father build up the Ivy Woolen Mills of the Roswell Manufacturing Company before the war. After being severely wounded at First Manassas, he had returned to Roswell, where he had become mayor. The seriousness of the current situation and the nearness of the federal forces was brought home to the community on September 21, when Roswell learned of King's death at the Battle of Chickamauga.[39]

On September 28, Anne Smith wrote to Willie, "Marietta & Atlanta are fill'd with wounded men & we are all at work preparing lint bandages &c. The Factory has given $5000 to each place. . . . I have not written to Father because I do not know where he will be but of course you will see him on his return. Do tell him he had better look after his corn in Marietta. I am very much afraid it will be seized. Mr King says corn is now $5.00 pr bush. & not to be had for Confederate money."

Far to the south, Archibald Smith, who had left Roswell on September 21, was having troubles of his own. From Clinch County he wrote in early October, "I find no place on my land in Clinch to encourage me to settle on one lot more than another as the clearings are so small & the houses have been blown down by a hurry cane. I can not well determine what to do." He was soon staying at the "refugee" home of Elizabeth Ann Maner Riley (1812–89) in Lowndes County, near Valdosta, Georgia, more than two hundred miles south of Roswell, almost on the Florida line. Elizabeth Riley had two daughters, Frances Morgandollar (1834–72), who married Archibald Smith Barnwell in 1862, and Gulielma English (1846–1921). Elizabeth Riley had left the family's plantation in Glynn County, called Sterling, to refugee in Lowndes County with her unmarried daughter, Gulielma English Riley (1846–1921), who his father seems to think would be a good wife for Willie.[40]

At that moment, Archie was wrestling with his sense of duty in the impending crisis. On September 28, Mrs. Smith told Willie, "Sometimes Sonny's feelings seem to be very bitter against himself for not being able to go into service (for he says he knows he cannot stand it). He feels degraded." Over the next months such sentiments echo through the correspondence.

Desperately attempting to protect her brood, Anne Smith seems to think that Willie can somehow pull strings to get Archie into the Signal Corps. If this plan fails, she hopes that Archie can get a commission in a newly formed unit. On October 5, 1863, she tells Willie that if their father can get Archie an exemption, "it will be safer for him to go into this new service. But I am afraid our plans are going to be broken up. Your Father met John Magill[41] in Macon & he came home with him. I suppose you know he is trying to get up a Battalion of Artillery & he is *detailed* to go round recruiting. The men who wish to have the commissions have subscribed $20,000 to get up the Battalion & so he is buying up men, many of whom Mr D.[42] expected to have. He has been to Alpharetta[43] this morning & got the promise of 40 at $10 a piece for the conscription officer who last week promised Mr D. his assistance. John is to have conscripts & those under age, Mr D. only those under 18 or in some way unfit for active service, but he has no money to buy them."

On December 4 she writes, "He feels degraded in doing nothing for his country (perhaps if he were older he might view matters differently) so that I fear the failure may be an injury to him." And on the 19th, "Sonny said yesterday if he could go into the service & had to be discharged he would feel more like a white man." These feelings will continue into the new year, when she tells Willie on January 15, 1864, that Archie "feels that it would be such a disgrace to be conscripted that he cannot bear it."

A very real characteristic of the Smith family surfaces during the storms that beset them. Their correspondence always breathes a concern for the natural world, for the normal cycle of the seasons, and for the small and intimate details that make life distinctive. On November 11, 1863, Willie writes to his sister Lizzie to ask for a textbook description of Ilex Cassina (Yaupon tea). Lizzie immediately complies with his request, adding that she planted the oxalis roots that he sent. All through the terrible month of November 1863, there are references to such matters as patterns for pants and sheet music.

On December 8, 1863, Willie's sister tells him, "When we hear a report one day that the army is at Kingston or Cassville, it is generally contradicted the next, so we are kept in a pleasant state of excitement," a state that was aggravated by an outbreak of diphtheria that would almost claim her. A Roswell friend, Rosa Dunwody, died of diphtheria on December 27, 1863, and when Helen herself later contracted the disease, her condition delayed the family's planned departure from Roswell.[44]

The Smith's letters tell also a sad tale of shortages, trials, and of rampant inflation that racked the South as the year ended. On December 11, Willie's mother writes him that she has just sent him some ham, sweetmeats, stewed and raw pears, okra, tomatoes, catsup, cucumbers, apples, and biscuits, adding in the next paragraph that the family was preparing to flee Roswell. She continues, "We shall not be able to carry any furniture I suppose, for it is almost impossible to have any thing hauled now, & if several trips have to be made to Atlanta the probability is that the first will be stolen before the others arrive, for Atlanta is literally cram'd with the off-scouring of the earth & it seems to be a den of iniquity." As if their problems were not great enough, she adds, "John M. drop'd down on us last Tuesday & has established his headquarters here again & has two sergeants reporting to him at any hour from day to night." Helen wrote to Willie on December 23 that "for a little flannel sack I am going to get $12 and other things in proportion." Yet she says, "This is a Xmass letter, but there is nothing very Xmass like going on. I expect it will be the saddest one we ever spent, and it may be the last we will ever spend here."

When Helen wrote this letter, Archibald Smith had just returned, after an absence of five weeks, from a second trip to Valdosta, having successfully rented a farm that could be cultivated but not yet having found a house for his family to occupy. In seeking out this section of Georgia, Smith was not alone, for refugees had been settling there for some time, considering it the area of the state most secure from enemy attack.[45]

Added to these worries were concerns about not hearing from their relatives in Arkansas, Anne Smith's sister Elizabeth Merrell and brother Charles Arthur Magill. Elizabeth Magill Merrell, known to the Smiths as Aunt Bet (1815–90), had married the Yankee manager of the Roswell Manufacturing Company, Henry Merrell. Mrs. Smith's brother, Charley (1817–84), had moved to Arkansas to serve as Merrell's assistant.[46] Merrell had recently completed a mission for the Confederate Department of the Trans-Mississippi and had moved the family group from his factory site in Pike County to a safer location in Camden, in the southwest corner of Arkansas.

The Smiths, together with the rest of Roswell, faced 1864 with a mixture of fear and hope. As the year began, sons of each of the original six families of "The Colony" were serving as Confederate soldiers, none providing more than the Kings, referred to locally with some justification as "The Royal Family." Six of Barrington King's eight sons performed some kind of military service, and two were killed in the war. In addition to Tom King, Colonel Barrington Simrall King (1833–65) was killed in one of the war's last battles, at Averasboro, North Carolina. Joseph Henry King never fully recovered from the wound he received at First Manassas. James Roswell King was almost captured during the Battle of Atlanta, and Clifford A. King was captured at Vicksburg and later served as a captain and aide on the staff of General William J. Hardee, on whose staff Willie Smith served as a telegraph operator. Ralph Browne King was seriously injured in the evacuation of Savannah.

The Bulloch family provided the Confederacy with James Dunwody Bulloch (1823–1901), its naval agent in England who had the raider *Alabama* built, and with his half-brother, Irvine Stevens Bulloch (1842–98), a midshipman who in 1864 fired the last gun that the ship discharged before sinking from its battle with the federal ship *Kearsarge* off Cherbourg, France. The Reverend Pratt's son, Charles Jones Pratt (1842–1924), served in Willie Smith's unit, the Savannah Volunteer Guards, and was eventually captured while serving with Morgan's Kentucky Cavalry in Tennessee. Horace A. Pratt (b. 1830) and Bayard Hand Pratt (b. 1838) were members of the same company of Georgia State Troops. Henry Macon Dunwody (1826–63) was killed at Gettysburg. His brother, Major Charles Archibald Dunwody (1828–1905), never recovered from a wound sustained at First Manassas. Catherine Hand married the famous Confederate physician and chaplain Charles T. Quintard (1824–98), who had nursed Tom King back to health, had telegraphed to Roswell the notice of King's death at Chickamauga, and had brought him home to be buried.[47]

Of the original families who had settled Roswell a quarter of a century earlier, only the Pratt family remained behind to witness the federal occupation of the town and the burning of the Roswell Manufacturing Company on July 6. Barrington Hall and Great Oaks served as headquarters for the thousands of troops in the area. Mimosa Hall and the Presbyterian church were used as hospitals, and Bulloch Hall became a barracks. The Smith house was spared any occupation and abuse, surviving, perhaps as it always has, because of its relative isolation.

Following its victories at Lookout Mountain and Missionary Ridge in late November 1863, the federal forces under Sherman stood poised at the beginning of 1864 to push into Georgia, to capture Atlanta, and to split the Confederacy. As we turn to their correspondence of 1864, the Smith family prepares for what will be its own wrenching part in the tragedy.

NOTES

1. As late as the Civil War, people referred to the northern third of the state as "Cherokee Georgia." Kennett, *Marching through Georgia,* 9.

2. The Smith family had originally come to Georgia with its founder, James Edward Oglethorpe (1689–1785). John Smith (1715–93) arrived in Savannah from England in 1735, according to Coulter and Saye, eds., *A List of Early Settlers of Georgia,* 96. The son of the Archibald Smith approaching Roswell, also named Archibald ("Archie," 1844–1923), writes around 1910 of the family tradition "that John Smith was urged by his family to become a clergyman, but that he did not feel that he was a suitable person, and that he was once in a sequestered spot praying over the matter, and that General Oglethorpe happened upon him and on conversing with him was so much pleased with his honesty and sincerity of purpose that he made him his private secretary" (Smith Papers, box 108). Family tradition held that this information was documented by Thomas Spalding's "Life of Oglethorpe" (1840), but this work makes no reference to John Smith as his secretary. Among other public responsibilities and of-

fices, John Smith was a trustee of the colony of Georgia; attended the earliest called patriot assembly, in Savannah on July 27, 1774; served on the Council of Public Safety; and represented the town and district of Savannah in the First Provincial Congress of 1775, during which he was one of several men chosen to give an account of the proceedings to the Continental Congress. In 1780, because of his rebel activities Sir James Wright, the royal governor, disqualified him from holding office under the Crown (Candler, ed., *Colonial Records,* 3:426; Knight, *Georgia's Landmarks,* 2:642–43; White, *Historical Collections of Georgia,* 39, 44, 65, 70–71, 77, 86, 98–104).

Archibald Smith (1758–1830), the son of John Smith and Eliza Williamson (c.1731–1809), first married Margaret Joyner (1772–94), by whom he had one son, John Joyner Smith, (1790–1872), known as "Uncle Smith" to the Roswell family. This Archibald was a merchant in Savannah and had a rice plantation and a large tract of land on the Carolina side of the Savannah River—including the Screvens Ferry, Blue Mud, and Nullification plantations—but he lived at least part of the time at Old Fort plantation near Beaufort, South Carolina, his wife's home. After his first wife's death, in 1796 Archibald married Helen Zubly, the daughter of David Zubly (d.1792) and granddaughter of John Joachim Zubly (1724–81). From this marriage came a daughter, Eliza Zubly (1803–46), who married Edward Barnwell (1785–1860) of Beaufort, and a son, Archibald (1801–86). According to his son, Archie, "After Grandfather left his house in Savannah to Uncle Smith and some small houses he had in Savannah to Aunt Barnwell, Father found himself and his Negroes and his wife out of doors. He sold his portion of the rice land and went to St. Marys" (Smith Papers, box 108). Archibald Smith kept "the Smith Wharf and Stores" on Factor's Walk, however, and had an agent named William Duncan (1799–1879) handle his affairs there.

3. The Jersey Point plantation is currently a large part of the U.S. Navy Trident Submarine Support Base.

4. Smith's son, Archie, wrote of these efforts, "About this time, say 1831, Father was infected with abolition ideas and designed to free his Negroes and send them to Liberia but attempted first to prepare them for self support and self government. In this attempt he overworked himself, destroyed all discipline and effectiveness among his people. Crops failed. Father had nervous prostration. Appenzelle was a failure." The father had apparently had such ideas from his youth, according to the son: "As a young man Father was zealous in giving the Negroes religious instruction, and he endured much heat and hardship teaching them in Savannah" (Smith Papers, box 108). It appears that Archibald Smith later succeeded in such efforts. Some of his letters after 1850 (e.g., one of October 8, 1856) make references to paying wages to men whose names are the same as those who appear on his earlier lists of slaves (Smith Papers, box 17, folder 2). Although the 1850 Georgia census lists Smith as owning twenty-one slaves, the 1860 census shows only four, all of them children and none over three years old (National Archives Microfilm Publications, *Population Schedules of the Seventh Census of the United States;*

2:621; see also National Archives Microfilm Publications, *Population Schedules of the Eighth Census of the United States;* roll 144, 93).

5. Archie's recollections are now in the Smith Papers, box 108. Future quotations from this work will not be cited.

6. His many observations on agriculture in Georgia include: "Oats grow finely from 20 to 30 bushels per acre; corn 10 to 30; wheat 3 to 10, being much injured by the Hessian fly, and subject to *rust;* rye so much affected by the same causes as to be neglected; the cow pea from 3 to 5; usually fed off by stock. Carrots suit the soil, but beets, cabbage, turnips and potatoes (Irish) do not succeed; the deficiency in the last is, however, made up by the sweet potato, producing 100 bushels; all this is the product unassisted by manure.

"There is, however, a considerable portion of creek and river bottoms very good, apparently the debris of Hornblende rocks; these last produce nearly double the above quantities per acre. The grey land is grateful for and tenacious of the little manure we have tried it with, and in addition to the above products known at the North, we have the staple product of the South, which gives very satisfactory return after the land has been cultivated a few years, producing from 1 to 5 hundred weight of clean cotton to the acre, according to the quality of the land, and being about 50 per ct. more expensive to cultivate than corn."

7. Earlier, on May 14, 1863, Archibald Smith had sent Willie, then serving in the Confederate Signal Corps in Savannah, some interesting details about the factory's income during the Civil War: "The factory has been doing full work, and increased the Capital Stock, by taking in the value of Improvements, hitherto placed on Expense account; and part of its floating capital; so that now each Share is $2000, and on this it has just been declared a dividend of 20 per cent. Also a large stock of Cotton bought at average of 8 cts, which is now worth 40 is made the ground of a dividend in part, of 30 pr ct. so that my last dividend up to 1 Ap[l] is $6000. As I have been investing the previous dividends in Bonds and 7[30] notes to a pretty good amount (9,000). I will be very willing to let you have this last div[d] or any part of it whenever you can find a good use for it."

8. Merrell's story, interesting in its own right, can be found in Skinner, ed., *Autobiography of Henry Merrell;* see 234–41 for the story of Willie's trip to Arkansas with Merrell.

9. White, *Statistics,* 140; Arnow, "History," April 27 and May 18, 1951. As for the academy itself, "the expectations failed of realization, and after a short struggle it ceased to be an academy, but it was from time to time rented for school purposes to private teachers" (Silva, *Early Reminiscence,* 27). The building was burned by Maine troops during the Civil War (Reddick, comp., *Camden's Challenge,* 109–11).

10. John Dunwody (1786–1858) was another of the founders of Roswell. He and his wife, Jane Bulloch Dunwody (1788–1856), had six children, most of whom rose to prominence as planters, ministers, merchants, physicians, and military leaders.

11. Archie made some very frank comments about his parents in his recollections that enable a better understanding of the couple and how they later coped with their son's death: "I think his sister made the match. They did not suit each other. It was more esteem and convenience than congeniality or passion. I think each one wanted someone else.... I think from what I have heard that he was in love with a girl but would not address her because she was not a professor of religion and that he never got over it." Archibald was "remarkably erect active and quick in every way, nervous and impulsive. [He was] very deaf and could not hear even the sound of ordinary conversation. His eyes were excellent and he read a great deal.... He had a fine voice and sang constantly, but all tunes were alike to him. He could and would rigorously deny himself what he wanted to eat but would never restrict himself to a little. It was plenty or none at all with him.... He was warmhearted and impulsive like an April day.... He lacked tact and did not cover the backbone of truth with the flesh of courtesy and moderation, nor the skin of charity for the different ideas and opinions of other people.... His theories to him were axioms, even if disproved by the experience of others and discredited by his own. [However,] he could not execute his own theories, could not control labor, and did not plan his work ahead. [He was] rather an extremist in all his views, especially about dress and worldly conformity, but he moderated as he grew older. He was very impatient of man but patient before God. He feared God and nothing else. His faith knew no bounds. His honor and word were impeccable." Archie also respected the fact that his father was an "enthusiastic agriculturist, especially for hay. His mind was scientific and his ideas and theories fifty years ahead of his time.... He was much taken with new inventions, methods and machinery. He invented the twin screw propeller for steamships about 1881. I do not know who else invented the twin screw and used it, but Father invented it independently about 1881 but had not the ability to test it.... His faith in God never shook, and he would have been burned at the stake sooner than discredit the Bible. He believed just 144 hours elapsed from the time space was vacuum till Adam and Eve were placed in the garden.... He could not oppose the evils which he saw by quiet calmness but set his face like a flint against evil and all that he thought to be connected with evil so that his truth and honesty were like a crabs shell.... He was zealous for missions."

His mother, Archie says, "was very handsome, 5 ft. 8 inches tall, rather slender but stately and majestic." [She] "had abundance of black hair, her eyes were almost black, they expressed calm strength of character but they were not very strong and she wore glasses as long as I can remember. Her beauty was that of a steel engraving and not that of a chromo. She had some injury to her back and though it did not diminish her erectness nor prevent her standing nor working it prevented her walking far.... She was blind for ten years from glaucoma and lame eighteen months from fracture of the hip."

Archie's view of her character prepares us for the way that she confronted her later trials. "She was heroic and tragic in mind and body. She was quiet and even tempered, calm and deep, but rather cold on the surface. She inspired confidence and respect rather than affection. She was ever kind and self controlled but never merry. She was a good manager in many respects but condemned policy and [was] destitute of tact toward Father. When his temper was not smooth she did not pour oil on it. She always took the heavy end of the burden, never selected the smooth side of the path to walk in. She would not turn aside for a stone nor lengthen nor shorten her step for a thorn. She would have adorned a high position in society. She felt and suffered deeply but would not wink an eye."

12. Smith Papers, box 4, folder 3; Skinner, ed., *Autobiography of Henry Merrell*, 447 n. 4. Woodrow (1828–1907) was a professor of natural science from 1853 to 1861 at Oglethorpe University, then located in Milledgeville, Georgia, and from which Willie had been graduated in 1855. Woodrow was the first teacher in the history of Georgia to hold the Ph.D. degree (Heidelberg). After serving the Confederacy as a chemist making medicine, he earned some notoriety, while a professor of Columbia Theological Seminary in Columbia, South Carolina, in attempting to reconcile the Darwinian hypothesis with religion. He later served as the president of the University of South Carolina (Tankersley, *College Life,* 38–42, 80–82, 104; Johnson et al., eds., *Dictionary of American Biography,* 20:495–96).

13. John Elbert DuBose (1836–58), like Willie, was from Camden County. He became dissatisfied with medical studies at the University of Virginia and returned to St. Marys to teach school. After a religious conversion, he wanted to study for the ministry and in October 1856 enrolled with advanced standing at Oglethorpe University. He overcame the problems outlined in the letter to graduate in 1858 and then enrolled as a ministerial candidate at Columbia Theological Seminary in Columbia, South Carolina, where his devoutness won him attention. He organized Sunday schools, preached revivals, and distributed books and tracts. When he fell ill and knew he might not live to continue preaching, he attempted to persuade others to become ministers. "His flaming zeal consumed him." This letter indicates Willie Smith's friends and relationships and substantiates George White's observation that the inhabitants of early St. Marys "have a high reputation for morals and intelligence" (Buist, "John Elbert DuBose"; Tankersley, *College Life,* 70–71, 166; White, *Statistics,* 140).

14. "Jennie" has not been identified. "Miss Mary," "Nanna," and "Miss Ria" are daughters of merchant John Bessent Jr. (1799–1885) and his wife, Maria (1813–1903): Mary Ann (1836–1911), Hannah McGillis (1839–75), and Maria (1838–1923). "Miss Julia" may be E. Julia Bessent (b. 1846?), the daughter of John Bessent's cousin, Abram J. Bessent, who was mentioned in Charles Magill's letter to Willie of August 20. At the corner of Bryant and Osborne streets, near to the place where the Magills and Smiths had lived in St. Marys, were a family of three sisters named Crichton: Eleanor (b. 1810?), Laticia Sophia (1825–93), and Louisa Jane (1829–99). According to Silva's *Early Reminiscence*, the sisters were "a remarkable trio of cultured women who had a large circle of friends. . . . The three presented a solid front of advanced single-blessedness which

seemed impregnable to matrimonial attack. Though not averse to the company of gentle-men, no 'Lord of Creation' ever dominated the home where they in their Adamless Eden enjoyed life in their own way" (57).

15. Skinner, ed., *Autobiography of Henry Merrell*, 218, 224, 285, 287–92, 482–83 n. 3.

16. Willie's early enlistment, seven months after the firing on Fort Sumter and four months after First Manassas, reflects the Smith family's loyalty to the Confederacy's cause. Although this first enlistment was for a period of six months, he had enlisted "for the war" by April 17, 1862 (National Archives Microfilm Publications, *Compiled Service Records of Confederate Soldiers Who Served in Organizations from the State of Georgia*; roll 141).

17. A Confederate ship named after the resounding Confederate victory at Ball's Bluff, Virginia, on October 21, 1861. Often used in supplying Fort Pulaski, the steamer was used in the Confederate defense of Whitemarsh Island in 1862 (U.S. War Department, *The War of the Rebellion*, 14:10. Hereafter cited as *OR*).

18. William Henry Elliott (1837–1919), a Savannah physician and cousin of Willie's. He was the son of Margaret Cowper Mackay Elliott (1810?–93), the granddaughter of Archibald Smith's aunt Anne Smith McQueen (1753–1809). This reference introduces another characteristic of the Smith correspondence. It contains scores of references to a warren of interrelationships typical of nineteenth-century Georgia families, particularly those of the planter class. Because the Smiths' original home was Savannah, because Willie was now there, and because he often ran across family members and friends, a good portion of his correspondence with Roswell includes cryptic references to these people. In addition to the Elliotts, prominent Savannah relatives that he mentions and visits are the Lows, the Stileses, and the Mackays.

19. *OR*, 3:32–33, 192; McGee, "Siege of Fort Pulaski," 214–22.

20. General Pierre Gustave Toutant Beauregard (1818–93), the commander of the Confederate Department of South Carolina, Georgia, and Florida, had published on February 18, 1863, a proclamation concerning an imminent federal attack on Savannah. As it appeared in the *Savannah Republican* on February 18, it reads, in part: "It has be-come my solemn duty to inform the authorities and citizens of Charleston and Savannah that the movements of the enemy's fleet indicates an early land and naval attack on one or both of these cities: and to urge that all persons unable to take an active part in the struggle shall retire. . . . Carolinians and Georgians! The hour is at hand to prove your devotion to your country's cause. Let all able-bodied men, from the seaboard to the mountains, rush to arms. Be not too exacting in the choice of weapons. Pikes and scythes will do for exterminating your enemies—spades and shovels for protecting your friends. To arms! fellow citizens. Come to share with us our dangers, our brilliant suc-cess, or our glorious death," vol. 62, no. 41, p. 1.

21. Mary Cowper Stiles Low (1832–63), the daughter of William Henry Stiles (1810–65) and Elizabeth Anne Mackay (1810–67). Mary Low's mother was the grand-

daughter of Anne Smith McQueen (1753–1809), Archibald Smith's aunt. Eliza Stiles is probably one of Mary Low's cousins, Eliza Mackay Stiles, whose father, Benjamin Edward Stiles (1794–1855), was the brother of Mary Low's father. "Maggie" is probably their aunt Margaret Cowper Mackay Elliott (1807–93). "Cousin Sarah" seems to be another aunt, Sarah Mackay (1815–76), a spinster who may be visiting her sister Margaret's son, William Henry Elliott (1837–1919) and his wife, Sidney Stiles Elliott (1840–1925). Sarah Mackay and her other unmarried sister, Catherine (1811–75), lived together in the family home on Broughton and Abercorn streets in Savannah. "Carrie" may be their sister Margaret's daughter, Caroline Elliott (1842–94). This information comes from many Smith family sources; see also Myers, ed., *Children of Pride*, 1588–89, 1610, 1693.

22. William Henry Stiles (1834–78), the brother of Mary Cowper Stiles Low, is whistling now but will receive severe wounds in the thigh and right side at Second Manassas (August 28, 1862) and Fredericksburg (December 13, 1862) (Myers, ed., *Children of Pride*, 1693).

23. Mary Read Clemens King, the only child of the Honorable Jeremiah Clemens (1814–65), a U. S. Senator from Alabama from 1849 to 1853, and Mary Talbot Locke Read. Thomas Edward King (1829–63), a son of Barrington King, was elected captain of the Roswell Guards and was severely wounded at First Manassas in 1861. He later died at Chickamauga on September 19, 1863 (Myers, ed., *Children of Pride*, 1585).

24. Ralph Browne King (1835–78) was the sixth child of Barrington and Catherine Nephew King. His wife was Florence Stillwell of New York.

25. Archibald Smith's half-brother, John Joyner Smith (1790–1872). He had been driven from his beautiful home in Beaufort in November 1861 when federal forces occupied the town and used the house as the headquarters for General Isaac Ingalls Stevens, who commanded the post at Beaufort. John Joyner Smith was never able to recover his home and his Old Fort Plantation near Beaufort. He lived with the Smiths in Roswell and in Valdosta, Georgia, during the Civil War.

26. These family servants can be identified in Archibald Smith's records as David Cold (b. July 25, 1834), Moses (b. March 1842), and Hannah (b. 1836). David and Hannah were brother and sister (Smith Papers, box 17, folder 2).

27. This letter has been dated from an internal reference. Most of this document is written in French. Some corrections to Lizzie's letter were marked in pencil by Theophile Roché, a Frenchman employed by the Roswell Manufacturing Company with whom Lizzie Smith, Helen Zubly Magill, and perhaps Helen Zubly Smith evidently studied the language.

A key French passage reads, "Je suppose que vous apprendîmes par la lettre de ma mère (mardi dernier) que la cuisine et le magasin brûlaient jeudi soir dernier. Il fut un grand malheur. Tout le porc sale et lard etc. étaient dans le magasin et tout fut presque brûlé.

"Par une bonne providence il pleuvait pendant que la cuisine brulûit car s'il avait été un temps sec notre maison aussi aurait brûlé sans doute.

"Tout nos amis sont très bon envoyant toute choses necessaire. Tout nos utensils de cuisine sont brûlés et nous ne pouvons pas en user.

"Quelques poulets étaient dans la cuisine et brûles. Un Coq avait peur de brûlait et s'il alla sous le pluies que [dégoûté?] d'appentis du porche il crue qu'il y [fut?] [sauf?] et cela fut. . . .

[I suppose that you have learned by a letter from my mother (last Tuesday) that the kitchen and the storehouse burned last Thursday evening. It was a great misfortune. All the salted pork and lard, etc. were in the storehouse and nearly all was burned.

By a lucky chance it rained while the kitchen was burning, because if it had been dry (weather), our house also would have burned, without doubt.

All our friends are very good, sending (us) all necessary things. All our kitchen utensils are burned, and we are not able to use them.

Several chickens were in the kitchen and were burned. A rooster was afraid of getting burned and if he went out in the rain (on) the roof of the porch, he believed that he was "safe" there] (editors' translation).

28. Bohannon, "Cadets, Drillmasters, Draft Dodgers, and Soldiers," 7–15. Moore, *Conscription and Conflict*, 13, 266–67. See also Bryan, *Confederate Georgia*, 143; Yates, "History of the Georgia Military Institute," 5, 30.

29. The Confederate garrison at Vicksburg, Mississippi, had surrendered to General Ulysses S. Grant on July 4, 1863.

30. On April 7, 1863, Rear Admiral Samuel F. Dupont (1803–65) led a federal attack of seven monitors in an attempt to capture Charleston. This attack failed because of massive firepower from Fort Sumter. On July 10 Charleston was subjected to a joint land and naval attack led by Major General Quincy A. Gillmore (1825–88), an attack that developed into a largely unsuccessful siege, again owing to fire from Sumter and neighboring forts. See Faust, ed., *Historical Times Illustrated Encyclopedia of the Civil War*, 131–32, 310–11.

31. Lee's Army of Northern Virginia entered Pennsylvania on June 25, beginning the train of events that would culminate in the Battle of Gettysburg, July 1–3.

32. Charlotte Cuthbert Barnwell was the daughter of Archibald Smith's sister Eliza Zubly Smith Barnwell (1803–46). Charlotte Barnwell lived in Beaufort, South Carolina, and suffered from curvature of the spine. After the Civil War, she lived in Baltimore and helped children with spinal diseases (Barnwell, *Story of an American Family*, 255).

33. This term seems to refer to the King family of Roswell. Four sons of Barrington King held commissions in the Roswell Battalion: Captain James Roswell King (1827–97), Captain Thomas Edward King (1829–63), 1st Lieutenant Ralph Browne King (1835–78), and 1st Lieutenant Joseph Henry King (1839–1917) (Hitt, *After the Left Flank*, foreword).

34. Great Oaks, the home of the Presbyterian minister Nathaniel Alpheus Pratt, was about one-half of a mile south of the Smith home, across from the church. On the same side of the street and about two hundred yards to the south was Holly Hill, built in 1842 for Savannah cotton broker Robert Adams Lewis (1813–96) and his wife, Catherine Barrington Cook, a niece of Roswell King's who had been named for his wife. An elderly couple who are surely Robert Lewis's parents, John and Margaret Lewis, are listed in dwelling 1333 (Holly Hill) on page 188 of the 1860 census of Cobb County, Georgia, while the Pratts' dwelling is listed on page 189 as number 1334. John Lewis (1784–1867) is listed as age seventy-four and Margaret as seventy-three.

35. General Braxton Bragg (1817–76) commanded Confederate forces around Chattanooga, Tennessee, until his defeat at Missionary Ridge on November 25, 1863, whereupon he resigned his command.

36. Rodgers, comp., "Roster of the Battalion of the Georgia Military Institute Cadets," lists a Captain John M. Richardson as Professor of Higher Mathematics and a Captain Paul Eve as Professor of Mathematics and English Branches. Rodgers must have confused the chief surgeon of the Army of Tennessee with Joseph E. Eve, who is listed as Professor of Civil and Military Engineering at GMI in Temple, *The First Hundred Years*, 196–97. Francis Withers Capers (1819–92), after a successful career in teaching at academies and universities in Kentucky and South Carolina, including a time as superintendent of the Citadel, became the superintendent of the Georgia Military Institute in 1859, with the rank of major. He was also appointed a brigadier general in the state militia in 1861 (Myers, ed., *Children of Pride*, 1484–85).

37. There were two prominent military schools in North Carolina at the time: the Charlotte Military Institute and the Hillsboro Military Academy (Barrett, *Civil War in North Carolina*, 27).

38. Confederate General Joseph Eggleston Johnston (1807–91) had not yet assumed command of the Army of Tennessee, having been in charge of the Department of the West. The town of Kingston is on the Western and Atlantic Railroad between Rome and Cassville, Georgia. The troop movement mentioned here is part of the impending Battle of Chickamauga, which took place on September 19–20 and resulted in a Confederate victory when forces under Bragg turned back a federal attack into northwest Georgia, forcing a retreat to Chattanooga.

39. Captain King had volunteered to become a part of the staff of General Preston Smith and was killed when they lost their way while inspecting their lines at night and rode into a federal unit (Myers, ed., *Children of Pride*, 1585; Faust, ed., *Historical Times Illustrated Encyclopedia of the Civil War*, 697–98).

40. On December 3, 1863, Archibald Smith wrote to William, "I find the Rileys clever hospitable people, and if you had Smith's views of getting a fortune with a wife you might take the younger daughter, tho S. has the best of the two. She is really a very

suitable wife for him, has good sound sense & is very affectionate and good tempered."
Gulielma later married Archie Smith.

41. John W. Magill (b. 1817) was the son of Anne Smith's uncle William A. Magill
(b. 1792). After enlisting as a private in the Chatham Artillery in 1861, "Jack" Magill became a 1st lieutenant in Captain Daniell's battery of light artillery in 1863–64 (drawer
254, rolls 51, 65, microfilm records of Georgia Civil War soldiers, Georgia Department of Archives and History, Atlanta). Jack Magill had previously been U.S. consul at
Sabanilla (now Baranquilla), Colombia (then Nueva Granada), from March 1860 to
June 30, 1861 (information courtesy of John Ziebarth). Jack Magill was a "black sheep"
Magill, was something of a rake, and was constantly imposing upon the Smiths' hospitality.

42. One of many references to a Mr. Dougherty who was attempting to raise a company. Possibly Captain William E. Doughtery, who left Confederate service in 1863 because of disability (Henderson, ed., *Roster*, 3:287). At least three Georgia Confederate
companies were named Dougherty.

43. A settlement a few miles north of Roswell.

44. Major Charles Archibald Alexander Dunwody (1828–1905) was a Roswell merchant and Civil War soldier who had been compelled to resign because of his wounds
(Myers, ed., *Children of Pride*, 1510). A daughter, R. M. Dunwody, eight years old,
is listed in his household in the Cobb County census of 1860.

45. According to Lee Kennett, "Most of the population did not see a blue uniform
until after Appomattox," and "the area eventually became the granary of the Confederacy, or more properly its corncrib." The huge crops of 1863 and 1864 "became the surest source of supply for the Confederate army in Virginia," and in late 1863 the
Confederate government selected this area for its new prisoner of war camp, naming
it Camp Sumter. But everyone called it by the name of a village nearby: Andersonville
(*Marching through Georgia*, 22–23).

46. See Skinner, ed., *Autobiography of Henry Merrell*, 343–44, 489 n. 9.

47. Quintard, chaplain-at-large to Joseph E. Johnston's Army of Tennessee, was
a physician who later became Protestant Episcopal bishop of Tennessee and Vice-
Chancellor of the University of the South. At the time he was chaplain of the 1st Regi-
ment of Tennessee Infantry. He was connected to Roswell through his wife, Eliza
Catherine Hand, the granddaughter of Roswell King (Myers, ed., *Children of
Pride*, 1653). See also Quintard, *Dr. Quintard*, 12–13, 89–90.

Correspondents

(IN ORDER OF THEIR APPEARANCE)

ANNE MAGILL SMITH (1807–87) *Willie's mother*

THOMAS CAROLIN CLAY (1841–97) *A military friend of Willie's*

ELIZABETH ANNE ("LIZZIE") SMITH (1831–1915) *Willie's older sister*

ARCHIBALD SMITH (1801–86) *Willie's father*

WILLIAM SEAGROVE ("WILLIE") SMITH (1834–65)
The focal point of these letters

CAPT. G. W. JOHNSON (?) *A grateful Confederate officer*

ARCHIBALD ("ARCHIE") SMITH (1844–1923) *Willie's younger brother*

P. D. GIVENS (?) *A Signal Corps friend of Willie's*

HELEN ZUBLY ("AUNTIE") MAGILL (1812–87)
Willie's maternal aunt, living with the Smiths

HELEN ZUBLY ("SISSIE") SMITH (1841–96) *Willie's younger sister*

BARRINGTON KING (1798–1866)
Head of the Roswell Manufacturing Company

GULIELMA RILEY SMITH (1846–1921)
The wife of Willie's brother, Archie

JAMES J. PRYOR (?) *An employee of the Roswell Manufacturing Company*

GEORGE HULL CAMP (1816–1907)
Agent of the Roswell Manufacturing Company

MARGARET COWPER MACKAY ELLIOTT (1807–93)
A Savannah cousin of the Smiths'

DAVID COMFORT (1837–73) *A Presbyterian minister in Valdosta, Georgia*

DR. RICHARD SHARP MASON (1795–1874)
An Episcopalian rector in Raleigh, North Carolina

BISHOP STEPHEN ELLIOTT (1806–66)
A cousin of the Smiths', living in Augusta, Georgia

WILLIAM DUNCAN (1799–1879) *The Savannah agent of Archibald Smith*

SARAH MACKAY (1815–76) *A Savannah cousin of the Smiths'*

JOSEPH M. ATKINSON (1820–91)
A Presbyterian minister in Raleigh, North Carolina

MARY ANN MASON (1802–81) *The wife of Richard Sharp Mason and author*

CHARLES ARTHUR MAGILL (1817–84)
Willie's maternal uncle, living in Arkansas

ISABELLA BACON MAGILL (1830–1907)
One of Willie's aunts, living in Arkansas
REBECCA E. MASON (?)
The youngest daughter of Richard Sharp and Mary Ann Mason
ANN ELIZA STEWART (b. 1810?) *A friend of the Smiths' from St. Marys*
SEAGROVE WILLIAM MAGILL (1810–84)
Willie's maternal uncle, living in Connecticut
ELIZABETH MAGILL MERRELL (1815–90)
Willie's maternal aunt, living in Arkansas
CATHERINE MARGARET KING (1804–87) *Barrington King's wife*
ARTHUR WILLIAM SMITH (1881–1960)
Archie's son, the last member of the Smith family
ROBERT G. STEPHENS (1881–1974)
An Atlanta physician and friend of Arthur Smith's

The Death of a Confederate

"A Time of
Anxiety & Apprehension"

MOTHER TO WILLIAM

Roswell Jan 1st 1864

A happy new year to you my precious child. There is little now in the out-
ward circumstances of life to bring happiness, yet I trust we all possess that
within which gives joy & peace under all circumstances. After a great deal of
rain it has cleared off intensely cold & I cannot keep my thoughts from the
sufferings of the poor fellows exposed to all its severity. At the same time it
seems to render any advance of the enemy impossible for the present & as
Mr Waldburg[1] declines letting your Father have [a] house it scarcely seems
worth while for us to rush down, either to be without adequate shelter or at
immense expense boarding in Valdosta & the fact is there are so many

Negroes in the neighborhood that I do not think it much better than remaining here. Sonny's sickness & now the weather have hindered so much that nothing has yet been done. It takes all the time of Luke & Jack[2] to cut wood & Father is in a constant state of hurry & excitement with no help & accomplishing nothing. We are thinking now that it will be better for him to go down & make some preparation for us & if a hurry comes before he is ready we can then go as we would now. God only knows what is best & we pray that he will direct us. Sonny keeps up & bears the change of weather better than we thought he would but is quite weak. C. Dunwody's oldest daughter Rosa died last Sunday, with diphtheria.[3] It is the only case we have heard of. H. Pratt expects to be with Col. Gordon's regiment. He will go down next week.[4]

Bayard is better. I am sorry to hear Percy's accident is so serious. I hope he will be able to come to his mother before long.[5] My cold is better. The rest as usual.

It is so cold I cannot write any more. May God bless you my precious child

Your aff

Mother

I hope Lizzie told all my messages about my sweet little basket.

1. There is no Waldburg living in Lowndes County, Georgia, in 1860. The likeliest candidate seems to be a Jacob Waldberg of Savannah, a planter who was sixty-six years old in 1860. The only other Waldberg living in the state in 1860 was in far-off Habersham County, in north Georgia (Genealogical Committee, comp., *1860 Census*, 381).

2. Perhaps family servants Luck (b. 1814?) and John (b. 1818). Luck seems to have been known as "Daddy Luke" (Smith Papers, box 17, folder 2).

3. Major Charles Archibald Alexander Dunwody (1828–1905) was a Roswell merchant and Civil War soldier who had been compelled to resign because of his wounds (Myers, ed., *Children of Pride*, 1510). A daughter, R. M. Dunwody, eight years old, is listed in his household in the Cobb County census of 1860.

4. Because Henry Barrington Pratt (1832–1912) was a missionary who went to South America in 1856 it is not likely that he is the "H. Pratt" referred to here. It seems more probable that "H. Pratt" is his older brother, Horace Alpheus Pratt (1830–70). Henry and Horace were two of the ten children of the Nathaniel Alpheus Pratt (1796–1879), minister of the Presbyterian church in Roswell. According to Confederate records, both Captain Horace A. Pratt and Bayard Hand Pratt (b. 1838), another brother, were members of Company A, 3d Regiment of Georgia State (Glynn County) Troops (Georgia, Confederate Pensions and Records Department, Georgia Department of Archives and

History, microfilm drawer 253, roll 50). Perhaps "Gordon's Regiment" is that of George Anderson Gordon (1830–72), colonel of the 63d Regiment of Georgia Infantry (Myers, ed., *Children of Pride*, 1531).

5. Bayard may be Bayard Hand Pratt. Percy is Percival Elliott (1840–65), a son of Margaret Cowper Mackay Elliott (1807–93).

MOTHER TO WILLIAM

Roswell Jan 8th 1864

My Dear Son

Your letter of Jan. 1st I rec'd on Wednesday & am glad to find you are able to keep warm for tho' the weather cannot be near as cold with you as it is here I know you mind a less degree as much as most of us do a greater. The weather continues extremely cold & wet. It is unusual for such severe weather to continue so long. It is almost impossible to do any thing but make fire. Your Father wanted to do most of the heavy packing before he leaves but it is so cold that nothing is done yet & yet cold as it is, it is a severe trial to leave our home & go where we shall have barely a shelter & probably meet with sickness, where there will be so little to alleviate it. Since Mr Waldberg declines to let him have his house your Father has concluded it will be best for him to go to his own land & put up a log house & what an undertaking it is for a man of his years & health to go into the woods without even a neighbor & do such a work. I feel very anxious on his account & would willingly go with him if it did not seem even more necessary for me to remain at home. He is very anxious that you sh[d] get a furlough & go to help him select a place for the house.

I wish very much that you could, for a great many things are to be considered & I think your quiet judgment would aid him very much. It will be very trying to be set down in a small house exposed to the burning sun & if there is any choice of a place it should be looked to. We have been talking of the hammock as most desirable on account of trees & good soil for a garden but that being surrounded by a swamp we fear would be sickly. If all could be reconciled to the change & resolve to make the best of it I could feel strong to encounter all the hardships incident to the removal. May our Heavenly Father guide us in the right way & my continual prayer is, "If the Lord go not with us let us not go hence."

I am glad to hear you had such a pleasant day in town & the opportunity of entertaining your friends with your microscope. You must have prepared a good many specimens. I hope I shall be able to remember to send some Mica. We think it will be best for Sonny to go down & see about getting into the Signal Corps, for the new conscript law will probably do away with the exemption of the Cadets. We hear nothing more of Mr D's company & if he is rejected by the Signal Corps on the score of health there will be more hope of his getting a discharge & if he gets in it will be a situation of less exposure than the common service. I hope he will be rejected if it will be the means of securing his discharge. Your Father went to see a surgeon of the examining board in Atlanta who told him there was no such thing as a discharge on account of Rheumatism. He has so far recovered from this attack better than from the previous tho' the weather is very much against him.

I am sorry to hear you are so much troubled about being groomsman. I do not see how you can refuse & you ought to overcome your bashfulness, for you know you can be very entertaining & agreeable to the ladies when you choose & it will be such a fine opp.ʸ for you to wear your smart new coat. There is no jean to be had now except brown which I think very ugly. I will continue to look for it. Have you heard nothing of your box? Even if you should get the money at which it is valued it will not make up to you the loss of the little home comforts it contained. We are as usual & all unite in much love to you.

May God bless & keep you my precious child
Your aff
Mother

Father thinks he may not go through Sav. in going down but he will write to you in good time & you can go to him if you can get furlough.

———

MOTHER TO WILLIAM

Roswell Jan 15ᵗʰ 1864

I sit down to write & my mind is so full of anxiety that I can hardly collect my thoughts. Here is the middle of January & we are no nearer to having a place of refuge than we were when we first became apprehensive for the safety of this place. The weather has been such that it has been impossible to do any thing in preparation for moving. Clarinda[1] has not been able to leave her house for several weeks & it is as much as the boys [can] make out to keep us in wood & it is impossible to hire a carpenter to box up furniture. Time is going so fast that spring will soon be here & the yankees again moving. So your Father will have to be off as soon as the weather will permit to try & prepare a shelter for us & then if the necessity comes we must just go & leave every thing.

It is hard to know what to do. We pray for light but no light seems to dawn upon us. There is no present cause for haste in leaving but it will take a long time for even a coarse log house & now it seems as if we would not have the means of boarding altho' we may have plenty to live on. Economically you know the Factory is our only means of support & the Legislature has put on such a heavy tax to take effect from *last* April that it will take all they can make for some time to pay arrears. It seems strange how such laws can be made but so it is.

In regard to our dear boy I am very anxious the act has not yet passed (as we thought it had) but no doubt it will, repealing all exemptions with some few exceptions, & he feels that it would be such a disgrace to be conscripted, that he cannot bear it. The government officials surgeons as well as others are so little actuated by principle that there seems little hope of his health being duly considered & it seems to me that there would be more hope of his being discharged from the Signal Corps than from the common service (if he should be conscripted) or getting an exemption on acct of health. At present he certainly is not fit for any thing but to be taken care of. Our present idea is that he had better go to Clinch or wherever your Father goes, stopping a few days with you if you can accommodate him. Your Father intends to go to Albany & from there take his mules & wagon across, as the least expensive way & Sonny could not stand the fatigue & exposure. So I want him to go to Sav. & stay until you hear from Father. . . .

I am so much stronger than I used to be that I hope to be able to walk to church.[2] I do not know if I wrote that we had a letter from Charley not long since. It was dated in Oct. They had all removed to Camden. Aunt Bet had her house & Belle still had her friends with her. C. mentioned that he was about uniting with the Episcopal Church & we hope he was actuated by proper feeling as he mentioned it in a very different way from what he did on several previous occasions when Belle was intending to have him confirmed.[3] We have just rec'd your letter of *Aug. 8* in which you notice your Father's offer to give you something to invest for yourself. I always thought it strange you did not say anything about it. It has stop'd raining at last & is not as cold as it has been but is still very uncomfortable. Oh! how I wish I could have you a little while to talk over matters, but I dare say I should not be satisfied with a little while. May God bless you my darling son

Your aff

Mother

1. Clarinda Richardson, according to Archibald Smith's records of his servants, had been born on February 10, 1834, and was apparently the daughter of Nanny Morris (b. 1791?) and Morris (b. 1780) (Smith Papers, box 17, folder 2).

2. The Roswell Presbyterian Church is one-half mile from the Smith home.

3. The details of these sentences concern the family of Anne Smith's sister Elizabeth Magill Merrell (1815–90), known to the Smiths as Aunt Bet. Her husband, Henry Merrell (1816–83), moved to Arkansas in 1856, and at the time of this letter, he had recently completed a mission for the Confederate Department of the Trans-Mississippi and had moved his family from his factory site in Pike County to a safer location in Camden, in the southwest corner of Arkansas. Anne Smith's brother Charles Arthur ("Charley") Magill (1817–84), had also moved to Arkansas to be Merrell's assistant. Charley married Aurelia Isabella ("Belle") Bacon (1830–1907), an Episcopalian, and converted to her church. See also Skinner, ed., *Autobiography of Henry Merrell*, 343–44; 489 n. 9.

T. C. CLAY TO WILLIAM

Ways Station Jan 19th 1864

Dear Smith

There are to be two stations out here one at Genesis pt, the other *here* (at Ways Station).[1] Try and get the Capt to let you come tell him we would rather be here than at the point. Go and see about it yourself. Don't fail. Clarke says there is no reason why you should not come & he wants good men. Thinks both you & Harden ought to be sent out here.[2] You here & Harden at the point. I will tell you about my talk with the Capt when I was in Sav. about you coming out here. Just tell him you have got to come. He said when the post was established at the point he would send you with me, & I think he will let you & I have this post. Try hard & go & see about it at once. Please don't fail. I want you out here at Ways with me

goodbye your aff friend
T.C. Clay[3]

He said this post was not a permanent one. Clarke says it is & it was only an excuse, & if the wagon had not gotten to Rose Dew, I think he would have changed his plans & let you come but it was too late when I got to him. Try hard, plenty of game & near at hand.

Your aff friend
T.C. Clay

1. Fort McAllister was at Genesis Point on the Great Ogeechee River south of Savannah. Way's Station, also on the Great Ogeechee a few miles northwest of Genesis Point, was Station 1¹/2 on the Atlantic and Gulf Railroad.

2. Privates G. B. Clarke and W. D. Harden were members of the Chatham Artillery in 1862 (Jones, *Historical Sketch*, 104). Harden, like Willie, was a member of the Signal Corps command of Captain Joseph Manigault in Savannah, District of Geor-

gia (National Archives Microfilm Publications, *Compiled Service Records of Confederate Soldiers Who Served in Organizations Raised Directly by the Confederate Government*, roll 118).

3. Thomas Carolin Clay (1841–97), a native of Bryan County, Georgia. After Georgia seceded from the Union, Clay left Yale in 1861 and enlisted as a private in the Liberty Independent Troop. He was detailed to serve in the Signal Corps and became a close friend of Willie Smith's (Myers, ed., *Childen of Pride*, 1492–93).

LIZZIE TO WILLIAM

Jan 22^{d} 64

Cher Guilliaume

... Sonny has his heart so set on staying with you a little while & do of all things don't say any thing about he *ought* to stay at home when Father is gone & helping.[1] He feels badly about that sort of thing enough already but he can do no good as he is & mother will be better off having him where she thinks he is getting well. So you had better talk as if that was the best thing for him to do....

Love from all
your aff sister
Lizzie Smith

1. Archie, apparently on leave from GMI, was on his way to visit Willie in Savannah. He was also apparently recovering from an illness and was concerned about not helping at home during his father's absence.

Dear William

I send this letter[1] to Archie to you as I don't know where to direct to him. I told him he must bring home lots of palmetto with him as we are going to make lots of things.

I expect he is enjoying himself very much. I wish he would stay all his time with you. He will enjoy it much more than being off by himself.

Mother is gone to Marietta today to see Maj Capers about him about getting an extension of furlough, how long he will continue to give them, & if there is any chance of an exemption.[2] I think the hope of Mr Daugherty's company is getting very slim tho it may come up some of these days.[3]

Love from all
your aff sister
E S

1. Enclosed with the previous letter. Archie is apparently on his way to Savannah.

2. Francis Withers Capers (1819–92) was the superintendent of GMI, but he also had the rank of brigadier general in the state militia.

3. Mr. Daughtery (or Doughtery or Dougherty) is a man from the Roswell area whose effort to raise a company of soldiers holds out the hope that Archie might get an officer's commission in the unit. His identity, however, continues to elude us. In the Kennesaw cemetery, east of Roswell and north of Marietta, lies one of the earliest settlers of Cobb County, James G. Dougherty (1812–84) (Shadburn, *Cherokee Planters*, 353; Temple, *First Hundred Years*, 764). The man mentioned here could also be a Captain William E. Doughtery, who was forced to leave Confederate service in 1863 because of disability (Henderson, ed., *Roster*, 3:287).

MOTHER TO WILLIAM

Roswell Jan 29th 1864

My Dear Son

. . . I hope [Sonny] will get to you safely about the time you receive this. It seems to me that the indications of Providence are that the army is not his place & only the fear of conscription would make me yield at all to his wish to seek a situation there. If he could be exempted in another way I should greatly prefer it to his going back to the Institute at present for I think his health is much injured by being there. It is only not quite as bad as being in the common service & the idea of returning there is a great burden to him yet I do not think that is the reason he wishes to go into the Army. I proposed to him to give up a year at the Institute if we can manage to keep him at home & perhaps with a change of climate his health might improve but he seems to think he is getting too old to lose a year, yet he may save time by doing so.

Young men in this country are in too great a hurry to take upon them the responsibilities of life & that is one reason why they are so superficial & grow old so soon. I want you to think about this & talk it all over with him & try & get him to talk freely to you. He has great confidence in your judgment & if you both think as I do I will try & see Gen Capers (Father will not be back in time) who seemed very willing to be obliging about extending his furlough & perhaps he will consider him a member & yet give him furloughs from time to time which will protect him & I do not think there will be any thing wrong in it. I am glad to hear Rose Dew is such a pleasant situation[1] & that Genesis Point is still your destination. I only know you seemed to think that would be pleasant for you & tho' if we go down Way's Station would be very convenient I am afraid for your health there.

Only think, I had some new stockings for you & forgot to send them & your knife that Arch. mended so nicely was put into Lizzie's work box & came back. How is it that you do not get any pay now? I am thankful Father is able to help you & hope you will let us know when you require any thing. Sonny has more than he will require, so do use any you want only leaving enough to bring him home. Father left on Monday with his large wagon (on springs), the buggy, 4 mules, Nanny Sue, & the children, expecting to take them on the R.R. to Albany & drive the rest of the way.[2] But he wrote me from Atlanta the day after he left that he found it so troublesome he had sold the mules for 400 less than he gave for them & the wagon for very little & was going to Valdosta by R.R. It is a great pity for he will want them very much down there. Sonny will tell you all about Harry & the small pox.[3] It makes me very uneasy about Father. The hotel keeper & physician ought to be exposed for it was a shameful piece of negligence if nothing worse. The weather is delightful now & makes us think how soon spring with all its beauties will be here & we must go & leave them all. Do keep an eye on Sonny. He is very easily over fatigued. If he has rheumatism rub his spine faithfully with the liniment he has in his trunk. It is apt to commence in his chest. Love to him & yourself May God bless you both

Your aff

Mother

Helen says if you wish a cravat say what colour & she will make it for you. This is for A.

1. The original name for this site on the Little Ogeechee River south of Vernonburg was Rose Dhu. It was the southwestern end of the Confederate line of defense that began at the Savannah River about four miles east of the city and swung in a rough semicircle to Rose Dew. Beaulieu, to which Willie Smith was often posted, was the next fortified position to the east of Rose Dew. It was situated where the Little Ogeechee joined with the Vernon River. Genesis Point is southwest of Rose Dew; Way's Station is northwest of it.

2. Nanny Sue seems to be the Smith's servant, Sue, who appears as twelve years old in one of Archibald Smith's notebooks in a "List of Negroes left to me by my father in 1831." She was the mother of Moses (b. 1842), Luke (b. 1846), and Nancy (1857–64), who may be some of the children mentioned here. Nancy died in Valdosta on February 5, 1864 (Smith Papers, box 17, folder 2).

3. Harry seems to be a Smith servant (b.1824?), who has been staying with Willie. The possibility that Archibald Smith paid his servants wages is raised in this sentence

from a letter from Anne Smith to Willie dated Nov. 2, 1863: "What arrangement did you make about clothing when you hired Harry? If you are to clothe him do not buy in Sav. It will cost you most of his wages. Let me know at once & I will send something when I send your box."

FATHER TO WILLIAM

Sav[a] Feby 1/64 at the Mackays[1]

My Dear Son

I am in Sav[a] & expect to stay until Wednesday, without there is hope of seeing you and that would keep me a day or two longer, do try and send me word somehow, whether you can come in and on what day.

I am anxious to get back to Lowndes to get to work but am very desirous of having a talk with you. I met Willis[2] just now & he told me that the lines were down, so I must try & get this out to you in some other way. I don't know if it is best to take Archy with me now or wait until he stays with you a day or two, I rather think he will be better with you a short time & then come on. I have not yet concluded whether to build in Clinch or on Brother's place.[3] The latter would be much the most convenient, but the former would be more out of the way of the numerous gangs of coast Negroes, who form by their numbers an inducement for a yankee raid, and might by their thieving prevent all stock or vegetable raising.

I am quite well & A. is doing well.

May God bless you.

Your affectionate Father

Arch[d] Smith

Tuesday   A. thought of going to see you in your wagon but the rain may prevent. Do let me know by teleg[h] if you can come up tomorrow.

I will call at the Barrack by sundown to see if you can send me a message.

A.S.

---

1. Archibald Smith's distant cousins Catherine (1811–79) and Sarah Mackay (1815–76) were unmarried and lived in the old Mackay home on the corner of Broughton and Abercorn Streets in Savannah (see Myers, ed., *Children of Pride,* 1610).

2. Private Francis William Willis of Company G, 5th Georgia Cavalry, who, like Willie, was detailed to duty in the Signal Corps (National Archives Microfilm Publications, *Compiled Service Records of Confederate Soldiers Who Served in Organizations Raised Directly by the Confederate Government,* roll 121).

3. Archibald Smith may be referring either to some property that his half-brother John Joyner Smith (1790–1872) owned in Lowndes County or to his "Blue Mud" plantation on the South Carolina side of the Savannah River, near the city.

MOTHER TO WILLIAM, UNDATED

My Dear Son

I am truly sorry you could not see your Father either time that he was in Sav.[1] It seems to me that the face of things is changing very much & the Yankees are rather turning from than toward us & if (as your Father writes me is probable) they take the R. R. below Savannah will we be safer down there where there is no military force to oppose them & such large numbers of Negroes who might be incited to diabolical deeds. I feel almost distracted by conflicting ideas. It seems to me things have changed very much since your Father first talked of going to that part of the country & there have been so many Providential obstacles in his way that it is almost fighting against God to go on. I should have been more willing to go in the winter, but it will be almost summer there before he can have a shelter for us & I think it is a sickly country. I want you to look at the matter in all its bearings & see what the movements of the armies are & write what *you* think about it as he says he wants the aid of your counsel. You know when he takes an idea he can see nothing else & mostly but one point.

Liz has violently opposed our going from here & I have not been able to get him to discuss the matter calmly. As soon as I try to say any thing not in favour of an immediate removal he says it is opposition to him. He wants to put up two log rooms & take us all down immediately to live in them & did not like at all that I was not willing unless we were driven off as fugitives. He thinks we shall not be able to take much more than our bedding & but little of that (& I suppose this is so for it is impossible to hire horses or wagons & he has sold all his) & if so why hurry away from all our comforts? I do not want to make you think as I do but I want to lay things before you & let you judge. I have no one to talk with about it & do not know what to think. I do not like to write to you in this strain & in most things I give up my opinion & will, but this is a matter of too much importance to yield without trying to come at the truth. Father writes that he hopes I am getting things pack'd but I have not done any thing at it yet.

Clarinda is not able to do much.[2] It takes the two boys all the time to keep us in wood & do the little necessary errands & I have not felt strong enough to undertake the work particularly as I do not know what to put up when every thing is in use. O! that God would deliver us from our enemies & give us wisdom for our present difficulties.

Sonny was anticipating a great deal of pleasure in being with you but from your last I fear it is inconvenient to you to have him. If so let him go on to Valdosta.

May God bless you my dear son

Your aff
Mother

1. Archibald Smith had not seen Willie on an earlier trip he had made through Savannah in October–November 1863.

2. Clarinda Richardson (b. 1834) was a Smith family servant who remained in Valdosta after the Civil War and corresponded with the family until the last decade of the century.

WILLIAM TO HELEN

Rose Dew Feb 9/64

Dear Sissie

I am surprised to learn by your last letter that you did not receive my answer to your former one for I am sure I wrote an answer to it.

It seems that my letters are getting like the newspapers, each one contradicting the former. Sonnie will go to Sa^v today and stay a day before going on to Fl^a. He has been quite well since he has been here, has not had any rheumatism.

I thought I had told Sister all about the wedding but it seems you want to know more. Well I wore my fine grey coat and blue pants, and a pair of new shoes which hurt my feet a little, had my hair brushed and moustache curled by a barber. I can't tell how sweet I looked for I did not see myself in a glass after I was dressed but you can just compare me to a barrel of sugar or a cane patch or any thing of the sort. I felt prime only D^r. Axson[1] was very long and boring in the ceremony. The ceremony was performed at the house in what used to be Cousin Margaret's dining room so there was not any long aisle to walk up.[2] The bridal party was formed in a sort of oblong so the couple was in the middle, Tom Clay and Miss Willie Law on each side of them Sam Law and Ellen Axson at one end Miss Dowse and myself at the other and D^r. A. in front just about under the gas burner.[3] No doubt we looked very pretty. The bride was dressed in white muslin or some sort of stuff made up very plainly with a puff of white concern round where the hem ought to be and ever so

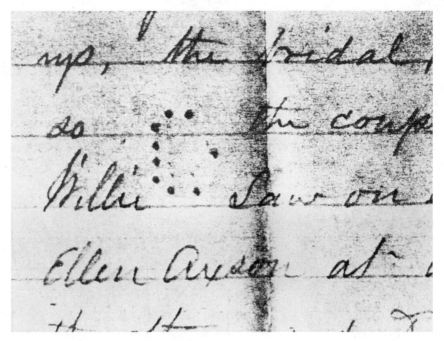

Willie's diagram of a wedding ceremony

much white lace hanging down from her head to the floor with a silk cord round the edge, and a wreath of shell flowers on her head.

I don't think I will fall in love with any of the others because the prettiest that is left is engaged to Tom Clay, and besides there is a very charming young widow worth $150,000 in town, that I have been thinking about lately, so you need not be scared of my admiration of Miss Law.[4]

You are the first one that has written to me about D[r]. G. So much espoir with Helen B.[5] The report here is that they are engaged, but of course her flat denial of it falsifies the report. I hope it is not so for he is not gentleman enough to marry into our family. I was very much surprised to hear it for I did not know when they could have met unless under the auspices of that woman Mrs. B.

It is just Capt. M's. meanness that I am not sent to Ways Station.[6] He took a man from this station who did not want to go, and then sent me here in his place. It has been a great disappointment to me, for I have been counting on having good times out there. Clay says that deer and turkeys are plentiful out there, but we niggers have to put up with any thing that officers choose to do.

A & I are quite well.

Much Love to all

Your afft Bro W[m]

My box has come. The apples and chestnuts and peas were of course good for nothing but the hams and cans were good and the gown and socks unhurt. The receipt of the box in any condition was an agreeable surprise.

1. The Reverend Dr. Isaac Stockton Keith Axson (1831–91) was the pastor of the Independent Presbyterian Church in Savannah from 1857 until his death (Myers, ed., *Children of Pride,* 1456).

2. The wedding of Willie's college friend James Smith Cozby (1837–94), a Confederate chaplain, and Mary Louisa Law took place on January 26, 1864 (Tankersley, *College Life,* 166; Myers, ed., *Children of Pride,* 1496). The wedding must have taken place at the home of Margaret Cowper Mackay Elliott (1807–93).

3. Willie's friend, Thomas Carolin Clay; Caroline Matilda Law (1842–1909), daughter of the Honorable William Law (1793–1874); her brother, Samuel Spry Law (1844–68); Dr. Axon's daughter Ellen (1860–1914); and Laura Philoclea Dowse (1835–99), a prominent Savannah spinster (see Myers, ed., *Children of Pride,* 1492, 1591, 1456, 1508).

4. Tom Clay later married Caroline Matilda Law on November 1, 1864.

5. Dr. Charles Atwood Geiger (b.1822?), who lived in Roswell with the family of Major John Minton (1797–1871), close to the Smiths. Geiger's *espoir* (hope) would be fulfilled later in the war, when he married Archibald's Smith's niece Helen Barnwell (1839–79), the oldest daughter of Eliza Zubly Smith Barnwell (1803–46).

6. Probably Captain Joseph Manigault. See Anne Smith's letter of November 24, 1863, n. 1, above.

FATHER TO WILLIAM

at Mrs Riley's 11 Feby 64

My Dear William

Before the door, in this retired place, as we all thought, presents quite a military array of the Troops going to repel the enemy in Florida.[1] There is quite a little army passing, what the yanks are at I can't divine, but I hope they will be destroyed or captured.

I have just concluded a bargain to hire a comfortable house with a garden spot, for $250 per an. the house has small rooms 4 rooms and two pantries too confined for sleeping rooms dotted and a good piazza in front & shade trees, altogether a snug *little* place, good out buildings of Logs. I want to write to Mother so must stop.

Your Affectionate Father
Arch^d Smith

Let Archie come on, I must go home soon.

1. The troops are passing by on their way to repel a federal advance from Jacksonville westward across Florida that was part of an attempt to bring Florida back into the Union. By February 20, some five thousand Confederates had gathered near Olustee (Ocean Pond), Florida, to repel that advance.

MOTHER TO WILLIAM

Roswell Feb. 12th 1864

My Dear Son

Your letter of the 7th has just come to hand. I am surprised to hear that Sonny had left you. He seemed so decidedly to prefer being with you to any other arrangement but perhaps it was not convenient to you to have him stay longer. . . . I was in hopes to hear from him today, what he wants to do about returning to the Institute. He thought if he was to return he had rather go at the commencement of the term tho' the Dr advises that he should not.

I went to see Gen Capers a few days ago & got an extension of furlough for him in case he wanted to remain longer in the low country & his first is nearly out but I do not know where to send it. I suppose you have not been able to do any thing for him as you say nothing about it & I am miserable about him. Gen Capers said he had better enroll himself & go before a board of examination & he promised a certificate (signed by Dr Setz[1] & himself) of his unfitness for military duty & he thinks no military board would refuse him an exemption. Dear Son pray for him & for me that I may have faith to leave him in God's hands & yet that we may all do what we can to secure what seems so desirable for him. He seemed very much pleased with your idea of his going to Genesis Point & learning telegraphing with you but unless he can get an exemption he cannot do it & I am afraid under the new law even the military Inst. will not shield him.

Helen has commenced making fans. They will use for "society" all those you sent up except two that Lizzie wants, one for Flo Bayard[2] & one for herself & I want one to send to the lady of the house where we stayed at Indian Springs who was very attentive & extremely kind to Helen. H. says you must remember she cannot have too many. They sell readily. We are now turning our attention to soldier's stockings & the society money is all spent for them. 50 prs were sent to Gen Foster[3] last week for Longstreet's men & we are trying to get more. We cannot knit enough. It is tedious work & the same time spent on fancy articles for sale enables us to purchase a great many more at $2.00. Just think before the war we gave 20 cents.

Archibald's diagram of a rented house

... We are as usual.

May God bless you & guide you in all your ways my precious child

Your aff

Mother

1. A Dr. E. J. Setze (b. 1830?) lived in Marietta in 1860.

2. The family of Nicholas J. Bayard (1799–1879), a stockholder in the Roswell Manufacturing Company who often signed its minutes, lived next to the Smiths in 1850, and they had a daughter named Florida (b. 1834?). However, they are not listed in the 1860 census of the county.

3. John Gray Foster (1823–74) commanded the Union Department of the South in 1864. Because there is no Confederate general named Foster who could have received these gifts, Anne Smith probably means that the stockings were sent to Foster for those of Longstreet's men who were his prisoners.

MOTHER TO WILLIAM

Roswell Feb. 19th/64

My Dear Son

We have during the last week had a fresh cause of anxiety out of which the Lord has mercifully delivered us. Helen was so sick with her throat last Friday & Saturday that I sent to Marietta for a Dr on Saturday afternoon. He did [not] get here until 3 O'clock Sunday afternoon & then pronounced it Diphtheria. He said it was a very mild case, but it such an insidious & dreadful disease & from the mildest sometimes suddenly becomes of the most violent character that of course we were very anxious until the membrane was removed & the throat began to assume a healthy appearance. She is still in bed & rather weak but by no means prostrated & we hope the danger is passed. There is still some ulceration but that is yielding to remedies.

I had a letter from Father by last mail & was much relieved to hear something of Sonny & that he was with him for I thought he might be in some danger at the Springs as we see that the Yankees are approaching in that direction. The opinion has been pretty general here that they would make an effort to reach the South Western counties of this state where such large numbers of Negroes have been sent for safety & if they succeeded to continue their march to Mobile things have looked very threatening in the part of the country where we thought of going. There were so many unexpected hindrances to our getting off that I could not but feel that they were Providential & now I am sure we have great cause of thankfulness that Father's early plans did not succeed for if they had we should have been established down there & found it difficult to get away but he seems only to think of getting away from here & not to see any danger any where else. He has even carried most of his garden seeds. . . .

May God bless you my darling & keep you from all the danger of the times & above all enable you to glorify him in all your intercourse with others.

Your aff
Mother

NOTE FROM CAPTAIN G. W. JOHNSON,
ADDRESSED TO "MR. ARCH SMITH HIRED HOUSE"

H^{d}Qrs Co "C" Geo Siege Train
Camp at Forks of Road Feb 22nd
Mr Arch Smith

My dear Sir

Please accept my heartfelt thanks and grateful acknowledgments for the turkeys and provisions which you have so liberally furnished me. Your generosity will long be remembered by me and my company with deep and affectionate gratitude. It has been our fortune to visit many sections of the country in the capacity of soldiers and I can safely say we have never before received such a hospitable welcome as we have here. We appreciate you as friends and patriots, and if it should be our fate to meet the enemy who are now menacing your beautiful country on the field of conflict I trust that we shall conduct ourselves in such a manner as will prove that we are in some measure worthy of the good cheer which we have received by the wayside. Hoping that we may soon conquer a peace, and that a kind Providence will reward the good Samaritan who feeds the soldiers on their weary march to battle,

I am my dear Sir
Very [Rept ?] & truly yours
Geo W. Johnson[1]
Capt. Comd'g

1. It is possible that Captain Johnson and his company were returning through Valdosta from the Confederate victory at the Battle of Olustee, fought on February 20 near Lake City, Florida. We have not been able to identify this officer.

FATHER TO WILLIAM

Hired House Near Valdosta 26 F

My Dear William

We are fixed here in a very comfortable house which I hired at $250 until Jany 65 but from present appearances it is just as near the enemy as Roswell is, tho there is not so great local attraction here for the yankees.

Archy got an extension of his furlough to the 15 March, but he is not well enough yet to go the Institute. He has a cough, quite troublesome at times, which hinders his improvement. I think he will stay here longer & try & get another extension of furlough. I suppose you have heard of Helen's sickness with Diphtheria. By last accounts (19th) she was better tho not out of danger. She will probably need a change when she gets a little better, and can come here, if the enemy has been driven out of Florida; if so, I will go for her and on the way will be glad to see you. I almost want to take the trip to Sav on purpose to see you, and talk over matters. I don't like the situation here for if the yanks overrun Flo.ª, as they threaten, this will be an insecure place & then over in Clinch will not be much better and if I want to go to the inner pine Counties there is the difficulty of getting provisions and of transportation even if I could get a suitable place. Perhaps I now have done all I can, and must wait on the Lord. I was reading last night Take no thought for your life &c but seek ye first the Kingdom of God & his righteousness & all these things will be added to you for your Heavenly Father knows you have need of these things & surely if any Family has been blessed with the protection and guidance of the Lord it is ours. All my Children are the Lord's, and it is well with us, whatever may betide "The Lord is my strength & refuge, my high-tower." Unto Him will I fly. In Him will I trust. May He bless you. Ever your affectionate Father

Arch^d Smith

LIZZIE TO WILLIAM, UNDATED

Dear William

I had intended to write you a long lettre francaise this morning but extortioners have no time to spare for such things. I have a piece of Extortioner's work on hand which has to be finished today so must be content with plain English. The "Extortioners" have bought with their "ill gotten gains" 120 pairs of socks at $2.00. 40 pairs already sent off & the rest to be sent this week. Don't you think that is doing well? By those crochet caps alone I have made $69 & have orders for $21 worth more. With the palmetto which you are preparing we intend to screw lots of money out of some poor creatures.

Sissy is a great deal better well you may say altho not yet allowed to sit up much, Mother is so much afraid of her getting worse again. But I suppose all danger of that is past. Now she looks considerably thinner.

I am delighted to hear that you had such a nice time at that wedding. I thought you would. The young lady must have looked very sweet dressed so "plainly" if it is Miss Minnie.

You pretend you don't care for society & all that & yet you are so anxious to go out to Bryan Co because Clay tells you there are plenty of "dears" out there. I think you must be coming out. I always thought all that was half pretense but now you are just coming out. As to that $150,000 remember old Mr Weller & his advice to Samivel. Take warning by the old man Villiam bevare of the vidders for you know what one vidder is equal to.[1]

Don't let Sonny forget how that basket work is done. I am very anxious to do some. Is it very quick work? Who taught you how to do it? I have turned gardener & have planted some mustard & Kale to make "biled vittles" for your marm, she is so bad off for some & am hoeing out the strawberries. Are you going to get a furlough this summer? You must come either in Strawberry or Azalea time. You will have to take your choice. You ought to come a little later than you did last year. Anyhow the azaleas which I found after you went were a heap prettier than any we found before. I wish for you at home now very often for the weather is just the thing for walking & Liverworts & Houstonia & Saxifrage.

Love from all

yours aff sister

E S

Do if you can find any pretty duetts get one or two & send up by Father or Sonny, whichever comes first & if you can get from the girls any new sleeve patterns. Any one which you think pretty you can ask for . . . & send it up. . . . How do you like my home made envelopes?

---

1. Lizzie is using the name and dialect that Dickens's Cockney father Mr. Weller uses for his son Samuel in *Pickwick Papers.*

Roswell Feb. 26*th*/64

My Dear Son

I have had no letter from you this week & I do not know what to make of it, but I try not to feel anxious the mails are so unreliable. I am thankful to be able to say that Helen is much better. Up to last Tuesday from Saturday she had a good deal of fever & seemed to grow weaker rather than stronger having fever every day but I gave her quinine & the fever has left her & her throat is now quite free from ulcers or any appearance of the false membrane. She sat up out of bed yesterday for perhaps 2 hours at different times but she is still very weak & last night appeared very much fatigued & today has no inclination to get up. It is a very trying disease for if a light case as the Dr pronounced it has had such effect on her what must a severe case be?

We all like Dr Setze very much. His manner is so pleasant & considerate though his personal appearance is any thing but prepossessing.

I hear Mrs Baker & Mr & Mrs. Ralph are going to Savannah next week.[1] I will send your Stockings by Mrs Baker & I hope you will call on her. She is always sociable & pleasant. I hear they are going to the wedding altho' I have heard that the family were not pleased with the match. If you have any of Sonny's half worn socks you had better give them back to him when he returns as they would not last you long & now you will have new ones enough. I thought it a very good plan for you to take his when you could not get your own new ones.

I have never heard whether Sonny gave you the piece of Jean or his pants. I am very anxious to know whether his large ones are cut right & how they fit you for if I could cut I could have your common clothes made for so much less than you can that it would be worth while for me to do it. I have had some very nice & good looking cloth made for Father & Sonny & woolen cloth is getting so scarce & high that I think it would be wise for you when the weather grows warm to have some cotton made up & put away your woolen for another winter.

I have a letter from Father to-day. I am glad to find he & Sonny are staying at the place he has rented for I did not like their being at Mrs. Riley's so long. He says "as things look now I do not know if it will be necessary for us to leave Roswell, yet here is a resort in case we are driven from home." As he has given up the idea of building I do not know why he remains down there. They are living very roughly but I dare say it will be of service to Sonny.

Smith wrote to your Uncle that the Sec*y* of War had withdrawn the authority wh. he had given for raising those companies & he was going to

Richmond to see about it.[2] The fact is I do not believe they ever had much authority. They were carrying on things in a very high handed manner & thought they would have every thing their own way & now they find the officers must be elected they do not like it. We see by the papers that there has been a fight near Lake City[3] & a victory on our side but I do not think the yankees will give up that desirable object very easily. The cutting off supplies from our army & obtaining them for themselves is a great consideration, besides the number of voters they will secure by taking the Negroes. Yet Father [says] we should be quite safe at Val.[a] & proposes that Helen should go down as soon as she is well enough. We hear there has been a fight at Tunnel Hill, that our army had possession of the field but the contest was not decided.[4]

Lizzie asks you to do a small piece of the basket work & send it up with a little palmetto if you have an opportunity before Sonny comes. I wish you would let me know if you want any underclothing. I think your common shirts must be wearing out by this time & I do not want you to use your nice ones for common new homespun would not be comfortable for the summer, but you have those thin blue ones & I can make some thick ones for winter. Will you be able to get a furlough this spring? It will soon be a year since you were at home. How was the butter that went in your box? & have you made any okra soup yet? I hope your peas were not spoiled by the decayed fruit. May God bless you darling.

Your aff
Mother

1. Catherine Evelyn King Baker (1837–1923), a daughter of Barrington King and the wife of William Elliott Baker (1830–1906), a Presbyterian clergyman (Myers, ed., *Children of Pride*, 1459). "Mrs. Ralph" may therefore be her sister-in-law, Florence Stillwell King, who is married to Ralph Browne King (1835–78).

2. Captain Archibald Smith Barnwell (1833–1917), Archibald Smith's nephew, began the war as a company commander in a mounted militia regiment stationed in South Carolina, but he now seems to be attempting to raise a new company. In March 1864 he became commander of Company C of Major J. A. Maxwell's battalion of light artillery, formed at Camp Pembroke, just outside Savannah. The unit eventually became known as Barnwell's Light Battery (Barnwell, *Story of an American Family*, 209).

3. Captain Johnson's letter of February 22, note 1, above. Lake City, Florida, is not far south of Valdosta, Georgia. On February 20, 1864, near Olustee, or Ocean Pond, Confederate forces from Lake City won the field and inflicted heavy losses on federal forces that had been sent out from Jacksonville.

4. A federal reconnaissance into northwest Georgia was checked on February 24–25, 1864, at Tunnel Hill, or Buzzard's Roost Gap.

FATHER TO WILLIAM

Hired house 4ᵗʰ March 64

My Dear William

I had intended to stay here with A. for a month yet, altho I was very anxious to go home on Helen's account and was afraid to take A. with me. Osborn B.[1] came here this morning & I have made arrangements for Archy to stay with him and let me go home. I want you to come to town on Tuesday 8ᵗʰ as I expect to leave here on Monday, but if I should miss getting off on Monday, try & arrange your leave of absence so that you may stay in Savᵃ on Tuesday night, so that if I come on Monday or Tuesday I may have either Tuesday afternoon or Tuesday night with you. I will go to the Mackays when you can hear of me at least.[2] We are both pretty well. May God bless you.

your Affᵉ Father
Archᵈ Smith

P.S. Last accounts from home (I think 22ᵈ) Helen was better tho' yet very feeble. May God preserve her to us, if consistent with her good.

A.S.

1. Probably Thomas Osborn Barnwell (1815–79), a son of Captain Edward Barnwell (1785–1860) by his first wife Elizabeth Osborn (1789–1824) (Barnwell, *Story of an American Family*, 81–82). Edward Barnwell's second wife was Archibald Smith's sister Eliza Zubly (1803–46).

2. While in Savannah, Archibald Smith stayed with his distant cousins, Catherine and Sarah Mackay (Myers, ed., *Children of Pride*, 1610).

MOTHER TO WILLIAM

Roswell March 11ᵗʰ/64

My Dear Son

Father reached home to-day quite well as you will suppose when I tell you he walked from Marietta & ate a hearty dinner of bacon & rice, our every day fare which we vary by sometimes boiling & sometimes frying. But we are thankful I hope that we have plenty of that. I am glad to hear you have nice oysters though I believe you are not very fond of them. We are quite disappointed that Sonny did not come. I do not like the arrangement of his staying with the Barnwells & as the severity of the winter is past I would much prefer his being with us if he cannot be with you. I do not know what is to be done about him. Gen Capers says the conscript officers have received no new instructions & he has extended his furlough to the 10th of April. If he is going back to the Institute he will be very much behind his class. I suppose by what Gen Capers said to me he felt that things had got too much at loose ends & he was going to try to straighten them out & he & Dr Setze both seemed quite rejoiced to be rid of their old commissary.

I am sorry to hear you could not call to see Mrs Baker. I hear Cliff expects to be up with his bride in a few days.[1] The family seem to think it quite a ridiculous affair, I suppose quite in keeping with the characters of the parties.

Major Minton was here a few days last week looking very badly.[2] I was in hopes we should be able to get his horse as I have no way of riding to church but he said he could sell him for 3 times as much in the low country & would take him down. I have walked to church twice but find it almost too much for me.

Helen is improving. She sits up more & in the last few days has walked about the room, but I fear it will be long before she recovers even her usual strength. The hyacinths are coming out beautifully though we have nothing like the number or variety of fine ones which we once had. Are you still expecting to go to Genesis Pt.? What has become of your dog? I thought you would have sent him up by Father. I have not time to write more. May God bless you my precious child.

Your aff
Mother

1. Possibly Catherine Evelyn King Baker. If so, "Cliff" may be her youngest brother, Clifford A. King (1842–1911), who married Mary Eliza Hardee of Savannah.

2. Major John Minton (1797–1871) settled near the Smiths in 1849, joining the Kings, Bullochs, and Dunwodys in coming to Roswell from Liberty County, Georgia. He had a distinguished military career, fighting in the War of 1812, the Indian wars, and in Texas before being wounded at First Manassas, July 21, 1861 (Myers, ed., *Children of Pride*, 1625–26).

MOTHER TO WILLIAM

Roswell March 18th/64

My Dear Son

You will perceive that I have changed my writing day from Tuesday to Friday as your regular communication with the city is on Tuesday. I sup-

The Roswell Presbyterian Church, completed in 1840

pose you receive the letters in a shorter time than if they were written on any other day. I have not heard any thing from Sonny since Father came. The girls are very much obliged to you for sending the palmetto. I hope the box will not take as long to come as it did to go, tho' it does not make much difference. . . . Father is very anxious for me to take Helen down to his establishment in Lowndes as soon as she is able to travel, but it will be getting hot down there pretty soon & I do not think it would do for him & me to leave home at the same time. God's providence has thrown your Uncle upon us to be taken care of & he is quite old & we do not know what may happen, & then there are no comforts about the place such as would be necessary for a person in Helen's state. He says he is going down again before long. I do not know what for as Mr Barnwell has charge of his affairs there.[1] I suppose you have seen Gov. Brown's message.[2] How can a man of sense try to create discontent in the country at a time like this? But I am glad to find there seem to be some men of sense in the Legislature. We have had some very cold weather this week. The trees are in full bloom & we fear the fruit will be kill'd but perhaps enough will escape. We are as usual. I do long to see you darling but I must not complain.

May God bless & keep you ever near to himself

Your aff

Mother

1. "Uncle" is John Joyner Smith (1790–1872), Archibald Smith's half-brother. He had been driven from his beautiful home in Beaufort, South Carolina, known to this day as the John Joyner Smith house, when federal forces occupied the town on November 7, 1861, and used the house as the headquarters for General Isaac Ingalls Stevens, who commanded the post at Beaufort. After the federal occupation of Beaufort, Smith spent the Civil War years living with his half-brother's family in Roswell and Valdosta, Georgia. John Joyner Smith's first wife was Mary Gibbes Barnwell (1795–1853), Captain Edward Barnwell's half-sister. Uncle Smith had also inherited the Old Fort Plantation near Beaufort, built on the ruins of Fort Frederick, which he was also never able to recover. "Helen" is probably Helen Zubly Smith rather than Helen Zubly Magill. "Mr. Barnwell" is probably Thomas Osborn Barnwell (1815–79), a son of Archibald Smith Barnwell's father, Captain Edward Barnwell, and his first wife, Elizabeth Osborn (1789–1824).

2. Georgia's governor, Joseph Emerson Brown, was outraged when the Confederate Congress suspended the writ of habeas corpus on February 15, limiting it to specified offenses. Brown raged against the suspension because it made efforts to call state conventions treasonable. According to Louise Billes Hill, "His opposition to the Confederacy henceforth became truly formidable" (*Joseph E. Brown*, 196–97).

MOTHER TO WILLIAM

Roswell March 25ᵗʰ/64

Yours of the 19ᵗʰ My beloved child has come to hand to-day it is a great satisfaction to me to hear from you so regularly & I often wonder how those mothers bear the cruel & dangerous separation from their sons who only write to them occasionally at long intervals & I often pity those whose boys are not like mine affectionate & attentive & above all servants of God. Oh my darling I feel that I have great cause of thankfulness & when I see & hear of so much sorrow occasioned by this cruel war it seems that it is too much to expect that we should pass through it unscathed & tho' I have so much anxiety on account of my precious baby I feel at the same time that I have abundant cause to bless God on his account & leave him in his hands who has promised that no evil shall come nigh him.

We see that the authorities have ordered all the able bodied men now in home situations to be enrol'd & the vacancies fill'd by men unfit for field service & we are in hopes our dear boy[1] may be assigned to some such place. It may be that it will be necessary for him to be examined in the district in which he was enrol'd as a cadet. That I suppose you can find out. We have been very much disappointed in not receiving a certificate jointly with Dr Setze & your Father wrote to him more than a week since about it but has rec'd no answer.

We have had very severe weather this week, on Sunday night & Monday a very heavy fall of sleet & snow more than we have had for years, lying from 2 to 3 inches altho' the ground was not frozen & a great deal must have melted as it fell & a little may still be seen in sheltered places. I fear the fruit is entirely lost for altho' the blossoms were not all open the ice was upon them so long they will hardly outlive it. It is a serious loss in these scarce times being not only an article of luxury but of food among the country people.

It will be six weeks to-morrow that Helen has been confined to her room. Only once last week she walked across to mine & looked out at the garden. Her appetite & spirits are better & it seems strange she does not gain strength. I wish she could have a change. Father wants her to go down to the place he has rented but she could not be comfortable there without a table chair or good bed & she is not willing to go without me & of course I cannot leave home at the same time that your Father does while your Uncle is here unless I felt that her life depended on it. I think this is the proper place for him & it is our duty to take care of him. I think it would do her good to spend a little while in Sav. if it could be accomplished, but I cannot see exactly how it can. She says tell Brother she is trying her best to get strong & she means to go down stairs as soon as the weather is pleasant. Father was to have carried her down last week to look at the hyacinths, but it was too cold. I suppose this weather will retard the movements of the armies & postpone the battle which is expected above us.

We had quite a pleasant visitor on Sunday evening. A soldier stop'd & asked to spend the night. He introduced himself as Dr Nicolson belonging to Martin's command (Cavalry) which had been crossing the Chatta[oht] on the bridges near here on their way to Dalton from Longstreet's army.[2] He was very gentlemanly & pleasant. After breakfast he asked if there was a piano in the house & said altho' it was not a suitable time for music he must beg to hear some, it was so long since he had had such enjoyment. He seemed to enjoy it very much & spoke of his wife's playing. When he told your Father good bye he said when he stop'd he expected to pay for his lodging but he had been so kindly entertained that [he] quite forgot to ask for his bill. It was really a pleasure to do a kindness for a soldier, particularly one who could appreciate the kind feelings altho' the entertainment is so plain.

I am sorry you had to give away your dog. I expected to make a pet of him because he was yours but it was not worth while for you to be troubled with him if you did not care about him & unless he has been in good hands it would hardly be worth while to get him back as he may have learned bad tricks & any one who would take pains to teach him any thing good would not be willing to give him up. I am glad to find you are so confident about being able to come up. I dare say it will be better for you to come in May than in April. We are all as usual.

May God bless & keep you my darling son

Your aff

Mother

1. Archie, who is still enrolled as a cadet at GMI.

2. William Thompson Martin (1823–1910) of Mississippi led a division of Joseph Wheeler's cavalry corps during the Atlanta Campaign.

LIZZIE TO WILLIAM, UNDATED

Dear William

What has become of you? We have not heard from you for a week. To be sure Sonny wrote a note but for all that was in it to satisfy folks Pete might have written it. What has got into him? One week he writes almost deranged to go with Morgan or join Smith & John's Co.[1]—of the two I think I had rather it be Morgan's but that is insane—& the next week he says nothing about either & talks as if his time was his own & he had a discharge. Does being in the Institute exempt him? I wish you would write us something for we are just in uncertainty & don't know. But Sonny may be caught up by a conscript officer any time & sent off any where.

Mother wants you to find out if there is any place on the salt water such as W. Bluff or Montgomery[2] &c where Sissy could go for a little while for a change, some place which would be safe you know & I want you if there is such a place to persuade Mother to go instead of sending me for I think she needs a change. She just has to stay here on the lot all the time except to *walk* to Church on Sunday & that you know tires her very much but don't you let on that I said any thing about it. Can people bring provisions up on the RR if they take oath it is only for their own uses?

The spring is very late this year. Scarcely any flowers are out yet—only Saxifrage, Stellaria, Liverworts, Thalictrums (I think that is it) & Houstonia.

I found our Anemone last time I went to walk. I wrote you could see the nemophyllas in the greenhouse. They are prettier than ever. I send you one or two. They are so very large this year. I am afraid my Olive will die. This winter has been so severe a good many of the things were killed. Has Cousin K a greenhouse iris?[3] You had better find out so as to carry one down for her when you go. Mr Benedict[4] is going to preach in the Church Friday night & they have invited me an outside barbarian to play with my unsanctified hands the organ. I am very glad of the opportunity to shew them that the bad feelings which have been "gwiny bout"[5] are none of my doings.

Your aff sister

Lizzie Smith

1. If Archie has visions of joining the dashing Confederate cavalry leader John Hunt Morgan (1825–64) in Virginia, Lizzie may well consider him deranged. It is uncertain if she is referring to another Morgan closer to home. "Smith and John's Co." would seem to be the company that Archibald Smith Barnwell had just formed near Savannah in March and commanded: Company C of Major J. A. Maxwell's Battalion of Light Artillery.

2. White Bluff and Montgomery were both settlements south of Savannah near Willie's duty stations.

3. Catherine Mackay.

4. Possibly David Benedict (1779–1874), a clergyman and historian who traveled the United States gathering materials for a history of the Baptist church. His *Fifty Years among the Baptists* had appeared in 1860.

5. Black dialect for "going about" or "making the rounds." Other letters indicate some conflict between Lizzie and one of the minister's daughters, Anna Pratt (1844–1937), concerning who would play the organ at the Roswell Presbyterian Church.

MOTHER TO WILLIAM

Roswell Apl. 15th 1864

My Dear Son

I know you are anxious about our boy & so I will tell you at once that he is gone to the Institute & will be allowed to remain there for a while until July, I hear, unless some new order comes out. We all feel very much relieved at this respite which is allowed us & which gives us time to consider what is best for him & try for a comfortable situation for him. I suppose while he is exempt he will be able to join any company he may prefer. We are all decided in wishing to have him in the Signal Corps hoping he may be allowed to be with you or at least near you. The Battalion in Augusta is to have an ensign & he wants to try to get that appointment if he cannot get the other place but he does not know how to go about it as it is by appointment & not by election. It is given it will not be necessary for him to be known to the company, but he would need some influence to secure it. . . .

I am quite in earnest in wanting you to go among the ladies & fix upon one that will suit you & be married as soon as the war is over. If we are not destroyed your Father will have something to give you. I would not have you look for money in seeking a wife but it is a very foolish idea that some romantic & morbidly unmercenary people have that money is an objection even if every thing else is suitable. We are more apt to find refinement & cultivation among the wealthy if wealth is an accompaniment of good blood. This last I should consider indispensable for whatever some may say I believe good blood is as necessary to the development of the superior qualities in man as in the inferior animals. There are exceptions to be sure, but where men or women seem to rise above their own class they are not to be depended on. Their instincts are not the same as those flowing from good blood & as circumstances lifted them up so circumstances may throw them back again. It seems to me that good blood would have kept Gov. Brown & Alex Stephens from their present hostile positions in regard to the Gov^t, that it would have given Stephens at least an intuitive perception of the want of propriety in his present course,[1] but it seems to me where a man is taken from his equals & lifted to a sphere above them he will never be satisfied until he can put his foot upon the necks of those to whom he once looked up. O! I am sick of a republican government. The majority always will be the ignorant & debased & they rule the country their only aim seems to be to put down those above them & stand in their places though they have not the education or talents to fit them for it. But you will ask why has Mother written all this to me & I answer I cannot tell. My thoughts glided into that channel very naturally when writing of the necessity of good blood in a wife for you as yours ought to be very good seeing you can claim it from both sides. But if you do not like it you need not read it.

Helen is gaining strength & I think if the weather were more favourable she would improve more rapidly, but it continues cold & we have a great deal of rain & damp cloudy weather. She has been to ride several times. Mrs. Camp is very kind in sending for her.[2] The last fine day we had she was brought down stairs & walked about the garden & tho' she was a good deal fatigued I do not think it injured her.

. . . Your Father took Sonny to Marietta & saw that your box was come. We hope to get it soon as the Fac. Wagons are going there now. Lizzie is talking of going to Rome but I do not know whether she will accomplish it. She has been talking more than a year. Father has been talking of going down to

Lowndes & I suppose would go next week if he had any way of going to Atlanta. If one goes by Marietta he will have to spend a night in Atlanta & that costs $15. I suppose he would not care for that if he could be comfortable & besides the stage is generally full & Charlotte intends to go to see the Osborn Barnwells when he goes.[3] I cannot imagine what he is going for, as Mr Barnwell has charge of his Negroes & all they will make won't pay his expenses, but I do not think he will ever be satisfied here again, though I think if we live he will be just as uncomfortable in the low country in a few years as he was before we left for I think that enervating climate will be much worse for him than the severity of this. Being there a little while in the winter is [a] very different thing from being there all the time. We have just rec'd a budget of letters from Aunt Bet & I will open yours & put mine in the same envelope. A letter from Sonny he says he was disappointed to get in so easily. He does not want to stay. Good bye darling

May God bless you. Your aff
Mother

1. With the suspension of the writ of habeas corpus in 1864 to enforce conscription, Confederate Vice President Alexander H. Stephens joined Georgia governor Joe E. Brown in attacking the Confederate government. Stephens was the power behind Brown's successful attempt to get the Georgia legislature to pass resolutions denouncing the habeas corpus act as "unreasonable and unconstitutional." These resolutions were directed through the legislature by Stephens's brother, Linton (Moore, *Conscription and Conflict*, 270–75).

2. Jane Atwood Camp (1830–1911), the wife of George Hull Camp (1816–1907), Barrington King's chief agent at the Roswell Manufacturing Company.

3. Charlotte Cuthbert Barnwell (1842–1922) was the child of Edward Barnwell's second marriage, to Eliza Zubly Smith (1803–46). The "Osborn Barnwells" refers to Thomas Osborn Barnwell.

ARCHIE TO WILLIAM

G.M.I. April 18th

Dear Brother

I got home safely on Friday the 8th. I had to walk from Marietta and the road was very muddy and it rained part of the way but I don't think the walk hurt me any. I only stayed at home till Monday and came on in a buggy. I found no difficulty in getting in as the Cadets are still exempt. They are now called the engineer corps of the state of Georgia.

As I only came in a buggy I could not bring more than a blanket and comfortable and I have not been able to get my things yet though they were sent over by the factory wagons on Friday.

I could not get into my old room and had to go to the very tail end of the whole concern in a very poor room with some new fellows. They are nothing extra but will do very well.

I feel the change of climate very much from the coast to this cold bleak hill and have taken a bad cold and cough. If I can't get a place in the Signal Corps I think I will try to get the ensigncy of the battalion that Mr Daugherty is in. Of course I would rather be in the corps if there was any chance of getting with you.

I have only one class mate this term and he is away on furlough so I have a good opportunity of catching up.

Tell Frank Neufville his things are here and if he says so I can send them to him.[1]

I did not get my trunk home but Father came over with me and he carried the palmetto cabbage back with him.

Professor Manget is dead.[2] He died very suddenly some time in February I believe it was. I am truly sorry for I esteemed him very highly and don't know but I even loved him.

I now have to recite mathematics to capn Eve which I don't like at all as he is a very poor excuse for a professor and I have a thorough contempt for him and wish him conscripted. I don't wish him any evil but I think he would do more good to the country than he does here. Reciting to him after Major Richardson is like drinking warm water with a few drops of milk in it.[3]

Remember me to all the fellows.

Helen was well enough to come down with help and be carried up.

Your affectionate bro

Archie

1. Possibly Edward F. Neufville (b. 1842?), the son of a Savannah clergyman. He was a 4th corporal in the Chatham Artillery in 1862 (Jones, *Historical Sketch*, 104).

2. Victor H. Manget (1813?-64), a native of France, was professor of French and history at GMI (Yates, "History of the Georgia Military Institute," 3).

3. John M. Richardson was a professor of higher mathematics at GMI (Rodgers, *Roster*). Although Paul Eve is listed in Rodgers's work as a professor of mathematics and English branches, it should be Joseph E. Eve, a professor of civil and military engineering (Temple, *First Hundred Years*, 197).

Roswell Apl. 22nd 1864

I do not know My dear Son how it is that your letters take so long to come to us. You write on Monday or Tuesday & unless there is an extra mail on Saturday we do not receive the letter until the next Monday. It made me a little uneasy at first to have the whole week pass & no letter. You are so punctual, but it has happened so often that I am ready to charge the P.O. Department with the delinquency. Sonny seemed quite restive when he first returned to the Institute, but by a letter we had yesterday he appeared better satisfied tho' he still speaks of remaining there only a short time. I suppose you have seen in the papers the position of the G. M. I. The Cadets are considered the Engineer Corps of the state & as A. is I believe the most advanced I suppose he would get a good position if called into service & he would not be a conscript. I do not know whether his graduating would be any particular benefit to him in time of peace unless he wishes to enter the regular army. Lizzie says he does but I have not heard him say anything about it. I hope not, for it is such an idle useless life in time of peace.

Helen with assistance comes down every day when the weather is pleasant, but has only gone up once on her own feet. The weather is beautiful now & we hope she will improve faster. If the winter & spring had not been unprecedented we should say, there would be no more frost as the full moon is passed & a mocking bird that "infalliable omium"[1] has been here, but we have had frost almost every night when it was not raining up to this time. As yet we have had only a small mess of asparagus 3 times for Helen & nothing else growing. I am glad you did not come up this month for you would not have enjoyed the visit.

Helen asks me to tell you she wished & intended to write to you very soon but she tried to write a little to A. to-day & it has given her pain in her back & fatigued her so much that she cannot write again until she is stronger.

I am glad you have copied the family tree, it was kind in Margaret to give you the old bible it is valuable for its antiquity altho' it is not a family relic.[2]

The box is come with the Palmetto & cans. The girls are delighted with the feathers. They say the down feathers will make elegant plumes with the downy feathers of the white owl which you brought from Arkansas. It is very gratifying to have you thinking of these little things for your sisters. Helen says tell you you *are* a good boy. But darling I shall not be able to send you any goodies unless you take better care of the cans. Don't you know they are of no use without the India rubber & I cannot replace those which are missing. You should have the tins washed very particularly & thoroughly dried by the fire or very hot sun & then screw them up before any salt or damp air gets to them. I like to send the tin to you because there is no risk of breaking but they require more care in washing &c. When you come try & bring the tube rose roots & let them be for Lizzie as well as Helen. I do hope you will be able to come it is now almost a year since I have seen you.

Do remember me to all the cousins when you see them. We are all pretty well. May God bless you my dear son Your aff

Mother

Aunty asks you when you come to bring that new Southern Botany which Father sent you by Dr Porcher[3] I believe.

1. A possible explanation of this curious Latin is "infallible omen."

2. A family tree showing many of the relationships between the Smith, Mackay, Williamson, and McQueen families was found in the Smith home in Roswell. An inscription at the bottom in Willie's hand indicates that he copied it on April 11, 1864, from an original made on January 1, 1844, "at Prairie on the Ogeechee River by Joseph Stiles and by him presented to his Aunt Elliott." Joseph Stiles was the son of Margaret Cowper Mackay Elliott's sister Mary Anne.

3. Francis Peyre Porcher (1825–95), a physician and botanist. A professor of medicine at the Medical College of the State of South Carolina and the founder of several hospitals, Porcher was known as an authority on diseases of the heart as well as on botany. The "new Southern Botany" was *The Resources of the Southern Fields and Forests*, (1863).

WILLIAM TO MOTHER

Rose Dew Apr 22/64

Dear Mother

I was very glad to learn by yours of 15 that A. had reached home safely. I did not think there was much danger of his being taken up, but still felt a little anxious about him.

I was very much amused at your matrimonial advice and when I conclude to follow it will get out the letter and read it over. But I agree entirely with you in what you say about good blood. Gov. Brown and the Stephenses are the most pertinent instances of men who wish to trample on those whom they feel to be their superiors in rank.[1] . . .

I hear that Woodie and a whole lot of Barnwell girls passed thro' Sav[h] Tuesday night on their way to Lowndes Co.[2] How is it that W. is down here again? I am sorry I did not know of their coming as I should have gone in to see them.

My visit to Jimmie Cozby yesterday was very pleasant.[3] Cousin Margaret, Phoebe and Mary went out to their plantation in the train so I had their company most of the way.[4] Jimmie has been living on Judge Law's place near Ways Station, but will move next week to the Parsonage on the salts. I suppose that it is the same place Uncle S. used to occupy.[5] Mrs Cozby is a very lovely person and is very much esteemed by persons who are well acquainted with her. As I came back Tom Clay put two Ladies under my care, Miss Tatnall and Miss Kollock. So I had the good luck to get a seat in the Ladies car both ways.[6]

When Father comes down please send some roots of the large Blue, and White Iris for the Elliotts. I believe you have both. I do not think Cousin Kate would care for them as her garden is very full, but I think she would like the Greenhouse Iris and some Nemophila seeds. The Elliotts have a large garden and spoke very admiringly of the Irides you gave Cousin Eliza.[7] ...

Did I tell you that we are now allowed to buy rations from the Commissary? We can get 10 lbs. of Bacon 8 lbs. rice 32 lbs Meal and 6 lbs Peas per month for $27.75 which is a very great convenience as heretofore we sometimes found it hard to get provisions enough even at market prices.

Much Love to all your afft son

W[m]

1. Governor Brown had told the Georgia legislature in Milledgeville on March 10 that the war was lost, that the Confederacy was a failure, and that it should dissolve itself into separate states. His fellow Georgian, and the vice president of the Confederacy, Alexander H. Stephens, supported him fully in an address to the same legislature. Both men were supported by Linton Stephens, Alexander's younger brother, who had introduced the measures in the legislature condemning Richmond (Foote, *The Civil War*, 3:92–94; see also Anne Smith's letter of April 15, 1864, n.1, above, and Moore, *Conscription and Conflict*, 270–75).

2. Probably Woodward Barnwell (1838–1927) and his sisters, Helen, Charlotte, and Leila—all children of Archibald Smith's sister Eliza Zubly Smith Barnwell and Captain Edward Barnwell. In July 1861 Woodward Barnwell joined the Congaree Troop of the cavalry battalion of Wade Hampton's Legion in the Army of Northern Virginia, a unit that later became part of the 2d Regiment, South Carolina Infantry. Woodie Barnwell was later detached from this unit to serve as a scout around Beaufort (Barnwell, *Story of an American Family*, 209–10, 255).

3. James Smith Cozby, the Confederate chaplain whose wedding was the subject of Willie's letter of February 9, 1864, above.

4. Margaret Cowper Mackay Elliott and her children, Phoebe (1833–66) and Mary (1838–1919).

5. Judge William Law (1793-1874) lived near Way's Station, station 1 1/2 on the Atlantic and Gulf Railroad southwest of Savannah on the Great Ogeechee River. Although "Uncle S." usually refers to John Joyner Smith, Willie's reference here seems to be to his mother's brother Seagrove William Magill (1810–84).

6. Willie's friends Tom Clay and Jimmie Cozby both married daughters of William Law. Miss Tatnall appears to be the daughter of Confederate naval hero Josiah Tatnall, who commanded the *Merrimac*. Miss Kollock would appear to be the daughter of Savannah physician Phineas Kollock.

7. Kate is Catherine Mackay; Eliza is her sister Elizabeth M. Stiles (1810–67).

P. D. GIVENS TO WILLIAM

Coosawhatchie[1] April 25

Dear Smith

Your long expected letter arrived this evening & as I am up all night tonight will amuse myself by endeavoring to answer it. Colquitt's Brigade is passing through tonight[2] and trains are running both ways and every office on this road are ordered open tonight to keep them from having collisions. . . .

My dear Boy I have just got the nicest garden coming on you ever saw. I will have lots of vegetables this summer. My irish potatoes look beautifully and will be flowering soon. I have everything you can think of and have just sowed the watermelons and muskmelons, so won't be dependent on anyone this summer, & won't have to hunt up a Livingston to go foraging. I have a lot of hens and am raising Chickens, have a fine chance coming on. Have 3 shoats which will give good bacon next winter. So you see I am coming out. What pay do you fellows get now & how do you fare generally? I am living on nothing but ham and eggs, the former I buy from commissary. I forgot to mention I have a cow too and get about 1 1/2 quarts of milk every day, and it comes in fine, I can assure you. I had 3 sometime back but the fellow came for them and then I took up this one. . . .

I suppose as you say Clay's Lady love will not marry him till the war is over and of course it is enough to make the old fellow mad. Ha Ha. Is Ways station on the Lake City line and what is the call for it? Our line is sometimes connected with it and I can have a chat with Clay. Do Remember me to West, Guerard and all the old Corps.[3] The fish will commence biting here and then I will go into their affections. Well I must say goodnight. I am going to try and take a nap now, if the trains mash themselves to atoms.

Write soon to your sincere friend
P. D. Givens

1. Coosawhatchie, South Carolina, is a station north of Savannah on the Charleston and Savannah Railroad. This letter represents several energetic letters to Willie Smith from his remarkable but unidentified friend and fellow telegrapher, P. D. Givens.

2. The infantry brigade of Willie's fellow Georgian Alfred Holt Colquitt (1824–94) helped to win the recent battle at Olustee, Florida. After the war, Colquitt served as governor of and as a U.S. senator from Georgia.

3. A. G. Guerard and Charles N. West, like Willie, were members of the Signal Corps command of Captain Joseph Manigault. (National Archives Microfilm Publications, *Compiled Service Records of Confederate Soldiers Who Served in Organizations Raised Directly by the Confederate Government*, rolls 118, 119).

HELEN ZUBLY MAGILL TO WILLIAM

Roswell May 11*th* 1864

Dear Willie,

I was very glad to receive your letter of April 30*th* especially as it had been so long since you had written to me. We have been hoping to have a visit from you before this time. Indeed Sissy was looking for you all last Friday. However, we must wait. You will no doubt come to us when the best time arrives, and when we think how many are deprived of their dear friends altogether; and how much suffering and privation thousands of the army are called to endure, we ought to feel so thankful for the favorable and comfortable situation in which you are placed, that we should not think of complaining, if you were obliged to be absent much longer. We have all been hoping you might come in time for the honeysuckles; which are now beautiful. . . .

You suppose "we are all working hard at palmetto, to get some hats ready for warm weather." I think there would probably be ready sale for all we could conveniently make, but as yet we have made but 3; & in verification of the old adage, "charity begins at home," they were all for ourselves; each of the girls has a *beautiful* hat, if I may be allowed to say so, seeing I had a finger in the pie; & Archie's finished, but waiting for an opportunity to be sent to him. Your Father has a very nice one made of Sissy's last summer one, ripped & sewed over by your Mother, & I have just commenced braiding a Sunday go to meeting bonnet for myself, as mine is not presentable, with summer fixings, & I have not $2 or 3.00 to spend for a new one. I wish you could have brought yours up here for some of us to sew. . . .

Among the palmetto you sent was some that was 'specially nice which I think must have been the *swamp palmetto*. Do try & get some more & if you come up bring it, or more of the other. We want to use up just as much as we have time for. We have 3 hats engaged, & I expect all the gentlemen would like them.

Lizzie says she wants you to come in time to make a frame for the "Fairy Bell," & if you do not make haste it will be too large. Also she wants you to bring some tube rose roots if you can get them even if sprouted. Sissy begs you to try & get her an apple geranium. Lizzie says she wants one too & if you come via Augusta you can go to Desmonds if there is time & get one.

Love from all

your affectionate Auntie

HELEN TO WILLIAM, ENCLOSED WITH PREVIOUS LETTER

Dear Brother

I have been expecting you to write to me for a long time as I was sick and could not write to you but the letter has not come. My hat is just finished. It is very pretty. The braid is quite fine and the palmetto is so beautifully white that it is the prettiest I have seen. Auntie did most of the braiding and sewed it for me. Palmetto hats seem to be very much in demand. Even "Old Barrington" thinks he will have to get one as his old beaver is about worn out.

I have been trying to make up some of the feathers which you sent but it is very slow work I am not strong enough to do much at a time. I have made an owl wing fan which is very nice indeed it is such a nice shape.

Wednesday May 11th

I begun to write this on Friday but got so tired before it was finished that I could not write any more and the next morning Mrs King sent for me to go to ride and I could not finish it so I mean to send it in an other letter as it is very small.

I have been painting some honeysuckles. They are only the common pink ones but I thought they would be easier to begin on. I will try and get some others but it has rained a good deal yesterday and the day before and I fear they will be much bruised. They are opening so fast that unless you come soon they will all be done.

People have been very good to me since I have [been] sick. Mrs Camp sent her buggy for me to ride every good day when I was first well enough to go to ride till her horse got sick and since that Mrs J. King[1] has been sending for me every day and I always drive down on the river so I can see the flowers. I am very glad to hear that you have copied the Family tree which Cousin Margaret[2] has and I hope you found out all she knows about all the old people.

You must make haste and come home. Every thing looks so fresh and sweet out of doors but if you don't come soon the hot weather will dry them all up.

Please if you can conveniently get me an apple geranium. All of ours are dead.

Your aff Sister

Helen

1. Frances ("Fanny") Price King (1829–81), the wife of Barrington King's son, James Roswell King (1827–97).

2. Margaret Cowper Elliott.

MOTHER TO WILLIAM

Roswell May 13th 1864

My Dear Son

Here is another mail & no letter from you. Perhaps you are so busy studying engineering that you have not time to write though I think it would take more than engineering to make you neglect home folks. We begin to feel quite impatient for your coming. The azaleas are blooming finely & the laurels opening & we are afraid you will be too late to enjoy them. The flowers are the only attraction besides the people that we can present to you. Bacon rice & bread are almost all we can get to eat, but though I like to give you something nice when you come home I know the visit will not be less pleasant to you that you do not get it.

We have had what you would call delightfully hot weather though we have not the additional luxury of mosquitoes & sandflies. Yesterday & today have been much cooler so that we have been glad of a fire in the morning & some entertained fears of frost, which would have been a calamity in these scarce times. Gardens are very backward. Only a very few strawberries have yet been found for Helen, I hope you will be able to get vegetables where you are. They are so conducive to health & yet people seem to think they must make all they can out of the poor soldiers if it takes a whole month's pay to buy a dinner of herbs. This is indeed a time of anxiety & apprehension. The movements of the armies seem to indicate a great battle which must soon be fought near Dalton. A body of yankees it seems have succeeded in reaching Resaca & have been repulsed.[1] We cannot but feel great anxiety for the result for though nothing is too hard for God yet what right have we to claim his interposition when we as a nation are so forgetful of his commands? He has stretched forth his

"Anxiety and Apprehension" 41

This page and opposite: Flowers painted by the women in the Smith home

hand for our deliverance many times but will his forbearance endure forever?

.... Helen is very anxious for you to come. She always has plenty of flowers but thinks she would enjoy them a great deal more if you were here.

All as usual & unite in love to you.

May God bless you darling.

Your aff
Mother

1. Sherman had begun his march from Chattanooga toward Atlanta on May 4, 1864. Confederate general Johnston moved his Army of Tennessee out of Dalton, Georgia, on the evening of May 12, then established new defenses to the north and west of Resaca. Sherman attacked on May 14, and Johnston withdrew to Resaca on May 15. Each day brought federal forces closer to the Smiths in Roswell.

helen Smith

Roswell May 21st

My Dear Son

In spite of all my brave resolutions I cannot help feeling uneasy about you as Monday will be three weeks since we have had a letter from you.

I dare say you are feeling very anxious about us but try darling to commit us to the Lord. We are packing our clothing & expect to leave on Monday or perhaps to-morrow if the news we get to-day makes our departure more urgent.[1]

We shall go by Augusta if we can get a wagon to go to Rock Mt. instead of Marietta.[2] May God bless you darling. We feel that in him is our only trust.

Your aff

Mother

Helen is very much agitated & could not sleep last night.

---

1. Johnston had abandoned his prepared defenses at Cassville on May 19, when generals Hood and Polk had convinced him that the position was untenable (Davis, *Rise and Fall,* 2:553).

2. The Smiths were considering two possible escape routes by rail. Rock Mountain, now known as Stone Mountain, was southeast of Roswell on the Georgia Railroad, which terminated in Augusta. Marietta was on the Western and Atlantic Railroad west of Roswell. In Atlanta, this road connected to the Macon and Western Railroad, which in turn connected in Macon to the Central Railroad, which terminated in Savannah.

"Driven from Our Homes"

MAY–NOVEMBER 1864

In leaving Roswell and in becoming refugees in late May 1864, the Smiths were just ahead of the tide. When Sherman started south in May, travelers in north Georgia had already begun to notice abandoned homes in the area. Most Confederates around Atlanta thought that the decisive battle would be fought to the north of them, and they had confidence in the great fortifications being placed around the city. Yet in May Sherman's army moved down the Western and Atlantic Railroad at a rate of a mile a day.[1] Federal victories at Dalton on May 14, Resaca on May 15, and Adairsville on May 17 had pushed General Joe Johnston's Confederates ever closer to Atlanta. Governor Joe Brown called out the state militia on May 18. Retreats from Rome and Cassville a day later left federal forces a mere forty or so miles from

Roswell. The Smiths were wise to leave when they did and somewhat lucky to have made it through Atlanta easily.

The day before the Smiths left Roswell was "a day of wild excitement in the city," with wagons rattling about the streets, engines screaming, and trains thundering along to get people and their possessions out of the city in a chaotic scene during which every possible means of conveyance was "bought, borrowed, begged or stolen."[2] May 25 could hardly have been less chaotic, and the Smiths were fortunate to have the help of Roswell's stalwart Barrington King in getting themselves and their possessions on trains to the south.

As they fled to their prepared refuge in Valdosta, they believed that Willie was safe in Savannah, but they were disappointed in not being able to see him as they passed through the city. Their concern for Archie mounted, for they knew that they were leaving him exposed at GMI, which lay directly in Sherman's path. Some GMI cadets may have participated in the Battle of Resaca on May 14–15, although Archie never mentions this fact.[3]

Superintendent Francis W. Capers made arrangements to move the institute from Sherman's path to Oglethorpe University at Midway, near the state capital of Milledgeville. Capers wrote to Dr. Samuel K. Talmage (often spelled Talmadge), president of the university, asking whether GMI could use university buildings—vacated when it had closed in June 1863—as a hospital for cadets and as a refuge for the families of the officers. Dr. Talmage had consented.[4] In his capacity as a quartermaster sergeant, Archie Smith was sent ahead to Midway on May 24, 1864. The cadets left their campus forever and boarded trains in Marietta on May 27, but they did not arrive at their new home until mid-August, for they were ordered to guard a railroad bridge near West Point, Georgia, then to participate in a skirmish at Turner's Ferry on the Chattahoochee River, and eventually to serve some time in the trenches around Atlanta. On August 12 they received orders to guard the state capital at Milledgeville.[5] Thus, they were squarely in Sherman's path once again, and Willie was at the end of that path in Savannah. The Smith parents waited and worried far to the south in Valdosta.

They also had to worry about the home that they had left behind. Letters from Barrington King and one of his employees gave them some scanty information about the conditions in Roswell, but they were not aware for many weeks of what had happened when Garrard's cavalry took the town on July 6, 1864, and burned the Roswell Manufacturing Company. Willie apparently received a furlough in late June 1864 that enabled him and his father to pay a flying visit to Roswell and to pick up some valuables just before the federals arrived. But about this same time, young Archie helped to fend off a cavalry raid in Gordon during which eleven locomotives and 140 railroad cars were destroyed, together with three rail factories and many homes.[6]

Such violence from those they termed the "vandals" and "vile wretches" must have seemed far away to Archibald and Anne Smith near Valdosta. Together with daughters Lizzie and Helen, Anne's sister Helen, and Archibald's half-brother, John Joyner, they were living in what was at the time the breadbasket of the Confederacy. The number of refugees in the area assured that they could not be evicted save by a huge army, and most of them did not see a blue uniform until after Appomattox. The huge crops grown there in 1863 and 1864 "became the surest source of supply for the Confederate army in Virginia."[7] The choice of nearby Andersonville for a prison camp must have seemed natural to the officials in Richmond. The recollection of Archie's future wife, Gulielma English Riley (1846–1921), demonstrates the pace and temper of life in south Georgia, where her own family had become refugees, living near the Smiths.

As Sherman closed in around Atlanta, the Smiths worried about their home in Roswell, their son to the north, their son to the east, and their relatives—the Merrells and the Magills—far to the west in Arkansas. When they heard that Atlanta had fallen on September 2, their worries had just begun.

NOTES

1. Kennett, *Marching through Georgia,* 84, 117.

2. Cyrena Bailey Stone (Miss Abby) Diary, quoted in ibid., 118.

3. Bohannon, "Cadets, Drillmasters, Draft Dodgers, and Soldiers," questions this contention, citing several wartime sources that make no mention of cadet involvement. (18n).

4. Tankersley, *College Life,* 107–8.

5. Bohannon, "Cadets, Drillmasters, Draft Dodgers, and Soldiers," 19–21.

6. Miles, *To the Sea,* 187.

7. Kennett, *Marching through Georgia,* 22–23.

─────────

MOTHER TO WILLIAM

25th We left our sweet home yesterday. Father to follow with the baggage & servants. There seemed to be a necessity for us to come off immediately as Mr King wanted his carriage to come off & it was only waiting for us. The wagon was at the door to be loaded when we left & we hope he will be here in time for the evening train tho' Mr King thinks there is small chance of our getting off. We expected to come all the way last night but a rain came on &

we were forced not unwillingly to stop for the night. Helen is better than we expected. The rest last night was a great thing for her she seems to feel better some. We left home tho' the determination that we must do so overcame her very much & she was quite unnerved during the preparation.

Atlanta is a jam. Mr King met us & succeeded in getting one room for us. He has been very kind. I had a letter from A on Monday. He seemed to be better satisfied. Had been sent to Atlanta to get accoutrements for the corps & expected to go to Macon soon. Their things were to be sent to Milledgeville & themselves to go when they were no longer needed, but I do not know what service they are performing. I feel badly to leave him so far but I hope he will only be put to some light duty. He wrote us a short time since that they had been ordered to report to Gen Johnston. Gen Capers went up & they are not gone so I suppose it is only something to talk about belonging to the state forces.

Father is come all safe & we expect to leave on the morning train.

ARCHIE TO MOTHER

Midway[1] Monday May 2[3]

Dear Mother

I arrived here Saturday morning but was too busy to write. I left Marietta last Tuesday at 2 at night with the cadets baggage in some chartered cars. Capt Griffiths[2] was in charge of the whole concern but I was in charge of the guard.

I have had a very fatiguing week. On Saturday I had to go to Atlanta to get some equipment and ammunition and did not get back to the hill[3] till about 10 or 11 oclock on Sunday. I had to go down to the train three times to look for the ammunition which was to be sent up and could not get back to bed till about eleven. On Monday I had to work hard packing cars. On Tuesday I was sent down to the cars about 10 o'clock with the guard. The cars were so full we had to ride on top. About sundown I was sent back to the hill to get some provisions and got caught in a soaking rain and had no way to change any clothes so had to keep them on till they dried. We managed to squeeze in to the cars till the rain was over which was about 12 o'c but the only sleep which I got was on a wet mattress in wet clothes on top of the car with out covering or overcoat.

We got to Atlanta just in time to see the train go off and had to lie over a little over 24 hours.

When we got to Macon we had to transfer the baggage to other cars as they would not let us carry the same cars any farther. This gave more hard work. We had to stay there till Friday morning and reached Milledgeville at night. Next day the cars were brought to Midway and unloaded when we had to get wagons and have the things hauled up and put away. There are eight of us here and we have to have two on post all night to guard the things. I and one of the others act corporal so I have to be up half of every night but can sleep as much as I wish in the day.

We are in the college buildings.

You can't tell how anxious I have been to hear of you all. I saw Mrs King's Brave boy in Macon who said he saw Father and some of the servants come down on the train and that he was staying at the Brown house or at the car shed but I could not see any thing of them. The rest of the cadets I left in Marietta waiting orders. We are now in service and I hate to be way off here guarding baggage when there is a prospect of a fight but it is my duty. I have to do it whether I am satisfied or not. I am pretty well.

Your affectionate Son Archie

Love to all Remember me to the folks at Mrs Riley's. Howdey to the servants &c

I carried this paper & envelope in my pocket about a week.

1. Some sources maintain that the GMI cadets were placed into the line of battle at Resaca on May 14 and returned to their campus by May 16. The plan was to move them to guard the state capital at Milledgeville. As a sergeant of supply for the cadets, Archie was sent to Midway, just to the south of Milledgeville, to prepare for the arrival of the rest of the corps. However, the cadets were then sent to West Point, Georgia, to guard a railroad bridge that linked Atlanta to Alabama (Yates, "History of the Georgia Military Institute," 7–9).

2. This Captain Griffiths (whose name Archie later spelled Griffith) was apparently in charge of commissary stores at GMI and was therefore Archie's supervisor.

3. "The hill" was a Marietta term for the Georgia Military Institute.

WILLIAM TO MOTHER

Rose Dew May 31/64

Dear Mother

I rec^d yours of 24 & 25 yesterday, I am very thankful to hear that you have been able to get away from R. in safety. Of course I felt very anxious about you, but not too much so as I knew under whose care you were, and that our Heavenly Father does all things for our good, and I rec^d yours of 21st saying that you were getting ready to start, and also the enemy seemed to be moving westward.

I went on Saturday to visit Smith at Isle of Hope, and enjoyed the visit very much. Helen was there which added to the pleasure of the visit.[1] I had seen her in Sav^h too the Monday before.

I am sorry you did not telegraph to me from Atlanta that I could have met you in Sav^h. However it would have been for a very short time and I hope soon to make you a visit as my turn for furlough comes the latter part of next week or the first part of the week after.

I suppose you brought but few things down with you but if the enemy came to Roswell, things would be destroyed whether you staid or came away.

I do not exactly understand about A. You say he is to go to Macon. Are the Cadets to be stationed there? He has his wish now. He is in service, it is most evident by the hand of Providence that has put him there. So altho' I can not help feeling very anxious about him yet I know he is as safe there as any wh[ere else]. . . .

Helen says tell Charlotte[2] that she is a bad girl for not stopping in Sav^h, but as Helen intended to take her to Grahamville[3] I am glad she did not stop, but I suppose Helen has written it all herself.

I am very well.

Much Love to all your afft son W^m

Do tell Momma[4] and all the servts howdye for me.

1. Willie's cousin, Archibald Smith Barnwell (1833–1917), commanded Barnwell's Light Battery on the Isle of Hope. He had a sister named Helen (1839–79).

2. Charlotte Cuthbert Barnwell (1842–1922), the sister of Archibald and Helen Barnwell.

3. Grahamville, South Carolina, lies north of Savannah between the Charleston and Savannah Railroad and the Broad River, with Port Royal Island and Beaufort to the east of the river.

4. Often referred to as "Mauma," or "Maum Mannie," she is an old servant of the Smith family, born about 1795, who apparently played a role in raising the children (Smith Papers, box 17, folder 2).

MOTHER TO WILLIAM

Valdosta Saturday

My Dear Son

We reached this place last night in safety & are going out to our place directly. We are pretty well but excessively fatigued & poor Helen seems quite overcome. Every thing so different from our home that now she seems to realize our situation & to despair of ever seeing it again, she says she needs a home more than ever & I fear she will suffer for want of the little corn paste she has been accustomed to. We brought the chair you made for her as it could be shut up & put in with a few blankets. That is all of [the] furniture that we have saved. She longs to see you & I am in hopes your visit will do her good. Of course you will come as soon as you can get a furlough. You have learned to sleep on the floor. We felt it hard to pass so near & not see you.

May God bless you darling pray for us that we may be upheld under this trial.

Your aff
Mother

———

ARCHIE TO WILLIAM

Midway June 4th

Dear Brother

I arrived here last Saturday with Capt Griffiths and some of the professors folks and 8 other cadets and three car loads of baggage and Institute property.

We left Marietta twelve o'clock Tuesday night and got to Atlanta just in time to see the train leave that we wanted to go on so we had to wait a little over twenty four hours for the next one.

We had to wait twelve hours in Macon and five or six in Gordon[1] and about twelve more in Milledgeville.

I had a good nights rest last night for the first time since I left Marietta as I had no good place to sleep while on the cars and have been on guard every night since I have been here. Thursday I got up at one o'c and did not go to bed till half past twelve and did not go to bed then as we were guarding some more things down at the depot which had just come. So I had to do the best I could on some bags of corn.

I am very anxious to hear something from the family. The last I heard was two weeks ago and then they were just expecting to run from the yankees. I suppose they are in Valdosta if nothing has happened to prevent but would like to know certainly and to know what they were able to carry with them. I am afraid it was very little and if the yankees burn the factory we will be pretty nearly "come to poorness." I am pretty hard up now as I have only about six dollars if that to pay for washing and all such expenses and have lost my knife and got my pen spoiled some how.

Georgia, northern Florida, and South Carolina at the time the
Smith family fled to Valdosta, Georgia

I saved most of my things but had to leave my table and box and a few odds and ends.

I believe the rest of the corps is at West Point[2] and I sincerely wish I was there too as I have had more work trouble and tiresome duty since I have left them than I would have in several months if things went on as usual.

Your affct bro

Archie

Do let me know all you know about the folks as they may not have got my letter and not know where to write.

1. A few miles below Midway, the junction of the Central of Georgia and the Milledgeville and Gordon railroads.

2. The GMI cadets had been assigned the task of guarding a key railroad bridge on the Atlanta and West Point Railroad, which linked Atlanta to Montgomery, Alabama (Yates, "History of the Georgia Military Institute," 8–9).

BARRINGTON KING TO ARCHIBALD SMITH

Atlanta 4 June 1864

A. Smith Esq

Dear Bro Arch—Yours of the 30th ult rec[d] this morning & glad indeed to learn that your family arrived at Valdosta without accident, and comfortable for the times: it is sad indeed to be driven from our homes by the vandals, but we must place our trust in the Lord, hoping all for the best. M[rs] King suffering much from head ache. . . . Trusting with God's blessing, we may be permitted soon, to return to Roswell. Gen[l] Johnston has had a general battle, skirmishing every day—the Yankees are working back to Alatoona, being short for provisions, man & horse: if forced back & that army whipped, we may escape at Roswell.

On Monday last the Factory at Lawrenceville was destroyed by fire, said to be accidental—sad loss to the country: when leaving home, I thought those mills would be safe, being distant from approach of the enemy—all moving on as usual at our mills yesterday, our teams hauling off all the usual production from day to day. Your bale of Yarn 50 Bundles was brought over & sent to care of M[r] Duncan Savannah via Macon 2nd Ins[t]—you had best write M[r] Duncan & give directions.[1]

The cadets from Marietta it is said are sent to West Point to guard the Bridge. I will inquire & send the letter for your son. God only knows whether we may all be permitted to meet & enjoy the comforts of this life, at our old homes—we must place our trust in him, discharge our duty & all will be well in another & better state. M[rs] King joins with me kind regards to yourself & family.

Your friend &c
B King

1. William C. Duncan (1799–1879), a merchant and factor of the firm of Duncan and Johnston of Savannah, played a major role in the Smiths' affairs beginning in 1865.

Midway June 6th

Dear Helen

I was very glad to receive Mother's letter last night as it was the first definite news I had heard of you since the Saturday before you left Roswell.

I wish very much I could have seen you all in Atlanta and would have looked about for you in the chance of your being there but Mother wrote word that you were going the other way so I had no idea you would be there.

The reason we saw nothing of each other on the R. R. [was that] I came on the freight train and you on the passenger but we passed each other a few miles from Macon and the people on one train spoke to those on the other.

I suppose you must have left Macon before I got there. I have only had two whole nights rest since I have been here as I have to act corporal of the guard half of every night. On Thursday I was up from one in the morning till half past twelve at night and did a great deal of hard work but slept about four hours in the day. I slept on a pile of corn bags that is bags of corn till about six and then had more hard work moving things from the depot as two more carloads had been sent down. When that was done I had to go to Milledgeville to see about expressing some tents and did not get back till after three. Then I slept from four oclock that evening till six the next morning.

I saved my trunk, bed, bucket, big tub, chair, dipper and I believe my bedstead but lost my table and box and my little tub got broken to pieces on the way.

The people about here are very kind and seem to think lots of the Cadets and there are more girls than anything else. I have several invitations to call and intend to make my first trial tonight if nothing happens to prevent. It is not very promising as far as the young lady is concerned but they have a big garden which looks as if there ought to be strawberrys in it.

I am very anxious to know what you were able to save and *think Father might save some more things* if he was to go up at once as it seems likely the yankees may not get to Roswell for some time yet. I would like to go myself and do what I could but there is no chance for me to leave here. How do you like Lowndes County, pine barren, and the Rileys?

I have a very hard time, have lost my knife and got my pen spoiled but am quite contented since I have heard of your safe arrival. I can spare my mattress very well if you need it.

Love to all. Howdy to the servants. Remember me to the Rileys & Barnwells.

Your affct bro Archie

RECOLLECTIONS OF GULIE RILEY SMITH[1]

We were at the old place only a short time after my father died. The war came on and we had to leave there. Very early one morning long before we got up a soldier came to the front door. A servant went to the door. The soldier wrote on a piece of paper and told my mother she must leave there immediately as the enemy was coming up the River. We were all sick with the measles. My poor mother did not know what to do. She knew it was very bad for us to go out before we were well over the measles but she dared not stay there with her daughters as they might have a battle right there. . . .

My mother bought a farm further up in the state where it was thought the enemy would not be so apt to come. . . . When we reached our log house we found the beds had in the confusion got lost, all but one. That one was put down on the floor and we all three slept on the same bed. We were on it most of the day with chills. After we had been there a week or more I was taken with pneumonia and was very ill. My mother and sister gave me the only bed. What they slept on I do not know. Perhaps they got some hay. I knew very little of what was happening outside of the room I was in.

We carried with us about forty of our servants. They were all sick except two or three. The few that were well had a hard time nursing so many sick. There was very little we could get to eat but corn meal or grits. This was very hard for us and for our servants. Altho' we had so many hardships we all recovered. The servants went to work willingly and planted all sorts of things to eat. Soon we had fine vegetables, melons, chickens, turkeys, and everything a farm affords, but until these good things came we lived very hard. When we had been there sometime my mother sent for more of her servants. Then a number of people owned several hundred servants. I do not know how many my mother owned.

My mother was an unusually fine business woman. She directed her servants who were obedient and faithful. They made large quantities of rice, corn, cotton, and potatoes. Much of these were sent to the soldiers. . . . We had a great many potatoes. I do not think they were ever sent to the soldiers. They were too heavy for them to carry probably. If they got any by the way, that was all right. I remember a regiment was going by our house on their way to Florida where they fought the battle of Olustee. Mother sent out and asked the officer if his men could stop and get potatoes. He sent her word they could not. Mother was anxious that they should have them, so she had the servants go and strew the road with them. Then the poor hungry creatures could pick them up as they marched along. When these men came back they gave us a number of little things they picked up on the battlefield.

Some of the wounded stopped by our house and had their wounds dressed. Mother's home was called "Soldier's Comfort" by those who knew it.

Except when these regiments passed we saw very few men. Every man that was able, old or young, was sent to the war. So the girls out in the country had rather a lonely time. I spent a great deal of my time riding horse back.

I was very fortunate in getting a very nice governess who taught me during the war. She lived in Virginia and had with her a younger sister about my age. We studied together and had all the fun we could. My governess liked very much to see the servants dance "the holy dance." She often went to the negro streets and had them dance. The servants' houses we built in rows which made streets between them. When my governess arrived at our house the first time, it was just after sundown. The servants were all at home from their days work, and had all their houses brightly lighted. As there were a number of them it looked very pretty. We sent a servant to the Rail Road to meet them (she and her sister). When she got in sight of one home she asked the servant what village is this? He said "dis ye de Mis plantation Ma'am." Soon after my governess left our home she went to China as missionary and has only been back on visits. If she is living she is a very old lady. I am ashamed to say I neglected to answer her last letter (from China) and in that way lost sight of her.[2]

We spent the four years of the war on the farm and had an abundance of everything that could be made there. We lacked salt, tea, coffee, and such things. Those who lived near the sea boiled the salt water and got salt that way. I remember once we had no salt and had to dig up the earth in the smoke house (where the meat had been salted and it had dripped). The earth was put in tubs of water that made the water quite salty. It was dark, and we would have thought it dreadful to use it any other time than during the war. At the close of the war our servants all with the exception of a few returned to the coast where they had lived so many years.

1. Gulielma English Riley, the future wife of Archie Smith, was the daughter of William Morgandollar Riley (1805–59) and Elizabeth Ann Maner Riley (1812–89). Shortly after her birth in Black Swamp, South Carolina, the Riley family moved to a new home at the Sterling Plantation, on the Turtle River in Glynn County, Georgia, from whence they refugeed to Valdosta. Gulie wrote this memoir about 1910–20.

2. A letter that Gulie Riley Smith received from China in 1901 proves that this governess was Lottie Moon (1840–1912), who has been called the "patron saint" of Southern Baptist missionaries (James, ed., *Notable American Women,* 2:570–71). One of Moon's biographers, Catherine B. Allen, reports that in October 1863, Moon, who lived in Virginia, was "seeking employment as a private tutor for a sixteen-year-old

girl in Valdosta, Georgia." This girl was almost certainly Gulie Riley (*New Lottie Moon Story*, 48).

MOTHER TO WILLIAM

Valdosta June 8th/64

My Dear Son

I have been so hard at work since I came down that I scarcely know how the time has gone & do not remember when I wrote to you last or what I told you, but I hope you will be with us before long & see all that I have neglected to mention about our situation here. You will find pretty hard times here, nothing but corn & bacon. Yet I know you will be glad to share it with us for a while.

The weather is very hot & we all feel the debilitating influence & miss our large airy house & cool spring. Yet we are thankful for this refuge from the dangers which threatened us. Helen appears better in the last day or two. She asks you to ask Mary Elliott[1] to lend her the Romance of a poor young man *in French*. We could bring so few things with us that they are at a loss for employment & would like to improve their French. We had long letters from Arkansas on Monday written after the Yankees had left Camden. They occupied it 11 days & Aunt Bet says no one who has not endured it can imagine the trials of their situation. The Yankees took every article of food which they could find, determined to starve the people into taking the oath. Mr Merrell had provisions concealed so they made out but many insults & indignities were offered to the people altho' Gen Steele is said to be very kind.[2]

The last I heard from Sonny he with 7 others was at Talmadge, in charge of the effects of the Cadets which had been moved to that place.[3] They occupied the College buildings. He seemed to feel badly that he was there only doing guard duty when the other cadets may be fighting. I rather think Gen Capers will manage to keep them away from the fighting altogether though they are considered in the service. Have you heard that Helen B. is engaged to Dr Geiger?[4] It is even so but I suppose it is a secret as yet. We have not seen any of the neighbors yet except the man from whom the house is rented[5] & who has been kind in lending us some chairs & tables soon. Mrs Riley has not called to see us tho' she has sent several kind messages. She is only a mile off. Father has been quite unwell since we came down. He was overworked before & during the journey.

All unite in love & hoping to see you soon

Your aff
Mother

Gulielma Riley Smith (1846–1921) married Willie's brother Archie. They became the parents of the last generation of the Smith family of Roswell. Courtesy of the Georgia Department of Archives and History

Archie Smith. Courtesy of the Georgia Department of Archives and History

1. Mary Stiles Elliott (1838–1919), the daughter of Margaret Cowper Mackay Elliott.

2. For Henry Merrell's eyewitness account of the Camden campaign in Arkansas, see Skinner, ed., *Autobiography of Henry Merrell*, 363–76. The federal general who led this attack was Frederick Steele (1819–68).

3. Talmadge was between Midway and Milledgeville, on the Milledgeville and Gordon Railroad.

4. Helen Barnwell (1839–79), the oldest daughter of Captain Edward Barnwell and Archibald Smith's sister, Eliza Zubly, married Dr. Charles Atwood Geiger of Roswell during the war.

5. The Smiths apparently rented their house from James Wisenbaker.

ANNE SMITH TO SARAH MACKAY, UNDATED

My Dear Sarah,

I thank you for the kind thoughtfulness of your proposal of aiding me from the Maryland fund.[1] It is like yourself to be thinking of the comfort of your friends. It is true we are very, very poor now & cannot expect to have even the comforts & indulgences we used to have when we thought we lived very plainly, yet there are so many who need and who are suffering for want of the necessaries of life that I cannot feel that it would be right in me to accept of what might be better bestowed. So far our actual wants have been supplied & I am able to have a cup of tea for anyone who is indisposed. I am thankful to say that Mr. S. & Charlotte[2] are the only ones who need it at present & those who are well might well come down at [once] & not try to bolster themselves up a little longer.

All is dark before us but we are not in present need & trust in Him who has promised that we shall want no good thing. Charlotte brought up some bacon which was at Mrs. Riley's for their use. It helps me in providing. She was quite distress'd at the loss of her tea & coffee, all of which was perfectly ruined by the leaking of a bottle of Kerosene oil. I have one servant, a common country hand, willing, but knows very little & who cooks & washes. Sister H.[3] & I do all the house work & I have to make all the bread & prepare most of the vegetables & iron the Sunday "Sunday" shirt & pantaloons (the girls have to put out any thing nice they have to do). So you see my dear Sarah, I have but little time on hand & must therefore leave to Charlotte to tell you about the girls &c, which [I] would do myself if she were not going to write to-day. . . .

1. The Maryland Fund seems to have been organized to benefit Confederate refugees and was apparently named for those who had a particularly bad time when they came

to Virginia after Maryland remained within the Union at the beginning of the war (Channing, *Confederate Ordeal*, 123).

2. Archibald Smith and Charlotte Barnwell.

3. Helen Zubly Magill.

ARCHIE TO WILLIAM

Midway June 20th

Dear Brother

I received your letter which was very welcome especially what it contained as I was truly hard up, not having a cent except a few stamps.

I hope you are enjoying your self at Valdosta now (I don't exactly know whether to call it home or not) and wish I was there too but am afraid it will be a long time first, how long I have no idea as I think very likely the cadets will stay in service a good many months at least, if not for the war and if that is the case there is no telling how long before I can come but I don't grumble. All I want is to be in service in earnest and not doing nothing here [is] so hard. But the rest of them are not in a much better place for as soon as the Yankees got near Marietta they were moved to West Point to a very safe distance and are now on provost duty and I suppose it is just as well to guard baggage here as to guard the town there. Either is a disgrace to a white man. What I want is to be really in service.

Please if any body is coming up this way send my pistol if it is convenient and safe and if you have no use for it as I may want it if I should happen to be called into active service.

Excuse this letter as I have neuralgia in my face. It is not bad but just enough to worry me.

Your affec't Bro

Archie

Love to all

I am taking quinine and hope to be well soon.

JAMES J. PRYOR TO ARCHIBALD SMITH

Roswell 29 June 1864

Mr Arch[l] Smith

Valdosta Geo

Dear Sir

When you were in this place, you gave me an order on Mrs Scoles[1] for six (6) bushels corn, as also an order upon the party living at your residence, for the *whole* of your corn at that place. I sent to Mrs Scoles but she had no corn whatever, and said that she had two bunches Cotton Yarn which she expected to exchange for corn, but that she had no corn belonging to you. The party sent (Mr Sherman)[2] called at your place and got all the corn at that place ten (10) bushels, *seven* of which you owed; and the balance three (3) bushels was placed to your credit on the books of the Ivy Mills, at Atlanta prices, i.e. Twelve & 50/100 Dolls per bushel. These are the figures given me by Mr B. King as being Atlanta prices.

Hoping that it will meet your approbation, I am Respectfully

James J. Pryor[3]

for J R & T E King

P.S. Very heavy artillery firing heard here yesterday and today. No results as yet heard in Roswell.

1. Perhaps of the family of Robert Scolds, listed in the 1840 census of Roswell, or of Jesse Scols, listed in the 1850 census.

2. R. E. Sherman, age forty-one, a carpenter from Rhode Island, is listed in the 1860 Roswell census.

3. James J. Pryor, apparently an employee of the Roswell Manufacturing Company with managerial status, is listed as a first lieutenant in the Roswell Battalion (Hitt, *Charged with Treason,* xvii). Pryor signs on behalf of the two sons of Barrington King who had built the Ivy (or Laurel) Woolen Mill of the Roswell Manufacturing Company, James Roswell King (1827–97) and Thomas Edward King (1829–63), even though the latter had been killed at the Battle of Chickamauga.

WILLIAM TO MOTHER

Rose Dew July 2/64

Dear Mother

I can not say I am glad to say I have arrived here safely for I have felt so bored all day.[1] I did not know what to do, after being free and remaining about so much it is dreadful to come back to routine and forced confinement and to feel that it must last for a long time, but I will get over this feeling in a few days and feel more cheerful. My furlough has done me a great deal of good. I feel much more like being contented and cheerful than I did before. We got to Sav*h* all right. The travelling was very hot but not dusty. Smith was not at the depot, as Charlotte went to the Cheveses to stay till he comes for her.[2]

If Sissie had come I could not have seen her much. Bacon[3] has gone off on 20 days furlough and I could not make the change to Isle of Hope until he gets back, and could not have gone over there very often. So I suppose on the whole it is as well that she did not come.

They have made a change in our pay. They give us $60 a month and give us rations and clothing. The rations are plenty except the meat, 10 lbs of bacon pr month to each. We get vinegar, sugar, rice, soap, grits and meal. I do not know how much clothing is given. Cousin Sarah is better.[4] She had a very good night last night. I did not stay in town last night. Came out to station.

The little bell that I brought does not do well on the instrument. I thought I was going to have the finest fixment on the line but it won't do.

Much Love to all.

My throat has got quite well.

Your afft son W^m

Do tell the servts howdie for me

1. During a brief furlough in June, Willie Smith joined his father in making a quick trip to Roswell to retrieve what they could and have it shipped south before Sherman's army arrived. Roswell was taken and its mills burned four days later.

2. Langdon Cheves (1814–63) was a rice planter on the Savannah River in the Beaufort District of South Carolina. An engineer defending Battery Wagner on Morris Island below Fort Sumter, he was killed on July 10, 1863, by the first shell fired in the federal attack that eventually involved the black troops of the famed fifty-fourth Massachusetts, led by Colonel Robert G. Shaw. Apparently Archibald Smith Barnwell and his sister, Charlotte Cuthbert Barnwell, planned to visit Mrs. Cheves at the family's plantation near Savannah on the Union Causeway (Myers, ed., *Children of Pride*, 1489; *OR*, 28, part 2: 180, 560).

3. Both Albert S. Bacon and Edward H. Bacon served in the Savannah Guards with Willie Smith: (Confederate Pensions and Records Department, Alphabetical Card File, roll 3).

4. Sarah Mackay.

ARCHIE TO MOTHER

Midway July 6th 64

Dear Mother

I received your letter the other day and was glad to hear that Father & Brother had got back safely. I think they were just in time as I hear the Yankees have taken Marietta but I am afraid Mr King did not have time to send the things off. I was very much in hopes they would get my things from Miss Sherrod and I am afraid they are entirely lost now. . . .

Do let me know if we have really come to poorness for if we have I won't spend any thing that is not absolutely necessary and feel much happier in denying myself than I would in spending any amount of money and knowing that you were skimping at home and after all to feel the loss of home less than any of you as I am just as comfortably situated here as I was in Marietta. About the only thing is being so much farther from home. I think very likely Father will not be able to support me at the Institute next term if the exercises are resumed and if that is the case I think I had better apply for the position of state cadet. It is no disgrace and I am not at all too proud. I am pretty sure Gen Capers or any of the professors would use their influence in my behalf.

I am having a pretty good time here now I don't have much to do except go on guard every other night and all I have to do is to sleep by the sentinel in an entry and he wakes me up when it is time to relieve him. I have become acquainted with nine young ladies and there are plenty more coming. We have greens for dinner once in a [while] and I get as many blackberries as I want, so on the whole I have a pretty good time. My greatest difficulty is having so few summer clothes that I can wear.

I think it is very likely the Cadets will stay in service for the war and I am more than willing as I have as good a position as I would be likely to get any where else and if they have an election of officers I am pretty confident I could get my present office again.

Love to all howdy to servants &c.

Your affectionate son
Archie

MOTHER TO WILLIAM

Valdosta July 6th/64

How a little indulgence spoils us My Darling. Since you left I have been feeling how hard it was to have you obliged to leave us so soon & by your letter received yesterday I find you too are feeling more the dull routine of your life & yet though we feel more keenly the trials of our circumstances after a brief respite I will not allow that the respite was not good for us. I think even a little relaxation makes us more strong to bear our troubles, as the bow unbent for a while is more efficient when strung again. I am not surprised that you found the travelling so uncomfortable. The weather has been oppressively hot since you left, very little breeze. I think that hot journey after a night in Valdosta would have been too much for Helen. She has had another boil on her leg & been more indisposed in other respects & since she hears you cannot make the exchange to the Isle of Hope she is more glad that she did not go. The idea of having you there was the only thing that reconciled her to going altho she consented where we all wished it. She said she would be willing to take the journey to have you with her all day in the car.

I had a letter from Sonny on Friday. He was well but sadly in want of clothes, so we all set to work & fix'd up some for him & sent them to the express yesterday. I sent him the linen coat you wore when you were here & another like it & 2 prs linen pants, also the knife you wished him to have. As he is now in service I suppose it will be no harm for you to buy a pr of Govt shoes for him when they are to be had. He will soon be in need of them but I do not wish you to have any made for him. He could probably have that done in Milledgeville. His bundle had to be express'd to that place. I do not know how far it is from Talmage.

We still get some blackberries tho' the hot dry weather has made them smaller. We had a fine rain yesterday which made the night & early morning very pleasant but it is very hot again. We heard from some soldiers passing last night that a telegram had been received in Sav. that the Yankees had taken Marietta. If so I fear the labour & expense of the trip to Roswell was only so much loss. J. K. is very tardy & forgetful,[1] yet we hope it may not be so, & if it is, God's will be done. As long as my precious boys are spared to me I feel that my portion of the trials of this war is light.

Last Sunday was our usual communion day & we felt deeply the privation of being driven away from our sanctuary, yet we trust in God's promise that he will never leave nor forsake & we know that he is not confined to temples made with hands.

Father seems not at all well. These spells of hard labour mental & bodily are too much for him & without the comfort as well as assistance of having you with him I think he would have broken down before he got home. The rest of us are as usual. We can hear nothing of our things which left when you did.

May God bless you darling

Your aff

Mother

1. This may be a reference to one of the sons of Barrington King, who Anne Smith may have thought was still in Roswell looking after the affairs of the Roswell Manufacturing Company. She is probably referring to James Roswell King, but she may be speaking of Joseph Henry King, who had been severely wounded at First Manassas and had not fully recovered.

Valdosta July 9th 1864

My Dear Son

Our minds are much relieved about our dear boy by learning that the Yankees have been checked in their approach to Milledgeville & so many captured as to weaken their force very much.[1] Yet we have not heard from him for more than 3 weeks & feel anxious to know how he is situated. It is indeed a disappointment for him to miss the place he has so long been wanting when it was almost within his grasp yet it is so ordered & must be best for him. I think it was rather a compliment to you & Mr B. to ask you to suggest the candidates. Young men of sobriety & reliability are so much wanted in such situations that I think if our boy's character were known the capt. would like to have him & would give time for the arrangement. Mr Barnwell returned last Saturday & told us the mail was not yet coming thro' so we suppose that is the reason we have not heard.[2] Your Father rec'd a letter from Mr Camp this morning.[3] He says they feel very insecure & had their trunk packed & ready to run if the Yankees should come. His letter was very old & we see that they have since crossed the bridge at Curtright but nothing was said about damage done. Our yarn reached Valdosta safely last Saturday. It is wonderful how all that we have tried to save has been preserved for us. The girls are very much in need of some dentist work & I think Lizzie would like to go to Sav. to have it done. Do find out if Parsons still works, if he would take gold dust or ore in payment or if he must have coin & also if it would be convenient to Kate to have her stay a few days with her she might go with Smith when he returns.[4]

We have plenty of melons from Smith's. I wish I could send you some. If you can appoint any way & time let me know & I will share with you. I do not half enjoy any thing my dear boys cannot partake of. We saw that the account of young Anderson's death on the *Alabama* was not true.[5] What a pity for people to be in such a hurry to publish such harrowing accounts. We are as usual & unite in love to you. Dr Geiger is clerk in a hospital in Macon. Mr B saw him. Helen is gratified at his being in service.

Your aff
Mother

1. Anne Smith clearly dated this letter July 9, but internal evidence suggests that she erred, for August 9 seems a more likely date. Readers may wish to return to this letter when they reach the middle of page 93 below.

2. Apparently Thomas Osborn Barnwell. See Anne Smith's letter of April 15, above, and Helen Smith's letter of July 23, below.

3. George Hull Camp (1816–1907), since 1849 Barrington King's assistant at the Roswell Manufacturing Company, fled Roswell at the last minute, even as retreating Confederates were burning the bridge across the Chattahoochee River south of the town. He removed to another textile mill at Curtright on the Oconee River above Milledgeville, also built by his cousin and former brother-in-law, Henry Merrell. Camp's first wife, Lucretia, was Merrell's sister; she had died in childbirth in 1845 at the Smith home in Roswell.

4. Elisha Parsons (1806–99) was reputed to be the best dentist in Georgia (Myers, ed., *Children of Pride*, 1640). Cousin Kate is Catherine Mackay (1811–79), and Smith is Archibald Smith Barnwell (1833–1917).

5. The son of former Savannah mayor and current artillery colonel Edward C. Anderson, Midshipman Edward Maffitt Anderson was on board the Confederate raider *Alabama* when, under its commander, Admiral Raphael Semmes (1809–77), it engaged and was sunk by the USS *Kearsarge* in the English Channel off Cherbourg on June 19. Edward C. Anderson received news that his son had been blown overboard, leaving a leg on the deck of his ship, but later received word that "Eddy was safe," having been only wounded and able to keep afloat until rescued (Lawrence, *Present,* 159; Sinclair, *Two Years on the* Alabama, (329–31, 343).

_____

ARCHIE TO WILLIAM

Midway July 9th

I received your letter some time ago and would have answered it before but I have not been in a condition to do business for over a week.

Last Saturday week there was a report that Milledgeville was about to be attacked so about ten cadets that were here and some men that were about the hospital here formed a company under Capt Manget and went to help the militia defend the town.[1]

We marched round town and started to come out this way to meet the Yankees but stopped to have dinner and after dinner thought better of it and went back. At night we lay out and next day they concluded as the Yankees would not come to us and we could not catch them on foot it would be best to get up a "critter" company to go after them.

The company was got up. Some had horses and some had mules and most had no stirrups but a rope or leather strap. None had any blankets and very few had cartridge boxes. Some had rifles, some had muskets and some had shot guns. When we started instead of going straight where we started the captain kept dodging about in by roads so that it took us about four hours to get about ten miles. In the mean time we had a hard rain which gave us a "right reverend wetting" and the captain went home to get some dry clothes and left us wandering about like sheep without a shepherd and when dark came we found ourselves faced about and going towards home but we met another company that had left after we did who were fortunate enough to have a captain who did not leave to go home every time he got wet.

So we turned round and followed him and after a while found our own captain along side the road and all started off for Eatonton. The other company went straight there and got there in time to have a skirmish with a squad of yankees but our captain preferred to go the crooked way so we could not get there that night but stopped about two oclock and slept out. We did not leave next morning till long after sun rise and did not get to Eatonton till long about eight or nine oclock but the yankees had burned the depot and gone long ago. We followed them a few miles but of course did not see them for they passed about the time we were getting up.[2]

We came back to Eatonton and stayed there till after dinner and then started home. We stopped about twelve miles from here that night and got home the next day which was Tuesday. We were off just about two days and in that time rode about eighty miles and had about two hours hard rain.

The horse of one of our men broke down and he had to stop when two stray yankees happened along and picked him up. After going with them a while he suddenly called on some imaginary Confederate troops to come and capture the yanks whereupon they ran off, but he called on them to throw down their guns which they did when he picked them up and ordered the yanks to halt which they did then quietly marched them into town. He was an Irish man and an old trooper.

The other company that went from Milledgeville captured two yankees but they were recaptured and five of their men taken, among them one cadet, but they all got back safely. One was a little fellow and they let him go. Two escaped and two were recaptured by Wheeler's men who almost annihilated the raid.[3]

The two fellows who last escaped each got a horse and a good carbine and one of them got a nice pistol and the other a first rate US blanket.

When I got back I took sick and had a right good fever for two days and I am still very weak from the effects of it but I don't think I had any rheumatism.

Mrs Talmage found out I was sick and was very kind sending me things. She sent me tea and coffee and okra soup several times.

Poor Dr Talmage has gone deranged and they have sent him to the asylum. I went to see Mrs Talmage this evening. She spoke very pleasantly of you and sent her kind regards or something of the kind to you when I wrote.

She asked all about you and seemed very much interested in you.

I think I may go to the front soon. I would have gone yesterday if I had been well as all that were fit for duty went up with Capt Manget.

Your affectionate bro
Archie

1. Victor E. Manget was the captain of the military unit created from the cadets of the Georgia Military Institute in 1864. He was the brother of Archie's beloved French and history professor at the Institute (Yates, "History of the Georgia Military Institute," 29).

2. Because the action that Archie is reporting would have taken place June 25–27, at exactly the same time that Confederate and federal forces were concentrated at Kennesaw, federal cavalry may have roamed as far as Eatonton to protect Sherman's left flank at Kennesaw. Brigadier General Kenner Garrard guarded that flank with orders to keep Confederate cavalry under Wheeler engaged. Garrard reported "much action and activity" in this regard, including six engagements with Wheeler, the last on June 27 (*OR*, 38, part 2: 804).

3. "Fighting Joe" Wheeler (1836–1906), whose cavalry exploits placed him second only to Nathan Bedford Forrest in the minds of many Confederates, provided most of the opposition to Sherman's march to Savannah.

WILLIAM TO HELEN

Rose Dew July 9/64

Dear Sissie

I was in hopes of having a letter from home to answer but as none has come, I must make my answer out of whole cloth. I spent yesterday at Isle of Hope and they all seemed sorry that you did not go but perhaps it is best not, as Smith has Bilious fever and may be sick for some time and there is a good deal of Typhoid fever among the troops. The Island does not seem to be so healthy as it used to be. It is very much overgrown and the turning up of the ground to make batteries may have made it sickly. The way about their having so little room in the house is that Smith hires only one half of the house, and one of his Lieutenants (Hill) was staying with his wife (Mary Maxwell) in one of the other rooms, but the Whites wanted it and so the Hills had to go into Smith's parlour.[1] Fanny said you would have had to stay in a small room with Charlotte until the Hills went, which they did yesterday and then you would have had plenty of room.[2]

In the afternoon Charlotte and I went to ride in the buggy and went nearly all over the Island and got some pretty wild flowers. The ride was very pleasant.

Woodie has been elected Lieut in the Company that John Magill is in.[3] They wrote for him to come on immediately but he has been sick and they do not know if he will be well enough to come at once. He nearly got caught on Beaufort Island the other day. He was within two miles of the town when he was chased by Negro troops and hid in a hedge. Two of them came where he was and opened the bushes, when he cocked his pistol at them and they ran one way and he the other and so got away. Ste Elliott has been made Brig^r Genl. since he went to Va. One year ago he was Major. That is rapid promotion.[4]

The D^r says that Cousin Sarah is much better. I have not seen any of them yet. I asked leave to go to town to morrow but Lt. H. refused so I will put it off until next Sunday.[5]

I will not be able to go to Isle of Hope now. Johnnie Elliott and Tom Clay are the only ones at that station.[6] The others have been sent away, and neither of them wants to change, but I do not care much about it now as you are not there.

I am quite well and have got over the blues that I had last Saturday.

Much Love to all.

Your afft Bro W^m

1. William H. Hill was fourth lieutenant of the Georgia Flying Artillery near Savannah (*Savannah Daily Morning News* (February 28, 1862), 1).

2. Smith Barnwell's wife was Frances ("Fanny") Riley Barnwell. Charlotte Cuthbert Barnwell was her sister-in-law.

3. Smith Barnwell's brother, Woodward (1828–1927), and John Magill (b. 1807), a cousin of the Smiths, may both have been assigned to Smith's independent artillery force known as Barnwell's Light Battery. After service with the Army of Northern Virginia, Woodward had been detached to serve in the Third Military District at McPhersonville, South Carolina, to function as a scout in the Beaufort area he knew so well. On June 25 he was nearly captured during a reconnaissance on Port Royal Island (Barnwell, *Story of an American Family*, 209–10).

4. Stephen Elliott (1832–66), the son of Protestant Episcopal Bishop Stephen Elliott (1806–66) and Mary Gibbes Barnwell (1808–37), died on March 21, 1866, from the effects of a wound received at Petersburg (Myers, ed., *Children of Pride*, 1514).

5. Willie was now serving under Lieutenant William R. Hanleiter, the son of the commander of Hanleiter's Company, Georgia Light Artillery, Army of Tennessee, the

Jo Thompson Artillery (Henderson, ed., *Roster of the Confederate Soldiers of Georgia,* 4:240).

6. John Mackay Elliott (1844–1929), the son of Margaret Cowper Mackay Elliott, enlisted in Company F, Fifty-Fourth Regiment, Georgia Volunteer Infantry, Army of Tennessee, the Savannah Cadets (ibid., 5: 682). He served in the Signal Corps along with Thomas Carolin Clay.

MOTHER TO WILLIAM

Valdosta July 12th 1864

My Dear Son

Helen received your letter of the 9th last night & I am sorry to find you were looking for a letter & had been disappointed. I wrote to you last week I cannot remember on what day but I certainly think early enough for you to have received it before you wrote. I cannot bear you to feel as if Mother neglected you even for a day, but I do not believe you feel so even if you do not get letters. We received the first installment which you and Father sent down but as yet have heard nothing of those you left to be sent. So I fear they were too late. We see by the papers that large numbers of families are leaving Atlanta so unless the things were sent very soon after you left so as to be shipped before the falling back of our army I suppose they could not be sent on even if they were in Atlanta. The barrel of pot ware came & I should feel prepared for baking any quantity of bread if the ovens had covers. We are glad of them however. They will be useful for many things. We [see] in one paper that the Roswell factory had been burned & in another that it had not but now that part of the country is given up it is only a question of time. It is sad indeed to think of our sweet & pretty home being destroyed, yet I thank God that we all have a good hope of a home in the better land & that he keeps us from dwelling exclusively on our losses. Even Helen who was so much overwhelmed by the anticipation of this calamity seems much more calm now that the loss is to her mind reduced to certainty.

I was very sorry at first that Helen could not go to Isle of Hope, but since I hear there is so much sickness there I am thankful she did not go. . . .

I had a letter from A. Saturday night. He seems more reconciled to his position or at least submits quietly to it. He says if the studies of the Inst. are resumed & his Father cannot support him there longer, he will apply for a place as State Cadet, but this I trust will not be necessary.[1] I was a little surprised at his giving it that turn instead of looking at it as an indication that it was time for him to go into the field. I am sorry to find you left your writing paper. Helen does not seem quite as well as when you were here. She has another boil. We got a fine piece of beef yesterday & I have been wishing you had some of our good soup. Father has been quite unwell, fever 4 days none now for 2.

Love from all.

Your aff

Mother

1. Georgia governor Joe E. Brown had raised a state militia, the Home Guards.

ARCHIE TO MOTHER

July 12th

Dear Mother

I received your letter night before last and the bundle last night. I was very glad indeed to get them especially the knife and sweetning and the clothes. I don't know which was the most acceptable.

I had an opportunity of airing some of my new clothes immediately as they had a sort of frolic up here last night.

There is a large hall belonging to one of the societys and the young ladies that stay here and about a half a dozen from Midway and a young fellow from here that used to be a class mate of mine at Marietta, Lieutenant Manget (brother of the professor), and three or four cadets met there to have a sociable. I had a pretty good time but nothing extra.

The brown linen pants are so long I can't wear them without having something done to them but I am in hopes they will shrink some as they seem never to have been washed and are a good deal longer than the white ones.

While I am talking about clothes I am very much in need of some socks. I have a very nice fellow to go visiting with. He is quite a gentleman and very much of a ladies man.

I consider the day lost if I don't go visiting or walk home with some of the ladies from the post office or something of the kind though I must confess there are a great many lost days. I hope if I stay here long I will be as good as the next man for I only began about two weeks ago and have made considerable progress. I think it is almost as improving and a great deal more agreeable than studying my regular lessons.

The cadets are gone to the front and it is very probable they will be in a fight before long. I believe they have been shelled by the yankees already but nobody hurt. If they are going to be in a fight I want to be with them but I would hate to leave here.

We are wishing I can hardly say hoping to be ordered up but you need not feel uneasy for there is very little chance of our leaving here.

I think it would be glorious to go to the front and get a wound that would give me about sixty days furlough and not keep me from walking. I could come through here and get my things and then come down to Lowndes and splurge. Excuse such a foolish letter. Love to all &c

Your affct son
Archie

GEORGE CAMP TO ARCHIBALD SMITH

Curtright,[1] Green Co., Ga.
July 13, 1864
A. Smith Esq

My dear Sir

The above direction indicates my safe exodus from Roswell, and arrival here, where I found all well.

The unfortunate providence which caused me to leave Roswell was also the cause of our determination to distribute to stock-holders (*not* sell to them) one Bale Yarn to each share, as a part of the available assets of the concern. This distribution will not subject you to taxation when you sell the yarn, for the Income tax is upon "profits derived from *buying & selling*." We have the yarn in Augusta and Macon, and as we desire an early distribution you will please, at once, let me know to which points you desire shipment of your yarn made. The yankees entered Roswell Tuesday. The day previous (Monday) I sent a team to your house and loaded it with such plunder as you had prepared, and sent the things to Atlanta, among the articles was Lizzie's Piano. I do not know if the things went any farther than Atlanta, but trust you will receive them all.

Jane[2] has recv'd a pleasant letter from Sister Helen and will soon reply, but I don't know that she will open her heart to all she knows or thinks of the portion of her letter. Time is a true revealer of the character and passions of all—sometimes to our terror—sometimes to the destruction of our happiness forever.

I do not know what my future will be, and do not know what is my duty. I am not able to perform regular field duty, and yet I ought to lend a hand to my country's cause. I am invited to the Presidency of the Curtright

Company, and may possibly accept—am not fully determined. With love to each member of your family

yours truly

Geo H. Camp

I remained in Roswell until the Bridge at Ivys Mill was burned.

1. After leaving Roswell, Camp went to this manufacturing village on the Oconee River, originally named Merrell after his cousin and former brother-in-law, Henry Merrell, who had built it. Both Merrell and Camp were from Utica, New York, yet both worked hard for the cause of their adopted country.

2. Camp's first wife was Henry Merrell's sister, Lucretia. After she had died in childbirth at the Smith home in Roswell, Camp married Jane Atwood (1830–1911) (see Skinner, ed., *Autobiography of Henry Merrell*, 70, 161–62, 164–65, 180–81, 183, 323).

BARRINGTON KING TO ARCHIBALD SMITH

Savannah 15 July 1864

Dear Bro Archy

I remained in Atlanta sending off Yarn &c, until the vandals took possession of Roswell—rec[d] a letter from M[r] Adams, saying the Yankees were running our mills, & promised to respect private property: since then they destroyed the Ivy mills, broke open M[r] Lewis' house, & distributed its contents to the operatives—heard nothing about your dwelling: it is reported that my house was destroyed, also the cotton mills, but nothing positive.[1] I consider all lost at Roswell, & should any thing be left, will be clear gain—Nothing from Bro. Pratt—but it is said M[r] Adams & M[r] Wood, weaver Ivy Mills, were taken prisoners, of this no certainty.[2]

What furniture &c I saved, was stored in Atlanta—should that place be taken, will be destroyed. Gen[l] Johnston had retreated to within six miles of Atlanta & we left via Augusta for this place last Monday morning—the rush from Atlanta was great, every one leaving that could get off, made it difficult to get away, cars all full. You acted wisely leaving with your family—there is no telling what is before us: all dark & gloomy, this cruel war is sad indeed. We hear nothing from Eva.[3] B. S. K. was slightly wounded in the shoulder, dispatch from Richmond informed us, that he was with his wife in Staunton—but no letters since the 5th June.[4] He was wounded about 14th. It is reported that Major Minton was killed, & Axon wounded about the same time—don't believe that M[rs] Minton has heard of it, & trust not true.[5]

Our wagons brought for you on 4th Ins[t] 4 Boxes. 2 Bundles Bedding 1 Box piano, which was sent to the care Duncan & Johnston Sav[h] hope rec[d] before this. It is expected that Kirby Smith is working to the rear of Sherman's army—we must trust in the good Lord for deliverance, & with his blessing yet hope the invaders will not reach Atlanta.[6]

Mrs King bears the trial very well, no headache for two weeks—she joins with me in kind regards to every member of your family. Hope your Brother is doing well.

Yrs truly

B King

Mr Camp left Roswell a little before the vandals entered, & has gone to Curtwright, where his family are.

We expect to make a division of yarn—do inform me what to do with yours & may divide some 4/4 Goods, so soon as our Books are posted. Mr Proudfoot, off^r.[7]

1. The 1860 census lists John and Margaret Lewis as an elderly Roswell couple living near the Smith family. They were the parents of the builder of Holly Hill, Robert Adams Lewis (1813–1906), who lived in New York during the war (Myers, ed., *Children of Pride*, 1594).

2. Nathaniel Alpheus Pratt (1796–1879), the beloved minister of the Roswell Presbyterian Church, had remained in the town following its occupation. Theodore Dwight Adams (1829–1901) was one of Barrington King's assistants. Jason S. Wood (1829–84) is listed in the 1860 census of Cobb County as a power loom boss at the Roswell Manufacturing Company.

3. He is probably referring to his daughter, Catherine Evelyn ("Eva") King (1837–1923), who married William Elliott Baker (1830–1906), the pastor of the First Presbyterian Church in Staunton, Virginia, from 1857 to 1884 (Myers, ed., *Children of Pride*, 1459).

4. Barrington S. King (1833–65), the fifth child of Barrington King to reach maturity, died in the last days of the war at Averasboro, North Carolina, on March 10, 1865.

5. Major John Minton (1797–1871), a native of New York but a resident of Roswell whose home was near the Smiths, was a veteran of the War of 1812, the Creek Indian Wars, the Mexican Wars, and the Civil War. His son, H. Axson Minton (1838–64), died on June 30, 1864, of wounds received at Nancy's Shop, Virginia, six days earlier (Myers, ed., *Children of Pride*, 1625–26).

6. Edmund Kirby Smith (1824–93) at the time commanded the Confederate Department of the Trans-Mississippi. Headquartered in Shreveport, Louisiana, he was nowhere near Atlanta at the time.

7. Hugh W. Proudfoot (1795–1871) was long a bookkeeper for the Roswell Manufacturing Company.

The Smiths' piano, photographed with Willie's flute, was a prized possession. When the family fled Roswell during wartime for the safety of Valdosta, they had the piano shipped along after them.

Sav^h July 16/64

Dear Mother

I rec^d yours of 12th to day. The opportunities for getting letters are so ir-regular now that no doubt they stay in town several days before I get them. The wagon only goes out once a month now and so it is only when one from the station comes to town that letters are carried out. I never could think of such a thing as your neglecting me in any way. Tom Clay did not refuse to change with me, I did not ask him. I am sure he would have done it if I had asked him to make a temporary exchange but circumstances prevented me from asking him. He was sent to another station to take a sick man's place and Bacon being away I did not think it best to ask it.

I went to Isle of Hope again last Tuesday, found Smith much better and expecting to get a furlough next week and will go to Valdosta as soon as he is able to travel, so I have come in to day to get the French books to send by him and I will send the Tea at the same time. Woodie arrived at Isle of Hope last Monday. He has been elected Lieut in J.M.'s Co.[1] He is quite well again.

Charlotte will go to Grahamville while Smith is off on furlough and they want her to come back to them when he returns. . . .

I wrote to A. the other day using all the arguments I could to satisfy him with his position but poor fellow he can not help feeling mortified at his position. I do not suppose that he will have to go into active service under Gov Brown's last call. By the bye is not it too bad that Gov B. can not let any opportunity pass without abusing the President and the Conf. Govt. His proclamation will do as much harm by encouraging the enemy, as his "Melish" will do good.[2]

I have a piece of tin on my telegraph instrument which answers very well but I thought the bell would be such a nice fancy arrangement.

I am glad you have had some beef. I hope Sissie's sickness is not from over-feed.

I have got some tea and think it is pretty good hope you will find it so.

17th Cousin Sarah is much better today.

Much Love to all.

Your afft Son W[m]

1. At this time John Magill's company seems to have been Company B of Daniell's Georgia Light Artillery.

2. Willie refers to Joseph E. Brown's July 9, 1864, proclamation calling all free white males in the state between seventeen and fifty years of age into the service of the state militia (Willie's "Melish"). In the proclamation, Brown said that correspondence with Jefferson Davis had left him with the knowledge that "Georgia is to be left to her own re-sources to supply the re-enforcements to General Johnston's army." While Georgians are on distant fields defending other states, he says, "it becomes my duty to call forth every man in the state able to bear arms." In reference to men who seem exempt from his call because they have been detailed by the Confederate government, he states, "It can-not surely be the intention of the Confederate Government to place a large number of young men to do service in the organization to keep them out of the bullet department" (*OR*, 52, part 2: 688–91).

ARCHIE TO WILLIAM

Midway July 19th

Dear Brother

I received your letter a few days ago and almost feel as if I owed you two letters as the last one I wrote to you was nearly no letter at all but I was suffering from neuralgia and that I think a sufficient excuse for nearly any thing.

I am much obliged to you for the knife which you sent me but I am sorry to say that I lost it the day after I got it. I had it just after dinner and went swimming in the afternoon and when I came out of the water it wasn't in my pocket and I have not seen it since. My pants were so tight I think the knife must have squeezed out of the pocket. I have had blades put into that large white handle that you gave me or that I hooked, I don't know which.

I am having a pretty good time here with hardly any thing to do. I have become acquainted with a good many young ladies and I am determined to improve my time in that way if I can in no other way.

I can have access to three libraries from the G.M.I. but they are all very poor ones and the Thalian hall has been broken open so I can get at that library.[1] I have not become acquainted with the [Thomases?] but I will try to do so soon especially as they have a fine apple orchard.

Have you heard any thing of Eugene Stiles lately?[2] I ought to have written to him again before now but we have been going ahead so much and there has been so much activity in Virginia that I suppose he has moved before now.

I have not seen any home folks since the twelfth of April. It seems like a long time to me and I am afraid it will be still a long time before I see them again. I want to get a furlough in September or the first of October but I don't know if I will be able to. It seems as if I was doomed to live in uncertainty. I don't know what will become of the Cadets, whether they will be kept in service for the war or if they will be disbanded or if the school will be opened at some other place. I hope we will be in for the war.

They say they are going to seize this place for a Hospital. I don't know what we will do exactly. If we are not turned out of our rooms it will be very disagreeable.

Your affectionate bro

Archie

1. Thalia, the Literary Society of Oglethorpe University, had been organized in 1839 to promote "oratory, declamation, debating, and other literary pursuits." Its hall was completed in 1861 (Tankersley, *College Life at Old Oglethorpe*, 45–49).

2. Eugene West Stiles was one of three sons of the Reverend Dr. Joseph Clay Stiles (1795–1875), a famous evangelist. Two of the Reverend Stiles's brothers had married sisters of Sarah Mackay, Catherine Mackay, and Margaret Cowper Mackay Elliott.

Valdosta July 20th 1864

My Dear Son

I am so tired I can hardly write & I believe I have no regular day. All days are so much alike with nothing to break their monotony that I never can remember what day I last wrote. I now write to tell you that all the things you & Father put up have arrived safely. We had about given them up when a letter came from Mr King mentioning that the Factory wagon had taken them to Atlanta on the 4th (the day before the Yankees entered Roswell) & he had sent them off immediately & by the same mail a letter from Mr Duncan mentioned that he had reshipped them.[1] I suppose if Mr K. had not been there to hurry them off they would not have come for he says there was a rush from Atlanta & they found it difficult to get off. Finding things looked so dangerous he sent the Piano down which we were very glad of for we had decided it had better come to Sav. & Father wrote to Mr Pease to send it down but Mr D. not knowing this sent it on.[2] I think you & Father accomplished a great deal in the time you had & have added very much to our comfort. Things generally have come safely tho' there was some breakage in the barrel which was packed with rice. It is a very unfit thing for packing. We have not opened the hhd. of crockery yet.[3] The things only came this morning & after unpacking all the other things I could not undertake the crockery. Mr King wrote that the Yankees were running the Fac^y & he heard Mr Adams & Mr Wood were taken prisoners. I doubt it for Mr A. said he would take the oath.[4] We hear since that the Facs. & all the dwelling houses except Mr Pratt's are burned. Aunty had a letter from Anna Pratt last night. She had had a letter from her Mother written the day the Yankees arrived. They broke open Mr Lewis's house & told the Fac. people to take what they wanted & they rushed through the streets shouting glory to God the Yankees are come.[5]

What can be the meaning of this change of command at such a crisis? It seems a distressing circumstance whatever view we take of it.[6] If it has been done from jealousy or any favouritism the effect will be disastrous on the troops & if from any mismanagement on the part of Johnston the consequences may be fatal to our cause. I suppose you have seen the shocking account of the loss of Col. Anderson's son on the *Alabama*. It seems to me Semmes ought to be a little crest fallen. He cannot justify himself for such an unnecessary fight.[7]

We are glad to hear Smith is so much better & also that Sarah is better. Give my love to them all. I often think of writing to Margaret & Eliza but what can I write about?[8] Only what is sorrowful & all know enough of that already. Helen seems a good deal better this week. Poor child she tries to bear up because it distresses me to see her give way but it is sad to feel that we have no home & not an article of furniture in the world yet we are not depressed. We feel daily that we have much to give thanks for. When you & Father left here I felt weighed down. It seemed that it was too much to expect you to be kept thro' all the dangers of the undertaking & yet you were brought back safely & all your exertions prospered & many times in the day my heart is lifted up in thankfulness for this comfortable refuge & now we have no room where to bestow our goods. You had better go to see Mr & Mrs King[9] if you have opp.ʸ They have been so very kind to us.

May God bless you my dear son.

Your aff

Mother

1. William Duncan (1799–1879), of the firm of Duncan and Johnston, cotton factors and commission merchants in Savannah, took care of most of Archibald Smith's business in the Savannah area.

2. Philander Pitkin Pease (1821–1900), an Atlanta grocer and commission merchant.

3. Abbreviation for "hogshead," a large cask containing from 43 to 140 gallons.

4. Barrington King's letter of July 15, 1864, n. 2, above.

5. Sarah Anna Pratt (1844–1937) was the daughter of Nathaniel Alpheus Pratt. The Lewis's house, Holly Hill, was close to the Pratts' Great Oaks.

6. Jefferson Davis relieved Joe Johnston on July 17 and replaced him with John Bell Hood on July 19.

7. See Anne Smith's letter to Willie of July 9, 1864, p.66, above.

8. Sarah Mackay, Margaret Cowper Mackay Elliott, and Elizabeth Anne Mackay Stiles.

9. Barrington and Catherine Nephew King, who were staying near Savannah with their son Charles Barrington King (1823–80).

LIZZIE TO WILLIAM, ENCLOSED WITH PREVIOUS LETTER

I am very glad to say the things all came safe & many more of my things than I expected. There are some little things which were worthless in themselves which are very valuable as mementos. I am sorry the Piano came down here tho it was nobody's fault. There is no good place to store it in Valdosta & there is no convenient place in the house here. I wish it could be opened as it is here. We might as well have the good of it but there is no place it could be put. It is put into Aunty's room all packed against the front wall. The braid came all safe & I shall go at your hat at once & have it to sent by Smith if that will not be too late in the season. I think perhaps as he is to have 30 days I am afraid it will be too late. I don't think there is much risk in sending by Express. The sprays of Fairy Belle are beautiful. I do hope the seeds will not all be destroyed. Do you think the heat of burning the house would kill them all? Do if any of your friends have any Mignonette seeds or any thing of that kind (Sweet alyssum) &c get some for me at once. August is the time for sowing them & if you could buy some Daliah cuttings they can be planted till the end of this month to advantage & if you could send some geraniums (cuttings) too they might do now. August is the time for them at home. I don't want you to put yourself to any inconvenience about it.

WILLIAM TO MOTHER

Rose Dew July 23/64

Dear Mother

I have just rec^d a long letter from A. and am glad to say it is written much more cheerfully than the last. He apologizes for writing so badly last time as he had neuralgia. He says that he has made several acquaintances and means to cultivate the ladies society but does not mention any names.

I had a note from Charlotte to tell me about Smith getting to town and her starting for Grahamville. She says Mr. Duncan says some more things have come down for Father so I hope that Jimmy King got some away before the Yankees got to R.[1]

We have this evening most cheering reports from Atlanta I am afraid too good to be true. It seems that Johnston was relieved because he wanted to fall back from Atlanta. Bragg was sent there to hold a council of war. It seems strange that Bragg should have a hand in relieving a Genl. who had only followed his example. I suppose you know more about these things than I do for I very seldom see a paper.

The Palmetto is coming out nicely now and if any is wanted I can get some very good and send it. Do write about it at once if so.

I saw some white flannel in town the other day and wanted to get some for A. but it is $20^{00} p. yard and I could not afford the luxury of getting it for him.

Eliza Stiles had a letter from Henry the other day dated 4 inst. he was well.[2]

Cousin Sarah is improving rapidly I hope that now she has begun to improve that she will get well.

Much Love to all

Your afft Son W^m

Do tell the servants howdye for me.

1. The people referred to are Archibald Smith Barnwell and his sister, Charlotte; William Duncan, Archibald Smith's factor in Savannah; and James Roswell King (1827–97), the third son of Barrington King.

2. Elizabeth Anne Mackay married William Henry Stiles (1810–65) in 1832. Her husband, the colonel of the Sixtieth Regiment of Georgia Infantry, had been forced to withdraw because of his health and, after organizing nonconscripted men for the defense of north Georgia, had resigned in April 1864. The reference therefore may be to their son, William Henry Stiles (1834–78), who had been wounded at both Second Manassas and Fredericksburg (Myers, ed., *Children of Pride*, 1693).

HELEN TO WILLIAM

July 23rd/64

Dear Brother

The last of the things have come from home and we are very glad to get some things from home but it is very sad to think that this little bit is all that is saved of our home. The barrel of china came very safely not a thing broken it was so nicely packed one bottle of catsup was popped and the wool was rather dirty but no other damage was done.

Sister says do get some violet plants if you can and all kinds of cuttings lantanas that you can beg or steal when the right time comes to set them out. Fannie has a very pretty lilac one and I expect we can get some from her. Fannie and Smith came and spent Saturday morning with us. We are very much pleased with her. She behaves so pleasantly and does not put on any fuss but behaves as if she knew all about people and is quite respectful to Mother more so than some other people who owe her more respect. They stopped as they passed the night and they got here and had a little talk. They came in a big wagon and when it got to the swamp it stuck in the mud and Smith walked the rest of the way. He would not wait for the buggy but he was much better the next day.

Mr Osborn Barnwell went last night to Atlanta (that is started) he says he knows he will be killed but still he went very readily. He did not know he had to go till Saturday and started off Sunday morning.

We are a little afraid that Sonnie will have to go but as the Institute is Gov Brown's pet pet we hope he will not interfere with this arrangement.

Can you remember whether there is anything in the barrel of carpets except the carpets themselves?

The tea and books came all safe and Mother says I must tell you that the tea is very nice and she wishes you would let her know the price. We are very much obliged for the books.

This ink I am writing with is some we made of gall berrys with a little copperas. I will send you some when Smith goes back if you would like to have it. Your pencil is so pale and your paper so blue that it is very hard to read it at night and we always get the mail then. So if you would like it I will send some.

Mrs King has been so very kind to us that we feel as if we want to do some things to let them know that we are sensible of their kindness though of course it is not any pay for what they have done. Mother said she wished I would finish the fan you began for her for Mrs King.[1] She did not need it here and she had one that you made for her and as you did not [will] it expressly for her she did not mind using it for that purpose so I am making a handle for it of walnut which came down with the things. Father did the cutting out and I am doing the polishing. I have filed so much to day that my hand is stiff and I can hardly write.

People send their love and Uncle S.[2] wants to be remembered to you. I am sure if you were to see him now he would never need to be remembered again. He has been shaving in all sorts of hideous ways and adding to his natural hideousness.

Your aff Sister

Helen

I am so glad you brought Mother's mirror that uncle Charlie gave her.[3] She was saying just a few days ago that she was so sorry to lose it.

1. Catherine Margaret Nephew King.

2. John Joyner Smith.

3. Charles Arthur Magill.

LIZZIE TO WILLIAM, UNDATED

Dear William

Is it not horrid to think what those vile wretches are after? To think of those vile feet polluting the streets of our peaceful village. To be sure that is not half as bad as their pollution of places made sacred by association with the great & good of former days. In fact I don't think altho the place is my home & they have destroyed all our present means of support or at least all our property which brought us any thing I don't think I mind half as much as their desecration of the White house & Arlington so consecrated with the memories of Washington & the idea of the wretches having all those valued mementos of him and his family. I should think the Lees would be perfectly savage. In fact the General must be a little less than a saint to be so perfectly temperate in all his dealings with the wretches. I don't see how he can. What a man he must be.

I should very much like to hear how Moses & his family came on.[1] We heard the other day that his house was the only one left standing in the place but that no one can tell for certain.

Mr Adams stayed there which I think a very suspicious circumstance for staying with his family could be no excuse as he must have known he would be taken prisoner or take the oath & altho he thought or said it would be right for a person to take the oath under such circumstances & he would do it yet I think when a man voluntarily puts himself in a place to do it his oath could not be regarded on either side.[2]

We heard the other day of poor Axon Minton's death. He was wounded & lived a week. He was lying in the trenches perfectly safe when a friend was shot & called for help & Axon went to his assistance & was shot while helping him in. The other fellow is now about. The Major was with him all the time & they seem to feel assured that he was prepared to go. Poor Mrs Minton is in great distress of course. I think she was very proud of Axon.[3] Miss Minton also mentioned the death of George Ladson.[4] I am sure he will be a great loss. I suppose he literally wore himself out.

There is no knowing or even conjecturing what will be the result at Atlanta. Heretofore I have thought when Gen Johnston reached the south side of the Chattachoochee he would be able to bring Sherman to a fight but the newspaper correspondents seem to be trying to prepare the minds of the country to the giving up of that place. I am afraid should he be compelled to give it up it would have a demoralizing effect on the army tho there is no knowing. Their faith in Joe Johnston is such that it would take a great deal to shake it. "Me ze same." I wonder if half the news we see in the papers about the invasion of Maryland is true.[5] The papers were certainly very reticent on the subject if it is so & deserve a great deal of credit & they may do more this time than at any other attempted invasion of those parts but I suppose it is only meant as a little "divarsion" for Gen Grant. I hope he will be pleased with these kind attempts to divert his mind for certainly he must be in need of it after his hard work before Petersburg and I think the least he can do will be to go to see the ploy. I hope some of our generals will make a little divarsion for Sherman. He will be jealous if Grant is better entertained than himself tho I should hardly like Sherman to go off without giving our people the opportunity of giving him some attention & entertainment, for his gentlemanly conduct certainly calls for some reward.

I think it is very well Sissy did not go to the Isle of Hope as they are having so much sickness there. She is a great deal better than she was. I think the change down here has benefitted her a great deal which I suppose would have been the case going to any place. I only wish there was some society for she wants some sort of divarsion, not Mrs Sherrod's sort for we have lots of that in the house but real amusement.[6]

I send you a seed of the Pinknia Pubens which you said you wanted very much to see. There is a pretty little flower about here grows in a little straggling bush with very small leaves, I don't know whether perennial or not. The flower almost exactly like the Kalmia. If you don't know it I will send you some.

We mean to make a garden here if we have to stay all winter. You must buy some plants for us particularly such as will flower in the winter & very early & an Olive if you can get it. I suppose Fuchsia would do out very well here so if you can get some cuttings of that & some Geraniums, any seeds which you can get. I don't know when will be time best to send them but at that season when the most of the things will be likely to do well. August is the time for Geranium & Fuchsia cuttings. Seeds you can send in a letter. I suppose there is very little doubt of our having to stay here all winter if the house is burned which is most probable. I don't know . . . what we'll do for there will be nothing to build a new one.

Aunty wants to know if you can remember if you put up her inkstand.

The oil barrel & four smaller ones, two bales & one large box & two small ones, have arrived. Very few things broken.

Love from all

your aff sister

E S

1. There are two possible candidates among Archibald Smith's servants. In one list, there is a Moses given as age twenty-six in a group he acquired from his sister, Eliza Zubly Barnwell, in 1832. Another list includes a Moses born to Sue in March 1842. (Smith Papers, box 17, folder 2; box 13, folder 2).

2. Lizzie seems to suspect the loyalty of their Roswell neighbor Theodore Dwight Adams (1829–1901) because he had been born in New York, and perhaps because he married Ellen Hamilton Seagrave (1836–64), in New York. Ellen Adams, with whom Lizzie enjoyed playing musical instruments, died in Ohio in August 1864 (Myers, ed., *Children of Pride*, 1450).

3. See Barrington King's letter of July 15, 1864, n. 5, above.

4. George Whitfield Ladson (1830–64) was adopted by John Dunwody of Roswell before becoming a student of the Reverend Nathaniel Pratt's at the Roswell Academy. While in Roswell and before becoming a student at Oglethorpe University and Columbia Theological Seminary, he worked to convert blacks in the area. Later, he

became a missionary to blacks in Columbia, South Carolina, where he died on July 4, 1864. (Cozby, "Rev. George Whitfield Ladson"; Tankersley, *College Life at Old Oglethorpe*, 71; Myers, ed., *Children of Pride*, 1587–88).

5. Beginning June 23, 1864, Confederate Major General Jubal A. Early (1816–94) began a raid into Maryland for the purpose of attacking Washington, D.C. He crossed the Potomac on July 5, captured Hagerstown on July 6, and was threatening Washington on July 11. Discouraged by reinforcements from Grant, he pulled back from Washington's outskirts on July 12 and recrossed the Potomac on July 14.

6. It seems that some of the Sherrod family stayed behind in Roswell to watch over the Smith home and that the wife of the family is with the Smiths in Valdosta. From Lizzie's remarks, we may assume that their social status is not the highest. The family of a John Sherod appears in the 1840 census of the Roswell area, and John and Nancy Sherrard, both age sixty, appear in the 1850 census, but there are no Sherrods listed as living in Roswell in the Cobb County census of 1860.

WILLIAM TO LIZZIE

Rose Dew July 26/64

Dear Sister

Your letter and Mother's of 20*th* were recd last night. I am very glad to hear that all the rest of the things have arrived. It is very sad to think of our dear home being destroyed but how much easier that loss can be borne than such as some are called to bear? The Neyle Habershams lost two sons in the late fight, Joe Clay and Willie. They say Mrs. Habersham is nearly distracted. They have not dared to tell her the whole loss yet.[1]

I suppose it will be very hard to know the truth about the fate of Roswell. I hope Hood will drive them back so fast that they will not have time to burn things, and I hope that they will have respect for Moses' age and calling and not annoy him. I think Mr. Adams was right to stay to take care of his wife as she was too sick to be moved but if he takes the oath he should take it in good faith and not stay in the South.

I could not say "me ze same" about Johnston after he crossed the Chattahoochee without fighting. See the result, the whole state is laid open to raids, the Ga. R.R. cut, Milledgeville and Athens threatened and the Prison Camp at Andersonville the object of another raid. I wish they would catch Joe Brown though, and carry him and the crackers off.[2]

I am afraid Grant enjoyed the "divarsion" too well. The only result seems to have been to help the Yankees to raise troops which would otherwise have been very hard to raise. I do not see that Grant was in need of amusement. To outgeneral Lee ought to be fun enough for one man.

The little pink flower you speak of must be Kalmia hirsuta. It is quite common and valuable as it cures mange on dogs.

I am pretty sure I put up Auntie's inkstand but do not remember where. I know I emptied it and put it out to pack up. Maybe it is among the pots.

I think you had better open the Piano. It may be damp. You know how damp that trunk was, and the Piano had not much airing before it was packed. You had better take it out even if you have to keep it in Auntie's room. As it is there you might as well have the good of it. I think it could stand against Uncle Smith's room.

I expect to be in town next Monday and will get some sorts of plants for you and send them by express. They will probably arrive Tuesday night.

I am to go back to Beaulieu soon. They are not satisfied to let us stay comfortable. They must have some divarsion. I do not like the move at all. The station is not at the same pleasant location and there will not be the same agreeable companions that I had last summer, but I ought not to grumble. I have for a year been very pleasantly situated and I might have been sent to a much worse station.

Do give me a list of the casualties among the crockery.

Have you had any frost? The weather here has been so cool that fire was very comfortable and I had to cover with two blankets.

I am very well. Much Love to all and to Fannie. I suppose you see her sometimes.

Your aff^t Bro W^m

1. There is listed in the 1860 census of Chatham County a William N. Habersham, age forty-three—a commercial merchant and planter—and his wife, Josephine C. Habersham, age thirty-seven. The couple appear to have two sons, nineteen-year-old Joseph C. and sixteen-year-old William Neyle.

2. Sherman's cavalry commander, Kenner Garrard, raided down the Georgia Railroad as far as Covington during and after the Battle of Atlanta, July 22–24. Willie's reference to "another" raid in Andersonville's direction must apply to Major General Lovell H. Rousseau's raid on July 10–22, for Major General George Stoneman (1822–94) had received permission for such a raid on the day that Willie was writing. Rousseau started from Decatur, Alabama, and tore up thirty miles of the West Point and Montgomery Railroad around Opelika and Auburn before entering Georgia through Carrollton and Villa Rica to join Sherman at Marietta on July 22 (OR, 38, part 2: 904–9).

Dear William

We heard from Sonny last night he had been out after the raiders two days & nights in rain &c & he was too sick to write at first. Is still too sick to go off with the Cadets some where, he don't say where. Mother thinks that it can't be to any where but Atlanta. She is just miserable one way or the other. Sonny must be dreadfully off, either very sick or gone to the front. I thought it would be good for Father to go on at once for if it is rheumatism the sooner he can be brought home the better & if he was made sick in any other way he is not fit to go to the front, but he will not go. He says people ought to have more faith &c but I think if it was for nothing else but to relieve Mother's anxiety he ought to go. Can't you do something, telegraph or go up? I don't think he ought to be allowed to go any where where he will be exposed just now, at least & I doubt not Gen Capers would do something to keep him back if it were represented to him. He is very reasonable about it.

Do what you can & write at once for you know how miserable Mother makes herself. She won't hear of any thing but his being sent directly to Atlanta altho there is no certainty & in fact I think he is more likely to be sent to Milledgeville or somewhere. Please don't let on that I said all this for Mother don't like me to say any thing about any thing of the kind & thinks it strange that I don't think as she does. . . .

your ES

I forgot to say Sonny's Letter was written on the 8th & he said he supposed he would have [to] follow the Cadets as soon as he was well enough.[1] If it was not Rheumatism he had, he may be gone. He did not say but we think it most likely to be rheumatism as riding & exposure pretty surely bring that on, so if you can telegraph that will be better.

The Piano would be too much in the way put up in Aunty's room. Where people have to live in trunks they take up so much room they have no room for Pianos. Your room is so large it could very well be put in there but then it would be rather damp in rainy weather & sunny in hot weather. We opened it however to air a little. The Music smelled quite musty & some was a little mouldy so I will take it out of the box entirely as it attracts moisture more than most any thing else. The Piano &c were in excellent order nothing like mould on them. . . .

Smith keeps us supplied with water melons very good ones. I wish you had some of them I suppose you cannot afford to buy them as I saw they were above every one but the darkies purses. Never mind, maybe you will get some some of these days. When are you going to Beaulieu?

1. This letter is not printed here. It contains much of the same information contained in Archie's July 9 letter to Willie.

LIZZIE TO WILLIAM, UNDATED

Dear William

I send your hat by express tomorrow so you must inquire for it & have it sent out to you by the first good opportunity. The only way I could find to put it up was to stuff your blue shirt in the crown, turn up the rim at the sides & tie it up in paper. So you will have to take it into town & get Cousin Kate[1] to have the rim pressed out flat for you. I wanted to put your quince marmalade in the crown but folks thought there was too much danger to the health of the hat. The other little article which is in the parcel you will no doubt find use for.

Gov Brown has done a little too much this time for the Gov[t] to put up with. I see they are forbidding some of their detailed men to go at his call.[2] I only wish he may be put down a little but am afraid there is no hope for any thing so good as that. I think the only putting down he will ever take will be putting down under ground. Gen Hood so far seems to have justified the selection of the President. I hope he will be able to do something. I am very sorry for Gen Johnston. I think often he has had all the blame so far. He could have got some of the Glory too. I saw in the paper last night that Gen Hardee had succeeded in getting into the rear of the right of Sherman. If that is really so I suppose it will be a very excellent thing & wish it may be so.[3]

What a scandalous thing this raid all about the state is. I wonder if the men in that part of the country are all gone away or what is the reason they don't seem to have been opposed any where? What can possess people?[4]

I hear that Mr Dougherty is down on Whitemarsh with his company. Woodie saw him in Savannah. He was on sick leave there. I should not wonder if the fellow should get sick down there tho perhaps Whitemarsh is healthy. You were down there once for a little while were you not? . . . Can you tell if the Piano stool was put up in the box? It was packed there when it was bought. I was laughing at the Rileys, who have a splendid piano & a "weaving bench" for a stool, & Mother said mind you don't have to use a weaving bench too but I said I know you had put it up. I am so distressed about the pretty little Music stand. Aunty wants to know if you ever had a chance to deliver the parcel to Mrs King. Sissy wants to know if you can tell her how

Mrs [Doty?] sells fans. Mother wants to know what was the price of that tea. It was very good indeed but it required to be boiled more than common tea.

Do if you can get us some Lantana seeds or plants get some for us. Fanny has a very pretty one (lilac) she is going to give us. I begun to think we might not want to make a garden here, after what Gen Hood had commenced but we hear nothing more. Seeing that some of the Yankee Gens had their head quarters at Roswell we thought they might not have burned the place & if they were driven off in a hurry they might not have time to burn. Do give my love to the folks I am very glad to know Cousin Sarah is so much better. Love from all. your aff sister

Lizzie Smith

1. Catherine Mackay.

2. Beginning in October 1862, the Confederate Congress allowed men with special skills to be detailed from the army, a practice that gave those with the authority to detail such men the power to exempt them from military service. Governor Joe E. Brown of Georgia was particularly insistent upon his right to detail state workers and even to raise a state militia by such details. Professor John M. Richardson, who taught at the Georgia Military Institute and who is mentioned by Archie Smith, estimated in August 1863 that the number of such exemptions in Georgia totalled about 29 percent of the number of troops in the field (Moore, *Conscription and Conflict*, 57–58, 76–79, 266–79).

3. On July 20 Hardee did indeed launch an attack from the Confederate right across Peachtree Creek in an attempt to catch General Thomas's corps as it crossed the creek. The attack was delayed, the federal forces stood firm, and Hardee's goals were not accomplished. Hood blamed Hardee for the failure of what came to be known as the Battle of Peachtree Creek (Foote, *The Civil War*, 3:473–75).

4. On July 27 federal cavalry under Major General George Stoneman rode east of Atlanta, and cavalry under Brigadier General Edward McCook rode west in an attempt to force the evacuation of the city. Joseph Wheeler's Confederate cavalry defeated these attempts.

WILLIAM TO MOTHER

Rose Dew Aug 2/64

Dear Mother

I rec^d Sister's and Sissie's letters on Sunday when I was in town but did not have time to write yesterday. Do tell Sister that my hat came very nicely. It fits exactly and has been very much admired. . . .

I went to see the Kings yesterday Mrs. K. sends her love to you. Mr. K. says tell Father that all his yarn is in Macon as is every bodies else. He tried to get it off but the R.R. would not take it. They had to leave their Piano and almost all their things in Atlanta. The Gov^t seized the cars the day after our things started.

I do not know what became of the cups. I could not find any at home, but I left plenty of plates of different kinds. In fact I should have put up many more things if I had really thought the Yankees were going to occupy the place but I like every one else had too much confidence in Johnston. The Kings say that they have not heard any thing reliable from Roswell. It was reported that theirs, Tom's, Jimmi's, Dunwody's houses and the Factories were burned but they do not know whether to believe it.[1]

I sent a bundle of such plants as I could get. You ought to get them to-night. I hope they will grow and bloom so as to make the yard more cheerful. I suppose you will know most of them by their looks.

Mrs. Tom, Jimmie & Ralph are in Macon. Mrs. Anderson is in Macon and the rest of the Bayards went to Lexington Va. just in time to be caught there by the Yankees. They have heard from the Bakers since the reoccupation of Staunton.[2] They were not much molested. I am glad Sissie is making the fan for Mrs. K. I think she will be very much pleased with it.

I am very glad Smith is so much better and that you like Fannie so much. I knew you would.

I have had such a disappointment about Arch. Capt M. sent word to Bacon and me if we knew any young men to recommend for the Corps as they want some new ones. So of course I put in for A. but Capt M. says he wants them at once and they must be here in some company of McLaw's command in a week and as the mails do not go to Milledgeville now I can not get A. down and even if a letter could get to him he would have to write to Genl. Capers and get a transfer which would occupy too much time.[3] It is a great disappointment to me, but I know it is all for the best. I will not mention it to him as he seemed to be more satisfied the last time he wrote to me.

Tell Sissie I will be very glad to get the ink. The Piano stool was put in the box but the Pedal was left out at first but Brunswick[4] said he would go and put it in. Is not there room in Auntie's room for the Piano? It would be better to put it there than not to have the use of it at all, or put it in my room. Much Love to all.

Your afft Son Wm

1. The homes of Thomas Edward and James Roswell King, as well as Mimosa Hall, the home of John Dunwody. Thomas Edward King rented Bulloch Hall from Martha Elliott Bulloch (1799–1864), who moved to New York City in 1856 (Clarece Martin, *Glimpse of the Past*, 24).

2. The references are primarily to the various branches of the Barrington King family: Marie Clemens King (Mrs. Thomas Edward King), Francis Price King (Mrs. James Roswell King), Florence Stillwell King (Mrs. Ralph Browne King), and Catherine Evelyn King Baker (Mrs. William Elliott Baker). The Bayards are probably the family of Nicholas J. Bayard, who moved to Rome, Georgia, at the outbreak of the war. His third marriage had been to Eliza Barrington King (Hand), Roswell King's daughter. Mrs. Anderson might well be Mrs. S. J. Anderson, the wife of R. B. Anderson, a Roswell physician listed in the 1860 census.

3. Major General Lafayette McLaws (1821–97) for a time commanded Confederate forces defending Savannah. As soon as Sherman's intentions became apparent, McLaws laid out a siege line west of the city. The GMI cadets eventually took positions in this line of defense. General Francis Withers Capers is the commandant of the Georgia Military Institute (Yates, "History of the Georgia Military Institute," 5, 15).

4. Brunswick seems to have been Barrington King's butler. His name appears in a ledger of King's that covers the years 1848–64, a volume kindly shown to us at Barrington Hall in Roswell by Lois Simpson.

MOTHER TO WILLIAM

Valdosta August 2ⁿᵈ/64

My Dear Son

We are all anxiety on account of the news received last night. We hear nothing from Atlanta as it seems that the R. Road & Telegraph communications are cut. We cannot hear from our dear boy & as it seems the party that is doing so much damage was a few days ago on its way to Milledgeville & no doubt will make a great effort to reach the Capital of the state & what will become of our dear boy? We cannot hear from him. At one time I hoped he might be sent off with the Inst. property but I believe there is but the one R R to Milledgeville. We can only leave him with God with hearts full of thankfulness that he is his.

Poor Helen is greatly distress'd though she seems more calm this morning. How strange it seems that a party of Yankees should be allowed to run about the state doing so much damage & as far as we can learn no effort made to arrest them when thousands of men are collected at Macon & might be sent off to any point. What an awful calamity it would be if they succeed in liberating the prisoners at Andersonville & it seems there is some danger about Lake City & that part, a considerable body of Negro troops with a few white having been there destroying the R. R. O[h]! What & when will the end be? This constant waiting & fearing the coming tidings seems more than we can bear.

Brother asks you when you see any of the family to mention to them that he wrote to M. Elliott some time ago. He directed it to Mrs Meta Elliott & he supposes she did not receive it. Do when you have told any of them let me know that I may tell him for he has been worrying about it for some time, poor old man. I am sorry for him but he worries me very much. He is constantly mishearing things that the servants say about the yard & it is entirely different from what he thinks. It might seem as if these were little things but when that or something else is going on constantly it is wearing to the spirit, & I am really afraid he will do some serious injury. He accuses them of saying such things as would really put evil into their heads. Fanny has been over twice to spend a morning. She seems very sociable & friendly & we all like her. Smith has sent us some fine melons & I do wish I could send some of them to you but you would have no way of getting them out. When are you to going to Beaulieu? I hope you will find it more pleasant than you expect though you can scarcely hope to find other companions as pleasant as you have had but we must not complain. If you are spared the miseries which so many are enduring we must be thankful. We are as usual, cannot think much about ourselves. Pray for our precious boy. If any thing should happen to him it will be a comfort to know that we did what we could for him & he has quietly waited where the Providence of God placed him. May God bless you darling.

Your aff
Mother

LIZZIE TO WILLIAM, UNDATED

Dear William

The plants all came in the very nicest order & it was a right pert bundle of plants. There were so many more than I thought when I saw the parcel. I got up early next morning & Mother & I planted them all out & we have made a little tent, at least Father has, of the farm sheets & it is put on in the morning & taken out at night. The place we have them planted is a narrow bed along the front fence from the orange tree to the corner. The Dahliahs, petunias, chrysanthemums & the English jasamine (?), & the olive, & lilys look first rate. Some of the other things may grow & some may die. The verbenas may grow, probably will. What was a curious looking plant, just a cutting, greyish green with very skeletonish leaves, some of that looks well. The Dahliahs look so well I am sorry you could get no more of them. I made 5 cuttings out of the two & they all look fine, tho the weather has been very trying very dry

& hot. The seeds came all safe last night & some are in the ground. I don't want to worry you, but if it comes in your way do get some pink seeds. If they are planted now they will grow & bloom in the spring & if any heartsease, even the long eared kind, do get some.

We know you had received your hat by the paper round the plants. I was very much afraid some one might sit on your hat or some accident happen to it going just so, but there was no help for it. I am very glad you have it. I was not sure about the shape. It suits me but I did not know if it would suit the fashion. I would be really distressed about that place in the corps for Sonny but the fact is we can see so plainly the hand of Providence in every thing concerning him since this war began that I can't say I feel disappointed at all & as he seems to be getting quite satisfied where he is, I dare say.

They were called out the other day when the "Raid" was riding about loose & that would help him very much. Was not it jolly that Roddy should come up just at the nick of time there at Newnan & help to take Stoneman.[1] I am so glad that old wretch is taken at last. I am sure he deserves all sorts of bad things. What a mercy it is the raid did not get to Andersonville & turn all those prisoners loose. What a horrid thing it would have been. Does not it seem strange that devoted as the army was to Johnston his removal has seemed to do no harm? They say they are as devoted to Hood as to Johnston & still love Johnston as well as ever. I know Hood was very much admired before & I suppose his natural bravery & his having only one leg yet still going on in his duty are things which would win soldiers hearts. You know they used to say a cheer from Gen Hood was equal to ever so many men. That was when he was Brig Gen: he must be a very brave man. To have risen so fast from Lieut since '61 he must be a remarkable man.... Do find out the price of the fans if you can for Sissy. Can you buy such a thing in Sav. as Brown paper by the quire what will do to make envelopes & what is the price?

your aff sister

E. S.

The casualties were 1 oldtime China cup & saucer broken (like yours), 2 finger basins broken, nothing else & those you know were packed with rice. Not even a handle broken off of one [of] the lemonade glasses. Aunty's inkstand was not among the pots but it was found in one of the boxes all safe. The Piano cannot be put up by Uncle S's wall for he makes such a fuss about all noises it would never do. It is put away under the bed in Aunty's room. I wish very much it could be put up for as you say it is just as well to use a thing when you have it. I wish with you that the raids would catch Gov Brown & the Crackers. I think Georgia might be worth something if that class all went off to the yankees.[2] Don't send any plants which you don't think will grow this time of year. We are going right to work to have the garden fixed. I think it is too bad to move you fellows about so but I'll bet they just want some of their friends to have your fine fixings on your instrument & the brass wire they think you will fix another place & then they will get that. Why have they moved the station at Beaulieu? I hope you will find some pleasant fellows there. I forgot to say the books came all safe & what I have read I like. . . . I begin to find it quite easy to read French. I wish I could have the chance of hearing it well spoken. That is much harder to understand than reading.

1. Brigadier General Philip Dale Roddey (1826–97), a Confederate cavalry commander from Alabama, was active in the Atlanta campaign under Major General Joseph Wheeler and went on to serve under Hood in Tennessee. Federal General George Stoneman (1822–94) had intended to rendezvous with his cavalry counterpart, Brigadier General Edward M. McCook, but was defeated after riding through Decatur, Covington, Monticello, Gordon, and Macon, and was captured on July 31 near Clinton, Georgia (*OR*, 38, part 2: 917).

2. "The word 'cracker' was used by Georgians to describe other Georgians whom they regarded as socially and culturally beneath them" (Kennett, *Marching through Georgia*, 19). The Smiths' disdain for Joe E. Brown was not only social, for they disapproved of his unwillingness to support the Confederate cause fully. "Brown's rigid defense of state's rights in the midst of a life-and-death struggle troubled a number of the state's leading political figures, particularly among the 'patricians' who had earlier run the state" (ibid., 32).

WILLIAM TO MOTHER

Savannah Aug 15/64

Dear Mother

I came to town yesterday and found a letter from you, one from Sister and one from A. His is very long and quite an entertaining account of his trip after the raiders. He closes by saying he expects to go to the post soon but does not say where the Cadets are so I can have no idea of what kind of service he will be put on. I am afraid it will not be possible to get him transferred to this District but will write to him to find out and then perhaps Smith can get Capt M to detail him. Capt M spoke very kindly about taking him and said he would like to have him, but the men were wanted immediately and he could not wait. There is a great deal of sickness in the Corps and new men are wanted to take the place of the sick. My letter from A. is dated 9th. He says he was quite sick with fever but had no Rheumatism. I see no way to get him out now but for him to apply for a discharge and he would not do that nor do I think he could get it. He said he would have gone the day before with Capt Manget but was not well enough so perhaps Genl Capers will still leave him at Midway.

Parsons does not work now but there was a very good dentist working where his office was. I will go after breakfast and find out if he is still there. If Sister comes with Smith I think I can go back with her for a day or two.

Mrs [Doty?] made a fan for Mary Elliott but would not tell what she charged for it nor send any bill but she said she had lost a good deal by bad money and was going to make up for it in charging now, so I suppose she will have a high price. They say she has piles of feathers to be made up. Cousin Margaret did not get Uncle Smith's letter. She will send to the office to enquire for it. She has a box and his letters are to be directed to Mrs. M. C. Elliott.

Cousin Sarah is well again. She looks thin and is weak of course but she goes down to meals and is more cheerful than she used to be.

They have concluded not to send me to Beaulieu, so I suppose I will stay at Rose Dew until November when there will be a general move round.

Please get about 15 lbs of honey for me. I will send or bring a tin canister to put it in. We get so tired of bacon that we want a change. The Tea cost $35.00.

Cousin Kate says it will be quite convenient for Sister to stay with her, and if she has not time to write before Smith comes just to come any how.

Much Love to all.

Yr afft Son W^m

If Sister comes she must send me a message by telegraph the day before she is ready to go back. I can not come in to see her when she comes if I am to go home with her.

MOTHER TO WILLIAM

Valdosta Aug 16th 64

My Dear Son

I know you are anxious about our boy & therefore write at once to let you know we heard from him last night. He is about well again with the exception of being very weak. It was fever & not rheumatism that he had. I am afraid from what Lizzie says she alarmed you very much about him for she was very much excited altho' she insisted that every body else was alarmed & there was no occasion for it. Of course I felt uneasy & wrote to him immediately to tell him if he was still sick & needed care to telegraph to you & you would write to us immediately unless you could go to him yourself. I am thankful to find no such necessity exists. He says their being sent to the front is now uncertain. He heard the cadets are to be stationed near Milledgeville which seems to me the most suitable thing to be done with them. But it is only "they say," yet I leave him with the Lord who has hitherto helped us.

Have you made any arrangement about those hats Mr Bacon's negro was to make?[1] A. is very much in need of one if you can get it done & say what weight of wool is required for a hat & his terms I will send it to you & would be willing to pay in fine wool if it will be any inducement. Perhaps he could make some slate colour. We had no letter from you last week. I wrote to you about sending some w. Melons & put aside 10 [of] the finest but they will not keep any longer. They got bruised in being hauled so far. Anna Pratt wrote word that Dr Talmadge was deranged.[2] It is sad indeed for such a good man's mind to go out in darkness & his poor wife is such a state but it is the Lord. We hear nothing of Mr Pratt. Mrs Camp wrote that a Mr Burney had come out from Roswell about 2 weeks before & he said all the houses were burned (except Mr Pratts) from Mr B. King's to ours also all the factories & the mill.[3] I believe I had a good deal more to say but Smith has just stop'd on his way to Valdosta & I must take advantage of the opp^y.

Your aff
Mother

1. Perhaps the servant of either Albert S. or Edward H. Bacon, who were serving with Willie (Confederate Pensions and Records Department, Georgia, roll 3).

2. Sarah Anna Pratt (1844–1937) was the eighth child of the Reverend Nathaniel Alpheus Pratt (1796–1879) and Catherine King Pratt (1810–94). Samuel K. Talmage (Talmadge) was the president of Oglethorpe College in Milledgeville. See also Archie's letter of July 9, 1864, above.

3. The 1860 census of Cobb County lists an Isaac H. Burney, age thirty-two, as a boss in the carding room of the Roswell Manufacturing Company. Although the mills themselves were burned or torn down, no Roswell home received either treatment.

BARRINGTON KING TO ARCHIBALD SMITH
Savannah 16th Augt 1864

A. Smith Esq

My dear Bro A. I have been very hard at work, trying to balance our Books, & see how matters stand with the R M C^o. Mr Proudfoot was here,[1] but his family being in McIntosh C^o, the late Yankee raid there, forced them into the swamp; he had to leave to see after them, expecting to return next Monday: his leaving has given me additional work, but thank God my health has improved. We are anxious to leave for Staunton Va[2] about 1st Septr, to return latter end of October—trusting by that time, the vandals may be driven from our State: until then, our movements undecided.

I requested Mitchel & Smith in July, to send you six bales Yarn, 2 Bales 8 & 10s 2 B. no 10. 1 B No 12 & 1 B No 14 care of Duncan & Johnson Savannah: the burning bridge on CRR with other difficulties, may have prevented the Yarn being sent off. I have written them to send you 2 Bales 4/4 Cloth No 27–877 No 28–883 yds making 1760 yds leaving 40 yds due, & will credit you at $2 50/100 pr yard $100. We charge nothing this division of the wreck, each share to receive 1 Bale Yarn & 300 yds Cloth, making all equal.

Should the vandals destroy no more cotton &c owned by R M Co, there will be enough left to repair damages at some future day I trust—we must leave all in the hands of God, looking to him for assistance & direction. Strange indeed no letters from Bro Pratt or any one at Roswell—nothing but reports & they contradictory about the houses destroyed: I expect no good from the enemy & presume [they] will do all the injury they can.

Mr Camp let Bob[3] visit his wife—if you can find employment for him driving wagon, or hired out to attend stock for his support, please do so. He must not suffer, any expense will be paid by R M Co. I gave him $10, to pay expenses to Valdosta—we have no use for him at present. Please hand the enclosed letter to Miss Magill. My kind regards to your Brother, Mrs S & all the family. I saw your son Wm at church last sabbath. He looked in good health.

Yrs truly &c
B King

1. Hugh W. Proudfoot (1795–1871), bookkeeper for the Roswell Manufacturing Company.

2. The Barrington Kings' daughter, Catherine Evelyn King, and son-in-law, the Reverend William Elliott Baker, lived in Staunton, Virginia.

3. Bob was apparently George H. Camp's servant.

WILLIAM TO MOTHER

Rose Dew Aug 20/64

Dear Mother

The mails seem almost as much out of joint between here and Valdosta as they used to be between here and Roswell. I wrote to you and Sister both last

Monday about her coming and thought that by this time at least there would have been an answer. Cousin Kate and the others were to return to Sav^h to day and if Sister will write to Cousin Kate in time Bob Stiles[1] will meet her at the Depot so she can come by herself very well and then I can have a good excuse to ask about leave to go home for a day or two. I am very glad to hear about A. If he is weak from sickness he ought to have a furlough. I hope it will prove true about the Cadets being stationed near Milledgeville. If they should be put into the field I do not think A. would take an exemption and am sure he could not stand service.

I should like very much to have had those melons but there is no way of being sure of getting them out. The Signal Corps wagon comes here only once a month now, and transportation is so irregular now that they would probably spoil in waiting.

Bacon says it is one of the field hands that makes the hats and he is only put at it in winter when there is not much out of doors work.

Do you get any wild grapes? That region of the country is said to produce them finely. We have had some pretty good ones the last few days. You had better have the boys look out for some as they are ripening now.

I have a fine lot of beautiful Palmetto, some is the whitest I ever saw. If I go home with Sister I can carry it. There is some of both kinds.

Has any body written to Aunt Bet since you left Roswell? She may have written to you there not knowing about your leaving or not knowing where to direct to.

I have not met Mr. Dougherty. I would like to go to see him but White-marsh Island is too much out of my way. It is almost at the other extremity of the District.

I am quite hearty.

Much Love to all.

Your aff^t Son W^m

You asked me some time ago about buying shoes for A. I can not even get them for myself from Govt. They issue one pair to four men.

I could not find any paper for making envelopes in town.

---

1. Catherine Mackay and her nephew, Robert Mackay Stiles (1836–74).

Milledgeville,[1] Aug. 23[d]

Dear Brother,

I received your letter yesterday, but was too busy to answer it.

I can resign or get a discharge—I don't know which they call it—if I have a showing from Father. At least, so the adjutant says and he ought to be good authority. I have not seen Maj. Capers[2] yet and don't think I will have time to see him as I will have plenty to do this morning.

We are camped in a very nice place on the state house square. We get good rations and enough.

Mother said something about you being sent to Beaulieu but I see you are still at Rose Dew. How is it? Excuse this short letter. I will do better next time.

Direct to Milledgeville.

Your affct bro.
Archie

1. The cadets of the Georgia Military Institute had just arrived in Milledgeville to guard the state capital of Georgia, which was believed to be in danger from further raids such as Stoneman's. The cadets attempted to resume their studies but were constantly interrupted by military duties (Yates, "History of the Georgia Military Institute," 10). From this date until Sherman's troops got to Savannah, Archie was in more danger than Willie, although no one was really aware of this fact. Ironically, Archie seemed to want to resign from the corps and join Willie in Savannah to get closer to the action.

2. Major Francis W. Capers (1819–92), the superintendent of GMI, also held the rank of general in the state militia.

Rose Dew Aug 25/64

Dear Sister

You are right enough about it being too hot for any thing in Savannah. Even I find it too hot there.

I think that the men detailed now will be permanently in the Corps, but they will be certain to get sick as they will be put on the same stations at which the others got sick. There is a great deal more sickness in the Corps this summer than there was last summer.

I do not think it probable that the exercises of the G.M.I. will be resumed soon, as the Cadets are now actually in service at Atlanta. Frank Neufville had a letter from one of them lately.[1]

I do not see that we can do any thing for A. I do not think he could be persuaded to apply for an exemption on account of his health tho I really think he ought not to go into the field. If he does apply for discharge on account of his health and can not get it then it is all right, for as you say we have seen the hand of Providence so plainly in his affairs that we can not but feel that he is safe wherever he is.

I have sent a tin canister for the honey. Do send it by next Tuesday if you can, that is send it so that it will get to Savannah Tuesday.

I have had a shake from my old acquaintance the chills but feel quite well again. Much Love to all. Your afft Bro Wm

The lock on the canister opens with the word Pride.

1. Probably Edward F. Neufville, fourth corporal in the Chatham Artillery (Jones, *Historical Sketch*, 104).

ANNE MAGILL SMITH TO MRS. RUTH S. TALMADGE,
UNDATED DRAFT

Though personally a stranger to you I feel your attention to my son (Cadet Arch Smith) warrants my taking the liberty of addressing you & assuring of the deep gratitude of his Father & myself for the many acts of kindness which he received from you during his recent indisposition. The obligation will long be felt by us & we trust you will enjoy the reward of those whose kindness is extended even to one of the least of Christ's disciples. It is with sincere sorrow that we have heard of Dr Talmadge's failing health yet we trust he will be restored & that after this cruel war is over the youth of our land may again have the privilege of sitting at his feet.[1]

1. This notice appeared in the *Savannah Republican*, September 20, 1864: "Dr. S. K. Talmadge, former President of Oglethorpe (Presbyterian) University, has lost his mind entirely, and has been placed by his friends in the Insane Asylum near Milledgeville, Ga." 63 (no. 222): p 2. Dr. Talmadge died in 1865.

MOTHER TO WILLIAM

Valdosta Aug. 25ᵗʰ 64

My Dear Son

I have been so interrupted by visitors (Fanny coming to spend the morning) that the day is almost gone but as the week is nearly gone also I do not like to put off another day. We have heard again from A. & he seems pretty well & I am thankful to find that the Cadets have been ordered to Milledgeville. I hope he will be satisfied for it certainly seems most suitable for the members of the state Institute to guard the State capital. I am looking out for some honey for you, hailing every cart that passes but I fear it is too late. However if you have an opp^y send your canister when Charlotte comes (in about 2 weeks). She will have a servant & can take care of it. I am still trying. Lizzie is very much obliged to the Mackays for their kind offer of sending to the Depot for her. She prefers not going while it is so hot as she could not take advantage of Smith's going. Do find out if it would be convenient to them for Helen to go at the same time. She is suffering as much as Lizzie for want of some dentist work & is so much better that I think she might have it done. I will cling to the hope of your coming back with them if only for a few days. Mrs Talmage was very kind to Sonny when he was sick, sending him Soup tea &c, & I wrote a note thanking her for it. I am so thankful to hear you are quite hearty.

May God bless & keep you my dear Son

Your aff

Mother

HELEN ZUBLY MAGILL TO ELIZABETH MAGILL MERRELL

Retreat near Valdosta

Lowndes Co. Geo. August 26ᵗʰ 1864

My dear Sister,

It seems almost useless to attempt to get a letter thro' to you, but I cannot be satisfied without trying from time to time. Since we came down, I have written once, & I think twice, to you; once to Charlie & Bell;[1] & once to Brother Henry. Sister has written once to you; & so has Helen. We have received, via Roswell, 3 letters dated Aug. Sept. & Feb. & the two long ones written by Brother H. & yourself, about the 5ᵗʰ May. Others may have crossed the river, directed to R. but of course they cannot reach there now; & if you have not received ours, you are ignorant of our present location. We saw in the paper a few days ago that a member of Genl Price's staff had

102 *The Death of a Confederate*

arrived from Camden, who left that place, I think, about the 24th July.[2] I have no doubt he has letters for us, but does not know where to send them. If I knew his name and his whereabouts, I would write to him, & enquire there too. It would be such a good opportunity to send a letter back. If you get any news at all from this side, you know of course that our home is, & has been for about 6 weeks, in the Federal lines. We can hear nothing at all *from* there, but there are of course a great many rumors, in which some place implicit reliance, & some none at all; for they are, as is always the case, constantly contradicting each other. Our dear Pastor (as I have told you before) remained there, with Mrs. P. & Jonie & her children; & we are exceedingly anxious to hear something of them; I cannot but trust tho' that he has remained unmolested.[3] There are many promises which apply to his case; & I doubt not he will act prudently. I cannot yet give up our homes either, for it seems to me when we ask any thing in prayer, as we all have of course for the preservation of our homes, we should not give up until we know God has refused our request; therefore I continue to hope & shall, 'til I know positively that they are destroyed; then, I hope I shall be entirely resigned to God's will.

I have told you what a comfortable retreat we have here, a nice, large, airy house, & delightful shady yard. I wish all poor refugees could be as well situated. We had 'til the dog days set in, plenty of breeze from the gulf, which I suppose will soon commence again. Helen's health has improved very much; she is much better in some respects than before she had diphtheria. We are about a mile from Mrs. Riley, the lady whose daughter Smith married. She has been very kind, in sending us vegetables & watermelons. Fannie B. is now at her Mother's; she has been with Smith on the Isle of Hope, but they lost their little girl there, & S. himself was quite sick, & got a furlough to come home & recruit; he stayed four weeks; & she concluded not to return with him, but wait 'til frost. We like her very much; & she is quite friendly & affectionate. There is a younger sister too, whom we like;[4] but we do not see much of them, as we have no way of riding, & while the warm weather lasts, it is too far to walk often, to make a visit. . . .

Woodie is at present 2nd lieutenant, in the company in which John Magill is first. I hear they are now stationed in Whitemarsh Island. Willie is still at Rose Dew island, about 9 miles from Savannah; his health is very good, & being in the Signal corps, has a very easy time. We had a good deal of anxiety about Archie when the reserves were called out, fearing he would be sent to the front, as a good many of the Cadets were, but as he was Quartermaster's sergeant, he had been stationed at Midway, in command of the detachment guarding the effects of the Military Institute; nevertheless they were sent to

Atlanta, & he of course would have had to go, but a few days previously, had gone off with a company in pursuit of a body of raiders, & exposure to rain, & hot sun, together with riding 80 miles on horseback, in a little over two days & nights; made him quite sick; & he had to be left. He now writes, that they are all to go into camp near Milledgeville, I suppose for the protection of the Capital. One of the Cadets was killed, & one severely wounded in the trenches at Atlanta. I don't know whether I told you where all our towns-folks are. The Barrington Kings are in Savannah, but expect soon to go to Staunton. The Camps are at Curtright, but he says he intends to place his family in Augusta, in the winter; & he remain at C. . . . Mrs. James and Mrs. T. King are in Macon, where they purchased houses sometime ago prospectively. Mrs. Ralph, I believe, is there also. R. is in the service. Miss Hamilton has been visiting the Baldwins and Woodrows in Columbia, but I have not heard of her for some time. The Proudfoots are in Valdosta. The Mintons removed to Washington in February. Axson was wounded & died in a week. The Adamses remained in Roswell with the Pratts. I believe I have told you all the news I can think of.[5]

No, let me tell you, Smith sent us from his plantation, forty watermelons at one time. Don't you think I enjoyed them? You know how fond I am of them. However they all managed to do them quite as much justice as I did, tho' they laugh very much at me, for being so devoted to them.

All send a great deal of love to you all. We long to hear from you but fear it will be a very long time first. Ever your affectionate Sister

Helen Magill

1. Charles Arthur Magill (1817–84) and his wife, Aurelia Isabella ("Belle," 1830–1907).

2. Sterling Price (1809–67) of Missouri was one of the foremost generals in the Trans-Mississippi Department of the Confederacy.

3. Joanna ("Jonie") Gildersleeve Pratt of Richmond, Virginia, was the wife of the Reverend and Mrs. Pratt's son, Henry Barrington Pratt (1832–1912), who had been a missionary in South America but returned to serve as a chaplain in the Confederate army (Clarece Martin, *History*, 33).

4. Gulielma English Riley.

5. Most of these Roswell citizens are members of the King family. Miss Hamilton and the Baldwins have not been identified. James Woodrow (1828–1907), one of Willie's teachers at Oglethorpe, had moved to Columbia, South Carolina, where he would become president of the University of South Carolina. The family of Major John Minton (1797–1871) lived across Norcross Street in Roswell from the Smiths. Their son, Axson (1838–64), died of wounds on June 30, 1864 (Myers, ed., *Children of Pride*, 1626).

Rose Dew Aug 29/64

Dear Mother

I find I am like the newspapers. This number has to contradict what I said in my last. I have just got a letter from A. dated 23ᵈ and find that the Cadets are really camped in Milledgeville. He says they have a pleasant situation and get very good food and enough of it. I wrote to him to find out if he could resign or be transferred so as to get into the Corps; I think that the men detailed now will be kept in the Corps, but if he comes now he will be put upon a sickly post immediately and before doing any thing more about it I will wait to see what you say about it, if you think it is best for him to come down now and run the risk of being sick. I think if he is satisfied to stay with the Cadets I think he had better stay. He could not be with me if he came into the Corps. The Cadets have been in service. One of them was killed and several wounded.

The Canister for the honey was not sent until today. I was in hopes it would have got off sooner so as to come back in time to come out here in the wagon this week, but as it is, it will have to come to Savh. and wait for an opportunity out here.

. . . . I am quite well again. I had three chills. I would not have so many but they came every day and I did not expect them in that way and did not take quinine in time.

Much Love to all your aff Son Wᵐ

Valdosta Aug 31ˢᵗ 1864

My Dear Son

I am truly sorry to hear that you have had chill again. It was so long since the last attack that I was in hopes it was eradicated entirely & that the situation you are now in would not give you a return. It is not half as bad as bilious fever & I am thankful it is not that. We hear from Miss Morel that Sav. is now very sickly, a great deal of bilious fever & if that is the case it will not do for the girls to go there before frost.[1] By dint of hard coaxing & paying an extra price we have succeeded in getting some honey for you, but your canister is not come yet & I am afraid by your appointing Tuesday for it to be in Sav., that that was your wagon day & you will have to wait for it another month. You did not allow time enough from the day you wrote for it to get to Sav. at the appointed time for it would have to be sent in on Saturday to go by Monday's train & I did not receive your letter until Monday night. Did you receive a bottle of honey I sent you by Smith to make Methiglin?[2] He told me he could not send it to you & I asked him to leave it at the office.

It must be a mistake about the Cadets still being in Atlanta. The letter you mention must have been an old one. We had a letter from A. Saturday night. He says they are encamped in the State house yard so they must have returned as he was the only one left. He seemed in good spirits, said he was in a pleasant mess but found the cooking rather hard to manage. I see by the papers they are working vigorously at the defenses of the Capital so I suppose they think the place in danger & hope Sonny will be satisfied there until there is some opening to better his situation. We have been very anxious about his getting into the Signal Corps but your being foiled in the last effort seems to me another link in the chain of providences which has surrounded him from the beginning & while I think it right to use efforts for his benefit & still wish you to embrace a favourable opportunity to help him on, I would not take matters out of God's hands. The dear child is very anxious to be in the Sig. Corps & with you but he has been so submissive to God's will concerning him that I am sure he will be bless'd.

You know you threatened to have chill this summer & if they continue I think you will have to get a furlough though you will not find here that delicious cool water nor a lemon from our dear greenhouse as you had when you had chill at home. I think you had better take a dose of medicine & some quinine if it is to be had. I wish I could send you a bottle of bitters made of bark of the Pinckneya Pubens. I have found it very good for Helen & for your Father when he had fever. We are having very very hot weather now, very little breeze & the nights not as pleasant but thank God none of us are sick & we do not hear of sickness around. You may hear something of insurrectionary movements here. We have heard a good deal of the discovery of a plot extending over several counties. Some Negroes have been taken up not far from us & several of them with one white man hung at Quitman but we do not feel afraid. I have no doubt that there are Yankees . . . prowling about making efforts of the kind but there seems a particular providence & such plans being always discovered.

Love from all howdy from the servants

Your aff

Mother

Father went to town again today & got your canister. The man has promised to bring the honey very soon & we will send it unless you stop it. I do not like the idea of its staying so long at the office. I think you might send your servant in for it.

1. Miss Morel may be one of three women listed in the household of Savannah banker William E. Morel in the 1860 census of Chatham County, Georgia.

2. A beverage made from fermented honey and water, similar to mead. It was often medicated or spiced for medicinal purposes.

HELEN TO WILLIAM, UNDATED, ENCLOSED WITH PREVIOUS LETTER

Dear Brother   I wrote you a note some time ago asking you if it was possible to get a low seated high back looking chair such as Mother used always at home. These strait chairs make her very tired when she has to sit in them all day and if she can have any comforts these tiresome sad times she might as well have them. You must not buy it just so but find out and all that, and some body near Mother's size should try it to see if it is comfortable before it is bought. It would not be worth while to buy it if it is not so, as mother would feel obliged to sit in it and it would not do her any good. The chair must *not* have arms, as they are in the way when you want to sew. Do see about this as soon as possible and write to me a private note in some letter so I will not have to shew it. Mother must not have any suspicion of it till it is bought or she will prevent it and say it costs too much. If you do not think it will suit well do not get it without waiting. Buy it if you can get it at any price. Don't wait to send word. It must have a *cane back,* stuffed is too hot. If you find one that you think would be suitable you had better get some of the people to try it so it can be sent soon. Did they not used to make chairs and things in Sav.? You might be able to have one made.

Your old can has come. It is very small. If you had sent something larger you might have got more honey. My pigeons are doing very well. They have got almost all their feathers new and look very clean and nice. One of them is so tame that it will light on my hand to eat. It is very hard to tame them though. I have been at it two months and they are still very shy. We have just had a great alarm of some birds on a tree. Father went out and killed one and wounded one. He says he thinks it is an Ibis. It is white in the body and has gray wings with some white underneath. . . . The bill is long and curved and the legs long. The wing will make a nice fan. I made the fan and sent it to Mrs King. She liked it very much, had come very near buying one that morning but did not. The fans I wanted to send to Atlanta I have sent with some others made of good feathers to Augusta to Anna Pratt to sell. I had ten altogether. She said they were in great demand there. Some men went out hunting the other day and killed two deer about a mile and a half from here but we did not get any.

Your aff Sister
Helen

LIZZIE TO WILLIAM, UNDATED

[after September 2, 1864]

Dear William

Before I forget to let me tell you Mother wants to know if you want a shrimp net & what is the length from center to circumference when it is spread. If you want one she will make you one. Be sure to say now the very next time you write.

I am sorry to tell you the honey has not come yet. The man promised & I expect it will come soon. I wish you had it now. I hope you have received a bottle which was sent you by Smith. You ought by now certainly. I think it must be very hard to have nothing but fat bacon this hot weather when you are sick & you never did eat fat bacon at home.

I don't know when I will go to Savannah now as I hear it is very sickly & I don't think we ought to do any thing imprudent as this is our first summer in the low country & things would make us sick which would not harm other people.

Mr Duncan wrote Father the other day that a dispatch had been received saying that Eddie Stiles had been killed at Front Royal. Is it really so? How many members of that family have died since the war commenced? Kitty & Sid will mind it very much, their last brother.[1] There is really no knowing where to look for the Yankees next. That fight at Jonesboro was such a very unexpected thing.[2] We are very anxious to hear more of it. I see that Gen Hood with a part of the army are still in Atlanta while Hardee commands in the field. I think it quite generous in Hood to give Hardee a chance. It is what all Generals would not have done.

I see you are putting your threat into execution, that is getting chill & fever so as to get a furlough to go to Suwanee. We were doing an extensive business at counting unhatched chickens. Mr Duncan was to buy a horse for Father & was waiting to hear something from Smith & in the meantime the horse got sold to some one else. Well our plan was for you to get a furlough & then we would (that is you & Sissy & I) take the horse & buggy & go down to Ocean Pond to kill cranes &c.[3] The Rileys were to go too & stay all night. Would not that have been nice? You get the furlough anyhow tho & maybe we may get a horse some of these days. I think it would be great fun. Some Ibises came & lit on a tree out here the other day & father shot one & that was what put us in the notion. I think it would be great fun to go down to Suwanee this fall for a little while so shake away as hard as you can & get a 60 day furlough. We could have a pretty good time running about here in that time.

Do next time you go to Savannah get some of those field poppys from Mary Elliott. You said she had such a great variety & ours are all gone. Of course I am in no hurry for the seeds only want to be sure of having them saved. You said you had a nice lot of palmetto. If you don't come soon I want you to send some. I am going to make a hat for Florida Bayard. I suppose it will be doubly valued when she hears who dried the palmetto. Don't send it too soon as I am not ready to begin yet & you may come or I may go before I am ready for it. The hat is only to be finished for next winter. You were talking of the fashion of bonnets when you were here. Have you seen any thing newer or prettier than those hideous high crowned narrow rimmed things? I want to make the hat in the newest style & I thought perhaps when the girls were shewing you bonnets they might have shewed you hats too.

We had a letter from Sonny the other day. He had made his first attempt at cooking & thought it no fun. Thought it would be far better to hire a cook as he would burn out more worth of shoe leather than his part of the hire of a cook would come to. He seemed quite disgusted with the whole mess. I am very glad for now I think he will be more satisfied to stay there, which is the best place for him .

We are having some really hot & parching weather. Almost all the things you sent have died since this weather commenced. Some were looking very well & putting out sprouts but this weather is enough to kill any thing. I think however if the things had had favorable weather at first they could have stood this. The German Star, petunia, Lantana, violets, lilys, spirea, [and] chrysanthemums are all alive & look well. The Olive is not dead but evergreens take so long either to start to grow or to die that you can never be certain about them.

Some few things which I got from Fanny are doing very well but they were taken up on a rainy day & set out in the rain & had a plenty of rain 'till they took root. That was two weeks after your things came. Do if you can get some sweet allyssum seeds & send some, for the plant died. It will bloom very nicely in winter if they are planted now.

I am glad to hear you have at last had warm enough weather. I think maybe you will have enough of the low country by this time you can go home like some other people. Begin to think up yonder is much better than down here. I am in hopes all will work out right some of these days. I don't know whether to say I hope your chills have left you or not for that I expect is your only chance for a furlough. I think it a very hard case that Bacon can get two long furloughs in the summer & you can only get one short.

Love from all

your aff sister

E Smith

What do you think of McLellan & the Chicago platform?

We heard from Anna Pratt last night that they had a long letter from her Mother. She says the yanks are camped up to their back & front doors & since they have learned to bar their doors they are not molested. The yanks send them fruit & vegetables & they have a few peaches of their own. They were all well. She does not mention Mr Pratt or Mrs H P only says all are well, but writes in very good spirits so we don't know what to think about Moses, whether yanks have troubled him or not I hope not. I am sure she says the yanks found a place they were sure something was buried & went & dug it up & it proved to be an old hog of theirs which had been buried a week or so before. Mrs Adams had gone north with the Eldredges & Mr A was going down to Augusta to try & get a place in the Niter bureau.[4] I don't think he ought to get it.

The penalty of molesting uninhabited houses was very great.

We heard dreadful news last night tho I don't think even the fall of Atlanta any thing to feel despairing about. It is certainly a terrible blow to our cause & I should think the soldiers would feel somewhat dispirited but now is the time to shew their true courage. I hope all things will yet come right & that not long hence. I am sure this time is dark enough to be just before the morning. The help of man seems vain indeed. I cannot but hope that God will help us in this Extremity. If people could only be brought to feel that I am sure he would.

1. Benjamin Edward Stiles (1836–64), the son of Mary Anne Mackay Stiles (1802–62) and Benjamin Edward Stiles (1794–1855), was killed at Front Royal, South Carolina, on August 16, 1864 (Myers, ed., *Children of Pride*, 1689). William Wallace, Joseph, and John McQueen Stiles, three other brothers of Katherine Anne Clay ("Kitty") Stiles (1832–1916) and Sidney Elizabeth Stiles Elliott (1840–1925), had died earlier.

2. The Battle of Jonesboro, fought south of Atlanta on August 31, 1864, destroyed Atlanta's last railroad supply line and forced the evacuation of the city.

3. Ocean Pond was a large lake southeast of Valdosta.

4. Augusta, Georgia, was one of the major centers in the Confederacy for the manufacturing of munitions. An arsenal, powder works, and niter bureau were located there.

HELEN TO WILLIAM, ENCLOSED WITH PREVIOUS LETTER

Dear Brother

I received your note about the chair last week but I had just written you another note. You must not think I mean to hurry you but I was afraid you had not received my last note. I do not think either you mention will do. Mother wants a chair to sew in and one with arms would not do and she dislikes stuffed back chairs very much they make her so hot. I think I will send to Anna Pratt to see if she can get one in Augusta and we can arrange about buying it when we see if it is to be had.

Your aff Sister
Helen

WILLIAM TO MOTHER

Rose Dew Sept 7/64

Dear Mother

I see by your of 31st ult that you had not rec^d my last in which I asked your advice about A. This is a sickly summer in Sav^h and this is the sickly season and I am almost afraid for him to come down and be exposed to the malaria on Sav^h River, as he will have to do. The new detail is to occupy the places of those who are sick; and A. would have to take his place with them. He could not get on station with me.

I rec^d the honey and ink last week and have had some very good methiglin, and am using the ink now. Many thanks for both. The canister of honey will not have to stay in Sav^h for a month. Mr. Kollock's wagon comes out to White Bluff nearly every week and we can get it out in that way.[1]

I have been quite well since the chills were broken. Any amount of chills would not do any good in the way of getting a furlough. I find that they do not give furloughs for chills. They keep the men in the Sav^h hospitals or send them up to Whitesville to recover but will not give furloughs. So I think I will not have any more, since they do no good. I can get Pinckneya bitters from the surgeon of the post. In fact he offered to make up a bottle of bitters to give me an appetite, but I found that I was always hungry enough and so did not send for it. We get milk and okra every now and then and manage to feed pretty well.

I went over to Montgomery and took dinner with Geo. Waring yesterday.[2] The Howards are staying with him. Miss Jane asked to be remembered to Sister. She says that the Yankees told them about burning Roswell Factories but did not say any thing about burning private houses. She thinks they did not do it as they have only burnt one house in their neighbourhood and that was because the people did some thing against them. They were very well treated especially by Gen McPherson.[3] The Yankees hauled all their things to Mrs Barnsley's. He has British protection and all his things are perfectly safe.[4] They do not even take his fruit. The Surgeon at Cartersville boxed up cousin Eliza's grand piano and sent it to his home in Chambersburg where it has been burned with his house by our troops.[5] They saw the train that had the factory girls from Roswell being carried North.[6]

Have you heard of Eddie Stiles' death? He was killed at Front Royal. I do not know the date. His poor wife I am afraid it will kill her. She has been very delicate indeed for some time and seemed very much attached to him.

Sidney Elliott has typhoid fever of a mild form.[7] The D^r says this has really been a sickly summer in Sav^h. I am thankful that I have been at this pleasant healthy place.

Much Love to all.

Your aff^t Son W^m

1. Mr. Kollock's wagon perhaps belongs to the same Savannah physician whose daughter is mentioned in Willie's letter of April 22, 1864. White Bluff was a town south of Savannah near Rose Dew, where Barrington King's son, Charles Barrington King (1823–80), was a clergyman at the Congregational Church (Clarece Martin, *Glimpse of the Past,* 28).

2. Montgomery was a settlement south of Savannah between Rose Dew and Beaulieu. George Houston Waring (1833–1902) was a Savannah druggist who served in the Signal Corps before becoming a cavalry major. His connection to Roswell and to the Smiths may have come through his partnership with William Henry King (1833–65), one of the sons of Roswell King, in the Savannah retail druggist firm of King and Waring. His wife was Ella Susan Howard, the daughter of a north Georgia Presbyterian minister (Myers, ed., *Children of Pride,* 1715, 1586).

3. General James B. MacPherson (1828–64) was commander of the Federal Army of Tennessee under Sherman. He was killed during the Battle of Atlanta on July 22.

4. Godfrey Barnsley (1805–73), a British subject who was a successful cotton broker in New Orleans and Savannah, built a famous home named Woodlands in Cass County, not far from Roswell, in the late 1830s. While developing northwest Georgia Indian lands, Barnsley conducted some pioneering agricultural developments. For business

reasons, he never became a citizen of the United States, and he contributed to the Confederate cause (Coleman and Gurr, eds., *Dictionary*, 1:58–59).

5. "Cousin Eliza" was Elizabeth Anne Mackay Stiles (1810–67), the wife of William Henry Stiles (1810–65) and one of the sisters of Margaret Cowper Mackay Elliott. Although they lived in Savannah, Mr. and Mrs. Henry Stiles also had a home in north Georgia in what was then Cass County (now Bartow County), whose largest town was Cartersville. Federal forces had taken Cartersville in May. Confederate cavalry under Jubal Early burned Chambersburg, Pennsylvania, on July 30, 1864.

6. In one of the most remarkable events of the Atlanta Campaign, General Sherman personally ordered the burning of the Roswell Manufacturing Company's mills and the deportation to the north of the four hundred workers, mostly women, who were company employees. He wrote to Chief of Staff Henry Wager Halleck on July 7, "I have ordered General Garrard to arrest for treason all owners and employés, foreign and native, and send them under guard to Marietta, whence I will send them North. Being exempt from conscription, they are as much governed by the rules of war as if in the ranks. The women can find employment in Indiana." Two days later, Sherman wrote to General Webster in Nashville, "I have ordered the arrest of the operators at the Confederate manufactories at Roswell and Sweet Water, to be sent North. When they reach Nashville, have them sent across the Ohio River and turned loose to earn a living where they won't do us any harm" (*OR*, 38, part 5: 73, 92). See also Hitt, *Charged with Treason*.

7. Eddie Stiles's sister, Sidney Elizabeth, married her cousin, William Henry Elliott (1837–1919), the son of Margaret Cowper Mackay Elliott.

MOTHER TO WILLIAM

Valdosta Sept 9th 1864

My Dear Son

I wrote to you a few days since but as we received some tidings from Roswell last night I will not wait for my usual time. Your Aunty had a letter from Mrs James King she said Mr K. who is somewhere in service sent her a letter which he had rec'd from Mr P. & requested her to let your Father know the state of things. Mr P. says all the mills are burned but the residences are not, though they have all been ransacked from top to bottom & every thing carried off mostly by the factory & Parkertown people, the church completely strip'd of every thing that could be moved except the organ & all the pipes were taken from that. Our house is occupied by Larkin Brown but every thing had been taken out of it—it is nothing more than I expected of those people when they had things in their power.[1] The Yankees destroyed all Mr Pratt's corn & wheat & took all his meat & molasses out of his smoke house but did not molest any thing in his dwelling house.

Mr Eldredge & Mr Roché were arrested.[2] Mr E. & family & Mrs Adams were sent off. Mr A. remained until he heard from Mrs. Seagrave who had come to her in Cincinnati where she was extremely ill not expected to live & had lost her little daughter.[3] It seems very strange that Mr. Adams should have allowed his sick wife to go without him & yet that he could go to her when he chose. The Yankees took all the Negroes which remained in R except Luke, Charlotte, Prince, Tira[4] & one sickly woman of Mr Camp's. I did receive your letter in regard to A. & wrote you that in consideration of the sickliness of the places to which he would certainly be sent I thought it best for him to remain where he is if he is satisfied for it seemed to me your not being able to communicate with him in time to get him to Sav. when there was an opp^y for him to get into the Corps was another link in the chain of Providence which had guarded him heretofore & yet if there should be any opening for him to be with you or in any other favourable situation I think it wd. be well to embrace it. They are now studying one lesson a day French & Mathematics alternately but I am afraid he will not do much even at that little. He says there does not seem any use in studying. He does not think he will ever graduate, he has been kept back so much. Do write & try to spur him up. I suppose the Yankees will soon be going there. Now there seems nothing to hinder their onward progress, & if they should succeed in reaching Andersonville it will inaugurate a reign of terror.

We heard of Ed. Stiles being killed. I feel truly sorry for his wife & Sisters & sorry more than all for himself for I have never heard of his having any preparation. Do my darling be careful & do not spend a night in Sav. again before frost. You had better get the bitters from the Surgeon, not to give you an appetite but to fortify your system against disease. If you are weakened by the chills you will be very apt to get Typhoid fever. Lizzie wants to know if the Magnolia Glauca is the common swamp bay & she asks you if you hear of any bantams find out the price. Gulie Riley wants to get some. I am glad to hear you will have some way to get your honey. The man has not brought it yet & I begin to feel uneasy about it tho' he is a man of some standing. There is a young man in Valdosta, one of the cadets on furlough. He came to see us & offered to take any thing to Sonny & Father has been trying to get a pr of shoes for him but cannot. John M surprised us by a visit the other day he is staying at the Rileys going to Suwannee on sick furlough. Looks ex. well. Has 30 days & does not intend to go back while his money lasts. He *made* Osborn Barnwell give him a recommendation to the board, said O I think must be an unprincipled fellow from what I have heard. Father is very poorly, the rest pretty well. Do not be afraid of too much appetite. Likely you may have less after taking the bitters. A person with chills has an unnatural appetite.

Your aff

Mother

1. "Mr. P" is the Reverend Pratt; "Parkertown" is no longer familiar to citizens of Roswell; and an L. M. Brown, age fifty-nine, is listed in the 1860 census of Cobb County, Roswell district, as an overseer at the Roswell Manufacturing Company. The 1870 census lists Larkin M. Brown as a millworker.

2. During the Civil War Olney Eldredge (b. 1807) was the superintendent of the Roswell Manufacturing Company's cotton mills. Eldredge was shipped, with his four hundred workers, as far as Louisville, Kentucky. Unlike many of them, he eventually returned to Roswell (Hitt, *Charged with Treason,* 156). Theophile Roché was a French employee of the Roswell Manufacturing Company who taught the Smith children French. His running up the French colors in an attempt to protect the company's mills angered Sherman and may have precipitated his shipping the employees to Indiana (*OR,* 38, part 5: 68).

3. Mrs. Theodore Dwight Adams was originally Ellen Hamilton Seagrave. She died in Cincinnati on August 12, 1864 (Myers, ed., *Children of Pride,* 1450).

4. All of these references are to older Smith family servants. Prince (b. 1800?) was the husband of Tira (b. 1806?). The older Luke had been born about 1819 and Charlotte about 1822 (Smith Papers, box 17, folder 2).

LIZZIE TO WILLIAM, UNDATED

Dear William

I had just done abusing you for not answering my numerous letters when yours came just to shut me up I suppose. I don't think you have received all my letters for I have asked you ever so many questions which you have never answered & I have now forgotten what they were so suppose they were no matter. You are mistaken I think in saying Sherman has outgeneraled Hood for I think Hood has done very well & I think outnumbering should not be set to the account of outgeneraling as far as we know things it was the outnumbering Hood which took Atlanta. I think it is a great cause of thankfulness that our army does not seem at all dispirited but only nerved for further resistance. I do wish we could retake Atlanta before Sherman fortifies himself too strongly.

What a savage thing Sherman's order for the expulsion of the people in the town in his rear.[1] I was surprised when I saw they were to be allowed to

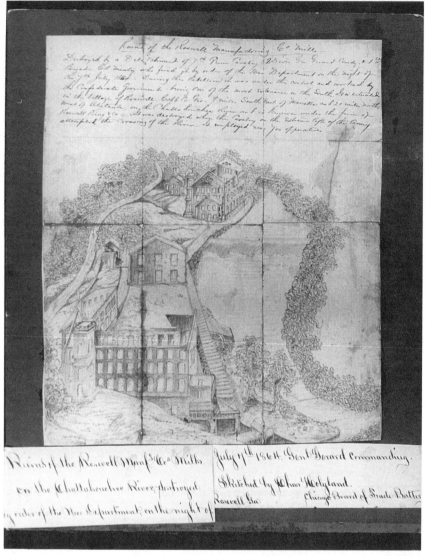

Sketch of the burned cotton factories of the Roswell Manufacturing Company, made by Charles Holyland of the Chicago Board of Trade Battery. Courtesy of the Roswell Historical Society

bring out some of their household goods but letting them come out with so little after all was all of a piece with his character, the vile wicked wretch.

I think you still seem to be trying still for the furlough. I suppose a spell of real fever would give you a furlough would not it? Mother says she wishes you would get some of that bitters & take it as she is afraid you may get fever & if you don't mind she will not let you go in bathing at all.

The reason I wanted to know about the magnolia glauca. Jack was sent out to get some of the Pinkneya Pubens. Mother shewed him a bush of it. It was in bloom & he went & brought the bark & it was used with very good effect & he was sent again to get it off the same tree & to bring some of the bush. Mrs Barnwell wanted some & Mother was going to send her some of the bush & he brought the Bag & it proved to be the thing Sissy had been taking all the time so I looked in Dr Porcher & it is highly recommended to be used in the place of Quinine & as good for colds & pectoral affections & Sissy had been saying she thought the thing was doing her good & so by accident altogether she took the thing which is more highly recommended than the Pinckneya. The Petunia which you sent is blooming nicely & the german star is full of buds. I planted some of the seeds which you sent & the sweet Basil is growing pretty well, only little plants tho, & now & then I pinch off a leaf apiece & we have a good time smelling. A violet bloomed yesterday & we took turns to keep it & smell it & when it was nearly defunct I told Sissy she could have it to put in some powder she had been making out of potatoe.

We received a letter from Sonny last week. He seems much better satisfied now that he is in camp round Milledgeville. I suppose he feels now that he is really in service & I expect the cooking is enough for him. He will not care for any more. I am really disappointed at McLellan. I was in hopes he would stand as Vallandigham has for so long & finally when the time came do as Vallandigham has, declare for peace any how.[2] I always thought Vallandigham was only waiting for the proper time to come out so I wish the Chicago convention would withdraw the nomination for I had much rather have Lincoln than McLellan elected but I believe, as I see a writer in one of the papers, that the only peace men are this side of the line & they are Lee, Beauregard, Hood, Kirby Smith &c & war, war is the only thing to bring peace to us & that at the present war is our business our duty & our salvation. We should adopt but one resolution that by the help of God we will achieve our independence & not depend on any peace party at the North or any exterior aid of any kind. That is what I call the true spirit for the times & if every one felt so we would soon be free but these good for nothing stay at home make money croakers are the hot fiends the yankees have any where. I do wish every one could be sent into the army or north of the Mason & Dixon & be hung if they were ever seen south of it. I hope that will be done with every one who *chooses* to go north under Sherman's order. I wish Sherman [&] all his friends & relations political or social, might have to suffer as the poor exiles he is turning out of house & home will have to do this winter. No doubt there will be a great suffering among them this winter.

If you can hear of any Bantams for sale find out the price. Gulie Riley wants some & I told her I would get you to see if you could hear of any.

Love from all
your aff sister
Lizzie Smith

1. Atlanta had been surrendered on September 2, 1864. Sherman's Special Field Order Number 67, dated September 4, required that Atlanta be evacuated, "being exclusively required for warlike purposes." On September 7 he wrote to the Confederate commander, John Bell Hood, that he had "deemed it to the interest of the United States that the citizens now residing in Atlanta should remove, those who prefer it to go south, and the rest north." He proposed to send those who chose to go south as far as the railroad stop at Rough and Ready. Hood had no choice but to accept, protesting that "the unprecedented measure you propose transcends, in studied and ingenious cruelty, all acts ever before brought to my attention in the dark history of war." When the mayor of Atlanta protested, Sherman replied, "War is cruelty, and you cannot refine it" (Sherman, *Memoirs*, 2:118–26).

2. Clement Laird Vallandigham (1820–71) was a states-rights advocate from Ohio whom Lincoln banished to the Confederacy. He became the Democratic candidate for governor of Ohio while living in Canada. A well-known Copperhead, he returned to the United States in June 1864 and helped to formulate George B. McClellan's "peace" platform at the Democratic national convention of 1864, a platform that McClellan subsequently repudiated.

MOTHER TO WILLIAM

Valdosta Sept. 12th 64

My Dear Son

At last I have got your honey & send it off this morning. I was in hopes of getting the canister full but could not get any more it is not as nice as old Mrs Lindburgher's.[1] I put it in a few pieces of hers that I had left. You must not let all the hindrances prevent you from sending another time. Being so late in the season makes it difficult to obtain now. If you had only brought some of my nice large canisters from home I could send you sometimes without your sending for it, if you would like some nice syrup. When the boiling season comes let me know & send something to put it in. Let me know whether the honey is for yourself or the mess. I will let you know price & quantity. Father is better able to ride to V. this morning.

Your aff
Mother

1. The 1860 census of Lowndes County, Georgia, lists a Saloma Lineberger, age forty-six. There is today a Lineberger Drive, which is south of Roswell Drive, which is in turn south of Smith Avenue. All are off Madison Highway within three miles south of Valdosta, the distance that Archie specifies as the location of the Smiths' rented house in some recollections that he wrote about 1910 (Smith Papers, box 107, folder 1).

ARCHIE TO LIZZIE

Milledgeville Sept 12th

Dear Sister

I received your letter some time ago and would have answered it before but lost my pencil and was waiting till I found it again.

I received mother's letter yesterday with the money in it. I think it was very kind for Griffin to go to see you. He is not exactly first quality but he is a very nice kind of a fellow.[1]

I went this morning to see about having my shoes fixed and they charged me $27.00 to halfsole them and patch two places so I concluded to try somewhere else. I think likely I can get them done more reasonably in Midway.

My hat is so pretty that I don't like to wear it in camp so I have not worn it much but will do so whenever I want to make an impression. If I had only had it when I was in Midway I think I would have gotten along a great deal better with the Ladies.

We engaged a man to cook for us by the week and when we had had him about a week he got negligent and we hired a boy by the month to cook and do just what we wanted him to do but we hired him from his mistress and in about three days his master came home he said something else so we had to give him up and have been afloat ever since. Some times we cook for ourselves and sometimes we get somebody to cook a meal or two but we are in hopes of hiring one of the Inst boys who is a good cook and a good honest boy.

We make biscuits out of our flour out of fried bacon gravey. Some of the boys make batter cakes of it.

Is that orange tree in the front yard dead yet? If not how is it coming on?

When Father and I were down there last winter an old cat used to come about the house and got to be quite tame. It was a very nice "manners" cat. The only objection I had to it was that it was a bob tailed cat. I would like to know if it still stays about. I am afraid its manners have been spoiled by eating in the kitchen.

From the time I entered the institute in 62 till we left Marietta in May last only three cadets died. Since that time six have died of disease, one been killed, one died from a wound and two been wounded not mortally.

I wish very much I could come home but see no chance of it yet a while and there is no knowing how long that while will be.

I have only seen three people that I was acquainted with since I left Marietta except the cadets and one of them was an old cadet.

Your affct bro   Archie

1. An S. Griffin was a fellow cadet of Archie's at GMI in 1864 (Yates, "History of the Georgia Military Institute," 29), and Samuel Griffin of Lowndes County is listed on a roster of the GMI battalion published in 1905 (Rodgers, comp., *Roster*). Also listed on this roster as his brother is J. W. Griffin. The Lowndes County census of 1860 lists a Samuel Griffin as the thirteen-year-old son of Thomas B. Griffin, a wealthy merchant and planter, but no J. W. Griffin is listed in that family. A marginal notation by Archie in his copy of Rodgers's listing seems to indicate that Rodgers may be mistaken in listing a J. W. Griffin. Thomas Butler Griffin (1816–77) was the great-grandfather and Samuel Griffin (1847–1902) the grandfather of S. Marvin Griffin, governor of Georgia from 1955–1959.

BARRINGTON KING TO ARCHIBALD SMITH
Staunton V^a 16 Septr 1864

Arch^d Smith Esq

Dr Bro Archy. . . . We arrived on the 13th & had a pleasant time, stopping 1 day in Columbia & 2 days in Richmond. Found Mr Baker, Eva & family quite well, with BSK's wife & children, also Mrs Stiles & [ ] , quite a house full of refugees. BSK with his regiment near Petersburg, expected soon here on a visit, unless the vandals should make an attack—at this time, all quiet on the lines.[1]

Our hope for Georgia, that Hood may not retreat from Jonesborough.[2] The taking of Atlanta will not benefit the vandals much—should Wheeler be active in cutting off their supplies, with the aid of Genl Forrest, they will have to retreat, or be captured: we must look to God for his blessing, at present all dark & gloomy. . . .

We expect to leave the latter part of October for Savannah should the way be opened. Mr Camp rec^d a letter from L McCall at Roswell dated 20th Aug^t—he mentioned that all the Factories were burned by the vandals, but *none of the dwelling* houses in the place: that Roswell was in a sad condition, old Prince & Tira with Negro woman & children left by Mr Camp, were well & he left them, but nearly out of provisions—that a woman hired by Mr Eldredge was at his house, her owner living near Greensborough & wanted to get her to the owner, being an expense to have—that no Yankees were stationed there, only one day that week some passed through the place. He said nothing about my Negroes. We left Bacon, Flour &c for 3 months supply—unless they have left of their own accord, presume our servants have not been taken off: and feel anxious to have them this side the line, as they may suffer from hunger.

Mr Eldredge & some others were taken & sent off. Mr Adams yet at Roswell, but he sent his wife & children with Mr Eldredge, his daughters promising to aid her taking care of the children.

Letters rec^d from my sister Mrs Pratt to 24 Augt. They were well, had not been treated rudely by the vandals—the officer commanding protected her house, but all the fencing &c outside demolished—so far no interference with Brother Pratt: but our home people did all they could to make them search the house, saying that goods &c were hid away—we have done much for that class of people, but they have no gratitude & now shew what we have had to manage.[3]

Mrs King Eva & all join in kind regards to yourself M^{rs} S & family.

Yrs truly &c

B King

The charge for board in the Female Sem^{y}[4] young Ladies $2800 for 9 months C. S. money on $15 pr month, payable in provisions at the price 1860.

1. BSK is Barrington King's son, Barrington Simrall King (1833–65), a Confederate soldier (Myers, ed., *Children of Pride*, 1459, 1579). Mrs. Stiles seems to be Elizabeth Ann Mackay Stiles.

2. On August 31 and September 1 Sherman had made Atlanta untenable for Hood by defeating General William J. Hardee south of Atlanta at Jonesboro and cutting the Macon and Western Railroad. Hood had remained south of Atlanta at Palmetto for almost a month before moving north and west in an attempt to cut off Sherman from the north.

3. Concerning the state of Roswell during the federal occupation, Dr. Nathaniel Pratt, the only founding colonist to remain behind, described the town's condition in a letter dated December 5, 1864, addressed to Barrington King's son Barrington Simrall King. After saying that Great Oaks, his own home, was "not much disturbed," Pratt told his correspondent that his father's Barrington Hall was "not much injured," that his brother James's house (Holly Hill, formerly the Lewis's home) and his brother Tom's widow's house (Bulloch Hall) were "not materially injured," but that the Minton house was "badly injured" and the Proudfoot home "nearly destroyed." Archibald Smith's house was "in pretty good order," but in all houses "the families living in them do not keep them very neatly." Further information that local people did not treat founders' homes well is provided on page twenty-two of a 1938 typescript entitled "Roswell and Those Who Built It" by Evelyn Barrington Simpson (1889–1960), a great-granddaughter of Barrington King, and Natalie Heath Merrill (1876–1938), a granddaughter of Dr. Pratt and great-granddaughter of Roswell King. They wrote that "women paraded in the streets in the clothes of Misses Lizzie, Helen, Belle, Anna, or Evelyn, as the case may be." The women referred to are Lizzie and Helen Smith, Belle and Anna Pratt, and Catherine Evelyn King (Barrington King Collection, Reel 71/61 [AH 1232], items 39 and 17. Cited with the kind permission of Lois Simpson of Barrington Hall).

4. Miss Baldwin's Female Institute, now Mary Baldwin College, in Staunton, Virginia.

ARCHIE TO MOTHER

Milledgeville Sept 22^d

Dear Mother

I received your letter the other day and the bundle by Griffin the next and I don't think I ever enjoyed anything from home so much unless it was the first letter after you got to Valdosta.

I had not had my shoes fixed as I was in hopes of getting them done more reasonably but they were in a very bad condition. One had a hole about an inch and a quarter wide and an inch and half long in one side and a small hole in the other side and the holes were so bad that they did not keep my feet dry and as the weather was quite rainy I was fully prepared to enjoy a nice pair of new shoes. They fit very well and are a very nice shape.

The candy was very nice but like all earthly things came to an end. A hog or something else stole about half the "lasis" candy and we ate all the rest.

The flag rapt is very good and if sister had not said so I never would have known that it ought to have been any different.

We have got a cook at last. He used to be a waiter in the mess hall in Marietta. He is a pretty good cook and a good honest kind of a boy.

I have not been able to find out about the cotton cards yet but a boy has promised to get me a circular which I will send.

It is on five months since I have seen any home folks and I begin to want to go home very much but I don't mind it like I used to. It used to be like going without my dinner to be away from home but now I want to go home like I want a piece of cake or something extra.

Love to all.

Your affct son
Archie

LIZZIE TO WILLIAM, UNDATED

[after September 25, 1864]

Dear William

I was very much surprised to see that you had been sent to the Isle of Hope.[1] For why have they made the change? I thought they told you you were to stay at Rose Dew 'till fall. It is not so healthy at the Isle of Hope, is it? Mother says she wishes you would get some Quinine & take a dose every day as there is so much tendency to bilious fevers. We hear there are cases of yellow fever in Savannah. The Cheves wrote Charlotte so & Mother begs that you will go to Sav as little as possible & not to stay in town at night unless it is absolutely necessary. Do you know how long you are to be kept at that station? Fanny says she is very glad you are going to be down there & hopes you will stay. She will not go I suppose 'till frost.

About the Bantams I just wanted you to find out about them & the price. I don't know which kind Gulie will prefer but just let me know if you can get any & all about them. I don't want you to put yourself to any inconvenience about them. I wrote to ask Sonny about them too.

Have you seen the speech the President made in Macon the other day?[2] I think he is vexed at last. I never saw any thing from him which was not perfectly calm but he really seemed roused by the yankees late doing. I tell you when he gets mad the yanks had better look out, for something will probably bring some of them to grief. I hope he will set matters to rights up there & Sherman & his army will be forced to surrender, for I would like to have the old wretch kept prisoner 'till the end of the war, notwithstanding his turning thousands of women & children out homeless wanderers with only a change of clothing & nothing to eat—is such a great piece of humanity. There were many of those as the Mayor of Atlanta said who could have fed themselves. Most of them could & they might have at least allowed people their choice.

The vile old wretch that he is, he is not fit to live & yet I would like him to live that he may "punitch" as he deserves.

A large basket went down to Smith the other day if he is going to send it back empty you might send the palmetto back in that.

Maybe if you cannot get a rocking chair to send Mother you might get one without rockers. Did the stuffed one have a high back or was it like the one at home? If you cannot get any such you may be able to get one of them such as you made for Sissy made. If you can let us know & we will send you the dimensions &c. We would only want the frame made. The cushions we would make at home. . . . Why don't you answer Sissy's letters? Don't say why but write to her & don't you say any thing in public about the chair. Put in a private note to Sissy all about it. Aunty sends the enclosed $2.00 change. She is much obliged to you for attending to the business for her. Look out for Cranes, crows, & things down there. They are worth their weight in gold.

Anna Pratt sold 3 of Sissy's fans at $20 apiece. That's pretty good.

your aff sister

E. S.

1. According to Willie Smith's service records, an order dated October 3, 1864, placed him on the muster roll of a detachment of men detailed in the Signal Corps at Savannah under the direction of Lieutenant George E. Harrison, Signal Officer of the Department of Georgia. This detachment was quartered on the Isle of Hope, southeast of Savannah. Although attached to the Signal Corps, Willie Smith remained on the rolls of the Savannah Volunteer Guards, subsequently named Company A, eighteenth Battalion, Georgia Infantry (National Archives Microfilm Publications, *Compiled Service Records of Confederate Soldiers Who Served in Organizations from the State of Georgia,* roll 318).

2. According to the *Savannah Republican* of September 26, 1864, Jefferson Davis arrived in Macon "quite unexpectedly in the Central train at 4 o'clock yesterday morning. Indeed no one in the city had the least intimation of his coming." In an address at the Baptist church to the refugees from Atlanta, Davis gave a fiery speech about absentee soldiers (1).

Valdosta Sept. 26*th* 1864

My Dear Son

I have been feeling a little anxious to hear again from you after your short attack of fever. I trust you had no return but you said you felt weak & when typhoid fever prevails it is apt to attack a person previously weakened. Do darling take that bitters faithfully. While we trust to God's care we should not neglect the means he places within our reach. I have been looking at old Dr Ewel's Materia Medica & find it contains all or nearly all the Medical plants mentioned by Dr Porcher & some others.[1] The Magnolia Glauca, it seems, is a very valuable remedy. We used it here by mistake, showed Jack[2] a branch of Pinckneya when it was in bloom & sent him to get the bark. He brought the other & I gave it to Helen as a tonic to your Father in the intervals of fever when he had a slight attack. In both cases it seemed to act well. Helen thinks it has been beneficial to her throat. After we discovered the mistake we looked in the book & found it was used in many cases. It was a mercy that it was nothing really poisonous. I cannot imagine how Jack could make the mistake.

I hope you have received your honey safely before this. When you empty it you must see how nicely Father mended the canister. After I had put in the honey & was ready to seal it up I found it was running out, so I emptied it & there was a little hole & Father soldered a little patch over it. If we live to see another season I will try & get some early for you when it will be better but how can we look forward a month or even a day in these troublous times. Oh! how much suffering there will be the coming winter among the poor exiles. Did you see in the *Republican* the statement of a *lady* from Atlanta of Gen. Sherman's great kindness in packing all her things & allowing her to bring out even her wash tubs & after 3 hours conversation he showed her that his order was entirely from motives of humanity.[3] Strange when so many were driven out & allowed to take but one change of clothing & yet by such a statement many will be beguiled into thinking the Yankees are not so bad & be ready to follow Stevens in a reconstruction.[4] Is it not good that McClellan has avowed his sentiments so soon, before Vallandigham & Long were entrapped into electioneering for him?[5] With his views Lincoln will probably be better for us than he.

John M. returned from the springs & *put up* here last Friday. On Saturday just as breakfast was coming in he walked out without saying a word & we heard nothing more of him until evening. He passed by on his way to town.

This morning he walked in, changed his clothes, asked for a saddle & walked out again. He acts just as if he was in a hotel. I am afraid he is looking after Mrs Riley's youngest daughter.[6] She is too nice a girl for him, but you know he can make himself very agreeable *when he pleases.*

Father succeeded at last in getting a pr of coarse shoes for A for $80. I wish you could make some arrange[t] for me to send you some chickens. I am not sure I could get them but perhaps I might. We are all pretty well.

May God bless you darling.

Your aff

Mother

1. In the library at the Smith home in Roswell was found a copy of James Ewell's *The Planters' and Mariners' Medical Companion* (1816). Ewell (1773–1832) was a South Carolina physician and one of the pioneers of vaccination in America. His book went through ten editions after first being published in 1807 (*Who Was Who,* 173). The Smiths were also familiar with the books of South Carolina physician and botanist Francis Peyre Porcher (1825–95), especially *The Resources of the Southern Fields and Forests* (1863).

2. Jack might be the Smith servant named John (b. 1818).

3. The issue in which such a statement was printed seems not to have survived. The only relevant issues of the *Republican* possessed by the Georgia Historical Society and the Georgia Department of Archives and History are September 17, 20, 21, 22, 23, and 26.

4. Either the name, image, and program of Thaddeus Stevens of Pennsylvania (1792–1868) had penetrated the pine barrens of Georgia by 1864 or the reference is to Alexander H. Stephens, the vice president of the Confederate States, who was rumored to side with Georgia's Governor Joe E. Brown in favoring secession from the Confederacy.

5. Alexander Long (1816–86) was a U.S. representative from Ohio from 1863 to 1865 who was an influential delegate at the Democratic convention of 1864.

6. John Magill apparently pursued Gulielma Riley.

ARCHIBALD TO WILLIAM DUNCAN

Valdosta 27th Sep[r] 64

M[r] Duncan Esq[1]

D[r] Sir

Yours of the 26th about the Horse is at hand. I am much obliged to you for taking a friendly interest about the purchase. I have been trying about here & the only decent looking animal I can get is held at $2000 & he is washy, balks, & has *blueish eyes;* so that I feel very willing to get the Turner horse at the price you mention or to go above it at your discretion. I am not afraid of his shying, as there is nothing here to shy at, & a plenty of room if he shies at nothing. I am in want of money to pay my Soldiers Tax, which must be in new currency. Please send by Express the balance on hand, from the cloth, after paying a/c—

My Brother keeps up astonishingly under his circumstances. He eats heartily of the simple fare, we are obliged to have; is thankful for our quiet refuge; has nothing of the petulance so common to old age; in fact makes me continually feel thankful that I have a home in which he can pass his days so contentedly, and let the light of the aged Christian shine so pleasantly; God grant that we may be undisturbed, by the enemy here; and that we here & in the Cities may soon be relieved from the chastening of the Lord & may have his favor & blessing in a godly prosperity.

A good idea, to get W. K. at Sherman.[2] He surely could not stand his influence.

Yours truly
Arch[d] Smith

1. There are many business letters in the Smith Papers from and to William Duncan (1799–1879), a cotton factor and commission merchant of the Savannah firm of Duncan and Johnston.

2. William King (1804–84), a brother of Barrington King, was also a cotton factor and commission agent whom Duncan would have known. Archibald Smith never forgave William King for becoming an intermediary between Georgia governor Joseph E. Brown and General Sherman, who was a friend of King's (Myers, ed., *Children of Pride*, 1585–86). See Willie's letter of October 18, 1864, below.

In William King, in Judge Augustus R. Wright of Rome, and in former Congressman Joshua Hill of Madison, Sherman believed that he had influential citizens of Georgia who could persuade Brown, who hated Jefferson Davis, to "issue his proclamation withdrawing his State troops from the armies of the Confederacy." In this event, Sherman would "spare the State and in our passage across it confine the troops to the main roads and would, moreover, pay for all the corn and food we needed" (Sherman, *Memoirs*, 2: 137–39).

King invited Brown to attend a conference with Sherman, later maintaining that he attempted to arrange this meeting for peace, not for Georgia's withdrawal from the Confederacy. The meeting never took place (*Atlanta Daily Constitution*, June 5, 1879, 4). Sherman wrote to Lincoln about his plan, saying, "It would be a magnificent stroke of policy if I could, without surrendering a foot of ground or of principle, arouse the latent enmity to Jeff Davis of Georgia." Sherman's plan included bringing

Alexander H. Stephens to this view, for Sherman had been led to believe that "Mr. Stephens was, and is, a Union man at heart" (*OR*, 39, part 2: 395–96). See also Avery, *History*, 300–303; Fielder, *Sketch*, 310–11; and Austin, *Blue and the Gray*, 145–46.

MOTHER TO WILLIAM

Valdosta Oct. 1st 1864

My Dear Son

As Robert[1] is going from the yard I wanted to send you something & could do nothing better than these cakes which by courtesy we call ginger-cakes. If you do not like such homely doings you must let me know & I will not send them again but I have the materials & it is no trouble to me to have them made if you like them though I cannot get butter eggs &c to make nice things. Would you like a pair of common shoes? Father has found out a man that makes much better shoes than those he got for Sonny & for just half the price, $40. He heard of this man & wrote to him some time ago but rec'd no answer & Sonny was so much in need & an opp^y offering he was glad to get the others.

Do my darling use all prudent measures in regard to health. We hear Isle of Hope is more healthy than it was early in the season, but you will be more apt to get sick than a person who had been there all the time. Do not be out late in the evening where the miasma is rising & if you can get quinine take a dose every morning & do not expose yourself to the heat of the sun & do not go to the city if you can possibly avoid it & on no account spend a night there. Sonny seems to be getting along very well. They have a cook now. He rec'd his shoes & they fit very well. He says he never enjoyed any thing from home so much except the letter telling him we were safe down here for he was in sad plight for want of them, his feet being almost on the ground. If you want a pr of shoes you must send your measure or number. The shoes seem very well cut, quite high round the ankle. Father finds it very difficult to get corn. Govt. has so much yarn & cloth to exchange that there is no demand for them & so many planters are bound for the sale of their produce, that refugees will find it difficult to live unless they can obtain permission to buy.

J. M. left this morning. He only stayed 1 day & night with us & had his mending & washing done here. We did not mind the loss of his company but it must appear strange to the Rileys for him to go & stay with them as we are his relatives. He expects to return to the Isle of Hope shortly. I intended to send my letter with the bundle but think it had better go by mail that you may know about the bundle. All pretty well. Love to all our kind friends in Sav.

May God bless you darling & keep you as he has hitherto done thro' all dangers.

Your aff

Mother

Write to Sissy next time. She thinks you do not care about her letters.

1. Robert was born to Tira on May 24, 1825 (Smith Papers, box 13, folder 2).

WILLIAM TO MOTHER

Isle of Hope Oct 3/64

Dear Mother

I failed to write last week as there were letters in town and I kept hoping every day to get them out so as to answer them. I was sick again last week but it was not that [which] prevented my writing, as it was only one day that I had much fever. I am quite well now, in fact feel much better than I have done before, since I came here. As I wrote before I rec^d the honey and enjoyed it very much, the last of it is now in a jug to make mead. I noticed the mend in the bottom of the canister and thought it very nice. Sister asks why I do not answer Sissie's letters. The fact is the letters generally come two or three at a time and I answer them all in one, as I have not enough say to make more than one letter a week, and I thought my letters were public property and it did not make much difference who they were directed to. I do not think that daily doses of Quinine keep off the fever. Johnnie Elliott tried it here and his fever returned. It is now so late in the season that I do not think there is much danger of any more fever.

Do tell Fannie I am looking forward to her coming as a very pleasant time and hope she will not put it off too long. It is probable I will stay here until next Summer. When they ordered me here they said it was permanent. I am very much pleased with the place and if Johnnie Elliott is not moved from here I shall not make any effort to get away. . . .

I should like to have seen Mr. Davises Macon speach. Any thing of the indignant order from him must be fine. I seldom see the papers and do not know what is going on in the country.

Much Love to all

Your afft Son W^m

Valdosta Oct. 7th 1864

I am truly sorry My Dear Son to find you have had fever again. I am afraid you have not used the bitters as I beg'd you to do & notwithstanding what you say about Johnnie Elliott, I believe if quinine is taken faithfully before the fever has possession of the system it would keep it off. Some people make such a fuss about taking quinine that unless they have some one to force them they will not take it. You are quite mistaken if you think because it is late in the season there is less danger. Where a place is at all sickly the danger increases as the season advances, until there is frost, so do my precious boy use proper precautions. . . .

I send you some *speeches* to read. Sister says take care of them, (how did you learn to spell speach?). I like Mr Davises less than any thing I have seen from him & I cannot believe it was correctly reported. It is not dignified enough nor considerate, but there is some excuse in his being hurried unexpectedly from a night journey to the place of meeting. I am sorry to find you have no access to news papers. Perhaps you have not heard what Forrest is doing.[1] No train came from Sav. yesterday. There seems to have been a good deal of apprehension for the safety of the Altamaha bridge. We have not heard of a guard there, suppose after it is burned there will be one sent there. Helen seems not so well, rather feverish. The rest as usual. A gentleman in Valdosta told Father he saw A in Mil^e last Saturday quite well. All send love.

Your aff
Mother

1. At the end of September, Confederate cavalry under Nathan Bedford Forrest (1821–77) began raids into northern Alabama and Tennessee to interrupt Sherman's communications and supply line to Atlanta.

Milledgeville Oct 11th 64

Dear Helen

Here is Tuesday afternoon and I am just writing the letter that ought to have gone on Saturday morning but it seems almost impossible for me to get time to write though I have not much to do. I have to recite in the morning and in the afternoon I generally have something to do which prevents me from writing. Friday, Saturday, and Monday I had to go after wood. We get a wagon from the Quartermaster and I go in charge of the detail to load it.

They are not going to pay us. They say the education we are getting is pay enough but I think that is only a conscience easer. I had rather have the pay and clothing which we ought to draw in a year than all the education I would get in five at the present rate, for we have been at work for about six weeks and recited two lessons in mathematics and read about thirty pages or so in *Télémaque*.[1]

Captain Griffith[2] is about to leave us and Capt. Eve is going to take his place and I am going to try to persuade him to persuade the Governor to give us a uniform if he won't pay us. What they owed us when we left Marietta and what they ought to pay us for the time that we did not pretend to study would buy us a very nice uniform. But it is the lot of Man-kind to be swindled.

This part of the country has been excessively gay lately. There have been four concerts in town, two by a brass band and two by the ladies &c of Milledgeville and one small "tea party" in Midway.

I did not go to the concerts for the best of reasons. Admission was respectively five and three dollars but as there was nothing to pay for the party and as I was invited I went and had a very nice time but we came very near not getting there at all. We got a little wagon to go in as it was some distance but we had four swot[3] breakdowns or rather break offs and finally we had to leave our fine turn out in a branch. It was about nine oclock when we got there but we had a good while to stay as we did not leave till three.

I believe there is going to be a ball tonight in town and a picnic in Midway to morrow and there is a rumor of another party in Midway.

We are having real fall weather this week and there was quite a heavy frost Sunday night.

I have been threatened with rheumatism for some time but am much better, not that it was at all bad but I had a pain in one hip for some days and my shoulder would hurt if I went to use my arm behind me.

A Mr Griffin from Valdosta was here a while ago and said that Cadet Griffin's[4] father and somebody else were going to make up a box and if there was any thing I wanted sent it could be put in. He said he would let Father know about it. It might be a good opportunity to send my over coat and at the same time. I wish you would send me some hair grease and some pepper.

This delightful fall weather makes me want to go back to Old Roswell. I suspect the trees are beautiful now and it is just about time for Spitzenburg apples to be ripe and for Gentians and all those beautiful fall flowers.

Love to all. Remember me to the folks at Mrs R's. Howdy to the servts.

Your affct bro

Archie

1. A romance (1699) by the French theologian and author François Fénelon (1651–1715). It tells the story of the son of the Greek hero Odysseus for the purpose of educating the young Duke of Burgundy, the son of the French king Louis XIV.

2. While no Captain Griffith (or Griffiths) is listed on the GMI roster, in a note written in 1922 Archie identifies a Captain Griffith, "our commissary," as commander of a GMI detail sent to the college campus near Milledgeville.

3. *Swot* is a British term for a hard worker, a drudge.

4. See Archie's letter of September 12, 1864, n. 1, above.

HELEN TO WILLIAM

Oct 12th

Dear Brother

I received your letter this morning (we do not send at night now except Saturday the mail comes so late) and I am very sorry to hear you speak of leaving the Isle of Hope. You must not go now for I expect to go there with Fannie. She is very urgent for me to go with her. In fact they all are. Even Mrs Riley told Fannie when she came here that she must not go home till I had promised to go. Gulie is going too. For some reason I do not want to go but when they are so kind in asking me and I have no reason why I can not go and so many things to make it pleasant they would have a right to be offended. So you must not think of leaving there till I come, which will be as soon as it is safe. Mother says she does not think you had better change because though we should love to have you near enough to come to see us she does not think it would make up for not being able to go to town and see the folks. You would be able to see us only once in a great while and you are able to go to town now and I think it must be pleasanter on the coast than up in the pine woods. You must consider all these things well.

There is no use to direct your letters to Smith's care. He does not get his letters unless they are directed to Capt Maxwell's care.[1] Do you want it sent to his care? I anticipate a great pleasure in seeing you so much if I go and I hope I will be able to bring you some little things. Mother is grabbling groundnuts at an old man's who lives near here. I don't know whether it is on shares or just so. Any how we will get enough for you boys to have some. I am very glad you have got even half a crow. When I come I hope you will have some more. I sent the fans I had to Anna Pratt to sell it was so late in the season that they were not much in demand but she sold three at twenty dollars apiece. I want to get plenty of feathers to make up by next spring, and get them out early in the season. I have two pairs of young pigeons and the old ones look very well. I am going to give Gulie a pair. She has been very kind to me and I am glad to have some thing to give her. When I come we can see about the chair and I can try the stuffed one, if there is no hope of getting another. Auntie begs you to plait a piece of six ply man of war and send it in a letter. She can't get it exactly right.

I hope you will get this in time to stop your moving, at least till my visit is over.

Your aff Sister
Helen

1. James Audley Maxwell (1837–1900) was a civil engineer on the Savannah, Albany, and Gulf Railroad until the war, and during the war he was captain and commander of Captain Maxwell's Georgia Regular Light Artillery Battery. In December 1864 he was named chief of artillery of McLaw's division, one of three divisions defending Savannah (*OR,* 28, part 2: 176, 247, 328, 469, 604; Myers, ed., *Children of Pride,* 1620).

WILLIAM TO MOTHER

Isle of Hope Oct. 18/64

Dear Mother

I rec^d yours of 7th yesterday and answer it at once so as to tell you about the shoes. I would like them what you call common dress shoes as I do not have any thing to do with salt water except to look at it occasionally so I do not want the ext. half sole. I have been taking Quinine and have continued very well since the last time which was three weeks ago. As usual the newspapers will lie about a thing. A few days ago the *Republican* had that there was no yellow fever in Savh.[1] There is not much but one of the Corps has it certainly. I do not think there would be any danger in Fanny and Sissie coming here and I wish they would come.

I am much obliged for the speeches. I am glad to have seen that one of Stephens as by it I see he is not quite as bad as I thought. It is no wonder Mr. Davis felt cross in Georgia. He knows Georgia soldiers to be among the best and bravest and then to come to the state and find it full of skulkers and fault finders was enough to provoke him. I take a paper now. I learned to spell "speach" logically, *speak* would naturally give speach but the Dictionary says not, so I give up.

What do you think? Mr. Wm King was one of Sherman's messengers. I should not be surprised if he proposed the whole thing and told Sherman what a strong Union feeling there was in the State. He must have had a good time talking unionism to the Yankees and if they believed him I suspect he made out that the state was opposed to Secession from the first.[2]

We are having a spell of N.E. weather and I hope it will clear off soon with frost. Much Love to all and howdye to the servts.

Your afft son

W^m

1. On October 14, 1864, the *Savannah Republican* published this article on its front page: "YELLOW FEVER—We hear there are many extravagant reports in the interior reactive to the prevalence of yellow fever in Savannah.— Some of the accounts represent our city as in a deplorable condition. In correction of all such statements, we would say that there is no epidemic of any kind here at the present time. A few cases of yellow fever have occurred, some of which proved fatal, and all originating, it is thought, with a soldier who spent several nights in Charleston. The cases are regarded by our own physicians as entirely sporadic in their character; there is no excitement here about the disease, and no fears felt of an epidemic at this late season. We have numerous refugees amongst us at this time, who seem quite content to remain" (1).

2. See Archibald Smith's letter of September 27, 1864, n. 2, above.

WILLIAM TO MOTHER

Isle of Hope Oct 24/64

Dear Mother

I suppose my letter from home this week has gone wandering about, as I have not yet rec^d it. Smith was moved from here to Whitemarsh very suddenly last week, and I suppose my letters will have to go down there and come back here.

I am very much disappointed at Sissie not getting here I had looked forward to her visit so anxiously but she may still come. Smith says he does not think he will be kept on Whitemarsh more than a month and if Fanny comes here when he comes back I hope Sissy will be able to come with her. The house is in a good sheltered place and will not be very cold, so she need not be afraid of that and even if I am moved from here I am pretty sure I can get one of the fellows to change with me for a while. Helen and Leila came here the night before Smith was moved but, as Woodie is here and Capt. Maxwell gave him leave to sleep at the house, they have staid and will not go until the latter part of next week.

Mr. Murdstone (Dr. G.)[1] writes to Helen that Mrs. Tom King and family are going to Europe under care of Mr. Roché and Miss Hamilton is going to her friends at the North.[2] Mrs. Adams died on the way to N.Y. but I dare say you have heard all this already.

Helen says "I don't see why you call Dr. G. Mr. Murdstone. I don't think he is like him." Don't you folks think it a pretty good nickname?

I am going to move to Beaulieu after a while to be there probably for a long time with Johnnie Elliott, but if Sissie comes here I can swap here while she stays, so she must come if she can.

I will try to send Elizabeth's Palmetto next Monday if not then some time soon.

Much Love to all. Your afft son W[m]

1. Mr. Murdstone was the disagreeable stepfather of Dickens's *David Copperfield.* "Dr. G" is Dr. Charles Atwood Geiger, who later married Helen Barnwell.

2. Theophile Roché was the Frenchman who angered Sherman by raising his country's flag over the Roswell Manufacturing Company. Miss Hamilton may be a relative of the recently deceased Ellen Hamilton Seagrave Adams.

MOTHER TO WILLIAM

Valdosta Oct. 24th 1864

My Dear Son

By your request I directed your last letter to Smith's care & now we hear he is gone to Whitemarsh so I suppose you will not receive it at least for a long time. I wrote to ask you about the pockets of your overcoat. I cannot remember where & how they were cut. Do let me know as soon as convenient whether they are cut as sack pockets usually are or whether more long ways of the coat & how far from the arm hole, also length of strap behind & how far below the arm hole measuring along the seam where it is put in. If it has only breast pockets measure the distance from the collar. Smith's leaving the Isle of Hope is a great disappointm[t]. It will put off Fanny's visit 1 month & if you should be removed I am afraid we shall not be able to persuade her to go, as only your being there reconciled her to it at first & we think a little while on the salt water will do her good. . . . We are having weather cooler than usual in this month, even in the up country & have had pretty heavy frost so as to kill the potatoes. I bought some chickens for you & intended to put them in with Fanny's. Hope still to do so & also have some ground-nuts for you. . . .

Your aff Mother

Milledgeville Oct 31st

Dear Brother

It is so long since I have written to you that I am ashamed to write but waiting will only make the matter worse, so there is no use in it. It is true that I do not have much to do but then what I do have is in little pieces and breaks my time up so much that it is hard to find time.

I am quite pleasantly situated here now. I am in a nice mess. There are four of us. The most serious objection is that we are all blessed with such appetites but we get a plenty of bacon and meal and draw one pound of flour, one half pound of rice, half pint of syrup, one tenth of a pound of soap in five days.

I have half a tent to myself I don't have to get up to reveille nor attend any roll call. I don't have to stay in bounds and have the counter sign, so I have a very easy time in camp. I have the very place for a lazy man.

We pretend to carry on academic duties but it is a poor pretence. Our class has recited one lesson in Mathematics and read about forty pages of *Télémaque* in about two months. I think it is only an excuse to pay the professors their salary and not give us any clothing or pay.

I wish I could get a place somewhere for I should not wonder if the battalion was to break up. They pretend to keep up the Institute and Army regulations both at the same time and then go by their own will. Nobody takes any interest in us and they have expelled one boy without any charges against him and another that was reported for breach of arrest was only confined to the guard tent for ten days but Major Capers rides his father's horse and lives in a house his father got for him.

I am in hopes of getting a furlough about the first of December and would like to stop a day or so with you but don't know if it can be done for I don't know how to get out to where you are nor what to do with my things, but if you could make some good arrangement I would be very glad. I want to carry the rifle home with me while I am there.

Give my love to Helen & Leila.

Your affct bro
Archie

Valdosta Oct 31st/64

My Dear Son

I was thankful to receive your letter this morning for we did not hear from you last week & as your last was written about the time of the periodic return of your fever I should have felt uneasy if we had not heard of you through Helen B. You mention Mr Murdstone as resembling Dr G. but as I have no acquaintance with either gentleman I cannot give any opinion as to the applicability of the name.

Helen is very much disappointed not to go down. At first we had to persuade her a good deal to go but now she is very anxious but still says she does wish to go if you are not to be there. She has improved very much since the cool weather commenced. Father also is quite smart. 5 or 6 of the planters in the neighborhood are going to the Florida coast for fish & he is trying to make arrangements to go with them. As yet he has not been able to get a horse, but he is trying to fix up a cart & has a kind of half promise of a mule to hire. If he cannot get any way of bringing home fish I think he will go on horseback. You know he likes a little frolic of the kind & I think it will do him good, though I am a little afraid for him to go & do not exactly like being left here without him.

You have not mentioned J.M.[1] Is he not at the Isle of Hope? Is it settled that you are to go to Beaulieu? You mention it pretty positively. You liked Beaulieu & were sorry to leave it but I am sorry for you to be so far from town. I like you to be able to visit the family frequently. It is beneficial as well as pleasant for you to do so. . . . Have you seen Mr. King's letter to Sherman? It is rather rambling & yet has more reasoning than I thought he was capable. I heard he thought he had great influence with S. & thought he could do a great deal for the Country by returning & communicating with him. Poor man, he must be cracked.[2] When the Yankees went into Staunton Mr B. King was off on a little trip with Mr Baker & so escaped them.

We are having a nice rain today. It has been very much wanted but the garden spot we have is so miserable that we do not expect much.

Love from all. Your aff

Mother

Howdy from Servts

1. John W. Magill (b. 1817), the son of Anne Smith's uncle.

2. We have not been able to locate this letter. The *Savannah Daily Morning News* of October 10, 1864, printed a letter to Sherman in which King states that he has personally

delivered his message to Governor Brown and to Vice President Stephens (Works Progress Administration, "Annals of Savannah," 163).

WILLIAM TO MOTHER

Isle of Hope Nov 4/64

Dear Mother

As I said in my last, I hope that Sissie may come here yet. I suppose I will be moved next week but that need not prevent her coming. I am much obliged to you for getting the chickens but do not wish them sent just now, until I get fixed at my new station.

After a long spell of most delightful weather (it has not been very cold here, only one frost) we are now having a N.E. rain which is very uncomfortable.

I was in Sav*h* on Sunday. All the friends there quite well, Cousins S. & K.[1] looking much better than they did in the Summer.

The overcoat has but one pocket. It is on the left side outside and slopes downward a little. It is 9 inches from the top of the coat 5 from the front edge and 3 from the armhole. I am afraid I will not be able to send the Palmetto for Sister this week. The opportunity I expected to have for sending it to town was tonight and it is raining so I am afraid it would be spoiled.

I will be very thankful if some of you will knit me a pair of cotton gloves to wear about this winter & keep my hands from chapping and be sure to put a seam up the little finger side so that I can know which hand to put them on.

I am very well Much Love to all
Your afft Son W*m*

1. Probably sisters Sarah and Catherine Mackay.

HELEN TO WILLIAM

Nov 4th 1864

Dear Brother

I am very much disappointed indeed that our visit has to be put off. I was promising myself so much pleasure in seeing you and the visit would be very pleasant in itself for I had not "made up my mind not to enjoy it" but expected to find it very pleasant though I might find some disagreeable thing, but now that it is put off I fear something will come in the way to prevent our going. Every thing is so uncertain and even if we go you may not be able to be there but I will hope for the best.

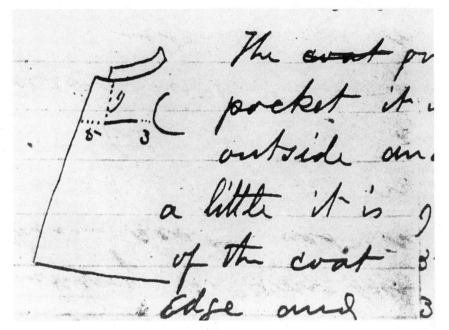

Willie's drawing of an overcoat pocket

Mother wants to know if you will want your overcoat cape again. She is making an overcoat for Sonnie and if you do not want the cape she will give that to him instead of making another, but there is no necessity to do it if you think at all that you will want it. Auntie says the piece of braid you sent is very pretty, also the palmetto. Father is going (if he can get any kind of "brute" to haul with) down to the coast with a party of men from this neighborhood to get fish. They carry wagons and pack them with the salted fish and bring a great many. So it is a very safe place and they expect to have a very nice time. Sister and I went out to walk this morning and found some beautiful "Indian pipes." Some were pink and some were white. The pink ones look like cactus flowers, not the shape but the texture and color. Have you ever seen them? I think I will try and paint one. I am very sorry you are to be moved from the Isle of Hope before Fannie's visit is over. It would be so pleasant for you to have her there. She is so kind and attentive to us all and behaves much more like a relation than some people who are really relations do and she expressed great pleasure at your being there. . . .

Nov 5th

This morning Auntie got a letter from Uncle Henry. He was in Shreveport and was to leave soon for Europe on business for the department. We cannot make out by his letter whether AmBet was going with him or not.[1] His health has not been good. He wrote under great excitement. Aunt Bell has gone to the North. Uncle Charlie was well. It is a very unsatisfactory letter indeed but lets us know that they were alive at that time, so it is better than nothing. . . . Mr Pratt says the crackers did more harm to the place than the Yankees. He seems more distressed and mortified at their behavior than any thing else. He says people are continually coming from miles off in the country and hunting iron and other things from the factories. Mrs King (Old Kate) has been so seriously ill from fright when the Yankees took Staunton but is now better.

Charlotte says she and you planned for me to go there and make a visit when she was there in the summer. How could you do that? I think Fannie was the person to do that.[2]

Write about the overcoat cape as soon as possible.

Your aff Sister
Helen

1. Willie's uncle, Henry Merrell, was sent to England by the Confederate commander of the Trans-Mississippi to purchase industrial machinery for the department. "AmBet" is the family name for Merrell's wife, Elizabeth Magill Merrell (see Skinner, ed., *Autobiography of Henry Merrell*, 379–90).

2. Charlotte Cuthbert Barnwell (1842–1922) and Frances ("Fanny") Riley Barnwell (1834–72), the wife of Archibald Smith Barnwell (1833–1917).

"The Vile Wicked Wretch"

NOVEMBER–DECEMBER 1864

In late 1864 the Smiths had two sons to worry about. No Confederate leader knew what Sherman had in mind after he had occupied Atlanta. When he left Atlanta on November 15 to begin his famous March to the Sea, Archie and the GMI cadet battalion that was guarding the state capital at Milledgeville constituted one of only a handful of military units in his path.[1] At the end of that path in Savannah, surrounded by other inadequate forces, Willie remained at the duty that had occupied him for almost three years. John Bell Hood, who had replaced Joe Johnston as the commander of the Army of Tennessee, pulled away from Atlanta and marched toward Tennessee in a vain attempt to cut Sherman's supply lines and to conquer Tennessee, leaving Georgia to the scanty mercy of Sherman's massive army.

Only four days after they had departed Atlanta, Sherman's army was threatening Milledgeville. Governor Brown and the legislature left in a hurry. Archie was an eyewitness to some events concerning Governor Brown on November 19 that have subsequently stirred up debate. While no less a figure than Sherman himself reported how Governor Brown loaded onto railroad cars even collards and vegetables from his kitchen and cellar,[2] a debate sprang up about whether he put his cows on that train while leaving behind ammunition, tents, and other state supplies. On what was said to have been the last train to leave the town were the GMI cadets, now under the command of Georgia's adjutant general, Major General Henry C. Wayne (1815–83), the son of a U.S. Supreme Court justice.[3] The train stopped at Gordon, where the railroad from Milledgeville joined with the Central Railroad to Savannah. Archie reported that he stayed behind and that the train returned on November 20, with about four cars. He was thus among the last Confederates to abandon the capital of Georgia.

Federal forces entered Milledgeville on November 22 and remained there until November 24.[4] Although Governor Brown tried to rally forces to block Sherman, only the regular Confederate cavalry under Joseph Wheeler (1836–1906), the Georgia State Militia under Gustavus W. Smith (1821–96), and the cadets stood between Sherman and the sea.[5] Charged with Savannah's defense was William J. Hardee (1815–73), the newly appointed commander of the Confederate Department of South Carolina, Georgia, and Florida. Hardee was a native of Camden County, Georgia, where the Smiths had lived before coming to Roswell, where Willie and his sister Lizzie had been born, and where Willie had tried to establish himself as a schoolmaster.

Under Hardee's orders, a small force under Major Alfred L. Hartridge was sent from Savannah to help General Wayne block the federal advance at Oconee Bridge. This force arrived at the bridge on the morning of November 20.[6] Archie Smith says that he and the other cadets got on the train to leave Gordon on November 21 around 2:00. A day earlier, Major Hartridge telegraphed that General Wayne left Gordon at 3:30 "and are now here. As we left Gordon the Yankees entered it. . . . General Wayne has assumed command here."[7] It should be noted that Archie reports a brief cavalry skirmish as they were boarding the train to Oconee.[8] The next day, Wayne says that "some of the militia are coming" and asked for arms and ammunition.[9] Placing his force that day at just over five hundred men, he numbers among them 145 GMI cadets.[10] It seems that Wayne actually turned over command of the bridge to the more experienced Major Francis

Withers Capers.[11] Capers placed his cadets on the west bank of the river, where the danger was the greatest, and reinforced them with a few Kentucky cavalrymen.[12]

One cadet was killed and five were wounded in the fighting that followed. They refused Wayne's offer to relieve them and maintained their position for the next two days, repelling federal attempts to burn down the bridge.[13] Following Wayne's orders, on November 23 Major Hartridge's forces drove the federal 1st Alabama Cavalry back across the Oconee River at Ball's Ferry, some four miles below the Oconee Bridge, where Archie and his friends were.[14] Early on the morning of November 24, General Wayne reported that he was still holding both the bridge and Ball's Ferry, but by 8:55 that evening he felt "I have held the bridge to the last extremity"; he reported the next day that he had been driven across it and had to retire.[15] The same day, however, Hartridge says, "We still hold the bridge, which is burning slowly at the other end."[16] Hardee himself arrived at Oconee Bridge early in the morning of November 25, and, fearing inevitable flanking movements from both north and south, ordered a withdrawal.[17]

While there is no possible way that this motley force could have slowed Sherman's thousands for long, their fight at Oconee Bridge was the only real resistance that Confederate forces staged between Atlanta and Savannah. Although he strangely omits reference to the fact in his letters, years later Archie proudly remembered his presence at this largely symbolic event.[18]

December 2 found General Wayne and the cadets at station 6 of the Central Railroad. A federal lieutenant colonel D. T. Kirby reported on December 4 from station 5 1/2 that General Wayne was making a stand at station 5 with four trainloads of troops and four pieces of artillery.[19] The same day, Confederate general Bragg in Augusta says that the Georgia Militia were last reported at Station 4 1/2 (Oliver), forty-five miles from Savannah, where there was a heavy skirmish.[20]

These events provide a fascinating background for a chance meeting between Archie and Willie, who was sent up from Savannah to serve as a telegraph operator for the retreating forces' rear guard. He may have come up with troops under Major General Lafayette McLaws (1821–97), whom General Hardee had ordered up the Central line to assume command of retreating forces, apparently on December 4 (Hardee had been called away to Honey Hill, South Carolina).[21] Also on December 4, Hardee ordered McLaws to withdraw his forces to the outer line of Savannah's defenses.[22] The GMI cadets left Station 4 1/2 on December 4, and federal forces occupied it on December 5.[23] There was skirmishing as far down as Station 2

(Eden) on December 7.[24] It seems, therefore, that Archie and Willie met at Station 1 1/2, perhaps on December 4–5.

Willie returned to his station with the Savannah artillery defenses, which were, according to federal General Jacob Cox, "a line of redoubts and strong detached forts along the interior channels connecting the Savannah River with the Great Ogeechee, from Fort Jackson to Fort MacAllister." These forts had been "sufficient for the protection of the town from expeditions by sea and naval attack."[25] They would also receive considerable Union attention in the coming weeks. That Willie was able to break away from his duties to find Archie at the cadet supply point about two miles outside of town testifies to the strength of Willie's love and concern for his younger brother.

Sherman was enveloping Savannah by December 9, when Beauregard met with Hardee and ordered him to sacrifice Savannah rather than allow troops to be trapped there.[26] Hardee laid his defenses across a thirteen-mile semicircle between the Savannah and Little Ogeechee Rivers. The GMI cadets under Major Capers were placed on the far right with Major General Gustavus Smith's Georgia Militia and held a position south of the river between three infantry brigades and the Georgia State Line Brigade. To General Smith's left were Major General McLaws's forces, and further to the south those of Major General Ambrose Wright, the lieutenant governor of Georgia, now a Confederate general. Major Hartridge, the hero of Oconee Bridge, was left with 350 men and the unenviable task of patrolling everything from Wright's left flank to Rose Dew and Beaulieu,[27] where Willie was the only telegraph operator and which was subject to constant federal naval shelling from December 14 to 21.[28] Rose Dew was in danger of federal land attack. It was there that Hardee had received Sherman's demand for the surrender of Savannah, a demand that Hardee had instantly rejected.[29]

Also present among the Confederate defenders were at least five of Willie and Archie's relatives: Archibald Smith Barnwell, whose battery had been divided between McLaws's and Wright's divisions; John Magill, who was serving in Daniell's Georgia Light Artillery in McLaws's division; Robert Mackay Stiles, who was an engineer working on the pontoon bridge escape route;[30] John Gibbes Barnwell Elliott, who was an artillery lieutenant; and Willie's fellow telegrapher John Mackay Elliott.

Although complimentary of some of the infantry and artillery forces arrayed against him in Savannah, Sherman thought that the city was also defended by "a mongrel mass of eight to ten thousand militia."[31] Hardee's entire force numbered 9,089 to Sherman's 69,627.[32] Hardee was thus outnumbered more than seven to one in numbers and was at an even greater disadvantage in relation to the equipment, training, and experience of his troops.

After holding his defensive position for almost two weeks, Hardee followed Beauregard's orders and planned to evacuate the city by crossing the Savannah River and moving his troops down a narrow causeway between flooded fields to get them to the Charleston and Savannah Railroad six miles north at Hardeeville.[33] Once it was determined that boats could not be used, Hardee had his engineers collect rice flats and barges seventy to eighty feet long from nearby plantations. These craft were lashed together end to end, then anchored to the river bottom with the wheels of railroad cars. Local wharves were stripped of planking to make floors for these makeshift pontoons, and many layers of straw were placed over the planking to deaden the sound of the retreating troops. This bridge was actually in three sections: the first extended from the foot of West Broad Street across to Hutchinson's Island, a portion of which Archibald Smith himself owned; the second section ran from Hutchinson's across the Middle River to Pennyworth Island; and the third crossed the Back River to Screven's Ferry on the South Carolina shore.[34] Although the original date set for evacuating the city was December 19, unpredictable events such as fog and ships running aground delayed the completion of the pontoon bridge.[35]

Finally, Hardee evacuated his army from Savannah during the night of December 20, 1864. To cover the sound of the retreat, Hardee ordered heavy artillery fire, wasting ammunition that could not be carried away. As the most outlying stations from which troops had to walk, Willie Smith's Rose Dew and Beaulieu were evacuated at dusk. Hardee then uncovered his main line from left to right, beginning with Wright's division and ending with Smith's.[36] Thus Willie Smith would have been one of the first across and Archie may have been one of the last, for the cadets "formed a part of a rear guard which covered the evacuation of the trenches between the Louisville Road and the Savannah river."[37]

All ammunition that could not be carried was to be dumped in the river.[38] As he crossed, Willie Smith threw in his rifle. A Smith relative who participated in Hardee's retreat, John Gibbes Barnwell Elliott, later wrote to his mother that the tread of the troops and the rumblings of the artillery "as they poured over those long floating bridges was a sad sound. And by the glare of the large fires at the east of the bridges it seemed like an immense funeral procession stealing out of the city at the dead of night."[39] When all had crossed, yet another Smith cousin, Captain Robert Mackay Stiles, was among the engineers who cut the bridge loose from the Savannah shore, crouched on the flats until the tide swung the structure downstream, then leaped to safety on Hutchinson's Island. When this maneuver was completed, Stiles noted that it was 5:40 A.M. and that when he looked across the river he saw Yankees running down Broad Street toward the Savannah waterfront.[40]

Archie and Willie Smith had participated in two of the Civil War's most remarkable events: as part of thinly stretched and inexperienced Confederate forces, they had helped to keep at bay the huge army with which Sherman had invested Savannah; they had also been a part of the most difficult and skillfully executed retreat of the war—Hardee's masterful maneuver conducted directly under Sherman's nose.

But such thoughts were probably not on their minds as they had trudged across the quaking bridges, out of their home state and into Carolina. Certainly, they must have noted the grim irony of their walk across Hutchinson's Island. Once they reached South Carolina, their route followed Huger's Causeway, which was virtually a dam that ran north to Hardeeville through the rice fields along the route of modern U.S. Highway 17, a narrow path just wide enough for the wagons and artillery.[41]

According to Archie, the brothers took leave of each other forever on the evening of December 22, 1864, although it may have been after midnight, for Willie reports leaving Hardeeville on December 23. If this is a variance, one may well understand that this was not a time to look for a clock, for it was late on a night that was so cold that half-frozen Confederate troops had to break up thick layers of ice in the Hardeeville water tanks and work in relays to get water into the locomotives' boilers.[42] Time must have meant little under the weight of such misery and such sorrow.

NOTES

1. Kennett, *Marching through Georgia*, 258.

2. *Memoirs*, 2:188.

3. Burke Davis, *Sherman's March*, 59.

4. Cox, *Sherman's March*, 27, 31.

5. Kennett, *Marching through Georgia*, 247.

6. *OR*, 44:873, 875.

7. Ibid., 44:879.

8. General Wayne reported to Governor Brown that there were "a few scattering shots as the train moved off," shots which "announced the entry of the enemy's Fifteenth corps into Gordon" (Rodgers, *Historical Sketch*, 93).

9. *OR*, 44:881.

10. Ibid., 44:882.

11. Capers was the superintendent of the Georgia Military Institute, but he also held the rank of brigadier general in the state militia.

12. Burke Davis, *Sherman's March*, 70–71.

13. Bohannon, "Cadets, Drillmasters, Draft Dodgers, and Soldiers," 23–24.

14. *OR*, 44:888; Scaife, *March to the Sea*, 64–67.

15. Ibid., 44:891.

16. *OR*, 44:892, 897.

17. Scaife, *March to the Sea*, 66; Wayne, "Military Reports," 95.

18. "I was in the fight at Oconee Bridge and the retreat to Savannah." Note made about 1922, apparently as part of a draft for an application for a Confederate pension (Smith Papers, box 107, folder 1).

19. *OR*, 44:104.

20. Ibid., 44:927, 622.

21. Cox, *Sherman's March*, 34. General Wayne says that McLaws arrived from Savannah at Station 4 1/2 on December 4 ("Military Reports," 95).

22. *OR*, 44:928.

23. Ibid., 44:632.

24. Ibid., 44:938.

25. Cox, *Sherman's March*, 45–46.

26. *OR*, 44:942.

27. Scaife, *March to the Sea*, 102–5.

28. *OR*, 44:2. The commander at Beaulieu, an officer whom Willie Smith mentions, was Cornelius R. Hanleiter of the Joe Thompson Artillery. He described his three-year duty at Beaulieu as being *always 'at the front,'* exposed to the constant assaults of the Federal navy" (Rodgers, *Historical Sketch*, 73).

29. *OR*, 44:957, 737.

30. Burke Davis, *Sherman's March*, 114.

31. Sherman, *Memoirs*, 2: 209–10.

32. *OR*, 44:974, 848.

33. Cox, *Sherman's March*, 47.

34. Hughes, *General William J. Hardee*, 264–65; Scaife, *March to the Sea*, 107–8.

35. Hughes, *General William J. Hardee*, 264.

36. *OR*, 44:967.

37. Rodgers, *Historical Sketch*, 96.

38. *OR*, 44:967.

39. J. G. B. Elliott to his mother, Charlotte Barnwell Elliott, January 10, 1865, in Habersham-Elliott Papers, Southern Historical Collection, University of North Carolina at Chapel Hill. John Gibbes Barnwell Elliott (1841–1921) was the son of Bishop

Stephen Elliott (1806–66), who wrote to the Smiths about Willie on July 15, 1865 (Barnwell, *Story of an American Family,* 160, 200).

40. Davis, *Sherman's March,* 114. Robert Mackay Stiles, second Regiment of Engineers, was the great-grandson of Archibald Smith's aunt Anne Smith McQueen (1753–1803).

41. Scaife, *March to the Sea,* 108.

42. Hughes, *General William J. Hardee,* 272.

WILLIAM TO MOTHER

Beaulieu Nov 9/64

Dear Mother

You see I am back to one of my old stamping grounds but not exactly at the same spot. We have an upstairs room in the house that Capt Hanleiter occupies.[1] It is very comfortable, being plastered and having a chimney. Johnny and Ralph Elliott are my companions. So I am very pleasantly fixed. I got here Monday evening. Smith Barnwell expects to be moved back to Isle of Hope about the 20th of this month. So I still hope to see Sissie there. He has spoken of it several times and my being here need not make any difference as I can change with one of the operators at Isle of Hope for the time she is there. J.M. is now in town sick, some severe catarrhal affection which has been troubling him all Summer. He had a letter from Aunt Bet lately. Mr. M and Uncle C are going to Europe with 8000 bales of Cotton to buy machinery for Govt.[2] I wish I could go with them. I dare say you have had letters too and know more about it than I do. The distance from town here does not make any difference about my going to town. We are not allowed to go oftener than once in eleven days so I go every other Sunday. The last time I was in Cousins K and S[3] were looking much better than they did in the Summer. Mary Elliott has diphtheria, a mild case. They do not apprehend any danger. She was taken sick the day after they moved into town from Montgomery.

I had a letter from Arch a few days ago. He expects to get a furlough in Dec. He is quite comfortably fixed he says. He wants to make me a visit, but I don't know yet how it will tally with my going to Isle of Hope. Perhaps it will be better for him to make it on his way back.

I am quite well.

Much Love to all your aff[t] Son W[m]

1. Captain Cornelius Redding Hanleiter (1815–97), although born in Savannah, was an Atlanta publisher who at this time commanded Captain Hanleiter's Company, Geor-

gia Light Artillery, of the Army of Tennessee, known as the Joe Thompson Artillery. He was headquartered at Beaulieu, living for a time with his wife there, and he kept a diary of his wartime experiences. Unfortunately, Willie Smith is not mentioned, and the pages referring to Sherman's attack on Savannah are missing. See *OR* (Navies, series 1) 15:493–94, 496–97. In 1890 Hanleiter published some recollections of the Joe Thompson Artillery and its service at Beaulieu, reprinted in Rodgers, *Historical Sketch*, 67–74.

2. Mr. M. is Willie's uncle Henry Merrell and Uncle C is his mother's brother, Charles Arthur Magill. Although Magill was Merrell's business partner, he did not accompany Merrell to England.

3. Catherine and Sarah Mackay.

ARCHIE TO LIZZIE

Milledgeville Nov 16th

Dear Sister

I received your letter the other day.

I suppose you will be very much disappointed to receive this letter instead of me but I did not make application for my furlough on Monday as I expected, as a bill has been introduced in to the Legislature to furlough us and there would be very little chance of getting a furlough approved till it is decided. If they do give us furlough I suppose it will be about the 20th of next month, if they do not I will make my application as soon as it is decided, which I suppose will be about tomorrow or next day.

I went to see about the paper as soon as I received the money but found it has risen to six dollars so I only bought one quire. I have not seen any brown paper.

I have not said any thing about the small pox as I thought it would only make you uneasy when there was really no danger. Three of the Negroes in camp have had it but it is two or three weeks since they were carried away and no more has broken out; there was an alarm the other day that one of the cadets had it but it turned out to be measles.

I hope the Legislature will pass our bill today if they are going to and decide the matter one way or the other. It is reported that the yankees are marching on Macon.[1] If this be so it will be almost impossible to get a furlough till they go back.

Love to all. your affct bro
Archie

1. Sherman's army had left Atlanta on its March to the Sea on November 15, the day before Archie wrote this letter.

In 1864 I was quartermaster sergeant of the Battalion of Ga cadets. In November of that year we were camped on the Capitol grounds at Milledgeville, and the legislature was in session.

On the evening of the 17th of that month came the rumor that the Yankees were approaching. The next day the legislature vanished without assembling and all was consternation and hurry to remove valuable property of the state and military stores.

All day of the 18th the commissary and quartermaster wagons were busy hauling commissary stores and ammunition from the magazine to the depot.

Saturday we struck our tents and they were carried to the depot together with a few of the effects of the Military Institute. We marched to the train Saturday after noon and the cadets got on board.

Governor Joseph E. Brown was on that train with his family and in the train was a car containing cows and hogs which one of the quartermaster wagon drivers told me belonged to Gov Brown that he and the other wagoners had brought to the train.

There was not room on the train for these cows and our tents, so the tents were left behind and Major Capers directed me to stay and see if I could not get them off.

The train returned to Milledgeville about midday Sunday the 20th. If I remember it consisted of 4 cars. One was occupied by some convicts who were not released together with their guards. The other three were loaded with powder much of which was in boxes containing 100 lbs each. One passenger car had one of these boxes laid on each seat and two stood up in front. There was a large quantity of powder left in the depot, I should think several car loads, and I could not get our tents shipped, so we had to lie out without shelter till we reached Augusta after Christmas. But Joe Brown's cows seemed to have a comfortable place in the preceding train.[1]

The Battalion of Cadets reached Gordon Saturday Nov 19th, I got there without our tents Sunday the 20th. I do not know what became of the cars of powder but Monday there was a train at Gordon.

About 2 pm Monday the 21st there was an alarm and we were ordered aboard the train, and as we got on there was a skirmish going on between some of our cavalry and Yankee cavalry who were firing at the train.

It rained while we were in the train going to the Oconee, which we reached about dark that night. There was a bitter cold wind.

Tuesday the 22nd the cadets were inactive.

Before daylight Wednesday the 23rd the long roll beat and we were marched across the bridge. After we left Oconee I had charge of a car of commissary stores, and we issued rations to the companies that were with us till we got to Savannah, when I was put in charge of the cook camp till we reached Augusta.

1. Hill, *Joseph E. Brown*, says that the famous story of Joe Brown's cows—including assertions that ammunition and the state archives were left behind—"probably was not true" but that it showed "the animosity toward the Governor which existed at the time" (243). Archie's eyewitness account may convince other doubters.

WILLIAM TO MOTHER

Beaulieu Nov 22/64

Dear Mother

I suppose you are feeling anxious as I am about our dear Sonnie. I wish I could change places with him and let him have my comfortable bed this cold night. I would like very much to know where he is, but do not see any thing in the papers about the cadets. What a dreadful thing this overrunning of the State is, but it was to be expected after Johnston gave up the mountains.

I was to have gone to Sav[h] today to meet Charlotte and take her to Isle of Hope as Woodie is sick and we did not know if Johnnie could get off, but Johnnie Elliott has been sent up to the Oconee Bridge on the C.R.R. to work a telegraph office and I can not leave and I suppose it will be a good while before Johnnie comes back so I am stuck here....

I am quite well. Much Love to all

Your afft Son W[m]

WILLIAM TO MOTHER

Beaulieu Nov 28/64

Dear Mother

Yours of 23[d] just received. You do not seem to have heard of my moving here as you say don't open the g'nuts at Isle of Hope. It is three weeks today since I moved. I had a chance to go to Isle of Hope last Saturday and saw Charlotte. She is very well. I was surprised to see how much Leila[1] was improved. I have been almost a prisoner here for the last week since J. E. went away, but the line was down on both sides of me on Saturday and so I took the chance to go to Isle of Hope.

There is so much prospect of Savannah being taken by Sherman that I have put up some of my clothes and will send them to town tomorrow to be shipped to you by Exp. You can open the trunk by shaking the top. My microscope is in it and the girls might as well take it out and use it. All the feathers I have been collecting are in the trunk, and some tobacco for Momma and Clarinda. There is a coat in the bundle that will do for Luke.[2] I have kept a plenty of clothes to make myself comfortable as long as I stay here and if I have to go into the field or am taken prisoner I will have to make out with what I can carry on my back.

This house is so comfortable that I have hardly felt the cold tho' it has been severe. It is much better than the Station at Isle of Hope and my companions here are far preferable to those I would have there. Tom Clay was married the first of this month[3] and has been off on furlough since he is to be stationed in town this winter. I do not think it could have been Diphtheria that Mary & Phoebe had as they have both been running about at night since feeding returned prisoners. Percy started for Va. last Monday.[4] He got tired of the Signal Corps and got ordered back to his Company. I think he chose a bad time of the year.

I send a small bundle of seeds and directions for preparing Indigo. The Soldiers on Rose Dew made a good deal last year.

Much Love to all. Your afft Son W[m]

1. Eliza Ann ("Leila") Barnwell (1846–1915), the sister of Charlotte Cuthbert Barnwell.

2. This trunk was found in the Smith attic in Roswell. The microscope was located separately, and the coat apparently had been removed. All the letters to Willie from 1856 through November 5, 1864, were found inside this trunk, along with various other personal effects.

3. Thomas Carolin Clay married Caroline Matilda Law on November 1, 1864 (Myers, ed., *Children of Pride*, 1492).

4. These references are all to children of Margaret Cowper Mackay Elliott.

BARRINGTON KING TO ARCHIBALD SMITH

Savannah 1st December 1864

A. Smith Esq.

My dear friend

We returned from Virginia last week, [were] detained by the sickness of M[rs] King, so soon as she could travel we left Staunton, stopping at

Richmond, Columbia & Augusta, taking it leisurely: thank God we arrived here in safety, & my wife continued improving. The vandals marching through our State & this place threatened: we thought of going to Macon via Thomasville yesterday, but having to travel in stage or wagons from Thomasville to Albany, would be too much for my wife, just from a severe attack Typhoid dysentery, and have concluded as we have comfortable quarters with my son Charly,[1] to remain here for the present: There is no place safe, & will trust for direction, to a kind providence. The R M C⁰ had some funds in Bank, which had to be drawn out. I thought best to divide amongst the stockholders near at hand, & sent you by Express C⁰ on the 29 Nov. one package containing $2500 to Valdosta & paid charge $28⁵⁰. May be of some service in these sad times: we must not despond, all will be right, we may suffer much from the enemy, but with God's blessing will gain our Independence in due time. I met one of the cadets yesterday. He left your son Archy at the 4 1/2 mile station with the command & was quite well. It was reported that Jaˢ R. King[2] was captured near Atlanta on the 13ᵗʰ Nov, but was much relieved to hear by letter from Fanny, that his horse stumbled in the charge, he fell much bruised, crawled to the woods and managed to reach Macon, after much suffering—expected in a few weeks to be well enough for duty. I wrote yourself & Brother from Staunton, hope recᵈ. Mʳˢ King joins in kind regards to Mʳˢ Smith & all the family. We want some corn if we remain here—could you procure 16 to 25 Bushels for me & send by Express? The sacks would be returned on arrival.

yours truly B King

1. Charles Barrington King (1823–80), Barrington King's oldest son and a Congregationalist minister at White Bluff, near Savannah.

2. James Roswell King (1827–97), the third child of Barrington King, had remained in Roswell to run the Ivy woolen mills of the Roswell Manufacturing Company. His wife was Frances Price King (1829–81). He was a captain in the Roswell Battalion, which was made up largely of workers at the Roswell Manufacturing Company.

MARGARET COWPER ELLIOTT TO ANNE MAGILL SMITH

Savannah December 1ˢᵗ 1864

I am in receipt of yours my dear Anne & hasten to inform you that if Archie should be wounded, my sisters or myself will take all possible care of him. I most sincerely hope that emergency will not arise & that he will be

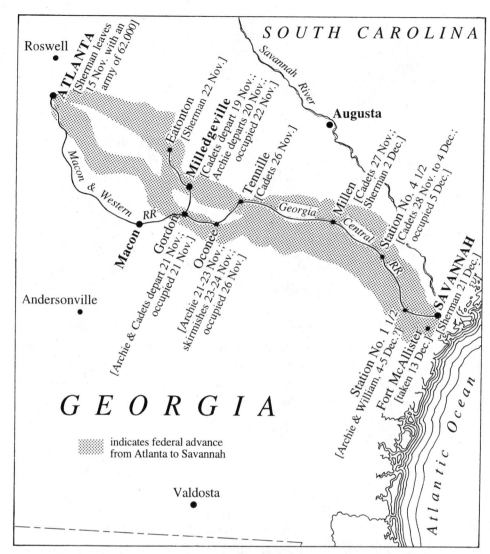

As Sherman approached Savannah, Willie's and Archie's paths crossed at the Central Railroad's station 1 ½. Willie proceeded to the front at station 4 ½, falling back with it to the city lines, while Archie, with the GMI cadets, took up a position in the line of the city's defense.

taken care of even in the midst of danger. People here seem to think Genl Wayne[1] retreats too rapidly to allow of any troops who are with him being much exposed. I don't know any thing of him lately. Indeed we are much in the dark not only about his movements but of those of the enemy & hear constant rumours which contradict & conflict with each other. My son John left here on the 20th to be telegraph operator to Maj Hartridge.[2] Maj H has come back. John was ordered off to join another command & I have not a line or word from him. I am glad my son Ralph has the benefit of being with

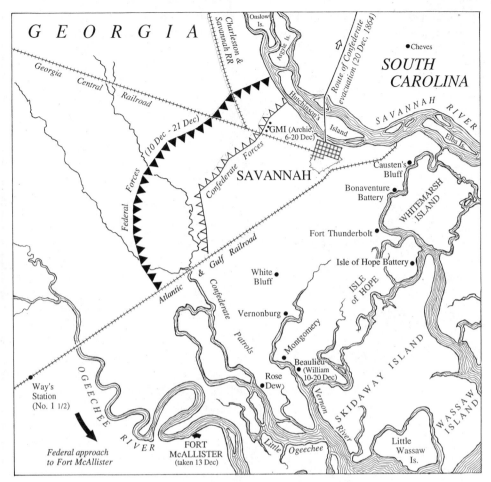

Savannah during the siege of December 1864. On December 6, when the GMI cadets took up positions just north of the Georgia Central Railroad, Archie was in the cook camp about a mile to the rear. Willie returned to Beaulieu on December 10, following a week at the front telegraphing for retreating Confederate forces. From December 10th to the 20th, he was the only telegraph operator on duty at Beaulieu, living in a bombproof shelter to survive the constant shelling by federal forces. All Confederate forces withdrew on the evening of December 20, crossing the Savannah River on a hastily constructed bridge supported by boats and pontoons. Sherman took the city the following day, presenting it to President Lincoln as a Christmas gift.

W.S.S.[3] John loves him so much & his influence has been so beneficial to John that I hope his brother may receive the same good. I have not seen W.S.S. for a long time. John being away I suppose he cannot leave the post as Ralph is too inexperienced. My daughter Mary is very much indisposed. She has been ailing all the fall & when the returned prisoners came she forgot her own aches & ails to minister to their wants & over fatigued herself.

She is confined to her bed not allowed to see any one & the D^r says requires absolute rest. . . . How are you all & how do you bear y^r exile? I was glad to hear y^r health was better than sometimes & the girls pretty well. Love to them from all here. Give mine to cousins I & A.[4] Remember me to Helen M & believe me your affc friend & cousin.

M.C.E.

1. General Henry Constantine Wayne (1815–83) was a native of Savannah who taught at West Point and served in the Mexican War before being appointed adjutant and inspector general of Georgia in 1861. As a major general of the militia, he resisted Sherman's advance toward Savannah (Myers, ed., *Children of Pride*, 1718).

2. Major Alfred L. Hartridge, who commanded the twenty-seventh Georgia Battalion, was the next level commander above Captain C. R. Hanleiter (Hanleiter War Diary, 5:2). On November 23 at Ball's Ferry, a few miles south of the Central Railroad bridge over the Oconee River, Hartridge had led Confederate forces to their only "victory" in Sherman's march to Savannah when, with a hastily assembled force of some two hundred men, about half of whom were from his battalion, he drove the federal first Alabama Cavalry back across the river. Archie and the GMI cadets were at the bridge that day (*OR*, 44:873, 879, 883, 886–88, 893, 897; Conyngham, *Sherman's March*, 270).

3. Her sons, John Mackay Elliott and Ralph Emms Elliott. "W.S.S." is Willie.

4. Her daughter is Mary Stiles Elliott (1838–1919). "Cousins I & A" have not been identified.

ARCHIE TO MOTHER

Savannah [December 7, 1864][1]

Dear Mother,

I received your letter by Cadet Griffin yesterday.[2] He could not find out where to go to join us and was pressed into the militia and went to Carolina, and my letter with him.

Brother wrote to you from No. 4 ½ C.R.R. Since then nothing particular has happened. We had a little skirmish there, but I was not in it. Then we fell back to 1 ½ Sunday night, and Monday night the cadets and some Militia came down as far as the out works about three miles from town.

Brother was sent from No. 1 ½ back to No. 4 where some troops were left, and I have not heard anything of him, and I suppose he will stay with the troops till they come down.[3] Col. Hardy, Dr. H.'s brother, was with them, and he was going to try to make his acquaintance.[4]

I am down at the depot with some things and have not been to town yet but expect to go this morning, get my new pants, and go to see white folks.

I saved my old pants, my jacket, two colored shirts, two pr. drawers, one pr. socks, one handkerchief.

Love to all. Your affct. son

Archie

Direct A. Smith.

    Batt. of cadets.

    Sav.

1. Although clearly dated November 7, Archie's letter bears a postmark of December 7. The events recorded in the letter also dictate that it must have been written in December.

2. See Archie's letter of September 12, 1864, n. 1, above.

3. Willie wrote on December 14 (below) that he had returned to Beaulieu from the front on Saturday, December 10, having spent "a week" there. Willie says further that he has not seen Archie "for a week" (since December 7?) and that he and Archie had been together "about three days." On December 7 Archie writes his parents that Willie had written them from 4 1/2 (the letter did not survive), that Willie had been sent from 1 1/2 (Bloomingdale) back to Station 4 (Egypt), and that the cadets had fallen back to 1 1/2 , about four miles from Savannah, the evening of December 4, leaving from there the next day. In his letter of December 16, Archie says that he had seen Willie at Station 1 1/2 (presumably on the 4th or 5th) and that Willie was "just going to 4 1/2," or Oliver, forty-five miles up the Central Railroad from Savannah. It is difficult to understand how Willie on December 5 could be going up to a station that had fallen into the enemy's hands, to understand how they could have been together at 4 1/2 or 1 1/2 for three days, and to calculate how the brothers could have been together for an entire three days anywhere at any time between December 3 and 7. If Archie did not arrive at 1 1/2 until December 4 and left it on December 5, they could have seen each other there barely two days. Perhaps both expanded their reports of their time together for the benefit of their worried parents.

4. This Colonel Hardy could have been the brother of Dr. John Gettings Hardy (1830–85), a Marietta physician whom the Smiths had consulted.

WILLIAM TO MOTHER

Savannah Dec 14/64

After staying at the front for a week and coming down with it to the city lines, that is telegraphing for the rear guard of our forces, I returned to Beaulieu last Saturday. I have not seen Arch for a week and feel anxious to know how he has stood this severe weather. I have come in this evening to bring some clothes for him and got in too late to see him. Wish I could have seen him to tell you about him. I hope however he is well as other wise he would have let me know. He is at present about four miles from the city behind the fortifications. The city is so closely surrounded that this has to go by couriers to Hardeeville to be mailed. Of course you were taken by surprise at hearing that you were cut off from Savannah. The papers have been lying so tremendously about things that many persons have been caught in the city who otherwise would have gone away and avoided the disagreeables of a siege. I almost hope that this will not reach you as I wish that you may have gone up the country. I am afraid the Yankees will ravage the whole of S Western Georgia.

I was with Arch about three days last week and he was in very good health and seemed to get along very well. I saw Maj Capers and thanked him for putting A in the place he did and he said yes, that he was a very worthy young man. Our friends in the town are all well. Cousin M. told me the other day that she had received your letter and would do any thing she could for A in case he was sick or wounded. I think he has recᵈ his over coat. It was not sent up to him and I think that when he was moved down near the city he came and got it. I had to furnish him with a blanket as he lost his at Ogeechee Bridge, and fortunately I have since drawn one from Government, so I have as many as I want.

I am very well.

Love to all and God bless and keep you.   your afft Son Wᵐ

ARCHIE TO MOTHER

Near Savannah Dec 16ᵗʰ

Dear Mother,

I heard yesterday that there was a chance of getting a letter through to you so I write though I am very much afraid it will not get to you.

I have been very uneasy about Brother since I got here, for when I left Nᵒ 1 ¹/₂ he was just going to no 4 ¹/₂ and I could not hear any thing of him till day before yesterday when I heard that he had got back safely to Sav and yesterday he came to see me.[1] He says he wrote yesterday by way of Carolina.

I received my bundle when I got here and was very glad of the things, specially the pants as I was getting pretty ragged and my over coat is delightful. I almost hated to wear it, it looked so nice and camp spoils any thing so, but I thought there was no use to keep it to look at. The other things were very acceptable too and the groundnut cake very nice. The Cadets are in the trenches between the C.R.R.[2] and the river. They are about three miles or a little more from town and I am at the cook camp about two miles from town.

I went to see the Mackays when I first came down but have not been to town since but expect to go today.

I have a bad cough but am pretty well otherwise and get along very well. I have been exposed a good deal since I left Milledgeville but have not had any feeling of rheumatism.

Love to all howdy to servants. Remember me to the folks at Mrs Riley's.

Your affct son

Archie

1. Willie must have been sent to Station 4 1/2 as a telegrapher on an expedition to slow Sherman's advance after the Confederate commander at Savannah, General William J. Hardee (1815–73), had sent Major General Lafayette McLaws (1821–97), with a brigade of Georgia militia and General Laurence Simmons Baker's North Carolina troops, to station 4 1/2. McLaws "found the position untenable and fell back, with Hardee's approval," to Station 1 1/2, about four miles from the city (Hughes, *General William J. Hardee,* 257).

2. Central Railroad, or Central of Georgia Railroad.

MOTHER TO WILLIAM

Valdosta December 30, 1864

It is so long since I have heard any thing of you, my Beloved son, that my anxiety & suspense are almost more than I can bear. We have heard of the evacuation of Sav.[1] (& that there was a severe fight) & that the troops were crossed into Carolina but who was left to go or who was wounded & remained in the enemy's hands we know not. It is three weeks today since the road between this & Sav. was cut & Sonny's note came the day before in which he mentioned that he was in Sav. & you had been back to remain with the troops left 40 miles from the city. Of course we conclude you fell back to the city before the Yankees came down but it is hard to have my two precious boys exposed to such dangers & not be able to hear from them. My only comfort is that you are both the children of God & he will do what seems good in his sight & that of course will be best for his children my daily & hourly prayer is for my dear ones & even if God should see fit to permit them to suffer that he will make up to them by his presence the absence of friends to minister to them.

It grieved us very much to hear of our darling boy being so destitute of clothing & I cannot but fear he may be suffering from exposure in the cold nights. Thinking about you both gives me many wakeful hours. I dare say you are anxious about us too but so far we are uninjured. There has been a great deal of apprehension of the Yankees coming this way for supplies but so much of the road & bridges are destroyed that fears are much allayed. Father got 150 bushels of corn last week, so we are supplied for the present. We hear the route is open to Charleston & I send letters hoping they may reach you. Do my precious child try & send me a line via Charleston. From there papers come by Macon. O if I could only know you were with my darling baby. I have written to both of you, but fear you have not rec'd, that if you should be taken prisoner & sent North you must write to *Aunty* Merrell.[2] We will most gladly repay any thing spent for you. May God bless you & enable you to look up to him & do all your duty.

Your aff

Mother

If you know any thing about the Barnwells mention it.

1. On the evening of December 20, 1864, General Hardee began the difficult withdrawal of the Confederate forces in Savannah across the Savannah River into South Carolina. Rose Dew and Beaulieu were evacuated at dark, and by the early morning hours of December 21 the withdrawal was complete. Of this masterly withdrawal in the face of an enemy that outnumbered him almost seven to one, Hardee said that there was no part of his military career in which he took greater satisfaction (Hughes, *General William J. Hardee,* 266, 270).

2. Harriet Camp Merrell (1799–1880), the mother of Willie's uncle, Henry Merrell, who was from Utica, New York. Harriet Merrell was at this time living in Sackets Harbor, New York, with her nephew, Walter Bicker Camp.

"The Failure of Our Hopes"

JANUARY–JULY 1865

When he left Willie, Archie and the GMI cadets had to endure a "long and tedious" march from Hardeeville through South Carolina before halting at Bamberg, then taking trains to their new duty station at Augusta, where they were to guard the arsenal.[1] Because of illness, Archie was granted leave and traveled to his family in Valdosta in mid-January 1865. By the time he was well enough to rejoin them, the war was near its end, and the roads were so choked with traffic and deserters that he could not get to his duty station. Willie was not as fortunate.

He was faced with a series of assignments that moved him up and down the South Carolina railroads that remained under Confederate control. He was in Pocotaligo until January 14 and went from there to Salkehatchie and

Charleston. By January 25 he was at George's Station, between Charleston and Bamberg, where he remained at least through February 2.

Sherman began his march from Savannah to Columbia on January 22, 1865. Neither Hardee nor any Confederate general knew his intentions, which were, according to one of Sherman's generals, to seem to threaten Charleston and Augusta while advancing all the while upon Columbia, "and thence to Goldsboro, where he hoped to open communication with Newbern and Beaufort, N.C."[2] On February 17, 1865—the same day that Sherman left Columbia in smoking ruin—Hardee evacuated the city to concentrate troops and join with Lee, much to the dismay of Charleston's citizens.[3]

All indications are that Willie Smith was now attached to Hardee's staff as a telegrapher. Hardee moved toward Florence on his only remaining railroad,[4] making for a junction at Cheraw, South Carolina, that would set him on the road to Greensboro, to which Beauregard had ordered him.[5] Willie wrote to his mother on February 24 from Gourdin's Station, on the Northeastern Railroad between Charleston and Florence.

The majority of Hardee's troops, like Willie himself, had never seen field service, having served all of their time in fixed emplacements in Charleston and Savannah. Nearly half of Hardee's command of two months earlier "had melted away through desertion, illness, and the withdrawal of various units."[6] Willie Smith himself was so disillusioned with his companions and with their leadership that he told his mother, "Our generals are drunkards and the soldiers black with profanity." He described all but Lee's army as "demoralized mobs." The fact that he did not desert testifies to his and his family's loyalty to the Confederate cause.

Hardee's army left Cheraw on March 3, and the town was occupied the same day by federal troops. Many Confederates were heartened on March 15 with the news that Jefferson Davis had recalled Joe Johnston to command the Army of Tennessee and all forces now gathering in North Carolina. Hardee reached Fayetteville on March 9 and found Johnston there. He left one night later.[7] Sherman's left wing commander, Slocum, entered Fayetteville on March 11.[8]

Sherman was on his way to Goldsboro, but at Averasboro on March 15 he collided with Hardee's rear guard, which Hardee had slowed for this very purpose. On his way to the concentration of troops that Johnston had ordered at Smithfield, Hardee made a stand to determine Sherman's strength and destination.[9] The Battle of Averasboro was fought on March 16. Stephen Elliott's brigade was there,[10] and there fell Barrington King's son, Colonel Barrington Simrall King.

The day after Averasboro, Willie Smith was admitted to the Peace Hospital in Raleigh. No longer attached to Hardee's staff, he may well have been unaware of the last major battle of the war, which took place near Bentonville March 19–21. Sherman's approach to Goldsboro became disorganized, and a gap between the wings allowed Johnston to hit hard at his left wing, commanded by Slocum.[11] This was the last gasp. Lee's surrender and Lincoln's assassination were rapidly followed in North Carolina by the federal occupation of Raleigh on April 13.[12]

Johnston surrendered to Sherman at Durham Station on April 26, and soon thereafter Peace Hospital was broken up. An angel of mercy then appeared to take Willie Smith to her home and to take upon herself the task of nursing him back to health, but she could not save him.

NOTES

1. Bohannon, "Cadets, Drillmasters, Draft Dodgers, and Soldiers," 25.
2. Cox, *Sherman's March to the Sea*, 164.
3. *OR*, 47, pt. 2: 1229.
4. Cox, *Sherman's March*, 170, 178.
5. Hughes, *General William J. Hardee*, 278.
6. Ibid., 282.
7. *OR*, 47, pt. 2: 1362.
8. Cox, *Sherman's March*, 178.
9. Hughes, *General William J. Hardee*, 281.
10. Ibid., 283.
11. Ibid., 286, 292.
12. Cox, *Sherman's March*, 214.

WILLIAM TO MOTHER

Pocotaligo, South Carolina Jan 3/65

Dear Mother,

I am afraid I have been very negligent in not writing to you before, but just about the time we left Savannah we heard that Thomasville had been destroyed and I thought there was no use to write but I have just found out that connection in that direction is probably all right.

We left Savannah during the night of the 20th of Dec. and marched to Hardeeville. I do not know how I would have got through if I had not struck up with Smith Barnwell and got a ride in his buggy. I did not go to see the folks in Savannah as it was in the night when I got there from Beaulieu. Arch stood the march very well. I saw him several times after we got to Hardeeville and when I left there (23ᵈ) he was expecting to be sent to Augusta since when I have heard nothing more of him but as he has stood service so well thus far I hope he will still keep well. I am here on telegraph duty but do not find it so pleasant as at Beaulieu yet it is a great deal better than being in the field. As I had to march from Beaulieu I reduced my wardrobe to a war footing 1 blanket 1 overcoat 1 jacket 2 flanel shirts 2 prs. drawers and a few socks. I now do my own cooking and washing and do not find it much fun.

As I do not know how long I will be here please direct to me Telegraph Office Charleston.

I am quite well Much Love to all

Your afft son Wᵐ

─────

WILLIAM TO MOTHER

Pocotaligo Jan 11/65

Dear Mother

Capt Geo. Elliott who is stationed here now recᵈ a letter from Charlotte yesterday,[1] so I suppose mail communication with you is open but it must be very slow and it will be some time yet before I can hope to hear from you again. It will not be worth while to direct to me here as I do not know when I may leave. I think the best chance for me to get the letters will be to have them directed to Telegraph Office Charleston. I have heard nothing from Arch since I left him at Hardeeville.

Smith Barnwell is about three miles from here with his Battery. He is quite well, he was slightly wounded week before last in a brush with the Yankees but is getting well. I see him every now & then. Johnnie is at Green Pond. I had a message from him the other day inquiring about you folks. I have not heard of Woodie since he passed here on his way towards Green Pond but I had a message from J.M.[2] at that place.

I have Bacon[3] stationed with me now which makes it much pleasanter than when there was only the regular operator at the place who was a stranger.

I have no idea what will become of me when I leave here but hope still to keep on telegraph rather than go back to my company.

Much Love to all

Your afft Son Wᵐ

1. Captain George Parsons Elliott (1807–71). He was the brother-in-law of Margaret Cowper Mackay Elliott, and at the time he was assistant commissary of the Beaufort Artillery of the third Military District of South Carolina. He had previously served on

the staff of Robert E. Lee when Lee was in charge of the area's coastal defenses. Charlotte appears to be Charlotte Cuthbert Barnwell (Barnwell, *Story of an American Family*, 145, 194, 209).

2. John W. Magill.

3. Either Albert S. or Edward H. Bacon, both members of Willie Smith's unit, the Savannah Guards (Confederate Pensions and Records Department, Alphabetical Card File, roll 3).

ARCHIE TO G. W. BROOKS

Camps, Augusta Ga
Jan 11th 1865

I Q.M. Sergt A Smith of Battalion of Cadets taking into consideration my present state of health and being confident that I will not recover it while in Camp, hereby make application for a furlough of thirty (30) days to visit my Residence in Lowndes County Geo.

A. Smith
Q.M.S. Batt of Cadets

I do hereby certify that I have carefully examined this officer & find him incapable of performing the duties of his office, reason of camp Itch. I would therefore respectfully recommend furlough of thirty days

G W. Brooks
Surgeon in charge

Hd.Qrs. Capers Command January 13th 1865 -
Approved & Resply. Forwarded

V. E. Manget
Captain

Exmd & Approved

J. A. Hill
Chr. Med Exmng Board

Approved

J.M. Douglas
Actg. Med. Director

HdQrs. 1st Div G.M.
Jany 14, 1865
Approved for thirty (30) days

By Command of Maj Genl Smith
S. H. Tobey
A. A. G.

Jan 14th 1865

Two days rations furnished

Jos. Darling

Capt & a.c.s.

No. 603 Jany 14 1865 Trans in kind from Milledgeville to Albany Ga

C.A. Bridewell Capt & a.q.m.

Rations furnished for three days Jany 16 1865

Jno A. Davis

Capt & a.c.s.

H^{d}Q^{rs} Post Albany Ga

Jan 16th 1865

A.Q.M. will furnish transportation for one man to Thomasville Ga

B F. White Capt

Com^d Post

#3674 Jan 16 / 65

Transpt^n in kind from Albany to Thomasville

R. K. Hines

Capt & a.q.m.

WILLIAM TO MOTHER

George's Station S.C.R.R.[1] Jan 25/65

Dear Mother

I have been running about so lately that I do not believe I have written since I left Pocotaligo. We left that place the night of the fourteenth and went on the cars to Salkehatchie a miserable place where the beef was tough and we had to sleep out of doors. Fortunately the weather was clear. After staying there two days we were ordered to Charleston and Harden was put in the office at Hardee's Head Quarters with John Elliott and I sent up here.[2] I suppose Charleston has been a handsome city but it now looks like a ten pin alley when the game is played out.

I came to this place on the 19$^{th.}$ I had been feeling unwell for a few days and the day after I got here I took to bed and broke out with measles and was quite sick for a few days. I have received every attention that I needed from a Mr. & Mrs Alston of Charleston.[3] They sent a servant to wait on me and kept me supplied with black tea and sent me nice things to eat, in fact just took charge of me as if I had been consigned to them by some particular friend. I am now nearly well again and thankful to say quite free from any of the after effects that measles sometimes leaves. I have just rec^d yours of 13th and a note from A written from Augusta I suppose he is with you by this time as I heard of him

Map labels:

TENNESSEE

Greensboro

Bennett's House
▲ [Johnston surrenders,
April 26, 1865]

Raleigh
[William arrives by 14 Mar.
Sherman enters 13 Apr.]

Goldsboro

NORTH CAROLINA

Bentonville

Averasboro
[battle 16 Mar.]

Fayetteville
[William early Mar.;
Hardee evacuates 10 Mar.,
occupied 11 Mar.]

Cheraw
[Hardee evacuates 3 Mar.;
occupied 3 Mar.]

SOUTH CAROLINA

Camden
[occupied 25 Feb.]

COLUMBIA
[burned 17 Feb]

George's Station
[Wm. 19 Jan.
to mid-Feb.]

Gourdin's Station
[William, 24 Feb.]

Roswell

ATLANTA

Augusta

Bamberg
[Archie 25 Dec.]

CHARLESTON
[Hardee evacuates 17 Feb.]

Milledgeville
[Archie 14 Jan.]

Salkehatchee
Pocotaligo [William departs 14 Jan., 1865;
Beaufort   Sherman, 24 Jan.]

Hardeeville
[Archie & William
bid farewell, 22 Dec.]

SAVANNAH [evacuation 20 Dec., 1864;
Sherman occupies 21 Dec.;
Sherman leaves 22 Jan., 1865]

GEORGIA

Atlantic Ocean

Albany
[16 Jan.]

Valdosta [Archie arrives
probably by 20 Jan.]

Thomasville

Archie - - - - - -
William ———
Federal forces ░░░░░

Hardee's retreat through the Carolinas. Willie and Archie last saw each other at Hardeeville, South Carolina, on December 22, 1864. Willie retreated with Hardee into North Carolina; Archie left with the GMI cadets to guard the Confederate arsenal at Augusta, Georgia.

on his way some time last week. I saw the account of the meeting in Sav^h and was very much disgusted at it, but I hear that all your part of the country is following the example of Sav^h and is going back to the Union is it not so?[24]

If I was alone I would not care much how this contest ended but I am troubled to know how you home folks are to live under Federal rule and negro equality. I can see no hope for our cause. Our armies except Lee's are demoralized mobs. Our generals are drunkards and the soldiers black with profanity. If our punishments brought anything like humiliation or improvement I could see some hope but they only seem to make us worse.

I have never heard yet if you rec^d the trunk and bundle I sent by Express in Nov. They contained most of my clothes, I did not lose many in Sav^h only my valise full which I sent to town and asked J. Elliott to take home for me but he had so much to do he forgot it. The last week I was there I was the only operator at Beaulieu and was living in a bombproof as they were shelling us, so I could not pay much attention to my things.[5] I had to throw the rifle into the river as I had no way of carrying it.

Much Love to all

Your afft Son W^m

Howdye for the servants.

I am very glad to get the gloves. My woolen ones are completely worn out in the fingers and do not do much good.

My letters had better be directed to care of Lieut Harrison Signal Officer Charleston S. C.[6]

1. Willie Smith was stationed at this location on the South Carolina Railroad until mid-February 1865.

2. Private W. D. Harden of the Chatham Artillery (Jones, *Historical Sketch,* 104). John Mackay Elliott (1844–1929).

3. Willie corrected their names to Austin in his letter of February 2, below.

4. Willie's and his family's loyalty to the Confederacy into 1865 seems exceptional. In late December 1864, Dr. Nathaniel Pratt said that there were "from forty to sixty" deserters in Roswell (Barrington King Collection, Reel 71/61 [AH 1232], item 39). Disasters such as the fall of Atlanta, the reelection of Lincoln, and the capture of Savannah meant, according to historian Archer Jones, that "confidence among southern citizens and soldiers dropped markedly. The significantly increased rate of desertion from the Rebel armies illustrated this." Some forty percent of Confederate soldiers east of the Mississippi deserted during the fall and early winter of 1864–65. "The Confederate armies melted away not because men lacked supplies but because they and their families no longer had the political motivation to continue" ("Military Means, Political Ends," in *Why the Confederacy Lost,* ed. Boritt, 73–74).

5. Forts Beaulieu and Rose Dew were subjected to constant federal shelling from December 14 to 21, 1864 (*OR,* 44:2). Captain Hanleiter's company, to which Willie seems to have been attached, was broken up after the retreat from Charleston (*OR,* 47, part 2:992). Willie himself was attached to Hardee's staff and sent virtually anywhere a telegrapher was needed.

6. Lieutenant George E. Harrison was serving as Signal Officer of the Department of Georgia, commanding the detachment to which Willie Smith had been detailed. By February 1865 Harrison commanded the Signal Corps in Charleston, South Carolina. See Lizzie Smith's letter written after September 25, 1864, n. 1, above (National Archives

Microfilm, *Compiled Service Records of Confederate Soldiers Who Served in Organizations Raised Directly by the Confederate Government*, roll 118.).

MOTHER TO WILLIAM

Valdosta January 31st 65

Day after day my beloved son we send to the P.O. in hope of receiving some tidings from you & only disappointment awaits us. Your last letter was of the 11th & since that we see there has been a fight at Pocotaligo. Thank God you are not in the field & yet you are in danger. I know you write but the mails are so slow & irregular. A wrote when he first got to Augusta & his letter did not come until he had been here some days. He is very unwell has a bad cough & has been in bed some days with fever. His "Camp itch" seems to be yielding to remedies. I suppose excitement kept him up for he is really weak & certainly will not be able to undertake the journey back next Monday which is the time he must leave to get back in time. He ought to have an extension of furlough but I fear there is no one here authorized to give it.

A tells me you have a lame foot what is the matter with it? I hope you have your pistol & that you carry it about with you. You know not what exigency may arise. It grieves me to think of your having such hard times doing your own cooking & washing. Your Father is anxious to send Harry[1] to you if you can tell how he may get to you safely. As you have nothing to steal now I dare say he will do very well. The other 2 boys having their wives here will not be willing to go & perhaps would not do as well & H. has been doing very well lately. Father can spare him perfectly well & it will make no difference at home except making us more comfortable to think you have some help.

I am glad to hear Mr. Bacon is with you again and hope he will continue. It is strange you have not heard from us. I have written 3 times before this & Lizzie once since you left Sav. In the first to Charleston I sent the gloves Sister knitted for you. Do let me know if you want money & how to send it. It is no comfort to us to have any thing & know that our dear ones are needing comforts. We are much more comfortable than when you were here (tho' we have no B. Berries). We have some nice pork of our own curing besides poultry with rice & wheat flour & the nicest syrup I ever tasted & Mr Waldburg[2] has just sent me a present of some butter.

Do my darling don't hesitate about taking Harry you know he is not worth much on the farm but is very capable & can do your cooking & washing very well. A is up now & seems to feel quite smart. It is a lovely bright day after a long spell of rain & severe cold. This is indeed a time of darkness, but let us look upward & trust in God who can deliver & may have brought us very low to teach us to trust in him alone. All as usual. May God bless & keep you my precious child.

Your aff   Mother

You seem uneasy about us but I do not think there is any cause.

1. Among Archibald Smith's servants was a Harry, who appears as age six on an 1830 list. A Harry also appears on a later "List of my negroes in Cobb" (Smith Papers, box 17, folder 2).

2. Perhaps another refugee from Savannah, a planter named Jacob Waldberg. See Anne Smith's letter of January 1, 1864, above.

HELEN TO WILLIAM, UNDATED

Dear Brother

It is a long time since I have written to you and we have heard so seldom lately it seems as if you were very far off. We are very delighted to have Sonnie at home once more. If you could only be at home too it would be so delightful we would hardly know what to do with ourselves. I do hope you will let Mother send Harry to you unless you think he will be more trouble than help. You know the negroes do very little at planting. They never make their feed & so his work will not be any loss and it will be a great relief to us to think you don't have to cook and wash for your self. Don't just say it is no use you can get along very well as you are. There is use to try and be comfortable and home people will be much better satisfied.

Sonnie is going in the morning to get his furlough renewed and Mother is going to Mrs Elbert.[1] Father has broken the horse and he does very well in the buggy. The hyacinth roots you brought down are growing very well and a few of the plants you sent are still alive and we have got some others from different people so we may have something of a garden. Last winter when Father came down to build a house I sent some plants to him to be planted at the house. As he did not settle any where he gave the plants to Fannie[2] so we are able to get some home things and among them one of our old sweet roses. We were quite distressed at the idea of losing it. Do you hear any thing of our friends in Savannah? We see by the papers that a good many refugees have come out.

your aff Helen

1. Perhaps the Elberts of Camden County. There seem to have been several Camden County refugee families in Valdosta with whom the Smiths were familiar from the old

days in St. Marys. In addition to the Elberts were families named Lang, Stewart, and Downs. It seems that the Smiths rented property on the lands of a James Wisenbaker. See Wisenbaker, "First Impressions," 5, 12.

2. Frances ("Fanny") Riley Barnwell.

WILLIAM TO MOTHER

George's Station Feb 2/65

Dear Mother

I have heard nothing more from home since my last tho' I suppose there is a letter in Charleston for me.

I have entirely recovered from the measles and feel quite well again. The family who were so kind to me are named Austin not Alston.[1] They invited me to dinner Monday and I spent the evening there too and enjoyed it very much as there is a young lady who plays on the Piano and sings very well. It was quite a treat to me to hear music again.

I am very pleasantly situated. The office is comfortable with a chimney and I board where they feed me well enough for $80 per month which is much better than cooking Gov^t rations for myself.

I begin to feel anxious about military movements. Sherman has begun his move on Augusta and I am very much afraid he will cut us off from Rail Road communication so that we will have to march from here which I do not fancy at all. I wish I could get a place on the Gulf Road or some line in Fla., but there is no chance. Tom Clay applied to be sent to #12 but Lieut Harrison would not consent as there is such a demand for Operators about here he could not be spared.

I have heard nothing more from Sav$^h.$ This Station is about 15 miles below Branchville. Perhaps it is not put down on the maps that you have.

Much Love to all
Your afft Son W^m

1. Although this Austin family has not been positively identified, there are two likely possibilities: the family of William Austin, a planter in St. John's Berkeley Parish, and the family of Philip Austin, a clerk who had been born in Scotland and lived in Charleston's second ward.

Valdosta February 17th 1865

My Dear Son   The enemy seems to be making such progress in Carolina & our last accounts were so unfavourable that before this I suppose we are entirely cut off from communication with you except by some irregular channel. Smith expects to go in a day or two to seek some way of joining his command & we trust this may reach you through him. I have felt very anxious to hear from you as you were just recovering from measles, & it was too soon after the appearance of the disease for us to feel at all confident that no ill effects would remain. I am thankful that I was permitted to receive that letter for altho' it has caused me some anxiety that has been more than counterbalanced by the comfort of knowing that God raised up friends for you in your time of need & I take it as an earnest that he will continue to do so. He has been very good to my precious boys tho' they have suffered there have been many alleviating circumstances.

When I wrote last I beg'd you to call on the Alstons & express your gratitude & mine also, let them see that their kindness was so much felt that you mentioned it to your friends. We used to think when Mr. D received letters from his Mother it was very strange that there was no word of thanks for what was done for him & though all was done for the *soldier* yet it is very pleasant to know that kindness is appreciated. Never mind not having nice clothes, the gentleman is readily distinguished even through very shabby clothing as we know from our own observation of those who stop'd to claim our hospitality at different times & while we were glad to extend it to the humblest soldier it was doubly pleasant to serve one who could appreciate the gentle kindness bestowed because he felt more the want of home & friends.

I feel now that the time is come for me to suffer the anxiety & suspense endured by so many Mothers thro'out our country, but I daily bless God for my more abundant consolation in the assurance that whatever I may be called to suffer it will be well with my dear ones & when my heart goes out after you in yearning tenderness then the promise comes to me "tho' a *mother* may forget yet will not I" & this comforts me when I feel the impossibility of doing any thing for you. I hope you will continue in the Telegraph Service but even that I must leave to the direction of Providence. Should you have a severe cough try your best to come home. A cough left by measles is very apt without care to fall on the lungs.

I thought of sending you some money by Smith but A. tells me you are supplied. If you should need any when you are about any where where

Smith is known, borrow & get S. to endorse for you. Your Father can meet the demand. There is no use in trying to hold back what we have. All will go probably by the time the war is over & we shall all have to work for which I trust God will give us stout hearts & willing hands. If he spares my best treasures I feel that I can let all else go. A. seems much better than when he came home & now & then we think he will soon be well but his disease shows itself again & gives evidence that it is in his blood still. He must have been in a suffering condition before he came home from what I have seen of the eruption & the extent of it manifested by his clothing. He is gone to town today to see a hospital surgeon about a longer stay here.

We see the DuBoses now & then they are quite sociable we all like Mrs Campbell best. I am very glad the Stewarts have not called on us for from all accounts they are very unladylike. Miss Downes & one of them stop'd at the fence a short time since to ask if you were at home.[1] The winter has been much more severe here than we expected & I have felt the cold I think more than I used to at home I suppose on account of the constant changes & partly from our being in a comparatively open house. Today it is quite warm & Father is busy planting some sugar cane some of which I trust you will eat. We are all in usual health. A. has returned with a recommendation of 30 days longer. Do darling look out for some way to write to us & try not to give way to depression. Remember the Lord reigns & tho' clouds & darkness veil his dealings all is light to him & he will bring to pass what is for his own glory.

All unite in love to you. I fear it will be a long time before I can hear from you or write again but I leave you with the Lord who is your ever present friend & parent & who can do more for you than even the Mother who loves you so tenderly.

1. The DuBoses, Stewarts, and Downses were all from Camden County. Ann E. Stewart, with whom Willie stayed when he taught school in St. Marys, had been Ann Eliza Downs before her marriage, and five members of that family were living with her when the 1860 census of Camden County was taken (Thompson, comp., *People of Camden County, Georgia*, 200). Mrs. Campbell remains unidentified.

P. RITCHARD TO F. W. CAPERS

Valdosta Hospital

February 25th 1865

This will certify that Cadet A. Smith of the Battalion of Georgia Cadets, is under my care & treatment and in my opinion will require the elapse of thirty days from date to restore him sufficiently for his return to and performance of military services.

P. Ritchard
surgeon in charge

HᵈQʳˢ Batt of Cadets
Milledgeville Feb 28, 1865
Extension approved for 30 days

F. W. Capers
Supᵗ Geo Mil Inst

WILLIAM TO MOTHER

Gourdins Station N.E.R.R.[1]
Feb 24/65

Dear Mother

I have just a chance to send a letter to *Georgia*. I passed from Georges thro' Charleston just in time to help evacuate and am temporarily here. The army is on the move & I go with it & do not think you will hear from me often. I am getting on very well. Have had a shake of chills but they were easily broken. I would like very much to hear from home but can not tell you where to direct in fact there is no use for you to write for a while.

Some thing will have to happen soon as things are coming to a crisis. Tom Clay has been so fortunate as to get himself ordered to Florida. I have made some efforts to the same end but have been too far from HᵈQrs. to effect any thing. I shall continue to try but soon the country will be too much occupied between here & Georgia for me to be able to get thro'. However Providence will direct all for the best. I have heard nothing more from friends in Savannah. Some of them wanted to come out but now there is no way for them to come.

I am now very well and weigh more than ever. Much Love to all

your afft son Wᵐ

1. This station was on the Northeastern Railroad between Charleston and Florence, South Carolina.

WILLIAM TO MOTHER[1]

Raleigh N.C. Mar 14 65[2]

Dear Mother

I believe my last was from Gourdins S.C. From that place we came up by R.R. to Cheraw, but as Sherman was pressing very close on our heels and Hardee had not more than 12,000 men, we did not stay there long but began to march towards Greensboro N.C. Circumstances however made it necessary for us to turn off to Fayetteville where our stay was shorter than at Cheraw and for the same reasons. I found the marching very fatiguing altho we only went about eleven miles per day and I managed to put part of my luggage on some of the wagons.

I saw Johnnie Barnwell and Lieut Heill in Fayetteville and heard of Woodie tho' I did not see him.[3] I heard that Smith was expected to be up with the army in a few days so I hope to have some later accounts from you the last letter I rec[d] was dated Jan 21st.

I can not say I am quite well as I had fever yesterday from the continued fatigue, but am well today and hope a day or two rest here will set me all right again and besides I think we will go by R.R. from this place. This place is about as large as Marietta and the surrounding country is about the same in fact reminds me very much of Cobb Co.

I tried again the other day to be sent to Florida or S.W. Ga. but Lieut Memminger[4] said he could not do it so I am afraid there is no present prospect of my getting home. All the hardships of marching have made me value and wish for home more than ever.

Much Love to all

Your afft Son W[m]

---

1. On the envelope Anne Magill Smith wrote, "Last letter from my darling."

2. Willie has reached Raleigh ahead of General Hardee, who arrived a day later before proceeding to Averasboro. Willie was admitted to a Confederate hospital in Raleigh on March 17.

3. Perhaps Dr. John Smith Barnwell (1836–87), a Confederate army physician and brother of Archibald Smith Barnwell, and Woodward Barnwell (Barnwell, *Story of an American Family,* 209, 255). We have not been able to identify Lieutenant Heill.

4. Probably 1st Lieutenant Christopher E. Memminger, a Signal Corps officer (National Archives Microfilm Publications, *Compiled Service Records of Confederate Soldiers Who Served in Organizations Raised Directly by the Confederate Government,* roll 119).

P. RITCHARD TO F. W. CAPERS

Valdosta Hospital
March 25th 1865

This will certify that Cadet A. Smith still continues in my opinion unfit for Duty or travelling, and I recommend an extension of *Thirty* days to his furlough, as necessary to restore him sufficiently for the performance of Military service.

P Ritchard
Surgeon in charge

ARCHIBALD SMITH TO REV. I. S. AXSON

Valdosta Lowndes C[o] G[a] May 30/65

Revd I. S. K. Axson[1]

My Dear Sir

I am in much anxiety about my Son W[m] S. Smith, and apply to you to assist me, in the confidence that your friendship & Christian sympathy will lead you to do all you can to aid me. The last account that I have been able to get of William, was, that he was sick of Typhus fever in Raleigh N. C. when our forces left that place.

If you can find any means of communicating with that city, please write to the Presbyterian Minister there, (who no doubt has been doing the Lord's work in the Hospitals) and ask him to find out the circumstances of my Son, if he is yet alive; and assist him until I may be able to send on the means of his coming home, & repay any expense which he may be at for him.

Or if he has gone to his rest let us know what he can find out of last moments.

William Seagrove Smith was a member of the Signal Corps in Savannah & left with the army when it evacuated Sav[h]. His last letter to us was from Raleigh dated 14 March. He had a fever the day before, & a Confed[e] Surgeon told a friend that he had left him ill of typhoid fever when our army left.

My family is comfortably situated in a hired house near Valdosta & we are all well at present.

M[rs] Smith joins me in kind regards to yourself & M[rs] Axson.

I am your Brother in Christ.

Arch[d] Smith

P. S. June 6th Since writing the above our Minister here[2] has been so good as to write to an acquaintance in Raleigh about William; the letter I enclose, and I will be obliged to you if you will send it by a different conveyance, from the one you may be pleased to write.

DAVID COMFORT TO REV. JOS. M. ATKINSON

Valdosta, Georgia
June 6th 1865

Revd Jos. M. Atkinson[3]
Raleigh, No. Ca.
Dear Bro,

Hoping that this letter may find you in Raleigh I write in behalf of a friend to request you to make some inquiries in your city about his son.

His name is Wm S. Smith, is a son of Archd Smith Esq, late of Roswell Georgia, an Elder in Dr Pratt's church, but temporarily resident here near Valdosta, Lowndes Co. Georgia; belonged to the Signal Corps of Genl Johnston's army, & was left sick with typhoid fever on the 9th of April last in the hospital in Raleigh, since which time his friends have heard nothing from him.

You will confer a lasting favor upon us all by writing to his father whatever information you may be able to get concerning him, & rendering him all the assistance you can if he still survives.

If he is dead, as they fear he is, it will gratify his friends here to know the particulars of his death. He has been for several years a consistent member of our Church, & was doubtless prepared to go, if in the wise providence of God he has been called away from earth.

A letter would be most likely to reach his father, Archd Smith Esq, if directed to Valdosta Georgia & sent by mail under cover to Wm Duncan Esq., Savannah, Georgia.

May the grace of God abundantly suffice to support & sustain you.

Your bro. in Christ
David Comfort

1. Isaac Stockton Keith Axson (1813–91) was pastor of the Independent Presbyterian Church in Savannah from 1857 to 1891 (Scott, comp., *Ministerial Directory*, 24).

2. David Comfort (1837–73) was the first regular minister at the Valdosta Presbyterian Church (ibid., 144). Archibald Smith helped to found this church and was chosen one of its three ruling elders when it was organized on December 3, 1864 (Carson, "History," 12).

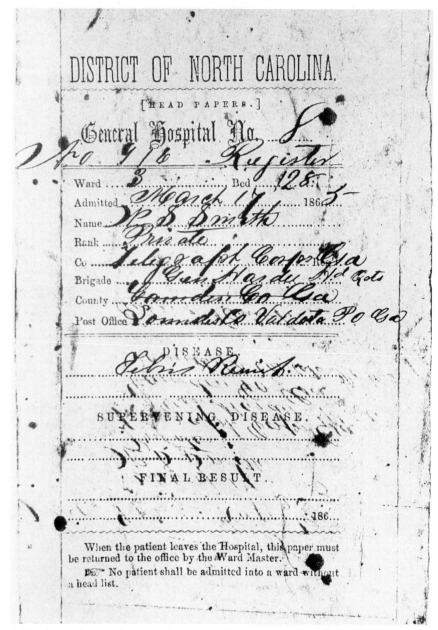

Willie's "Head Papers," concerning his admission to Confederate hospitals in Raleigh, North Carolina. The form indicates that he was at the time attached to Hardee's head-quarters. On the back of the form he wrote to a Mr. Johnston, "Dear Sir, Gen. Hardee's Headquarters has been broken up and I have been ordered back to my company. Had not you better make out a new head paper in case of exchange. I cannot be found by this. Yours respectf., W.S. Smith."

Willie's oath not to take up arms, dated May 9, 1865, and signed with an X

3. Joseph Mayo Atkinson (1820–91) was the minister of the First Presbyterian Church in Raleigh, North Carolina, from 1855 to 1875 (Scott, comp., *Ministerial Directory*, 23).

MOTHER TO WILLIAM

Valdosta June 6th 1865

Beloved Son

Our hearts & our faith are sorely tried on your account as the only intelligence we have had of you is that you were left ill in a hospital in Raleigh when our troops left that place. This we heard from the Barnwells who all reached here safely. O! my son if we had not the assurance of your being a child of God how could we endure this agony of suspense. It almost breaks my heart to think of one so kind & affectionate being left without one earthly friend to minister to your comfort, yet I daily bless God for the assurance that tho' even a Mother may forget yet he never will, & our constant prayer is that he will be with you & make up by the manifestation of himself for all your trials & privations. He does uphold us & enable us to cast this our heaviest burden on him. Since the failure of our hopes for our country we have so earnestly longed to have you with us that you might aid us in council as to our future, & we feel if you are taken away the strong staff on which we hoped to lean has been wrenched out of our hand, yet we know that our loss would be to your unspeakable gain & we try to leave you entirely with God & say thy will be done. We are as well as usual. A. still with us.

May God bless & keep you my precious child & raise up friends for you in your time of need. If you should be raised up it will be long before you can endure the fatigues of a march. Try & induce the authorities to send you by Steamer from Wilmington to Sav. or Jacksonville. From the latter place there is less difficulty in your reaching us.

Your aff
Mother

MARGARET COWPER MACKAY ELLIOTT
TO ANNE MAGILL SMITH

Savannah June 2nd 1865[1]

I have delayed answering your letter to the last moment my dear Anne in the hope that my son John would arrive from Augusta & be able to give me some tidings of William that might relieve your anxiety, but I am sorry to say John has not come. He was detained in Augusta by chill & fever. Ralph is here. He was separated from the others at the fall of Charleston and has been very sick with typhoid fever at a village in N C called Lanesboro'. He travelled as long as he could combat the sickness but broke down entirely on the 6th April. He remained there more than a month & then resumed his journey. In the mean time John had reached Augusta & hearing of Rs sickness, Habby E. & himself returned to N C for Ralph.[2] They met him on the road & all went to Augusta together & R came on at once to me. He says John had heard that William S. was better but cannot tell who John heard it from or give any particulars. He has been so sick & is so reduced that he does not know much. This grieves me my dear Anne. I know how very trying suspense & uncertainty are and I am distressed that you should feel it. May God support & comfort you & grant that you may hear good news of him soon.

. . . I met y^r brother Seagrove[3] in the street about two months ago. He did not know me but I recognized him at once. A strong impulse came over me & I spoke to him. I believe the reason was he looked so much like you. I could not help it. He had just come out of the old Methodist church which is now used as a school for darkies. He is or was superintendent. He was quite polite when I introduced myself but I am afraid I was not very cordial as the interview lasted only a few seconds. I was so disconcerted by his not asking me a word about you or your family that I did not know what to say. I only asked if he intended to remain here long. His answer was that his time was limited & he did not know if he might prolong it. He had called on my sisters, when he first came, as the agent of a Soc^y to assist those in need & asked C to help him to find proper objects but she told him she did not know of any one. He did not ask her a word about you which I thought extraordinary so I was sure he would ask me.

Our family is smaller than usual, Caroline is in Augusta her husband with her, they are staying with Mrs Carmichael & I dont know if they will return here before fall, in the meantime we have a Yankee lodger (not boarder) who pays 15 a month for the use of a room! This helps us to pay servants' wages. We have very few & live so strangely that it would be very amusing if it were not too sad. An ignorant plantation boy for waiter, two old crones for chambermaids & nurses, and a cook, comprise the only four to feed which is a great consideration. Leila keeps house now P. is gone & does a great deal. Mary makes up bouquets & baskets of flowers & sends them out to sell.[4] She has made more than 50 dollars in this way which is quite a help. Give all our love to your sister & daughters and to the men too. I am truly glad Archie is with you. If I should hear any thing I will try to inform you. My sisters all send love & sympathy in this your trying suspense believe me my dear friend

Yours ever very aff^y MCE

Do remember us to the Barnwell girls if they are in y^r neighbourhood.

1. This letter has been placed out of sequence to maintain a logical flow of events.

2. Margaret Elliott's children, Ralph Emms Elliott (b. 1846) and John Mackay Elliott (1844–1929), along with their cousin, Robert Habersham Elliott (1846–1936), the fourth child of Episcopal Bishop Stephen Elliott (1806–66) of South Carolina and his second wife, Charlotte Bull Elliott (1810–95) (Barnwell, *Story of an American Family,* 145).

3. Before the beginning of the Civil War, Anne Smith's brother, Seagrove William Magill (1810–84) had removed from his native Camden County, Georgia, to Connecticut, from which the Magill family had originally come to the South. He returned to Georgia to organize freedman schools for the American Missionary Association (correspondence with his great-great-grandson, Walter E. Ziebarth of Hamburg, New York).

4. Margaret Elliott speaks of her children. Caroline (1842–94) had married her cousin Major Robert Woodward Barnwell Elliott. After the war, they moved to Texas, where he was consecrated bishop of West Texas and founded twenty-seven parishes before his death in 1887. Her daughter Leila had lost her husband, Frederick Augustus Habersham (1831–63) at Fredericksburg. Mary Stiles Mackay (1838–1919) married twice. Her first marriage was to Robert Habersham (1838–62), an infantry lieutenant until his death in Atlanta. She later married Joseph Alston Huger (1842–1919). "P" is her daughter Phoebe (1833–66). Her other son, Percival (1840–65), had been severely wounded at Sayler's Creek, Virginia, on April 6th, only three days before the armistice, and died on May 30th, only three days before this letter was written. Clearly Margaret had not yet heard the tragic news of her own son's death (Barnwell, *Story of an American Family,* 232, 150).

Raleigh June 20 '65

Dear Sir

It is with great pain I am compelled to inform you of the continued and dangerous illness of your Son, Mr. William Smith, formerly a soldier of the confederate army. About four weeks [ago] your son with two other fellow soldiers was brought, for his greater comfort as we hoped from the hospital to our house; and we have endeavored to render him every attention in our power. I say this to relieve any apprehension you may entertain that he has suffered from neglect. One of his fellow soldiers has died, the other has recovered and gone home. Your son was afflicted when he came to us with chronick diarrhoea, occasionally assuming the form of dysentery. He has had medical advice from Confederate surgeons to within a day or two, but the disease has not yet been successfully arrested; and as his strength is continually decreasing, I very much fear for his life, should the complaint continue much longer.

I know my dear Sir, that sympathy must necessarily be a much feebler emotion than original distress, but I can assure you that we, my family, have felt that sympathy very deeply for your son, not only from his situation, but from the interest we have taken in him personally from his Christian character, and from his superior manner and attainments.

Be pleased to let me know if there are any wishes respecting your Son you desire should be carried out, either if he should recover, which, I pray, if God's will may be, or if the contrary should seem good to Him to inflict you with so severe a distress as the loss of your son.

I remain, Sir,

With sincere sympathy

Yours in the gospel

R. S. Mason

Address
Rev. Dr. R. S. Mason
Raleigh
N.C.

1. The Reverend Dr. Richard Sharp Mason (1795–1874) was the rector of the Protestant Episcopal Church of Raleigh. His wife, Mary Ann Mason (1802–81), had found Willie in a Confederate hospital that was breaking up after Joe Johnston, near Durham, North Carolina, on April 21, surrendered the remaining Confederate forces east of the Mississippi.

Augusta July 15, 1865

My Dear Sir

The accompanying letter from Dr Mason of Raleigh, N.C. was enclosed in one to me of the date of *June 20,* but only reached me this morning. I forward it to Savannah immediately, under cover to Miss Mackay, requesting her to get it to you with all dispatch.

It relates to your Son William who has been under the hospitable roof of Dr Mason, the Episcopal Clergyman of Raleigh, N.C., since about the middle of May. His disease, which is chronic Diarrhoea, does not yield to medicine & Dr Mason has become very uneasy about his condition. I regret that there has been so much delay in the transmission of this letter, but the fault has been in the postal arrangements. It reached me only this morning.

If I can be of any service to you in this matter, please make use of me. I shall be in Augusta until about the 8th of August.

With sincere sympathies for William's condition, I am Dear Sir, very sincerely

Stephen Elliott

P.S. It may comfort Mrs Smith & yourself to know that Dr Mason's family is one of the pleasantest & kindest in the Southern Country & that William has received, under his roof, as much attention as he could have received any where, except at home.

S. E.

1. Bishop Stephen Elliott (1806–66), whose marriages had been to two of his Barnwell cousins—Mary Gibbes (1808–37) and Charlotte Bull (1810–85)—was the father of the Habby Elliott mentioned in Margaret Cowper Mackay Elliott's letter of June 2.

WILLIAM DUNCAN TO ARCHIBALD SMITH
Sav^h July 17 1865

Mr A. Smith
Valdosta
Dear Sir,

I applied for & got control of the Wharf & Stores, but they are in a miserable condition the wharf head, all broken out—the stores terribly injured— locks broken, windows out—doors battered—&^{c} & will require a considerable outlay for repair, the stores not so much, but the wharf, 2a 3000$ I judge, at the least. How do you propose to meet that? I will try & rent the Stores & get the occupants to repair, deducting from rent, or renting at a reduced rate. I got possession on my statement, that the property is undivided, & belonging in part to minors. I have written you 3 letters about your Son, and in one I sent you, his letter to me. I must suppose that he is with you ere this, & wonder you have not written me saying so.

Mrs D has written twice to Mrs Smith.

Yrs
W. Duncan

SARAH MACKAY[1] TO ANNE MAGILL SMITH

19 July

My dear Cousin

We have long been very anxious about Willy & in a most uncertain state concerning him. Any thing definite is better than all you have undergone since hearing of his illness. The Bishop's letter tho of an old date is the last news we have had.[2] I feel the chances are against him & yet we are not entirely hopeless, such wonderful cures do sometimes occur I cannot help *hoping* it may please the Almighty yet to restore him to his family. Poor fellow he must have undergone great suffering & we feel deeply for you all to have been separated from him & denied the comfort of nursing & soothing him in his illness as none can do like his own parents and sisters.

But one comfort you have which nothing can deprive you of, living or dying. You are sure Willy is God's child & a Father's love will only send what is best for His dear children. We grieve for you all & this suspense is truly fearful, be assured of the warmest sympathy of us all. I don't know if you have heard of Percy's death on the 30th May at the Lincoln Hospital in Washington D. C. Phoebe was with him & we never gave up hope of his recovery till the end came.[3] The poor boy had his leg taken off & lived three weeks after. He was cheerful happy & resigned all thro his suffering & his mind was kept in perfect peace trusting in Christ his Saviour. My dear Cousins may the Gracious Lord sustain & comfort you as He has Margaret & all of us in all our trials. My dear Sister & her children are cheerful not withstanding their grief, they feel so sure of Percy's happiness they suffer willingly the loss of his dear presence among them. Phoebe met with great kindness from friends in Baltimore.

I am so thankful to feel God has raised up so kind a friend for Willy in his hour of need but I do indeed wish you could (some of you) be with him both for your sakes & his. If you have an opportunity do let us know how you all are. Mr Duncan sent us a note to say he could forward a letter for us so I send this. Robert is going to no. 9 next week when we will write again should we hear any thing but this is scarcely possible.[4] Your trial is greatly increased by suspense but I know you feel, dear Cousin, [the] Lord directs it all & will suffer patiently all He sends. Perhaps He will yet raise your boy up. Nothing is impossible with him. . . . I could write a great deal more about the family but will not intrude now as I know Willys state will occupy you entirely. You must not attribute it to want of feeling for you that I have written so much of other subjects. My sisters all join me in love & sympathy & so do the young people. John & Ralph are both so much attached to Willy they feel much his illness Love to Cousin John Helen & the girls.[5]

Yrs affy S. Mackay

1. This letter was written by Sarah Mackay (1815–76), the sister of Margaret Cowper Mackay Elliott.

2. Bishop Stephen Elliott's letter above of July 15 is not "of old date." She may be referring to Dr. Mason's letter of June 20, which the Bishop had forwarded.

3. Her sister Margaret's son, Percival, and daughter, Phoebe.

4. Her sister Elizabeth's son, Robert Mackay Elliott (1836–74).

5. Margaret's sons, John Mackay Elliott and Ralph Emms Elliott. The last words in the sentence seem to refer to John Joyner Smith, Helen Zubly Magill, Lizzie Smith, and Helen Zubly Smith.

REV. DR. R. S. MASON TO WILLIAM DUNCAN[1]

Raleigh June 30 '65

Sir

I just now received your letter, and am sorry to tell you that Mr. Smith is at present unable to travel. He is still at my house, to which he was removed about five or six weeks ago from the hospital, with two other fellow soldiers, one of whom died soon after being with us, and the other has recovered and gone home. I think Mr. Smith's situation is precarious. As the doctor expressed it, he has a good deal of vitality, his pulse and voice being both good, but he does not gain strength, while his disease still continues. He has been afflicted with diarrhoea, and occasionally dysentery, now one or other chronick.

He is in no need of money at present, as we endeavour to administer to all his wants. When he does need it, I will endeavour to supply him, though at present it is very difficult to be obtained.

I remain Sir
Yours with regard

W. Duncan Esqr   R. S. Mason

P. S. Mr. Smith begs his kind regards. Perhaps it would be as well to send him money, as I am afraid he would hardly be able to travel before it reaches him. He needs at present summer clothing.

1. This letter to Duncan was enclosed with the one that follows it, from Duncan to the Smiths.

WILLIAM DUNCAN TO ARCHIBALD SMITH
Sav^h July 21, 1865

M^r A Smith
Valdosta

Dear Sir, I have just rec^d the enclosed letter from Mr Mason of Raleigh and although the intelligence is not as favorable as you would wish, let us hope that the vitality, good pulse & voice, of which the D^r speaks, are indications of his ability to struggle through the disease.

Currency with me is a scarce article, but I managed to send by this days mail to Mr Mason a dft on N York for $50, which I hope will be needed for summer clothes for W^m.

It is gratifying to you to know that he is well cared for, as I am sure he is by the Revd Gentleman.

I sincerely hope we shall have better accounts of W^m, in the meantime I sympathise with you, in your present uncertainty. I send this to Blackshear, (to be forwarded,) by Genl Brannan's Courier to Genl Washburn.[1]

I am with kind regards
Yr obt S^t
W. Duncan

to your brother—
Mrs Duncan & all my family, have gone to Madison Ga

1. Mr. Duncan is referring to two federal generals who now oversee affairs in his area, John Milton Brannon (1819–92) and Cadwallader Colden Washburn (1818–82).

WILLIAM DUNCAN TO ARCHIBALD SMITH
Savannah July 24, 1865

Mr A. Smith

Dear Sir   Your favor of 17th with accompanying documents rec^d to day and can only acknowledge the rec^t as I have but a short time to embrace the opportunity of a party going out in the morning. The letter which I mentioned having sent to you, in my letter to Smith was one addressed to me (not to you) by W^m. I dont recollect by whom I sent it but think it was sent to Mr Macdonald.[1] At same time I wrote to you and Uncle John.

I have since, (three days ago) written you again, and enclosed a letter from Revd Mr Mason to me, giving quite unfavorable accts of W^m which I trust you will receive—it is addressed care of RRoad Agent Valdosta. In that letter I mentioned having sent Mr Mason, $50 for William's use, and told him I w^d be answerable for whatever more might be needed. I told him also, that W^{ms} Parents would take the first oppty to express their appreciation of and warmest gratitude to him for his kindness to their boy. . . .

Yrs Wm Duncan

1. The Smiths apparently never received the letter in question. Mail service at this time was irregular and unreliable.

MARGARET COWPER MACKAY ELLIOTT
TO ANNE MAGILL SMITH

Savannah July 24th 1865

I grieve for the distress in which you have been plunged my dear Anne by the sad accounts from Raleigh of the continued illness of your dear son. John arrived soon after I wrote you, but the account he brought was of so old a date that I was certain you had more recent tidings. Indeed I hoped most sincerely that William had reached you via Augusta & Macon especially after we knew that Mr Duncan had rec^d a letter from W^m himself. It seems John had been sent to some other point and was only in Raleigh part of two days—he heard William was quite sick in the hospital & then he immediately went—he thought him *very* sick and was with him a great deal for the short time he was there read the Bible to him frequently at William's request & did hate to leave him but was obliged to go where he was sent. This was on the 27th March. On the 5th April some others of the Signal Corps saw William in the same hospital & reported to John that his condition was not improved so John continued very anxious but hoped the best. After that he had no certain information only vague reports that W^m was better until he heard after his arrival here of the letter Mr Duncan had rec^d as late as the 19th May—so we were sure all was right—and our own grief was pressing very heavily upon us. My dear Percy's sufferings were ended by a peaceful & happy death on the 30th May. His sister would not leave his precious remains on the soil of the enemy so she went with them to Baltimore & then our friends the Glenns gave him Xtian burial & a grave, among their kindred. Phoebe was dreadfully worn out mind & body & remained for two weeks to recruit before she came home which she was obliged to do via NY she is now well & so are all except John. His constitution seems to be much injured by the hardships of the last campaign. He is gone into a counting room at 20 dollars a month (George gets 5 per month in the same place which I am truly thankful for as it saves him from idleness)—We are *very very* poor & have the most forlorn servants that I ever saw they are neither able nor willing to do much & the girls have to work too hard.[1]

Our heavenly Father is trying us severely but there are a thousand mercies mixed with all the greatest of which is that my darling was ripe for heaven when God took him. If you my dear Friend should have the same trial to undergo you will have the same consolation, but I hope you may not have your suspense ended as mine was. With much love to you all in which the family join I am ever yours aff^c

MCE

I saw Dr Masons letter & the Bishop's to Sarah which have been forwarded to you—you know you are much in our thoughts.

1. Margaret Elliott's references in this paragraph are to her remaining children, John Mackay, Phoebe, and George Herbert (1849–82).

JOSEPH M. ATKINSON TO ARCHIBALD SMITH
Raleigh, N.C. July 10th 1865[1]

My dear Sir,

It gives me pain to be obliged to communicate to you the fact of the death of your beloved and most excellent Son.

I received not only your letter in regard to him but one from Dr. Axson and two from the Rev Mr. Comfort. I made inquiry without loss of time at the only hospital where Confederate Soldiers now are without success. Afterwards I found him on the premises of the Rev. Dr. Mason, the Ep. clergyman here. Your son was specially favoured by a gracious Providence in falling into the hands of a most excellent Christian family from whom he received those attentions which are so soothing and so needful to an invalid. He remained for more than two months in a perfectly comfortable tent in Dr. Mason's yard and had the attentions of one of the most eminent physicians in the State, Dr. Johnson.[2] His death was very unexpected to us all: for though no one thought he could recover no one thought he would die so soon. I had a very satisfactory interview with him the day before he died and was greatly comforted to find him in a cheerful and most Christian frame of mind looking forward to the prospect of his approaching death without the least apprehension, in humble reliance in the ministry and grace of the Redeemer.

I conducted his funeral service which was attended by Dr. Mason and his family and other friends: his pallbearers were Confederate soldiers and his interment decent and seemly.

With the deepest sympathy for your grief, I remain

Very truly

Yr. friend & brother

Joseph M. Atkinson

1. The Smiths first learned of Willie's death by means of this letter, probably received in Valdosta at the very end of July. Although its date falls out of sequence with several of the letters above, we have elected to place it here by reason of its content. The lack of sequence in the 1865 correspondence is, of course, owing to the disruptions in all communication following the Confederate surrender, a disruption that must have caused the Smiths untold anguish as they waited to learn of Willie's fate. According to a note penned by Helen Zubly Magill at the top of Mary Mason's letter of July 20, the Smiths did not hear directly from the Masons about Willie's death until August 18.

2. According to the 1870 census of North Carolina, Charles Johnson (1812?–76) was a physician who lived near the Mason family in Raleigh.

MARY ANN MASON[1] TO ANNE MAGILL SMITH

Rec'd Aug. 18th 1865[2]

Raleigh July 20th

My Dear Madam,

It has become my painful duty to tell you that our efforts have all been in vain to save your excellent Son from the lot of martyrs. He died as he had lived, calm, peaceful and resigned to the will of Heaven. He came to me in the latter part of the month of April, and never for one moment has he evinced the least impatience or discontent at the decrees of Divine Providence in his disposal. I found him with two other sick soldiers in the Peace Hospital near my house,[3] and became very much interested in them, so that when the Yankees were about to remove the inmates of this Hospital to another some distance from here, I resolved to take them to my own home. As the weather was getting warm, and they had been accustomed to a tent, I thought as they did, that it would be best for them to continue in one, and according one was obtained and placed in my front yard under the shade of trees.

One, quite a boy, came in a settled consumption and only survived a week. Another as I thought the oldest of the three with typhoid fever recovered and returned home in S. Carolina some four weeks ago. So that for the last period my whole attn has been given to your Son.

At first his disease I am told was typhoid fever; then erisypelas, which continued to affect him more or less to the close, though an unconquerable diarrhea completed the exhaustion of his life.[4] Every thing that medicine could do was done, but nothing could stay the fatal disease. At six o'clock on the evening of the 7th of this month your truly pious son slept with Jesus. All our family were constantly with him, and near him. My husband and five grown daughters were his constant attendants. And to assure you of his well being with us, I must tell you, he said on one occasion to one of my daughters, "If it were not to see the dear ones at home I should like to stay here always."

He used to tell me I reminded him of his mother, and he felt like calling me Mother all the while. But alas now that I have lost my patient, I feel as if I had never done half enough for him. But when these misgivings come over me, my comfort is to recall his own words to me. "My mother could not do more if she were here." These things I tell you dear Madam only to assure your mother's heart that your son was not neglected. But Oh I can not tell you how ardently he longed to see you and all his "dear ones at home" as he continually said. How reverently, how tenderly he spoke of father, mother, sisters, and brother. His heart was with you always, but he said to me he had no doubt it was for his eternal good that God had thus tried him & kept him from his home and friends. The day before he died he received your letter. It was indeed a cordial to him. He could scarcely contain himself for joy. That night just before she retired one of My Daughters "Annie" stepped to his tent door and said how do you feel tonight Mr. Smith?

"Oh Glorious!" he answered. "I have heard from home."

On the following morning I found he was growing much weaker and his disease overpowering. All hope was gone by noon. He lay in unconscious quietude. Once I called to my Son William who was outside the tent, and he opened his eyes, fixed them full in my face and answered "Mother!" This dear word was the last he ever spoke. I think he supposed his own mother called him.

Tranquilly as an infant he breathed for the last three or four hours and passed into the world of bliss, without a sigh. But Oh Christian Mother I bid you rejoice in laying up this precious treasure in heaven. Doubt not to meet him there.

Ambrotype of his mother in Willie's locket

My dear Madam think me not remiss, in performing this sad duty earlier, for indeed I have been in a sick bed from the day of your dear Son's death. I commenced a letter the next day while he lay tranquilly awaiting his interment. I tried to write while he lay within my sight but such was my weakness I found I could not write anything that you could read. I could not read it myself. So that I was forced to postpone the duty. . . . 6 confederate soldiers young men from the first families here, all in their grey uniforms, act[ed] as the bearers of their lamented comrade in arms. My daughters sang "I would not live alway!" to: (Home Sweet Home). O! I wish you could have been there it was lovely. A bright wreath of fresh flowers graced his coffin. We all followed him to his last resting place. A kind friend loaned me his carriage for I was too sick to walk. I sat on a stone by his grave till all was as it should be.

He had a coffin ordered by myself. It was colored like black walnut varnished and lined with fine white muslin cushioned at the bottom and a nice little pillow, with book muslin on the face.

I closed his eyes myself. I assisted in bathing him as tenderly as you could have done it yourself. I am also, a mother. I helped to put him in his coffin.

I have put away his knapsack and some little valuables which await your order. I can think of nothing more necessary to be done. He rests in our cemetery where he wished to be "with a community of pious dead." Oh! how I wish we could have communicated with you, & you could have been here. But we must acquiesce in the dispensations of Providence as our dear departed one said.

At your convenience dear Madam I hope you will let me hear from you and know if you have received this letter and how to dispose of what is in my charge belonging to your son: and may a gracious God and Saviour comfort your afflicted heart and those of your remaining family. Present my regards to your husband and my warmest sympathy in his affliction. To his brother and sisters say my children took their places and did all they could to cheer and enliven their beloved brother while passing to his heavenly reward. He was attached to them all as they were to him. We trust to meet him in a better and happier world.

That God will please to comfort and console your hearts in this great bereavement is the earnest prayer of yours the bonds of the blessed Gospel of Christ

Mary Mason

1. Mary Ann Bryan Mason (1802–81), the wife of the Reverend Dr. Richard Sharp Mason, was an author as well as the mother of five sons and five daughters. *A Wreath*

The Reverend Dr.
Richard Sharp Mason
(1795–1874)

from the Woods of Carolina (1859) and *Her Church and Her Mother* (1860) were published by the General Protestant Episcopal Sunday School Union and Church Book Society in New York. In the Smiths' library in Roswell were found copies of *Spring-Time for Sowing* (1860) and *The Young Housewife's Counsellor and Friend* (1871), which was published by J. B. Lippincott in Philadelphia. Mary Ann Mason was also a painter, musician, and sculptor whose cameos were especially admired. We are grateful to Elizabeth Reid Murray of Raleigh for information about Dr. and Mrs. Mason.

2. This line is in Helen Zubly Magill's hand at the top of the letter.

3. In addition to private homes and the basement of the First Baptist Church, the unfinished building of the Peace Institute, now Peace College, in Raleigh served as a Confederate hospital for the wounded from the battles of Averasboro (March 16, 1865) and Bentonville (March 19–21, 1865) (Barrett, *Civil War*, 375).

4. During the Civil War, "diarrhea in its various forms, including dysentery, claimed more lives than battlefield wounds" (Faust, ed., *Historical Times Illustrated Encyclopedia*, 484).

REV. DR. R. S. MASON TO ARCHIBALD SMITH

Raleigh July 26 '65

Dear Sir,

At last I am obliged to communicate to you with much pain, the death of your excellent Christian son, who after struggling with his disease, or I should rather say diseases, has finally fallen a victim to them.

About the beginning of last May, an hospital in our neighbourhood was broken up, and the greater part of the patients sent to another hospital in our town. Some of the patients who were sickest were received into families in the neighbourhood of the hospital which had thus been broken up, by the U. States authorities. Among the other neighbours, we received three of the sick in a spacious and comfortable tent sent from the hospital. Your son was one of the number. The youngest of the three died soon after being with us in spite of all the care we could give him and the hope we entertained at one time of his recovery. Another recovered after some weeks from a severe attack of typhoid fever, and returned home. Your son appeared at first the least diseased of the three, and indeed rendered some assistance in the beginning to his fellow sufferers, but I soon began to fear that his disease would prove fatal, as I found that it was not at all removed while his strength continually diminished. At length, after various fluctuations of appearing somewhat better, and then getting worse, life ceased on the morning of the 7th of this month, and he was buried on the afternoon of the 8th by the Presbyterian minister of this place, as I supposed it would be more in conformity with the religious opinions & feelings of his friends to have a clergyman of the denomination to which his family and as I understood himself belonged.

I and indeed my whole family, became very much interested in and attached to your son not only from his having been so long with us, but from his gentlemanly bearing and great intelligence, showing his superior breeding and education. What gave confirmation to these impressions was the pious resignation which your son manifested through the whole of his complaints, a desire to recover if it was the will of God, and to return to his home, but ready to depart and to be with Christ. He died as I fully think in Christian faith and hope.

As I judged that his parents would be desirous, as he was himself, of receiving not a pompous or extravagant but a respectable funeral, I took care that such would be the case.

The particulars of the expense incurred I have sent on to Savannah to Mr. Duncan who I understand is your agent.

Mary Ann Mason
(1802–81)

With the trust that the gracious Lord whom we serve will enable you, dear friend, to support the great loss you have sustained, and with the sincerest sympathies of me and mine.

> I remain
> faithfully Your friend
> in Christ Jesus
> R. S. Mason

P.S. I hope I shall have the satisfaction of hearing from you direct to
Rev. Dr. R. S. Mason
Raleigh
N. C.

2nd P.S. I ought to have mentioned that the diseases with which your Son was afflicted were Erisypelas, & chronick Diarrhoea alternating with Dysentery. From the former he nearly recovered but the latter proved fatal.

> R. S. M.

2. P. S. I was near omitting a very important part of this communication. Your son left several little articles, some of value, as for instance his mother's likeness, and a gold chain. How can I convey them to you Shall I send them by express to Mr. Duncan?

DRAFT OF ANNE MAGILL SMITH TO MARY ANN MASON, UNDATED

Dear Mrs Mason

For so you will allow me to address you as the benefactor of my beloved departed son. But one long weary day has passed since the rect. of Dr Atkinsons letter giving us the heartrending intelligence. He says "your son was specially favoured by a gracious Providence in falling into the hands of a most excellent Christian family"—We feel that we can never thank God sufficiently for opening your hearts to a sick & destitute stranger, & words would fail me were I to attempt to express a tithe of the gratitude to your family for the kindness long continued to our precious one. In early youth our dear son gave witness of being a child of God & in manhood was a devoted Christian & I know that [for] him to depart has been great gain yet it is hard for the flesh to acquiesce in the manner of his removal, that during those long months the task of waiting on him should have been imposed on strangers when each member of the household would have esteemed it a privilege to perform the most menial offices for him. Oh yes, he was the darling of the household, so domestic that he was always ready (when not engaged in business) to promote the enjoyment of the family & such a devoted son that his parents can remember no one act of disobedience during his life & never had one anxious thought for him in regard to morals.

Perhaps you will ask why should I write all this to strangers? My answer is that you may see that your kindness was not misplaced & that you may excuse the boldness of my asking you to add yet one more favour to the great debt we already owe you which is that you will write us the particulars of our dear son's death. All we know is that he was with you, was kindly treated, & died. We know not even the date of his departure nor the disease which was the messenger sent to bear him away. Please say whether he suffered much, & whether he spoke of us. He was naturally taciturn & was probably not less so in his weak state but it is hard to believe that with all that wealth of love which he cherished for his family he left not one message for us.

We should be glad to know by what means he was placed under your care. We hope to return in the fall to our devastated & now truly desolate home, where we should rejoice to welcome any of your dear family for we should love to look upon the faces of those who had looked kindly on him & now dear friends we can offer you nothing but our prayers in return for all your kindness & we do most earnestly pray for Gods choicest blessings upon you & yours & O may you ever be spared such an affliction but if our Heavenly Father should see fit to try you thus may you have the same abundant consolation.

CHARLES AND ISABELLA MAGILL TO THE SMITH FAMILY
Camden, Ark
Aug 30/65

Dear Bro & Sister
Nieces & Nephew

My heart is very sore for you all, for myself. Dear Willie-boy, how we all loved him! But to us all what an unspeakable consolation there is in the fact that he was God's own child a consolation that so many, many thousands of Southern hearts have not. How few can say the only pain he ever gave us was his leaving us. So singularly pure a young man it would have been very hard to find. While this enhances our grief, it should, at the same time be a source of Thankfulness that our merciful Saviour has taken him to be with Himself. Dearest Willie so good & kind, but so unfit to struggle with this world. . . . Indeed I think if God would take us all together what a cause of Thankfulness it would be. What has any Southern man or woman to look forward to? Our Country is gone our property gone and thousands of us left to struggle on with a hard world, in middle life & in old age to begin the world anew.

The terrible weight of taxation which the government has fixed on us we can never pay. I do not think the property in the State will sell for enough to pay the taxes if the Yankees force the collection of it. In this State we have, in addition to the U.S. tax, to pay State taxes back to the time when the Yankees came to L Rock, & Establishd a bogus Govt $1^{50} on each $100^{00} dollars the property was worth before the war. In another point too we are worse off than you in Georgia, for the bogus legislature passed a law that no one concerned in the rebellion, directly or indirectly, could vote: so you see we, the rebels, have no way of having the laws changed. . . . I presume Bet has written you all about Mr. M. I mean all she knows. What I shall do, is yet uncertain. I would like to go to Brazil but I hate to go when I shall probably ne'er see any of you again & I hate to take Belle away so far from her father & mother who are old. If there was an opening she would like to unite with Lizzie in teaching; but no one has money to pay. . . . Best love to every one of you from

Yr aff C.

My Dear Sister

What can I write but that my heart is full of sorrow & sympathy for you in your great affliction. While the loveliness & purity of dear Willie's character makes *our* loss the greater, it only increases the conviction that he was unfit for this world. If at all times it is a blessed change when one of God's own children is called home, more especially is it so *now*. I know it does not our sufferings lessen to contemplate those of other people, still it *is* an alleviation that our dear Willie was as well cared for as he was: that he did not linger in a prisoner's cell with all the hardships attending such a death; that altho' the loved ones were not with him, he had *Christian* friends to nurse & take care of him. Oh! how I do want to see you all. I do so wish that whatever may be our future destiny we may all be together. I have never been so *sad* in all my life, as I have in the last few months, & it has not been merely on my own account. When we talked of you all, & wondered what you would do, we have thought "They have lost almost everything, but Willie & Archie are spared." How little we expected this great sorrow. My *best* love to *all*. As ever your

loving sister Belle

The Monument

SEPTEMBER 1865–FEBRUARY 1867

Following Willie Smith's death, the Smiths and Masons maintained a fairly regular correspondence for the next two years, a correspondence that is dominated by details of his sickness and death and preparations and negotiations for a stone to mark his grave. Owing to the disruptions in communications noted earlier, and perhaps because they thought that their earlier letters had miscarried, the Masons repeated in September much of what they previously had told the Smiths of the circumstances surrounding Willie's death. These letters between Roswell and Raleigh, although replete with Victorian sentimentality, breathe a respect and understanding between the Masons and the Smiths about the meaning and significance of what they had experienced.

Archibald Smith even purchased a print of the famous Confederate painting by William D. Washington (1833–70), *The Burial of Latané* (1864),
which depicts the burial by a southern woman and her family of a
Confederate captain who had fallen far from home. The message of the
painting is that if your son falls somewhere in the South, surrogate families
will take care of him. The parallel between Washington's painting about the
Brockenbrough family of Hanover County, Virginia, and the Mason family
of Raleigh, North Carolina, was obvious to the Smiths.

Their correspondence with a family of strangers who shared their belief
in the southern cause and who shared their pain in their loss was offset in late
1865 by hearing about and later from one of Anne Magill Smith's brothers,
who shared neither their beliefs nor their experiences. Seagrove William
Magill, whose name Anne had given to Willie, had left the South for New
England before the war and had returned to Savannah after the war to organize American Missionary Association schools for newly freed slaves. Icy and
tense letters between sister and brother followed Seagrove's encounter on a
Savannah street in 1865 with Archibald Smith's cousin, Margaret Cowper
Elliott.[1] Seagrove Magill's son, William Alexander (1836–99), served as a
Union sergeant in Mississippi and Louisiana.

Anne Smith's other brother, Charles Arthur Magill, and his wife, Isabella,
were sympathetic both to the southern cause and to loss, and they wrote
from Arkansas in an attempt to bring some comfort. Charles Magill had gone
to Arkansas to be a part of the enterprises of Henry Merrell, who had married Anne's sister, Elizabeth.

Elizabeth and Henry Merrell largely bore responsibility for the conditions
under which the bulk of the 1866 Smith family correspondence took place.
To spare the Smith daughters the pain and hardship of returning to their
desolate home in Roswell, Uncle Henry and Aunt Bet arranged to take them
on a European tour that began in April 1866. The Merrells journeyed from
Camden, Arkansas, to Valdosta, where Lizzie and Helen joined them to travel
to Savannah. From Savannah the party traveled to New York to visit Merrell's
Yankee relatives in Utica and Watertown before embarking on their transat-
lantic voyage. Archibald Smith did not want Merrell to introduce his daughters into the circle of a family that had supported and even actively raised
troops for the armies that had invaded their land and had helped to kill their
son. In these letters such feelings are mixed with poignant reminders of
Willie, including those that crop up when Merrell's relatives remembered
Willie from the trip across the north that he took with the Merrells in 1860.

Other letters in this section, such as those from the Barrington Kings, attempt to help the Smiths in their exile and desolation, suffering what they

termed "the failure of our hopes." But the letters from Europe, above all, demonstrate that the memory of Willie never left them.

1. See her letter of June 2, 1865, above.

MARY ANN MASON TO ANNE MAGILL SMITH

Raleigh Sept. 7th

My Dear Mrs Smith

I hope long before this, you have received my letter informing you of the circumstances of your son's death. I was quite sick, and feeble for several weeks after he died, so that I could not write in a legible hand, nor could I sit up long enough, so that I was compelled to defer the letter till my strength some what returned. This I was very much distressed at, on account of the terrible suspense I knew you were suffering. I wrote at last and the letter was sent to the care of Mr Duncan of Savannah. Since receiving your letter I have been quite feeble again so that its answer was deferred till now. Indeed I am afraid you will find it difficult to read this. You have my deepest heartfelt sympathy dear Madam on this sad occasion—so you have of my whole family. Dr Mason was very fond of your son and spent a great deal of time in conversation with him. We were all fond of him, My Daughters were his constant companions; with them he was always very cheerful and happy. He and I used to have some nice long talks together, and his theme was often his "dear ones at home." His Mother especially. But he was taken quite unexpectedly so it was that he left no message for home.

A few days before he died the Doctor told me that he had too much vitality about him to die—that he would surely get well & indeed I believe he told Mr Atkinson so the very day before he died. I always told your son every thing I could to cheer him and keep up hopes of reaching his dear home, so I told him of this assurance of the doctor. So it was that he did not expect the heavenly messenger which called him to his heavenly home. When the fatal shaft was sped, he became almost immediately insensible, and was only once aroused from that state once, when I called my son William. He thought it was his Mother and opened his eyes, saying "Mother!" It was his last word.

He died in his tent in my front yard in sight of my chamber window. We were all around him and that night the girls and two Confederate soldiers watched by him all night. There were lights in the tent, and the moon shone gloriously all night long. I was up at my window often in the night looking at his tent and his gentle watchers, those whose company he delighted in when alive & I thought how pleased he would be if he could see them there, and hear them converse about him.

On the following afternoon just at sunset his funeral commenced at the tent door. It was a beautiful scene. And I could not but hope his quiet happy spirit was present too. The girls sang "I would not live alway" delightfully to the tune Home Sweet Home, while I sat looking at the bright wreath of roses on the coffin of my dear departed patriot. I could not sing. Of course my heart was too full for that. I could only weep as I know his Mother would do were she present. Indeed dear Madam I felt as if I was in your place acting & feeling for you all the while he was with me.

There is but one regret I feel that I had no room in my house for him. It was unusually full at the time, and he assured me from time to time that it was better as it was. Still I regret that he was not in the house that I might have been more constantly with him myself. He said too it was cooler in the tent and easier to keep prim. But if I had doubted the prospect of his recovery I should have made a greater effort to have him near me. But we felt confident of his recovery. His death was a very great surprise.

If you have not received my letter dear Madam let me know and I will write another giving you a full account of all the circumstances of his illness and death. I hope however you have received it ere this. I have written to Mr Rountree[1] at Wilson to say I am ready to send your son's knapsack &c with some valuables, to his directive but I have as yet received no answer. Shall I send them by express to Savannah?

May the blessed God who has sustained you dear Madam and all your family on this trying occasion still support & comfort you till you again join your dear son where parting will be no more. Present my sincerest sympathies and regards to your honored husband and to all your family. And believe me ever Your

sincere friend
Mary Mason

1. According to the 1870 census of North Carolina, there was a dry-goods merchant in Wilson, North Carolina, named Willie Rountree. Also, a Louis Rountree family from North Carolina had moved to Lowndes County, Georgia, near the Smiths and had attended the Presbyterian Church there. It is therefore possible that the Smiths had met Willie Rountree in Valdosta. See Wisenbaker, "First Impressions," 44, 52.

Raleigh Sept. 20, 1865

My dear Sir

I hope by this time you have received the letters Mrs. Mason and myself wrote to you and Mrs. Smith a few days after Mr. Atkinson had written, but lest this should not be the case I write to you again to give you the particulars you ask in your recent letter of your Sons being with us, and of his death. Let me first say that if my family afforded any comfort to your son during his sickness it is repaid manifold by the kind expressions contained in yours and Mrs. Smith's letters, and by the hope that such attentions as we were able to shew him have been a gratification to you and his mother.

There were three hospitals in our town, for the reception of our sick and wounded soldiers.[1] Soon after the U. S. army entered this place two of the hospitals were broken up, and the inmates all sent to the third one. One of the hospitals thus broken up was in our immediate neighbourhood, and my wife being at the hospital at the time the patients were sent off, desired to receive some of the sick who in consequence of the great distance of the hospital to which they were to be taken could least bear the removal. Some of our neighbours followed the example. As our house was too full to accommodate our patients within; the authorities of the hospital furnished us with a large and excellent tent which was with every necessary convenience erected in the front yard. As the weather was not well settled we had a small stove placed in the entrance of the tent, so that if the air should be chilly or damp or there should be any rain, our friends could have the benefit of a fire. As the tent was a spacious one we received three in it. Your Son was one of the number.

The youngest of the three soon died. He was very young, and his constitution had been completely broken down. Another who lived in a village not very far from Charleston recovered sufficiently to return home. We have heard from him since his return, but are sorry to learn his health is not restored, perhaps never will be. Your son who at first appeared least ill of the three, did not get better, he gradually became weaker, while his disease chronick diarrhoea, assuming often the character of dysentery could not be checked. We had for him the best medical attendance we could procure, first of the Confederate surgeons, and after their departure from Raleigh, of the Physicians of the town all rendering their service gratuitously.

Your son had at the hospital been afflicted with Typhoid fever. Recovering from that, he was attacked with Erysipelas, and then diarrhoea and dysentery. We all soon became very much attached to him, as we found him so intelligent, so gentlemanly, and as we believed with a piety sanctifying a natural amiable and noble disposition. Some member of the family was almost constantly with him; and we took care that he should not suffer for want of night attendance. I hope and believe that he was well satisfied with what we could do for him, although, indeed, from the kindness of his temper it was not difficult to satisfy him. I prayed with him, and talked with him on the subject in which we were both so interested the service of God and our Saviour, and I felt convinced that his heart was deeply imbued with the love of the Redeemer. He never repined was always patient and resigned to life or death as God was pleased to determine.

He appeared to have but one strong desire, to see his family especially yourself and his mother before his death.

Thinking it would be agreeable to you to have a minister of his own faith to attend his funeral, I requested the Rev. Mr. Atkinson the pastor of the Presbyterian congregation in this town, and who had previously visited him to do so. As I had no doubt you would desire a respectable funeral for him, some expense was incurred for this purpose. Many of the neighbours with of course my own family attended the services, and he was borne to the grave by returned Confederate Soldiers & officers, natives of Raleigh who volunteered their services for this purpose.

From Mr. Duncan I received fifty dollars, for your Son's benefit, but this did not reach Raleigh till after your son's death. I have appropriated it to the payment of the funeral expenses. It nearly covers them. I sent Mr. Duncan the account sometime ago and will now send him the receipt.

Hoping, my dear friend, that he who has been pleased in his providence to bring upon you the heavy calamity of the loss of such a son will give you strength to bear it.

I remain affectionately Yr. frd.

A. Smith Esqr   R. S. Mason

1. Mrs. Elizabeth Reid Murray of Raleigh informed the editors that the three Confederate hospitals were Peace, Pettigrew, and Fairgrounds. Mrs. Mason discovered Willie in Peace Hospital.

REBECCA E. MASON[1] TO LIZZIE AND HELEN SMITH
Raleigh Oct 14th

Dear Young Ladies,

We count it a great privilege to have been able to render to your much loved brother, the little service that lay in our power. Never have I seen even a cup of cold water, given in the name of the Lord go unrewarded, & surely we have met ours in having made so many warm friends. It was but a little thing, a labour of love, for what southern woman would not joy in administering to the sufferings of any sick, southern, prisoner. It was some comfort when our enemies were round us, to see his good, honest, noble face, & know that *he* was a friend. Besides he had not been with us long, when it became a pleasure, for his sake alone. When he first came he was able to walk about a little, & often sat in front of his tent enjoying the fresh air, watching me take a sketch of the tent and yard. He was very thin & used to laugh & tell me, not to put him in the sketch until he recovered his flesh or he would be taken for a grim skeleton. He was in the house once or twice, & I played for him on the piano. He however preferred staying in his tent & having us to see him there. There was a Mrs Johnston, who was very kind to him before he came to us. He seemed to like her very much. Indeed she is a lovely little woman, so quiet & gentle. He was fond of flowers too & I often dressed a little flower pot & put it on his table where his eyes could rest upon them when he awoke.

He read a great deal, & told me little anecdotes of his home life. A few weeks before he died I was quite sick & obliged to leave town for a short distance in the country. I came home the next Sunday & went straight to see him. When I entered the door, he said "I knew you had come for I heard your voice when you first entered the gate, you are so bright. Oh! if I only had just enough of your life to get home to my mother & family, if I could only get home to die among them I would be more willing to die." Then he said "that was wrong in me to say that. I would not take one spark of life from you even to get home. It was selfish in me, besides you are all so good to me here; but I do so long to see my friends."

I believe if ever there was a good & unselfish man, he was one.

There were three Confederate prisoners in Raleigh while he was sick, & they went to see him almost every day. He had a Confederate Doctor to attend him. I was not at Home when he died, being in the country where Mother had sent me again to recover my health. But she told me all about his death & burial and truly it was peaceful & holy. She has already told your Mother of it & it would be useless to repeat it. Besides I was not here & could not tell you as if I had seen it all. I too feel the loss as if it were a friend & brother. He had endeared himself to every member of the family. Do not then think that you owe us a debt of gratitude. Ours it is to thank you for a blessing. Your Mother feared that my Mother's health had been somewhat impaired. If it had not been for your son I fear she would have been quite ill for fear & anxiety during the first two or three weeks that the Federal troops occupied R——had disturbed her mind so much, that if she had not had something to interest & draw her mind off from the troubles, we all think she may have been seriously ill & looked upon his coming as a Godsend. With kindest regards to your Mother & family & hoping to hear from you again.

Believe me
Truly Yours
Rebecca E. Mason

1. Rebecca Mason was the youngest daughter of the Reverend and Mrs. Richard S. Mason.

MARGARET COWPER MACKAY ELLIOTT
TO ANNE MAGILL SMITH

Savannah Novr 14th 1865

My dear Anne,

. . . My heart is full of sympathy for you. I often think of what you have lost. John says he was "the best man he ever knew." I answered, that is a strong speech. He repeated, "Yes, the man most governed by conscientious high principle, and there never was a man more highly valued by those who associated with him. Even the bad had to acknowledge his virtue & goodness."

Give my love to all including your sister H. I write in great haste but I cannot do otherwise ever yours

M.C.E.

BARRINGTON KING TO ARCHIBALD SMITH

Roswell 30th Nov 1865

A. Smith Esq
Valdosta
My dear Friend

Yours of the 15th is just received—the mail arrangement out of town, & but few letters reach this destination. We are about having a tri-weekly mail to this place, in the mean time our letters are directed to Roswell, Marietta. Happy to learn that yourself & family in usual health—we have had mild weather thus far, but so late in the season, if you are comfortable at Valdosta, *best spend the winter at the low country,* and return in the spring: by that time the R. Road will be in better condition, & the change more beneficial to your family. . . .

M^r [Cassels?] remains at your house, I told him that you were expected, & he must make arrangements to be off on your arrival:[1] no prospect of renting for the winter—if you decline coming, he had best continue there until spring. Your house is in pretty good condition, but will require some work no doubt before your family returns: the kitchen, Stable &c require fixing up, but lumber so scarce & high $35 pr [ ] that but little could have been done, the past season. Atlanta is building up rapidly & large stock of Goods there—by spring many will be setting out at a loss, & would prefer making purchases there than in Savannah; many of your articles can be found in the country hid away, by getting out search warrants when you return: I mentioned in one of my letters, that your small trunk with some Titles &c, was brought to me by Major Minton, for safe keeping.[2] I rec[d] Archys letter & would have replied to it, *but pressed for time,* & could not give him any encouragement about work—glad to see such good spirits of industry, but too young for hard work: when you return would be of great service assisting you to fix up, and should we have any employment that would suit him at some future day, will do all in my power to aid him. . . .

Glad to learn that your Brother in usual health—would be pleased to see him again at Roswell.

M[rs] King has much improved in health, better now than the last 2 years—our place has been healthy, no death here since our arrival.

1 Dec—I commenced this yesterday, but must close as C. Pratt[3] [is] waiting to take this to Marietta. M[rs] King & all join in kind regards to yourself, M[rs] Smith and every member of the family. Brother Pratt & family as usual. The sabbath school is kept alive & preaching every sabbath—we miss you much in the work here & [were] in hopes that your family would have returned this fall. Best for you all to remain in the low country until next spring, than coming to this climate so late in the season.

Yours truly

B King

Letter enclosed for M[rs] Smith.

May the blessing of God attend us all, & permit us to meet again at old Roswell, is my prayer.

1. The family of a Thomas Cassel, an elderly factory hand at the Roswell Manufacturing Company, appears in the 1860 census of Cobb County, Georgia. A Lorena Cassel, age twenty, is listed in his household; and in a letter of July 31, 1866, Anne Smith refers to Rena Cassels having stayed in their house.

2. Major John Minton (1797–1871), who lived near the Smiths in Roswell.

3. Charles Jones Pratt (1842–1924), the son of the Reverend and Mrs. Nathaniel Alpheus Pratt, was a student, a private in the Savannah Volunteer Guards, and then a junior first lieutenant in the Roswell Battalion. In 1864 he joined Morgan's command as

a private in the Kentucky Cavalry. He was taken prisoner and exchanged in September 1863 (Myers, ed., *Children of Pride,* 1648).

MARY ANN MASON TO ANNE MAGILL SMITH, UNDATED

My dear Mrs Smith

I send you here all the effects of your lamented Son. I am sure he had no watch when he came to us, nor did I see one with him while at the Hospital. I am sincerely sorry that it should have been lost.

My Son William is a man of thirty five years of age and I did not think he ought to have so precious a relic of your beloved and departed son. I have therefore sent them with the rest with many thanks for your kind intentions.

Dr Mason returned from the North quite sick and I have too been very ill since so that we have not yet attended to all your requests, but be assured all shall be done. Dr M received 50 dollars from Mr Duncan. We will appropriate it that is a part of it as you requested & the rest can remain till you find it convenient to have the monument erected. We have a marble yard here & Dr Mason will take pleasure in attending to it for you.

With much respect to your good husband and love for the young ladies I remain

Yours most sincerely
& affectionately
Mary Mason

A. E. STEWART[1] TO ARCHIBALD SMITH

Mr. A.[M.?] Smith

Dear Sir

Your note requesting a return of a lock of hair given as a memento by your Son to my daughter is received. Enclosed please find same cherished relic. Willie had endeared himself very much to our family, and in bidding us adieu exchanged parting gifts. In returning his hair we are only glad we can furnish his bereaved family with a testimonial of the worth of their estimable Son. We are obliged for the rings sent.

Yours with Great respect
"A E Stewart"

1. A. E. Stewart is very likely Ann Eliza Downs Stewart of St. Marys, an old friend of the Smiths. She had three daughters: Sarah E. (b. 1843?), Lillian (b. 1844?), and Laramie

N. (b. 1847?). Laramie, apparently also called Miranda, later married Archie's fellow cadet Samuel Griffin, and her grandson, S. Marvin Griffin, served as governor of Georgia from 1955 to 1959 (Huxford, *Pioneers,* 5:419; Wisenbaker, "First Impressions, 5, 44, 52).

SEAGROVE WILLIAM MAGILL[1] TO ANNE MAGILL SMITH AND HELEN ZUBLY MAGILL

Waterbury Nov. 21st, 1865

My dear Sisters

It is a great relief to feel that "the calamity is overpassed," and we may now look forward to the time when old arrangements shall be readjusted and old relations & opportunities restored, and we shall be, thro'out the land, as we always should have been, an undivided people, dwelling together in unity. And, if the Spirit be poured out upon us from on high, the alienations, which these terrible years of conflict have been fostering, may be dispelled, and they who love God, will love their brethren also, and so the things which are impossible with man, shall prove possible with God, and Divine grace will be recognised, as the great pacificator, and Jesus be adored with fresh delight, as the Prince of Peace.

I perceive that the government is reestablishing the mail routes in the So. States, and so hope a letter may reach you, and the same is the case of our lonely sister, in the far-off regions beyond the Mississippi. I have made several attempts to reach you by letter, during the war, but my letters were returned, and have received but one letter from you. I was in Savannah last winter, and heard of your whereabouts and your general welfare. Willie, I learned, had been in Savannah, until the departure thence of Hardee's Army, and had usually enjoy'd good health. Whether you are still in Lowndes Co., or have returned to Roswell, and whether your dear boys are restored to you in safety and health, or may have fallen on the battlefield or in the hospital, I am not definitely informed. I shall send this to Roswell, care of Mr. Pratt, who, I understand, remained there & was entirely undisturbed.

Our son is located in Lyme, in this state, where he has a boy's boarding sch. They have a sweet little girl, now about 1 year old. Matilda has not been in her former health, since the birth of the child, but is gradually gaining. Aunt Margaret in Middletown, is very infirm & nervous & has but little use of her eyes. Cousin Eliza is somewhat broken, but enjoys tolerable health. My wife's health, for several years, has not been good.[2] I am blessed with good health, tho' I find old age creeping in my bones, as our dear Mother

Seagrove William Magill
(1810–84)

used to say. I shall be happy to hear from you speedily, and to learn particulars respecting each and every member of the family, and of the wider family circle, embracing the kindred in Beech Island, Marietta, and those that formerly dwelt in Beaufort. I sailed by Old Fort, last winter, & saw the old oaks & palmettos, and thought of the days departed with deep sadness, saw also the houses & yards in Beaufort, but did not enter them. The refrain of that most plaintive melody "Oft in the stilly night,"[3] which I used to love so much in the days of our childhood, was ever coming back to me, as I passed along those old & once so tenderly cherished places. But alas! the change. Well, heaven is the same, its beauties change not, its fellowships are never interrupted, and God shall wipe away all tears. And my dear sisters, it is an abiding source of comfort to me, in connection with so much that has been most grievous, during the past 4 years, that to so many of us, has been granted, thro' the grace of God, the hope, that we have in heaven, a better and an enduring portion.

My most affectionate regards to all.

Yours truly, S.W. Magill

1. Born in St. Marys, Seagrove William Magill (1810–84) studied at Amherst, Yale, and Princeton before returning to a pastorate in Bryan County, Georgia, from 1834 to 1840. He then became a Congregational minister in Vermont, where he remained until 1847. He came back to Georgia to head two female academies, then returned to New England to serve a Congregational church in Connecticut. In 1864 he resigned to come to Georgia again, this time to organize freedman schools for the American Missionary Association. Two years later he returned to New England, where he remained until his death. We are grateful to Mr. Walter E. Ziebarth of Hamburg, New York, for providing us with information on his great-grandfather.

2. Seagrove Magill's son, William Alexander Magill (1836–99) married Matilda Wakefield Smith in 1860 and served as a sergeant in the twenty-fifth Connecticut Infantry, taking part in campaigns on the Mississippi and in Louisiana. Margaret Clay Magill (1788–1866) was the sister of Seagrove and Anne's father, Charles Arthur Magill (1782–1854). "Cousin Eliza" could be Elizabeth Denny, Elizabeth Magill Goodwin, or even Sarah Elizabeth Magill of Chicago. Seagrove Magill's wife was Helen Twining Magill (1812–1905). See *Obituary Record*, 174–75.

3. The first line and title of a poem by the Irish poet Thomas Moore (1779–1852). The first four lines are: "Oft, in the stilly night, / Ere Slumber's chain has bound me, / Fond Memory brings the light / Of other days around me."

DRAFT OF LETTER FROM ANNE MAGILL SMITH TO SEAGROVE WILLIAM MAGILL, UNDATED

Not having a mail we are dependent on travellers who may pass thro this place for the transmission of letters to & from the nearest point to which a mail has been allowed & so your letter of the 21st [Nov.] did not reach us until 24th January. We are glad to hear of the welfare of your family & hope altho' you have arrived at the dignity of Grandfather, the old age which you feel creeping upon you will prove a green & vigorous one that your family comforts may long be continued to you, your son as a prop for your declining years & his little ones grow up as olive plants about you.

We thank you for your inquiries about us. Those who remain are in usual health. You may have learned that my son Wm is gone to his rest. I cannot but regard those who urged for the unjust & cruel war against us as his murderers. I must say I am rather surprised that a thinking man should say the calamity is over past when weak & helpless people are ground in the dirt by the iron heel of tyranny which affords them neither support nor protection even wresting from them ground they might have cultivated [for] food or support.

Our Brother J.J.S. has been with us since '61. The Barnwells are in this neighborhood, all well.... Of the B[eech] I[sland][1] people we hear nothing. Mr & Mrs P. did remain in Roswell having put their daughters to a place of safety & if to escape personal violence & have their *dwelling* house spared when all else was stolen or destroyed....

1. Beech Island was a town on the Port Royal River in Aiken County, South Carolina, not far from Augusta, Georgia.

REV. DR. R. S. MASON TO WILLIAM DUNCAN

Raleigh Jan. 4 '66

Dear Sir

It must have appeared strange to you that I have not before acknowledged the receipt of your letter enclosing the check for $54.50, but I hope my explanation of the delay will prove to some extent if not wholly satisfactory to you.

Your letter reached this place either, as my daughter thinks, before my leaving home for the Gen Convention, but while I was suffering under an attack of intermittent fever, so that if she is right, I had totally forgotten the circumstances, or it did not arrive till I had gone from home. I was absent several weeks partly from attendance on the General Convention of the Episcopal Church in Philadelphia, partly in visits to my friends and relatives, and much beyond the time I proposed by a renewal and continuance of my attack. On my return home I was much enfeebled by my sickness besides having a short relapse. I hope you will accept this as an apology for my delay.

Next week I will attend to the request Mr. Smith makes in his last letter, but after I shall have expended whatever money may be necessary to carry out his wishes, the far greater part of what you sent me will still remain no doubt; what disposition shall I make of it? Shall I return it to you, which I would prefer; or shall I retain it to aid in erecting the monument Mr. Smith contemplates putting up over the grave of his noble son?

As soon as I execute Mr. Smith's wishes I will send you an account of the sum left, that you may make the disposition of it you prefer.

With most respect
I remain dr. Sir
faithfully Yours

W. Duncan Esqr.   R. S. Mason

My dear friend R, your very nice and kind letter I received some weeks ago but I have been very unwell since and not able to answer it. I thank you very much for telling me of yourselves. We are so deeply interested in each member of your family. We are glad to hear some thing of them personally. You hope your letters have led me to form a good impression of you as you do not know how to describe yourself. I wish I could tell you how sweet an impression your letters as well as your kindness have made. . . .

It was so good of you so good of them all to treat my dear brother as you did. All those little familiar home kindnesses are so much to those who feel as he did and love home and home ways. It was so good in you to go for him to see you when you were dressed doubtless it reminded him of home for he always noticed our things very much and was interested in all that we did and had.

We are so thankful for your thoughtful kindness in carrying him his meals and talking to him while he ate.

You ask that I will tell you some thing of our family there are so few of us there is very little to tell. My Father and Mother you already know of. Then there is an Aunt who has always lived with us and taught my brother Archie and myself when we were children.

My Sister is older than either of us and smarter also and she is always ready to do every thing for every body. She has grey eyes and brown curling hair. Of course we think our boy is a very nice fellow and very good and it is not only our blind love that makes him appear so to us. Other people think so of him too. Though he is very amenable he has not such a quiet gentle spirit as my brother that you know and so is better able to endure this life of hardship and oppression which we have to live now in the south. Archie has beautiful black eyes and we think he grows like William as he grows old, but his face is not so intellectual.

I am the baby of the house though Archie is younger than I.

Raleigh Feb. 8

My Dear Mrs Smith,

Yesterday evening I had the pleasure of receiving your very kind letter, and the assurance of the safe arrival of the box, containing the effects of your lamented, excellent Son. . . .

His voice was so strong to the last, his bodily vitality so apparent, his cheerfulness his hopes so bouyed him up, neither he or we doubted that he would recover—so that we did not endeavour to draw him out to speak of his home and relatives only as he chose, and this he was always backward in doing. In that this is one of my grievous regrets. And then my family was sick all the while some times most of them at once, and I could not stay with him long at a time. I often lamented this to him but he always said "Oh Mrs Mason dont say a word. My Mother could not do more for me if it were she." This alone is my consolation but then I think this was because he was so patient and so easily satisfied. He well knew how to take the will for the deed, and he knew I had the will. And my means too were so limited I am afraid I [did] not make him as comfortable in all respects as I could have wished. I often now think of many things he ought to have had.

But these are now vain regrets, and I must try and drive them from my mind. I was utterly surprised when I found he must die.

But I am sure he was fully prepared for the change. Dr Mason spent part of every day with him. Had long conversations with him constantly, and he is well satisfied of his immortal happiness now. He spent most of his time reading his Bible and other religious books.

I have some times reproached myself for speaking with bitterness of the Yankees before him for he never in one instance replied in one word coinciding with my sentiments. He was always silent in those occasions. I was always rebuked sufficiently by his silent charity. Sometimes it was hard to bear, when they refused nice comforts for my sick soldiers and I could not be silent. But still I persecuted them till I obtained something. It mattered not to me how much trouble I gave them. Ice I would have and as long as they had it, in any quantity, I obtained it for my sick. How often I was ashamed of my want of charity towards them one can guess but their insolence it was hard to bear.

I did not admit them into my tent, so my soldiers saw none of it, thank God. Their physician was always a Confederate. . . .

Dr Mason will attend to the monument with pleasure. Let him know in what style you wish it & at what cost. It can be done here.

Mr Duncan lent him 50 Dollars the second time; and only owes 4,50. I shall at your request give the servants who waited on him 5 and the remainder can go towards the Monument. I believe also the express bill was $6,50.

We were very much grieved to hear of the health of Mr. Smith, and hope he will soon be restored, and that your family will be enabled to return to your home. We are much obliged for the oranges. They have not yet arrived.

I wish you could come on next spring when the Monument is done and pay me a visit. We shall all be very glad to see you.

We are much obliged to you for your kind invitation, but money is scarce in these times and precludes much travelling. Nothing would give me more pleasure than to pay you a visit except that of visiting my distant Son, who is a clergyman in *New Jersey*, I am sorry to say. . . .

Your letters are delightful as coming from so dear a friend, but dont praise us any more. We do not deserve half and you are indeed under no manner of obligation to us. Your son was our son in the Lord and in love of Country. We did not do *half* our *duty* to him. His merits *entitled* him to far more.

ever, yours,

most affectionately

Mary Mason

MARY ANN MASON TO ANNE MAGILL SMITH

Raleigh Feb. 27.

My Dear Mrs Smith

I herewith enclose you a photograph of the old woman who had the care of your departed son. You may judge perhaps some what of the eyes that looked with so much interest upon his fading form. Perhaps the countenance may not express, but the heart was full of kindness as well as anxious solicitations for his recovery and restoration to his "loved ones at home" (Always his mode of designating them). This old lady is 63 years of age, grey headed, and her eyes are, some say, blue, some, gray bordering on blue. She is rather above medium height, carries some what of the elevated head (I trust) of the bred and born Southerner, not a semblance of a drop of Puritan blood in the veins. She loves the South with all her soul and trusts to see her righted yet. (Many sweet talks had she with her dear departed sainted Charge in the quiet tent, beneath that spreading elm tree.) English to the core, but not a drop of Puritan blood (therefore not yanky.)

This old woman was the mother of five sons and five daughters but the Good God was pleased to take three of the sons, ripe for Heaven before this cruel Puritan War. I trust your dear Willie and mine, has embraced them in their Heavenly home, and brought them tidings from their earthly home. Might not this be so? Why not? I feel that it is. I know his generous affectionate soul performed this Saintly office if permitted. And is there any thing in the blessed Scriptures to forbid such a comforting thought?

But enough of this intrusive old woman. Egotistical I should say. Forgive it dear friend, for Willie's sake.

I received his photograph from his loving aunt Mrs Merrell. It is like him but not quite so handsome. Perhaps his approach to the condition of an angel may have given it to them but his eyes were glorious, unearthly bright. They seemed to take in at one glance the whole horizon of natures loveliness as well as Gods unbounded goodness, Christ's unbounded love. . . .

Hoping to hear from you soon my dear Mrs Smith I am as ever your

Sincerest affectionate friend

Mary Mason

P.S. Best regards to your honoured husband, and love to all the girls, also to your son.

M. M.

REBECCA E. MASON TO LIZZIE SMITH, DATE OBSCURED AND LETTER INCOMPLETE

I hope you will not my dear Miss Lizzie think me forgetful of your request, but the sketch[1] was done on an old torn & soiled piece of paper & I delayed sending it until I could copy it. Not knowing any thing about drawing it is very poor, but if it will be of any value to you I am glad to send it. As you said, that you wished it because your brother saw me draw it I have sent both the original and the copy. On looking again, at this little drawing that I spoke to your sister of, I find that I had best not send it as it was done to make him laugh at a time when we had little doubt of your brother's recovery, you might not like to see it. Mother is writing or has, I expect, told of this beautiful dress sent her by your Aunt.[2] We were particularly glad to get the photograph of our "soldier." It was like him, but not so handsome. His glorious brown eyes were not taken to advantage, their expression was not so fine there was a depth & exalted look from them which the likeness fails to give. Yet it is like him & we were all very much gratified that your Aunt should have sent it. I assure you we will always prize it very highly. He was with us so long; it grieved us deeply to part with him. He was like a brother.

1. If a drawing was sent and still exists, it has not yet been found or identified.
2. Elizabeth Magill Merrell.

Raleigh March 28th

My Dear Mrs Smith,

I received your very kind letter some days ago. It is always a pleasure to hear from you or yours. I am glad to hear Mr Smith is so much better and rejoice that you are about to return to your home. May you never be deprived of its blessing again.

I received the letter containing the drawing of the monument you desired, but as I understood you that you could not conveniently afford the means at present, I concluded it would be best to defer the matter till further instructed, particularly as such things are at this time high. I thought after a little time the prices would fall. Mary my daughter did inquire of a stonecutter and he told her the price of such an one as you mentioned was 700 dollars. The spring is advancing now and we hope to have flowers blooming around the resting place of your dear one, and soon the monument will rear its graceful and protecting proportions above that cherished spot. Make yourself perfectly easy with respect to it. Those who love him are still near. I will write you soon again after I have made further inquiries. . . . In a short time you shall hear all about the monument, or slab and the pieces. I like the slab very much placed as those of my little boys.

. . . . Rebecca is anxious to know if your daughters have received her letter and the drawing of the tent. Both left Raleigh before my last letter. Remember me affectionately to your sister Mrs Merrell. . . . Give my love to all your children and best respects to your good husband, and believe me dear Mrs Smith ever truly and affectionately

yours
Mary Mason

LIZZIE TO MOTHER, UNDATED [APRIL 5, 1866][1]
[Savannah, Ga.]

Dear Mother

We reached here all safe but very tired, Sissy quite tired out but she thinks it is a good healthy tired. Charlotte had written a note to Uncle H to say the Mackays house was so full we could not go there & so he just brought us along to Mrs Duboses they seem to be doing very well have every thing very nice. Aunt Bet & I went round to the Mackays this evening. Only Cousin Sarah was at home but we intend all of us—Aunt B, Sissy , & I—to go in the morning to see both the Elliotts & the Mackays. Cousin S is as bad as all of you. She says we ought by all means to go & you will get on better without us. This is the anniversary of the day the battle was fought where the Guards were so cut up & all the Ladies have made wreaths & bouquets & were at the Cemetery dressing the graves of the Soldiers.[2] The Elliotts were gone there & that is why we did not go to see them this evening. I should have liked so much to see the cemetery. The Elliotts are selling flowers again this winter. Cousin Sarah says Mary refused to sell flowers to any one today who wanted them for dressing the graves. . . .

The steamer sails at 12 tomorrow & Uncle H says we must be down at 11 or so we will not have much time for visiting in the morning. I hope you got off today as you will not miss us as much. I am too glad you determined to go by way of Albany.[3] This road is so very fatiguing. It is a steady jarring (which keeps your teeth chattering) more than half the way. I know it would have tired you out. Remember you are none of you to work too hard because you have promised not.

your aff daughter
Lizzie Smith

write as soon as you get home

1. Lizzie and Helen Smith accompanied their uncle and aunt, Henry and Elizabeth Merrell, on a tour of Henry Merrell's native New York and then Europe. Archibald and Anne Smith were about to return to Roswell after an absence of almost two years. The Merrells traveled from Arkansas to Valdosta, where they met Lizzie and Helen and then departed for Savannah. At the same time that the Merrells left with the daughters, the parents and Helen Magill began their journey back to Roswell. This letter has been dated from events recorded in a travel diary kept by Elizabeth Magill Merrell (Smith Papers, box 103).

2. The Savannah Volunteer Guards, a unit that had first been organized in 1802, were mustered into Confederate service in March 1862 as the Eighteenth Georgia Battalion. Willie Smith originally enlisted in Company A of this unit before being detailed to the Signal Corps. The guards served around Savannah and Charleston until May 1864, when they were ordered to Virginia, where they were badly cut up at the Battle of Sayler's Creek on April 5, 1865, only a few days before Lee's surrender (Lee and Agnew, *Historical Record*, 113–14).

3. The Smiths seem to have returned to Roswell by traveling by road northwest to Albany, Georgia, and by taking the railroad from there to Marietta, twelve miles west of Roswell.

Albany Apl. 14th/66

My Dear Children

We have just reached this place & will stay over Sunday. We could not get off last week. Sonnie was so broken down on Friday with his hard work that we had to let him rest & then it rained Sunday & Monday & we left on Wednesday. We got along very well, found good places to camp every night & are all well. I had a note from Charlotte & she mentioned that you got down safely but she had not seen you. I am sorry she did not wait until afternoon to write & then she might have told us about your sailing & how Lizzie's face was. I have been very anxious about it. We hope to find a letter when we get home. Ask Aunt Bet to get Uncle H. when he is making his money arrangements to get $100 for me & give it to you. I will write to you further about things I may want. I forgot I only gave you your own money, there was so much confusion. Tell Aunt Bet Niddy[1] has behaved very well & did not give us any trouble. I hope you are enjoying yourselves & are getting over the sea sickness.

All unite in love to you

May God bless & keep you my dear children

Your aff

Dear Mother

1. Niddy is Mrs. Merrell's young servant, the daughter of her former slave Helen, who was herself the daughter of two of her former slaves, John and Tabby Marion. Niddy remained with the Smiths while the Merrells traveled. See Smith Papers, box 100, folder 8, and Skinner, ed., *Autobiography of Henry Merrell,* 508 n. 11.

[New York, N.Y.]

Dear sister H.,

Lizzie has written once & is writing again. We have had lovely spring weather since we have been in the City, but to-day is cloudy & cold. The girls seem to be enjoying themselves very much, we have been out all the time. It is astonishing how Zubly stands better than Lizzie. We did expect to go up the North River to-day but there were so many things Mr. M. wanted them to see he concluded to stay until Monday. I hope we will hear some good preaching to-morrow; we are going to try & find Dr Van Dyke.[1]

It seems an age since we left Valdosta, & it is only a week yesterday. I hope you got comfortably home & did not find things as bad as you expected. We long to hear from you, & I hope we will before leaving the country. We are living in a Hotel after the English plan, order what we please & eat where & when we please. We breakfast at the house at 9 (so you see the girls have a chance to sleep late) & then go off & where hunger takes us we eat. I suppose the girls wrote you of our stormy voyage; they look badly after it so we have not had their likenesses taken; but they may have it done before we sail. They were quite disheartened about going, but Mr. M. tells them they might cross the ocean a dozen times & never have such a blow; he went in March & came back in Septr. and had no such weather. The Steamer that left Sav. when we did had a much worse time than ours; she was aground in Sav. river a long time & then had 60 hours of gale & had to lay off Sandy Hook in a fog 20 hours.

New York is literally running over. We have not seen any body we know yet. We think it better to keep from finding out friends we can be so much more free without. We have not shopped any. Mr. M. carried us all over Lord Taylor & Co.'s splendid dry good store this morning & into Stewarts & from top to bottom of Ball & Blacks splendid Jewelry & fancy store & we spent some hours in a picture Gallery.

I feel sad at every step though for the last time I was in N. Y. our precious Willie was with us. In our ride through Greenwood yesterday I had him in my thoughts all the time. I am so sorry since we came, that it had not been planned for us to get that monument here, & if I had known the Inscription think I should have ventured to get it any how. Mr. M. priced one which he thought a pretty style; it was an upright slab about 8 in. thick 4 1/2 feet high 2 ft. wide, arched at the top & standing upon a thick heavy block of granite, the price was $125,00 plain; & three cents a letter. I almost felt like getting it any how & letting the Inscription be sent on but Helen thought perhaps the arrangement might have been made for the one in R., & it would hardly do to venture.

. . . I am sitting by the window looking out into the City Hall Park & cannot keep my eyes off the moving mass passing all the time. A great deal of love to all. your aff. sister Bet

1. Henry Jackson Van Dyke (1822–91), pastor of the First Presbyterian Church of Brooklyn from 1853 to 1891.

CATHERINE MARGARET KING TO ANNE MAGILL SMITH
April 21st 1866

My dear Friend

I am very glad to know that you have arrived safely at your old Home, once
such a happy one, but O! my Friend what changes have come over us since
we last parted. I have thought often [of] you and prayed that you should be
sustained under your great affliction. But what shall I say of myself, words
would fail me to express the sorrow of my poor heart at my overwhelming
bereavement. I had lived a long, and happy life with my precious Husband,
but in a moment when I thought not, he was taken from me.[1] I can write, but
will tell you all, when we meet. Eva[2] leaves me on Monday, her duty calls her
away; I shall miss her more than ever, she joins me in love to you all. . . .

Your affectionate friend
C. M. King

1. Catherine King is reporting the death of her husband, Barrington King, on
January 17 after having been kicked by his horse.

2. Catherine Evelyn King Baker.

LIZZIE, UNDATED [AFTER APRIL 21, 1866]
[Sackets Harbor, N.Y.]

Dear Folks at home

I don't know if I can tell you any news as Sissy wrote this week before
me. We reached this place last Friday & it is the old fogiest place I ever saw.
You would never imagine it at the north. The place is so quiet half country
half city. The houses look old & not as if they were all just done making as
they do every where else. The people walk & don't rush round as they do in
other places & they don't gabble but speak. There are beautiful walks round
here. I walked down to the lake the other day & I would have imagined myself in the country. When I looked up to one side is a beautiful bluff & all
covered with grass. I do think the grass at the north is lovely. It grows every
where. I wish we could have it so but we can't expect to have all the good
things. I would not be a yankee for all their grass & all other nice things into
the bargain.

We took tea at the Camps last night. We did not want to go but could not
help it very well. There is Old Mr & Mrs Camp & then their married son
George who is Miss Hattie's father & Mrs Camp is the one who wrote to
William.[1] The old gentleman is over 80 & is a little childish but when I was

introduced to him he said when they told him who I was, Ah yes the sister of that young man we all liked so much & the old lady was quite glad to see us because we were his sisters. Poor old lady. She has neuralgia in her back, & has had it for a good many years. . . .

Aunty Merrell[2] is just the same as ever. She has not grown a bit older than she was the last time I saw her. I expect she has about as easy a time here as she will care every thing comfortable & such a good servant & Mr Camp[3] so kind & attentive to her which of course he ought to be. However I think it is a mutual accommodation society they have for they both are kind to each other. She says send a great deal of love to them all every time you write.

I am very glad Sonny has commenced with the violin. I hope he will be able to do something at playing by the time I get home. I will write to him soon. I will write him the first letter from abroad. I don't know when we will sail but there is one comfort. There is no Cape Hatteras on the way & May is the least stormy time to go over. . . .

Lizzie

1. Henry Merrell's relatives, especially those on his mother's side, remembered Willie with great affection from his 1860 visit with the Merrells.

2. Henry Merrell's mother, Harriet Camp Merrell (1799–1880), was known to the Smith family as Aunty Merrell. Lizzie Smith would have met Harriet when she visited Henry in Georgia about 1850, while he was the head of two textile concerns in Greene County.

3. Henry Merrell's mother was living with her nephew, Walter Bicker Camp (1822–1916), in Sackets Harbor, New York. During the Civil War, Walter Camp had been energetic in raising federal troops from New York. As a result, Archibald Smith feared that his daughters would have to visit the home of someone who had their brother's blood on his hands. See letter of May 2, 1866, Elizabeth Merrell to Anne Smith, Smith Papers, box 100, folder 8.

LIZZIE, UNDATED [AFTER MAY 2, 1866]

[Niagara, N.Y.]

Dear folks at home

Aunt Bet received your letter (Aunty's) Saturday. We were very glad to hear you had got home safely at last but I am very sorry you were detained so long in Valdosta & in Albany. You must have found it horrid in Albany. I do wish I was at home to help with all the work which I know you have to do & will do notwithstanding all the promises to think of all the time I idle away & you all working hard & if all my idle time was used for some good what a lot of work I might accomplish. I am too glad to hear even two of the tables are safe for I know how much Mother valued them & then we will not have to eat off of pine tables.

We stayed at Watertown[1] till Tuesday morning & then left for Niagara where this letter is commenced. We will stay here tomorrow & in the evening go to Rochester to take the boat to Lake Ontario for Sacketts Harbor. Mr Walter Camp was at Watertown Saturday & gave us a very cordial invitation to go to his house & stay. They (he & Aunty Merrell) had before sent us a very pressing invite to go there so I suppose we will. Aunt Bet saw Mrs Geo Camp[2] & some other of those ladies who William knew & they sent us very kind messages & said they were very anxious to make our acquaintance on his account. They must have admired him very much. I am afraid they will not think me worthy to be the sister of such as he was. It makes me feel very sad going all about where he has been & thinking his eyes looked on all these things & will never look on them again. I always thought if ever I went off travelling it would be with him & we would enjoy it together but alas for us not for him. He could not enjoy any thing here now his eyes have seen the beauties which fade not.

We went this morning to Goat Island & rode round & saw the falls on the American side went up in the tower & saw the Canadian falls. Then we went over the suspension bridge to Canada & saw the falls there. Generally people are disappointed they say. But I was not at all. The falls are much grander & look a great deal higher than I expected. We enjoyed being in Canada hugely. We talked secesh & Jeff Davis & abused yankees & you dont know how much better physically one feels over there. I really think it is so for the people look more independent & don't have that mean sort of yankee look which they do here.

The ban of silence with regard to our journey is removed.[3] You may tell any one we are going to Europe. Oh my heart fails when I think of it. It is so far off. It seems as if we had been gone six months already I wish I was coming home instead of going. . . .

I send also a piece of birch bark which I picked up at the falls in the Black river at Watertown. That is for Sonny specially. . . .

your aff Lizzie

1. Henry Merrell's brother, Samuel Lewis Merrell, was a minister in Watertown, New York.

2. Perhaps Elizabeth Hitchcock Camp, the mother of the George Hull Camp mentioned earlier.

3. The Smiths had agreed that they would keep secret from their Southern friends the fact that they were touring the North so soon after the war.

LIZZIE, UNDATED AND UNADDRESSED

You need never fear my dear [   ] that I shall disgrace the memory of my brother by any such alliance as you speak of. Do you think I could ever feel complacently to any one with his blood on their hands? No indeed if you could know how I feel it you never would suspect me of any such thing. It goes against me to look at much more to speak to a yankee. It gives me a crawly feeling to be near one just as tho they were horrid reptiles & I always imagine the blood on their hands. To be sure I know there are many exceptions & I saw several such at the north which did me lots of good. 2 ladies in Utica who called on us just because we were southerners. One told us she had many relatives in the Southern army & 1 I think in the northern which she did not like tho she was very proud of the former & she did make great lions of them. Mrs Camp said when they went to see her, she was Mrs Seymour, sister in law to ex gov.[1] The other one was Mrs Miller, sister to ex gov. I did so like to hear them praise the southerners & turn up their noses at the yanks & that before Mrs Camp too so not just to please us. I hope you will get over any of those foolish ideas about me for I can assure you they are groundless.

1. Henry Merrell knew Horatio Seymour (1810–86), who served as governor of New York from 1852 to 1854 and who ran against U. S. Grant for president of the United States in 1868.

MARY ANN MASON TO ANNE MAGILL SMITH
Raleigh May 12.

My Dear Mrs Smith

I have received your letter and that of your sister Mrs Merrell. I am very glad to find your daughters will travel this summer, I think it will greatly benefit their health. I sincerely sympathize with you, in your sad feeling on returning to your injured home. But dear friend we must have to forego much in this lower world, in anticipation of that bright and enduring blessedness, with our divine Saviour, and those we love already participants of those untold joys. . . .

As respects the monument. Dr. Mason has seen the stonecutter and he says he can prepare a slab and two uprights—of granite at 75 dollars. Of

Marble about 100. Dr Mason had one of this kind done for a young clergyman who died at our house and it looks very well indeed.

I like this very much. (*not the drawing*)

Dr Mason says he has in his hands now of yours about $40 dollars, which can go towards the stone. If you say so he will have it done at once. Send on the inscriptions you wish at once—if you conclude to have it done now.

A few days ago in cleaning up my dressing room—I found on the top of a wardrobe an over coat of your son, his cap & blanket. I had forgotten these. How shall I send them to you? Please let me know.

. . . . It was a mournful pleasure to bestow my care on so good, gentle, and superior a man as your son. There is nothing I would have grudged to do for him, in my power and this from real regard as well as a sense of duty to our heroic martyrs. You do not know what a comfort it is to me to recall his own precious words to me "My own Mother could not do more" "and I feel like calling you mother."

And this is now one of my regrets—when he said this I was telling him something & forgot at the moment to say "why do you not?" And then it passed out of my mind. He died soon after this. In truth I had heavy cares pressing on me at the time, and my visits at the tent often had to be cut short suddenly so that I frequently intended to renew conversations with your son which afterwards would pass out of my mind. But he knew how it was, and sympathized with me in all my cares. As a son would have done. . . .

I wish you could come & see me. I should enjoy a visit from you so much & do write to your sister & daughters and tell them it will be very easy to return to Savannah by land & stop in Raleigh. I hope they will.

I send you a Raleigh paper containing the account of the floral visit to the tombs of Confederate dead. I think it will interest you.

Your Willie's grave of course was among the number of graves visited. Only three weeks ago my daughters had his grave sodded over and flowers planted again. But they die. The grave yard is at a distance from us. I shall have violets planted and grasses. The rose bushes do not seem to survive so well. But when the stone covers the place there will be no danger of interruption of any kind.

I like the kind I have mentioned to you best—on that account nothing can trouble the grave, when the slab is placed entirely over it. . . .

Best love & respects to your husband and all the family

ever affectionately
yours
Mary Mason

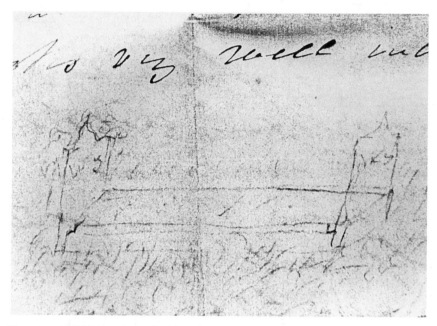
Drawing of Willie's tombstone by Mary Ann Mason

LIZZIE, UNDATED [AFTER MAY 17, 1866]
Dear Folks at home

I suppose we may say we are started as we are now on our way from Kingston to Montreal & Quebec. Our tickets are bought on the steamer to Londonderry I am very glad. We will land there instead of at Liverpool it makes the voyage so much shorter. On Saturday 19*th* at 12 oc we sail. I wish I could just fly home & see how you all are before we sail. I don't know if I could be driven off if I did get there. I am too distressed that we could not hear something definite about your fixments before we have. I hope we may find one at Quebec as Mr Camp was to send any letters that might come after we left by rail which would reach Q a day before we do by boat.

I commence this letter on board the *Magnet* on the St Lawrence. We have been going through the thousand isles & it is perfectly beautiful now. I don't know what it must be in summer. The little islands remind me very much of the little islands in the Chattahoochee which you see on the new Marietta road. This boat is the same one which they all went down the St. L. & up the Saguenay in when William was here. I have thought so much of him today the same boat & the same scenery which he gazed on but he has gone. I can't enjoy it half as much as if I thought we could talk it all over when I go back home....

your aff   Lizzie

[May 19, 1866]

This is the last opportunity which I will have to write home till the wide ocean rolls between us. We are on board & have very good accommodations not nice looking by any means but clean & our staterooms tho small are in the best part of the ship as regards ventilation & motion.

The weather is fair & we hope to have a good voyage.

At any rate we can trust tho' storms should come to him who rules in storm as well as sunshine as we have proved before. You must not all of you feel lonesome & low spirited at home. Now I am afraid you do but you must think of what good times we will have telling you all we have seen when we come home if we are all so happy as to be spared till then. Uncle H has pretty well decided to return in Oct. I am very glad of that....

.... I am afraid we will not hear from you till we get to London. You must all try not to feel lonesome & badly & we will do the same & when we get excited seeing things I don't feel so but somehow I don't enjoy things as I did before. I always used to think how much William would enjoy them.

There is a young man on board so much like William. I can't keep my eyes off his face & yet it makes me feel so sad to look at him. He has not as fine eyes as William's but still there is something about him alike too. I hope he is not a yankee. I could not bear the idea of such a thing.

We were looking at the evening star yesterday evening & wondering if you were looking at her too & I thought we could always think of each other when we see her & you can always think that I am looking at her & thinking of you.

I look forward to October & pray we may all see it in peace & health & comfort tho God knows best & I hope that whatever is his will I shall have strength to bear & for you all the same.

your aff daughter

Saturday eve 19th   Lizzie

Lizzie and Helen Zubly Smith, on their trip to Europe in 1866.
Courtesy of the Georgia Department of Archives and History

Roswell May 23rd 1866

My Dear Children

Your Aunt Bet said in her last letter, you might not sail before the middle of this month & as that time is now past I suppose you have left the country. When I think of the wide ocean separating us I feel sad, but when I think of the advantages which we so confidently expect from the trip the sadness is entirely overcome & I rejoice & thank God & your kind Uncle & Aunt that you have such an opportunity & I hope you are not backward in letting them see that you appreciate their kindness.

We have received your letters from Sackets Harbour. I am much obliged to Mr Camp for his politeness & yet I could not help hoping you would somehow avoid that visit though it would not have done to insist on not going as it would have been at your Uncle's expense. The weather is delightful & we are getting along very well but I am amused at your ideas that we are getting fix'd. We cannot put to rights until we can get moderately cleaned & while we were without a servant that seemed impossible. I have hired 3 different persons to scour but all they do is to make a great swash all over the floor & sweep it out after splashing round with corn shocks on a long handle & only the "big dirt" is taken off. One woman scoured the paint very well, but how we shall get the walls & ceilings cleaned I do not know. I tried one man & he only smeared the ceiling. Wages are high & they make the days work very short both coming & going when the sun is from 1 to 2 hours high.

What nice people your Uncle Henry's friends must be & how pleasant it must have been for you at the McAlpin's but I am afraid your Uncle was ashamed of you. How is it you have not got travelling dresses? While I think of it let me beg Lizzie to write with ink. Her letters are very interesting but I have to study very hard & I realize the truth of what the scripture says about "much study" & when she writes on thin paper it will be impossible for me to read if she continues to use a pencil.

I am very glad to hear the ban of silence in regard to your travels is removed. Persons seemed to think [it] so strange that you should be travelling at the North. Mrs C. Dunwody said it was quite a relief to her mind when Mr Camp told them you were going to Europe. She could not see how you could go to travel at the North but Charley said if it was for health you might.[1]

I had a long letter from Mrs. Mason yesterday. . . . She says "do write to your sister and daughters & tell them it will be very easy to return to Sav. by land & stop in Raleigh & I hope they will." She sent a drawing of a tomb

Lizzie Smith. Courtesy of the Georgia Department of Archives and History

stone which she said would cost about $100. I do not exactly like it, but a handsome slab will not cost more & as she says protects the grave better than any other. I do not like to have it left so long undone as to wait until you come back & I do not like to have one that any of the family does not like & yet it seems to me better not to wait....

Willie[2] has grown a good deal & looks pretty well but his arm is still bad tho' he seems to use it very well. I am sorry you did not take your watches & have them well repaired. Neither of them is of any use to me. Your Aunty's clock goes but it is very inconvenient to me to have to go up stairs every time I want to know the time.

I do not think it worth while to write about all kinds of things as I am doing when the letter is to go so far but after I passed the half sheet I did not want to send blank paper. Hereafter I will be short. The Mintons send love. The Major is quite flattered by being remembered.

We are all well & unite in love to you both with your Uncle & Aunt. May God bless & keep you my dear children & not allow your hearts to be drawn away from him....

Your affectionate Mother

1. The references seem to be to Ellen C. Dunwody (1827–95); to her husband, Major Charles A. Dunwody (1828?–1905); and to George Hull Camp.

2. A slip. "Archie" was obviously intended.

HELEN TO MOTHER, UNDATED

We have had a very good trip and were so fortunate as not to have a storm though we had some very rough disagreeable weather and it was very cold indeed. So we had to wear our little black shawls under our others all the time and I wore an undershirt of Uncle Henry's all the time. I was more sea-sick than I was coming from Savannah probably because I tried to sit up more. There were only two days I think that I was not on deck most of the day. We used to find it very hard to dress in the morning but after we were once in the fresh air we did very well until we had to go down again. Almost every body was awfully sick. Ambet went to bed the day after we left the St Lawrence and stayed most of the time. We did get her on deck one very smooth day but she had hardly got up when it commenced to rain and she went down again and never came up till this morning when we left the steamer. Saturday was an awful day not stormy but terribly rough. They said it was because there had been a storm and the sea had not gone down. We were very thankful that we did not get in the storm itself.

The passengers were a very dull set. They did not get up any entertainment but they were mostly sympathisers with the south. The yankee Gen Neal Dow was on board,[1] and when he first came on he had a great deal to say against the south but he soon found that people did not agree with him and he subsided entirely and we hardly heard or saw any thing more of him. Uncle Henry took him up one night when he was telling some of his big stories and told how it really was. Some of the English men came up and shook hands with him and expressed their sympathy with us. It does not do any good but it is pleasant to find people who speak well of the un-successful and give them credit for good motives and courage and under-stand the meanness of the yankees.

There was a Confederate Col. on board who had captured Gen Dow dur-ing the war. He is a funny little fellow [who] has come to Ireland to see his re-lations. He was quite delighted to meet some countrymen and we saw a good deal of him when he was not too sick to be visible.

Our steam up the lock this morning was perfectly delightful. I never imagined beautiful green grass and the trees all freshly put out and the swell of the "May blossom." It was enchanting. I do wish you could all have en-

Helen Zubly Smith.
Courtesy of the Georgia
Department of Archives
and History

joyed it too. "The gem of the sea" and "Emerald Isle" are not by any means extravagant names for this country.

Aff

Helen

We have not much time for writing as it is late and we have to start early.

1. Former federal general Neal Dow (1804–97) is better known as a temperance advocate and father of the Maine Liquor Law than as a military leader. For a time he was commander of the District of Florida, with headquarters at Pensacola. He had been captured, imprisoned, and then exchanged in 1864 (Warner, *Generals in Blue,* 130–31).

ELIZABETH MAGILL MERRELL TO ARCHIE

Londonderry, May 29th 1866

Dear Sonny. Your letter was addressed to your sister & the other folks so as I suppose I am one of them, I will answer it. We arrived here about 3 hours since, after a prosperous voyage of 10 days. Lizzie wrote by the Pilot who left

Elizabeth Magill Merrell (1815–90) and Henry Merrell (1816–83), circa 1855

us on Sunday night in the Gulf of St. Lawrence. We left Quebec at eleven A.M. on Saturday. It was charming going down the river & out in the Gulf & we were on deck all the time, but on Monday morning your poor giddy headed aunt Bet had to keep her berth & was up very little more until this morning after we got in. We had no storm at all but some days great rolling & pitching and all the time pitching enough to make me sick if I was up. We had a very fine ship & excellent & attentive officers, & waiters. We were out nearly 2 days longer than was expected, had but one day fair wind & unfortunately as we thought a bad lot of coal, & were inclined to murmur at the delay, but afterwards had cause of gratitude & learned how much better our Heavenly Father can order things for us than we can, for we had 2 days & one night of most distressing rolling & pitching & waves terribly high from a storm which we would have been in if we had come any faster.

Those were 2 horrible days & nights & almost every body had to keep their beds because they could not sit up; or stand up. Your sister was not seasick I believe at all, & Helen only a few times. They sometimes spent whole days on deck never coming down at all, & I believe even those rough days they went up & took their seats on the floor & staid some hours. They are real sailors; Sissy stood the whole voyage even better than your sister for *she* had one of her nervous spells one night. We have been out since we came &

*Golden anniversary portraits of Archibald and Anne Smith, from an 1880 locket found
in the Smith home*

seen some of the places of interest in this old Town, been in the Cathedral
where the people used to assemble every day during the siege & Walker used
to preach.[1] It is a splendid old building; walked on the wall of the City & saw
some of the old guns that did such execution. You will think we are smart to
have seen all these things already, but we went out as soon as we got here. We
stopped here instead of going on to Liverpool because we avoid one day at
sea; & your uncle wanted us to see this old Town. . . .

How much I have had your dear precious brother with me since I commenced my traveling; the last Journey I took he was with us; & never having
seen him since under other circumstances I have gone back the 6 years &
seem to have him with me in all the places we visited in N York State, in our
trip down among the Thousand Islands; down the Rapids, visiting the
places we visited together in Montreal & coming down to Quebec just about
such an evening as we came down together & just such a glorious sunset on
the water, sometimes I could almost imagine I heard his remarks on the passing scenes. Then the sad reality would come over me that never more would
I hear that voice again or see that sweet face in this world. But oh! far more
rapturous scenes does he now behold; then let us not weep that he is not
here. Dear Sonny, walk in the footsteps of that precious brother that you may

attain to that glorious inheritance which is most surely his. Give a great deal of love to Father Mother Aunty & yourself from uncle H. & myself. . . .

your aff aunt Bet

1. Always a Protestant center, Londonderry held out in 1688–89 against a siege from the forces of James II. The clergyman-governor George Walker was killed in 1690 at the Battle of the Boyne.

ARCHIBALD SMITH AND ANNE MAGILL SMITH TO LIZZIE AND HELEN

Roswell Cobb Co G^a North America
5 June 1866

My Dear Daughters

See what an undertaking, a sheet of super-royal-letter-cap, close lines; well I don't suppose I can strike it off at one sitting, or work in one vein thro'out (is it so, or throout, or so, through-out or so, throout.) but intend to be at it and at it, until I fill it, even if it should prove to be only as a puddle of tadpoles, to amuse you with their wiggle-*tales*. . . . Little troubles which pressed on us when we first got home are passing too, or we are getting more used to the burden, or are having them lightened by looking at the blessings we have; and among them the most striking is the wonderful manner in which we are all standing the hard work we have done, indeed our strength appeared to grow as it was needed; and it was needed to keep up for more than a month without a servant. Aunty did most of the cooking & sometimes bro't water from the spring, tho A & I did that mostly: I used to look with wonder at Mother taking off or putting on a kettle to the fire; where was the old pain in the back, well God helped & we all got so tired that we sleeped the sleep of the laborer and were refreshed and your sweet letters came to us so often that our toils were lightened and we have not only got thru it, but I think are all better in health than when we left Valdosta. . . .

I am amazed, & you would be to see how I work. I have kept your wish and have not *over*-worked. You see I would work & *get tired, healthy tired,* and come in & rest, and sometimes I would find dinner ready, and eat not too much, for several reasons, and would feel so fresh that I w^d go & get tired again, & then w^d be ready for supper quite sleepy, & so off & on till now I am quite hearty; I often felt how glad I am that the girls are not here, we are getting along finely, & it may be if you had been here we would not have worked so steadily & having time to fret would have all broke down together,

& then your letters were so full and gave us so many pleasant things to think about, that I really think we have done better with you where you were, I am truly thankful to God for the dealings of his providence in this matter. I have wanted to write to you often, and at last I determined I will write next week. Well here is Tuesday & to help me there is a steady pour down of rain. There has been before [us] one of the rainiest seasons I ever knew, & it has extended over the whole land. Grass is king, and cotton by its failure will like Sampson destroy his enemies in his dying struggles. Unless I know nothing of the Negro character there will not be picked 100 lbs to the hand in all the States. The Negro will run away, wages or no wages. We have a Cook on trial. She found it hard last winter to feed her children, appears desirous to please, & to keep her place, washes & irons, scrubs, & cleans up, at spare times, & is cleanly, don't know much, but wants to learn & is quite elated at being employed by Quality folks.

I do hope the cotton crop may fail; the South can not be much injured by it, she is brot so low already; and the cruel Yankee and western man may have some of the trouble brot home to him: the worst of it is that the poor Negro will bear the brunt of it, and there has been an official investigation, into the affairs of Freedmans Bureau, by order of Pres^t John^n, and it has developed some Yankeeism, the rogues are quarreling about it & I suppose it will lead to recrimination, and a slight exposure of their misdeeds in other matters. Your letters were interesting, especially where they tell of your kindly greeting by Southern sympathisers, and the hospitality you received from the Camps. The latter has been turned into chagrin since I heard what Mr G. Camp said about his bro' Walter's conduct in the war; Bro Henry's charity must be very large if he knew the *active* part which Walter took *raising troops* for the war,[1] and then led you, whose Brother had been murdered by those troops, to accept his hospitality: I can't suppose he knew it: he knew my sentiments & your feelings too well to put you into such a degrading position. . . .

You must not fret, or be fearful about us, or yourselves. We are all partakers of the Covenant thro faith in Christ, and it is well with us whatever may be appointed for us, for it is all in love. I fear that Liz is not resigned as she should be that our dear one is not with her in all the wonders & beauties she is beholding. Try & think of Him dear as in far happier scenes, and let this assurance draw forth your heart to God in praise for his redeeming love; and you may be assured of the continued fellowship & that the theme will be taken up by him in heavenly strains of joyful praise & adoration. Oh dear child rather praise God that you have spiritual union with one who is perfect, and in the full enjoyment of scenes more glorious than any earth can boast,

& where there are no rude alarms of raging foes, no sorrow, no sin, no more death. May God give us all grace gladly to leave all things here below at his call knowing that those we love will soon follow & we shall part no more.

Tell Bro. H. I am negociating with Mr Davis & have sent him those bills. I leave a little space for Mother to make up deficiencies, love to all, from
your affectionate Father   Arch^d Smith

Father has written you such a long letter that I think there can be nothing left for me to tell. . . . I have sent a description of the stone Aunt Bet sent me. We all liked it so much & told them if it could be had $200 covering all expenses to put it up immediately if it could not be had for that, get a large slab resting at the corners on granite pillars 18 inches high inscription Ps 17–15. . . .

1. Walter B. Camp had been energetic in raising federal troops from New York (Skinner, ed., *Autobiography of Henry Merrell*, 393).

ANNE MAGILL SMITH, UNDATED
>William S. Smith
>of Roswell Geo. Co A. 18th Geo Batt^n
>Obt. July 7th 1865 At 30 yrs and 7 mos.
>As for me I shall behold thy face in righteousness
>I shall be satisfied when I awake with thy likeness.

LIZZIE

London June 23^d 66

Dear Folks at Home

We have been today to the British museum but I despair of ever getting through with it. We were there from two to 5 ½ & only saw a little & were so tired standing & walking we had to come away without seeing any thing to speak of. There were rooms & rooms of stuffed animals & birds & fish. Minerals & gems in every state of formation & of preparation for setting. I thought how William would have enjoyed that part of it. He loved such things so much. Aunt Bet was looking over that part while we were some where else. She made the same remark when we came back, & the books too how he would have liked them. . . .

I received two letters from Rebecca Mason very nice letters. I am glad you will not get that monument at the north. I could not bear the idea. I am very willing you should do what ever suits you. That will please me as far as I am concerned. I am much obliged to Mrs Mason but I had rather for my part not go home that way. . . .

your aff Lizzie

REV. DR. R. S. MASON TO ARCHIBALD SMITH
Raleigh July 7. '66

My dear Sir

Mrs Mason received a few days ago Mrs Smith's letter of the 20th of last month. I have had copied from a book owned by the stone cutter three such monuments as I supposed would be most nearly in accordance with the wishes of the family. Will you be pleased to select and return the one you most approve of. The stone cutter has promised to execute it immediately.

No. 1 is 6 feet high, four inches thick and will cost $160 exclusive of the wreath at the top of the stone. The wreath would be $25.00 and the lettering 6 cts. a letter. No. 2, five feet high 4 in. thick $125 exclusive of lettering. No 3. $185.00 exclusive of lettering 6 feet high 5 in thick.

I have in hand from the money sent me by Mr. Duncan about $42.00.

It will give us great satisfaction my dear Sir, if we can do anything to gratify you in the erection of a suitable monument to your noble Son.

With kindest remembrances from all the members of my family to you and yours

I remain
My dear Sir
with great regard & esteem
very truly yr friend
RS Mason

ELIZABETH MAGILL MERRELL TO ANNE MAGILL SMITH
[JULY 1866]

London

Dear sister I fear you will think I am very remiss about writing but Lizzie generally has her Envelope so full that I cannot put in much, & I know she must write every thing that is worth writing. We are still here as you see & I don't know how long we will be here. The war has sadly interfered with our plans of travel and I fear we will not be able to go to any countries but France Scotland & Switzerland.[1] Mr. M. thinks as that is the case we better spend more time here where there is a great deal to see. He intends to spend

4 weeks in Switzerland thinking that the pure mountain air will invigorate us all. We are getting very anxious to hear from you all. It is about 3 weeks since we heard & your letters were no later than the 8th of May. I fear they have not been directed right, as Lizzie writes so indistinctly; and we will lose them altogether.

We have had very cool weather the last week; cold enough for fires, & cloaks. It makes it much more pleasant for our excursions that we take every day. We spent several hours at Kew garden one day last week & saw a great many beautiful & rare plants & flowers of which I suppose Lizzie has written you. We went by Steamboat up the Thames about 3 hours run & spent several hours in the greenhouses & Park then walked over to Richmond to dine at 7 & back to London by Cars at 10. It is so strange to see it light here at that hour, as light as it is at home half an hour after sunset. We are beginning to know London so well that the girls & I make excursions without Mr. M. We went last week to the Tower, & also to a fine Picture gallery. The family with whom Mr. M. lodged are very attentive to us.[2] They are very pleasant & refined people. 2 young ladies very pleasant. They often go about with us & we have taken tea with them several times. The mother is very much of a lady. . . .

How much I thought of you all on Saturday; the anniversary of our dearest Willie's death; & knew how you were all feeling. We were very sad & could not go any where; but spent the day in the house in quiet. On Sunday evening Mr. M. struck up "How blest the righteous when he dies." I tried to sing it but could not. The words carried me so forcibly back to that calm & quiet deathbed scene in that tent. How those beautiful words describe the closing life of that lovely character. I shall never again hear them without thinking of our precious Willie. But why grieve when he is so blest? I sent a paper to Archie last week. I hope he received it. I am sorry to hear he is not so strong as he has been. We do not hear from Charlie, they are very bad about writing. Mr. M. joins me in much love to all. . . .

your aff sister E. M.

1. The Seven Weeks War between Austria and various German states under the leadership of Prussia lasted from June 16 to August 23, 1866.

2. On his journey for the Confederacy Henry Merrell lodged with a Hinton family that lived at 35 Bedford Street, Covent Garden (Smith Papers, box 7, folder 2).

ARCHIBALD SMITH TO REV. DR. R. S. MASON, DRAFT
Roswell 14ᵗʰ July 66

Revᵈ R. S. Mason

My Dear Sir

We received yesterday your kind letter, written on the anniversary of the death of our dear William that was a day of deep feeling to me, in which, on review, of my feelings for the past year, of the consolations vouchsafed to us, in recalling the Christian love, and most kind attentions of yourself, and family, to the departed, the tender sympathy of all of you to us as expressed in your letters, I was constrained, submissively, yes joyfully, to say, blessed be the name of the Lord, goodness & mercy have followed me all my days, & I shall yet lie down in peace.

The drafts you sent us have given us a better idea of what we wish than we could otherwise have, tho neither of them exactly suit our taste, and means. We have therefore selected, from two of them, different parts, supposing the change can be readily made; and send a draft. You see we have adopted the upper part of No 2, and the lower part of no 1, which we like better.

We would rather the expense should be put on the solid than the ornamental parts & therefore prefer the thickness to be *Six* inches, if that can be obtained, and the marble part above the granite block to be five feet with *proportional* width. I believe Mʳˢ Smith has already sent to Mʳˢ Mason the inscription we wish.

When you let us know the full cost, I will send you the amt. either in Bills, or a check on N. York as you prefer.

MARY ANN MASON TO ANNE MAGILL SMITH
Raleigh Aug 15ᵗʰ

My dear Friend

I have been wishing to write to you for some time, but have not been able to do so. For several weeks I was suffering with neuralgia and as soon as I became able to stir about I must needs fall down stairs head foremost and narrowly escape breaking both neck & back. Since then I have been in bed most of the time. I am much better now, and my general health is much improved. (I do not say by the fall.)

Dr Mason bids me say to you that the stonecutter had no marble to suit and so he has to wait till it can be procured from N York. I am hurrying them all I can that the monument may be in its place before your sister and daughters arrive. You must insist upon their coming this way and paying us a visit. I am very anxious to make their acquaintance, and also to make friends with your sister on account of the dress. It is a beautiful dress and if I am in health to wear it I must try and have it ready by the time she comes. I have not yet made it up for I was afraid I should spoil it in summer. I have five daughters and two sons all single and I tell them it is a shame some of them do not get married and give me a chance to shew off my elegant dress. At any rate I will let them all see how grand I look in it, some day.

Rebecca is greatly pleased with the kind attentions of your daughters all the way from beyond the seas, and so are we all. And this makes us hope the more that they will not pass us on their way home. It will only be taking the land route instead of by sea.

I am writing at the window where I used to sit and watch the tent of my patient last summer, and listen, (as an old mother bird for the least chirp from the nest of her little brood) for a word or a sign from my baby. And some times I shut my eyes, imagine he is sitting out before the tent door. But alas when I open my eyes I miss the bright smiling inviting countenance, that used to hasten me down to minister to his wishes or wants. You don't know what a pleasure it was & how mournfully I miss that pleasing occupation.

But there we must all remember how our loss is his immense gain. I know it is far better to listen to the melody of his Saviour's voice, and bask in the bliss of His glorious gladdening smile. We must not wish him back in this uncertain world. We must try for his sake to be happy without his company for a little while. It will be for only a little while. If ever a soul was prepared to meet his Master surely he was. The night before he died he received yours and his father's letters and I never saw such happiness. It seemed as if that was all he wished to make him supremely happy. Dr. Mason was with him till two or three in the morning and he was still in a sort of ecstacy of happiness. Then he slept, and Dr. M left him, for he said he knew he should sleep till morning after taking his usual confusing draft.

But on the next morning the messenger was sent to bear his ransomed soul to the bosom of the Redeemer he had so loved, and trusted in. And there he surely is in rest and peace waiting the coming of his dear ones from earth. The girls have again and again planted flowers on his grave but they have died, but they still visit and adorn the hallowed spot and will do so till the monument is on the grave.

Our church is on a small lot in the heart of the town, so there is no grave yard attached to it. But your son was laid in the city cemetery.[1] There is no other place. None of the churches here have burying grounds attached to them. . . .

Present my best respects to Mr Smith & all your family and believe me
ever truly your affectionate friend
Mary Mason

1. Willie's body now rests in the Mason family plot in the Oakwood Cemetery, Raleigh, North Carolina, having been moved from its original location in the nearby City Cemetery.

MOTHER TO LIZZIE AND HELEN

Roswell Aug. 28*th* 1866

My Dear Children

Writing day is come but there seems to be nothing to write about except that it has been raining most of the time for 36 hours. I hope it will do some good to the potatoes & peas tho' it is too late to help the corn. We cannot understand your movement for in a letter dated 31*st* July you say Aunt Bet thinks she has received some benefit to her hearing & we are to remain in London another week for her to be with the Aurist & two days later the newspapers were mailed from Lewes. . . .

So many of our letters must have been lost that I should be afraid to send money even if your things could be sold. I cannot set down & tell you at one time what I want. I must just write as I think of it so I wish you would keep a piece of paper & set down every time a letter comes. Do get some seeds of the best French Artichoke & get what fine flower seeds you can. How lovely the carnations must be. Would it be possible to find out the mode of cultivation? You will be disappointed when you see our garden, I wrote you before that the beds on the east side of the house cannot be traced out, but you have rec^d so few letters, your Aunty has written every other time & altogether we have not miss'd more that 2 weeks if that. . . .

. . . We are having not a great many, but very nice nutmeg melons[1] & it makes me think so much of Dear William when Sonny cuts one in two & digs it out. You remember how W. used to sit on the porch after dinner & feed the ducks with the seeds, but O "I would not call him back to earth & the strife of earthly things." . . .

Love to all May God bless & keep you
Your aff
Mother

1. Cantaloupes.

Milan Septr 25th 1866

Dear sister . . . . Switzerland is so lovely I wonder our ancestors could have left it. Miss M.G. has given us a letter to a Madame Tolverger who can speak a little English. She is the only person of her acquaintance in Appenzell who speaks any thing but German. She will introduce us to the Toblers there who no doubt are the same family as we are.[1]

The day after Lizzie mailed her letter to you we came here; we came part of the trip on Lake Maggiore. It is a lovely trip but unfortunately it rained & we did not see it in all its beauty. It is thickly & beautifully settled. Sometimes we were in sight of 6 or 8 towns at one time; they settle towns away up on the hill sides. Sometimes we would pass a convent or church up on a steep hill & the ascent to it would be dotted on each side with shrines; once we counted 15; at each of these, the poor creatures have to say so many prayers in their ascent.

We got here by rail at 8 oclock saturday night. There is one Protestant Church here English; we were to go to last night; but on enquiry Mr. M. found it was 1 1/2 miles off & he did not like to venture so far with ladies in a strange Italian city which is at present full of discharged soldiers going to their homes. This morning I went to the window & there was just going by a soldier's funeral; the coffin borne by his comrades; his grey coat exactly the color of our dear Willie's & his cap were laid upon the coffin. I could not contain my tears, it made me think so much of that scene in Raleigh. I do not like to see the coats of that colour. It makes me think always of the sad scenes we have passed through so lately. Oh how many sorrowing hearts are associated with the Confederate grey. . . .

We have been very much favoured this summer; not one day have we been obliged to stop on account of the indisposition of any member of the party. I hope we are thankful for it. The time draws near when we must begin to think of returning home. O! how I dread that sea-voyage; The girls & Mr. M. send much love to all; with your aff sister E. . . .

1. In the intermarriage typical of planter families in the South, Anne Magill Smith and her siblings have the same maternal great-grandparents as Archibald Smith: John (or Johann) Joachim Zubly (1724–81) and Anna Tobler Zubly (1725–65). Anna Tobler was from the canton of Appenzelle in Switzerland, the name of which Archibald Smith had used for his first plantation in Camden County, Georgia. John Zubly was from St. Gall. The Zublys' son, David, had two daughters, Helen and Elizabeth. Helen was Archibald Smith's mother, and Elizabeth was the mother of the Magills.

Raleigh Oct 22

My dear Friend

Dr Mason received Mr Smith's letter a few days ago with the bills on N.Y. He will attend to every thing with pleasure, and write you a full account. I am sorry to tell you we have not yet succeeded in getting the monument put up. The man wrote to N York some time ago but it has not yet arrived. And then it will have to be executed to your order.

I hope it will be finished before your sister & daughters arrive. We will do our best to have it so.

I have written a short note to your sister Mrs Merrell which I enclose with this, and beg you to forward with yours to Europe. I ought to have answered her before but I have so many infirmities and multitudes of engagements when I can work that I have not found myself till now in an humour to write.

I think they are wise to remain till spring particularly as the World's Fair in Paris will come off then, and it will improve the young people so much, to see the curiosities of the old world. My dear Mrs Smith we feel deeply your kindness in wanting our daughters to see you, but I am afraid such will not be their good fortune, as two of them Annie & Rebecca propose going out to teach, and Martha our eldest can not be spared from the care of the parish & the old folks her parents. Sally is a permanent invalid with a weak spine and Mary I believe in the spring will leave the state of single blessedness. So that for the present we must be content to think of you all with our best love & postpone the pleasure of a personal acquaintance. I wish you could come & see us. And if not we hope to know you in a better world. . . .

We are all pretty well at present. D^r M who is now in his seventy second year has gone through the summer quite comfortably and I think is in as good health as I have known him for many years.

I hope you and Mr Smith are well and all your family. Remember me to them all with sincere regards and esteem and for yourself

> dear friend believe me
> ever full of love and kindness in the
> bonds of Christ our Lord
> Mary Mason

Raleigh Nov. 12. 66

My dear friend

I had the great pleasure of receiving your letter of the 9th of Octr. and owe you many apologies for not having before replied to it, but I hope you will be kind enough to excuse me, as I have had lately many letters to write, and have indeed twice before begun a letter to you but have been prevented from finishing it.

The checks you sent me were readily received on deposit by the national bank of this place, and I have now $142, one hundred and forty two dollars to be applied to the erection of the monument one hundred last sent & forty-two remaining from the fifty-four fifty $54.50 sent me by Mr. Duncan of Savannah of this

$4.50 were applied for the payment of some burial clothes

3.50 for the transportation of articles left by yr. Son

2.50 for sodding and otherwise dressing the grave

2.00 to servants for attendance

Be pleased not to send any more till the monument is complete.

I have feared sometimes you might think me remiss, although you have given me no intimation of the kind, in not sending you before this an account of the progress of the monument. But I am sorry to tell you it is not yet begun. The stone cutter had on hand no slab of the thickness you wished and sent for one immediately, as he assures me. He has been promised again and again that it should be sent at once, but he has not yet received it. He tells me that being so often disappointed in getting this slab from New York, he has written to Philadelphia for one, and is in daily expectation of receiving it. I have been repeatedly to him, and really believe he is anxious to do the work. I sincerely regret the delay, and I must be patient as there is no other stone-cutter in the place.

I am truly gratified, dear friend, with the expression of your friendship for me. It would be an unalloyed gratification to me, were it not accompanied with the remembrance of the sad loss of your noble son. But, pardon me, dear friend, for saying I think you value much too highly the little attentions, and few comforts we were able to afford him. We hoped at one time it would have pleased God, we might have been the instruments in his hands of sending him back to you restored to health, but He whose ways must necessarily be wisest, fittest, best, saw fit to determine otherwise, and to take one whom His grace I believe, had so well prepared, from this world of care and trouble to one of rest and peace, & final joy. He became very much endeared to us by his fine natural disposition sanctified by grace, and his truly gentlemanly demeanor. We felt his loss very much, and could well suppose how much more that loss must have been felt at home.

I hope your dear daughters will return to you with all the pleasure and advantage they expect to derive from so agreeable and so improving a tour. To see mankind in their varied appearances, manners, customs, laws, habitations, countries, what a delight! what an enjoyment! what an enlargement of the mind!

. . . As soon as the slab of marble arrives and the monument is begun, I will write to you again. In the mean time present my kind and respectful regards to the members of your family at present with you especially to Mrs. Smith; also if you please to the travelers when you next write to them.

With true esteem & regard
I remain dr. friend
very sincerely yours
R. S. Mason

REV. DR. R. S. MASON TO ARCHIBALD SMITH

Raleigh Decr. 26. '66

My dear friend

I have at last the pleasure to inform you that the slab of marble for your Son's monument has been received, and the stone cutter has promised me to have the monument completed in a week or ten days. I have no doubt the work will be well done, as they who have engaged to do it are Scotchmen regularly trained; and all the graves-stones and monuments which they have prepared have been well executed. As soon as they have completed your son's monument, I will let you know.

My daughter Rebecca has received her box with all the pretty things contained it in. Give my best thanks to your daughters for their kind remembrance of me in the prettily carved paper-folder they have sent me. Rebecca will write in a very short time.

With sincere regards
I remain dear fnd. truly Yours
R. S. Mason

Raleigh Feby. 6. '67

My dear friend

Enclosed I send the account for the monument which is completed and erected. I think you would be pleased with its appearance. The stone is a handsome one, and the execution is good. I hope we shall have the satisfaction of seeing yourself or some member or members of your family in Raleigh before a long time, and that you will have the melancholy gratification of seeing your noble son suitably remembered. With our best regards for your family

I remain dear friend
faithfully Yours
R. S. Mason

Archibald Smith Esqr.

T. King & Whitelaw D^r

T. One Tomb Stone for the Grave of W.S. Smith	$160.-
Lettering & putting up	15.-
	$175.-
Paid	142
Balance due	$33

Feb. 14th/67

Rev Dr Mason

Dear Sir, your letter of the 6th came to hand yesterday & in Mr Smith's absence you will excuse my addressing & thanking you for all the trouble you have taken in regard to the monument & again reiterate our gratitude for all the kindness & sympathy of yourself & family toward both the dead & the living whose only claim was their suffering & sorrow; words are poor evidence of gratitude yet they are all we have left unless it may be fervent unceasing prayer that God will reward you & in that day when he makes up his jewels will give you brighter crowns inasmuch as you for his sake ministered to his afflicted ones. There is a satisfaction in knowing that the monument is completed & yet it is sad to feel that there is nothing more that we can do, that the last act of love for our darling is performed. Pray for us dear friend that we may be truly submissive to the will of God & even rejoice in it though all our other hopes are as nothing compared with this one. I hope you will have no further trouble on our acc^t yet I cling to the acquaintance the

The grave of Willie Smith in the Mason family plot, Oakwood Cemetery, Raleigh, North Carolina

friendship which has grown out of this great sorrow & trust it will only end with life nor even then for I hope to renew it in that world where no changes come.

Please find enclosed thirty three dollars balance due on the monument.

─────────

ANNE MAGILL SMITH, INSCRIPTION
IN THE SMITH FAMILY BIBLE

William Seagrove Smith
Sweetly fell asleep in Jesus, on
the 7th July 1865, in Raleigh N. C.
where he was received into the
family of Revd R. S. Mason D. D.
an Episcopal Minister, & tenderly
nursed with Christian sympathy
for months, to the final issue of
diseases contracted by exposure
in the service of the Confederate
States, into which he early and
heartily entered.

"The Last Time I Saw Him"

1869–1956

The only member of the Smith family who is known to have visited Willie's grave site in Raleigh was Archie. In May 1869, while on his way to attend Baltimore Business College, Archie stayed with the Mason family. "We think he scarce needs a letter from us to certify who he is," wrote Archibald to the Reverend Mason, "for I feel that you have the remembrance of our William so fresh in your mind that you will at once recognize the Brother. He is indeed very much like him & more perhaps in gentleness and sincerity than in personal appearance." Archie wrote home that he had successfully completed the mission of planting seeds and laying flowers at the grave, and included in the envelope some flowers and grass that he gathered there. He said the Masons "seem like real nice people and I wish we lived nearer to each other. All the daughters are married except the oldest. I went there about 12m and took dinner and tea there and helped the Dr take some honey and admired his garden to his hearts content."

Whether Archibald, Anne, Helen, or Lizzie ever ventured to Raleigh is not certain. However, in a letter written in 1880 to an old Roswell friend whom they had not seen in years—James A. Rainwater[1] of Sardis Panola, Mississippi—Archibald mentions that they did on at least one occasion meet the Masons. After speaking of Willie's death far "from home from disease contracted in the war," and after describing Willie as "a lovely Ch^n whose light shone"—one who someone had told the Smiths "was the only Ch^n in his Co."—Archibald says that "at the end of the war he was kindly nursed by a family in Raleigh NC who cared for him like as a Son. We afterwards saw them in Virginia, an Episcopal Clergym^n a lovely old man & his fam^y. We shall meet them above."

In the same letter, Smith says that he is now "quite deaf" and then gives Rainwater an account of other members of the family. Mrs. Smith is "totally blind," but her infirmities and advanced years have apparently not prevented her from maintaining domestic activity. Archibald says that she "is today busy hem^g a wool shirt of mine wh h^d to be made shorter, & often sews the seams of skirts &c." Lizzie, he continues, "is more than 18 and 30 years old, a good musician, & well educated." Helen "was born at the old farm, was educated at home, is not musical, but a stay to her old Parents & a real treasure." Finally, of Archie he writes, "my remaining Son named after me, born also at the old farm, at 36 years old was educated mostly at home & during the war, & therefore has not much literature, was a Cadet in the Geo. M^y In & saw some service, just enough to ruin his health so that he can not work hard. He married a suitable good wife. They have 2 Ch^{n,} *white crows*, well grown boy & girl."

The "suitable good wife" was Gulielma Riley (1846–1921), whom Archie married in 1870. At first Archie and Gulie lived in Roswell not far from the Smith house, and for a time Archie owned a small business in Roswell making spokes and hubs. The two "white crows" were young Archibald (1874–1947) and Frances Maner (1875–1939). A third child was born in 1881, and given the name Arthur William Ambrose. Following the birth, Elizabeth Merrell wrote from Arkansas to her sister, Helen Zubly Magill, and did not seem pleased with the choice of names: "With regard to the young stranger's name, I cannot agree with you that it is pretty. Arthur & William are both very pretty names, but I cannot think Arthur William Ambrose (why not Zubly?) Smith is. I felt real disappointed when I heard the birth of the baby. I felt sure the name would be Willie & just that."

Five years later, in January 1886, the oldest Archibald Smith passed away, leaving a void in the Smith household. News of his passing reached Valdosta, and Clarinda Richardson,[2] one of the Smiths' servants who had stayed in Valdosta at the conclusion of the Civil War, sent a letter to Lizzie on March 16. Dictating her letter to one of her grandchildren, Clarinda said, "I take this Oppertinity of Writing you a few liens to let you know that we are all well at this time, hopeing thes few liens may find all well. That we heard that Old Mosser was dead. And I rite to find out whether no it was is So er not."

The remainder of the letter discusses some of the Smiths' other former servants and indicates something of Clarinda's relationship to the Smith family. "I Would like to no How all the family is getting along. Mass Archy I did not no you Was in Valdosta untill you was gone. I would like to of Seen you verry much. Tell Miss Lizzie Maria, Maria has 5 Children. Moses family all Send much love to you and they all are well and Silvy has a 11 Children.[3] Dinah was married and was in Savanah Ga and She has 3 Children. Dinah died last October. Please write as soon as you get this. And Pleas to send me my Age. Age. You sent me my age once but it got misplace. Please to send me Maria age. They all must. Miss Helen. Miss Lizzie Mass Arch they all must send me Something. Tell me when you Write. Pleas Direct in the Care of Mr. Middleton. This Maria oldest Child Writing Heattie. I will close by saying Remember me. Please Write to me as often as you can. Clarander Richardson."[4]

The following year saw the deaths of both Anne Magill Smith and Helen Magill, events that may have caused Archie and Gulie to feel that the time was right for them to remove to another part of the state, leaving Lizzie and Helen to keep the Smith home in Roswell. Archie and Gulie moved their family, with Grandmother Riley, to LaGrange, southwest of Atlanta and close to the Alabama line. Archie farmed seventy-five acres in LaGrange, but in a brief memoir written in 1918 Arthur William Smith said the farm was "not profitable." As time passed Archie and his family relied increasingly on leases and sales of land, timber, and turpentine from their properties throughout Georgia and Arkansas to supplement their income.

Their oldest son, Archibald Smith III, was graduated from the University of Georgia in 1895, received his M.D. from the University of Pennsylvania in 1899, and ultimately became a prominent physician in Atlanta.[5] He never married. After attending the Lewisburg Female Academy in West Virginia, their daughter, Frances Maner Smith, for many years kept house with her brother Arthur, and also did not marry. Arthur William Smith was the only one of this generation of Smiths to marry, and he did so late in his life. Because he had no children, he became the last surviving member of the Archibald Smith family.

Like his father before him, Arthur Smith attended a military institute: the Citadel, in Charleston, South Carolina, in 1898–99. There in May 1899, he witnessed a parade of Confederate veterans, and he wrote to his sister, "It was an incident that I will never forget, the troup of veterans passing by, some in the old uniform with musket and canteen, blanket and nap-sack, here and there one proudly bore a Confederate flag, torn to shreds by many a battle, maltreated by the hand of time, but bearing still the stars and bars as did its loyal owner. Or perhaps a large old eagle resting on a field of blue, but over his head there would be written: "Captured at Bull Run." In striking contrast to these tattered flags and heroes in handsomely decorated carriages came the fair daughters of the 'ante Bellum' South, the sponsors of each camp. Then sometimes, although few and feeble with his white wooly locks uncovered you would see a relic of the past indeed, an old Confederate negro. . . . Thursday afternoon we gave an exhibition drill which was quite a success. The skirmish drill with blank cartridges was what tickled the 'vets.' . . . Nearly all the boys tried to make it as pleasant as possible for the 'vets' and we spent much of our time bumming around with them, giving them directions in town, and talking up the school." Arthur also reports having gone to the school auditorium to hear speeches from the old Confederate veterans. He heard General John B. Gordon (1832–1904), whom Lee had asked to lead his troops to the formal surrender at Appomattox, introduce "Fighting Joe" Wheeler (1836–1906), whose cavalry, along with Archie Smith's GMI cadets, provided the only real resistance to Sherman's March to the Sea.[6] "I wish you could have seen Old Gen. Gordon introduce him. . . . When he announced 'the great victor of Santiago' and the people commenced to cheer, he called the house to order saying, 'Wait till I finish.' Then he spoke of the noted commander of 'Wheeler's Cavalry' and allowed the people to express their feelings."

Soon thereafter Arthur enrolled at the University of Georgia, graduating with the class of 1902. While at the university, Arthur met Robert Grier Stephens (1881–1974), great-nephew of Alexander H. Stephens, vice president of the Confederacy. In 1905 Robert Grier Stephens obtained his first medical degree from the Atlanta College of Physicians and Surgeons (now part of Emory University), and in 1907 he married Lucy Evans, the daughter of Confederate general and Civil War historian Clement A. Evans. Stephens became a well-known physician for thirty years in Atlanta, and for thirty years more in Washington, Georgia.[7] He also became one of Arthur's closest friends.

Arthur studied architecture at the Ecole des Beaux Arts in Paris from 1907 to 1909 and subsequently became a prominent Atlanta architect, working first as chief designer for firms such as P. Thornton Marye and G. Lloyd Preacher and later as partner in the firm of Wilhoit and Smith. Most noteworthy among the designs for which he claimed credit was the Atlanta City Hall, which he executed while working for G. Lloyd Preacher. He also designed a new educational building for the Roswell Presbyterian Church as well as the old Roswell City Hall on Founder's Square.[8]

Throughout their sixty-year friendship, Arthur Smith and Robert Stephens shared a fascination and a reverence for the Old South, and as the few letters that follow show, they often wrote wistfully of the bygone days of antebellum plantations. They shared a particular interest in the period of the Civil War and sometimes wrote each other letters commemorating the events of July 22, 1864, and April 9, 1865, dates in southern history that seemed to have faded from public memory.

A frequent visitor to Roswell for much of his life, Arthur also cared a great deal for the Smith house, "his ancestral home," which had been closed up and looked after by caretakers following Lizzie's death in 1915. Arthur ultimately reopened and occupied the Smith home with his wife, Mary Hatton Norvell (1890–1981), following their marriage in 1940. Arthur had considered giving the Smith home to the Presbyterian church, but the offer was declined. In 1940, Stephens wrote to Mary Norvell Smith applauding the turn of events that enabled Arthur "to keep the old place with a clear conscience." He continued, "I do not believe in things 'just happening,' but I am firmly convinced there is an Intelligence that directs things and I am sure it was intended this old place should be retained by Arthur for some better purpose than an old preachers' home."

Stephens had removed from Atlanta to his own "ancestral home" in Wilkes County just a year earlier, and Arthur and Bob began to correspond with some regularity until Arthur's death in 1960. Late in the course of this correspondence, a fragment of a 1912 letter from Archie to Lizzie was recovered, and the memory of William Seagrove Smith suddenly and enigmatically resurfaced.

NOTES

1. In Archibald Smith's farm records, there is a November 1849 entry referring to his employment of one P. F. Rainwater as an overseer. The 1850 census lists Pinkney F. Rainwater as a thirty-eight-year-old laborer. James may be his son and may have been too young to be aware of the births of Helen and Archie (Smith Papers, box 17, folder 2).

2. According to Archibald Smith's records, Clarinda Richardson was born on February 10, 1834, and was apparently the daughter of Nanny Morris (b. 1791?) and Morris (b. 1780). Maria was born in 1850 (Smith Papers, box, 17, folder 2).

3. The Smiths' servant Sue gave birth to Moses in 1842 and to Dinah in 1859. Silvy may be the subject of a note in Archibald Smith's records after 1859 that reads, "Silva given to Mr. G." There is also a bill of sale for a Sylvia, age eighteen, and child Lot from John Joyner Smith to Archibald Smith, dated July 21, 1863 (Smith Papers, box 17, folder 2). A letter to Archie from A. Wisenbaker of Valdosta, dated "Rebel Hall, June 16, 1866" says at the end, "Clarander, Silvy, and Mose sends more howdies."

4. Clarinda wrote to the Smiths again in 1892, this time addressing her letter to Archie: "My dear young Master, I take great Pleasure in riting to you to inform you of my Present health. Hoping when these few liens reach you they will find you all enjoying the Best of health as it leaves me and family all well and Please to rite and tell me how the young ladies are and where they are, and let me no if they are with you, and give my Best regards to them. . . . Maria has six children and they are all getting along verry well, and she has moved to savanah Ga to live. The oldest one is marid. Tell miss Lizzie, and miss Hellen, and you Massie Archie and Miss Julia you all must send me something before I die. I ever remain your affectionate old servant Clarander."

The letter continues, "And you all must come to see me. I can't come to see you all and Luke died in Savanah with consumption and John is there with it. And Moses Bowens is gone crazy with his head he had a verry serious attack of it. And they sent him to the silence at Millidgeville last friday night. Silvy and her family is still here in Valdosta Ga and Mass Archie when you direct your letter Please direct it to Mr Mydelton."

We assume that "silence" is Clarinda's rendering of the state asylum at Milledgeville. "Mr. Middleton" is very likely Robert T. Myddleton (1845–1912), clerk of the Superior Court of Lowndes County for thirty-one years (*Valdosta Daily Times,* December 2, 1912, 5; Wisenbaker, "First Impressions," 5, 21, 52). There is no record of any response from Archie to Clarinda, nor any record of Clarinda's death or burial in Valdosta.

5. Following Dr. Archibald Smith's death, A. Worth Hobby, the secretary of the Fulton County Medical Society, sent Arthur Smith a copy of a resolution that the society passed on February 19, 1948, concerning Dr. Smith. It refers to his authorship of "several papers" pertaining to his speciality in gynecology, to another paper in 1914 on intravenous medication, and to his establishing a clinic after World War I "in which were trained some of the leading gynecologists of Atlanta today." The resolution also mentions his service in the medical department of the Georgia National Guard, from which he retired as a lieutenant colonel in 1938, as well as his contributions of time, talent, and medical equipment to the various programs of the North Avenue Presbyterian Church, of which he was a member. He must have represented the Smith tradition well, for his colleagues referred to his fifty-five years of "selfless service to the people of this community," calling him "doctor, patriot, Christian."

6. Following the Civil War Wheeler became a cavalry officer in the U.S. Army and commanded the cavalry attack at Guásimas early in the Spanish-American War. As the Spanish broke into a full retreat, leaving the road to Santiago open, Wheeler is said to have shouted, "We've got the damn Yankees on the run!" Soon after this address at the Citadel in May 1899, Wheeler took up his final battlefield assignment when in June President McKinley ordered him to report to General Arthur McArthur at Manila to help subdue Emilio Aguinaldo (Wilson and Ferris, eds., *Encyclopedia*, 664; Dyer, *From Shiloh to San Juan*, 230–31, 256–57).

7. General Clement Anselm Evans was the author of the *Military History of Georgia* (1895) and the editor of the important twelve-volume *Confederate Military History* (1899) (Stephens, ed., *Stephens Family Genealogies*, 2166; *Washington (Georgia) News Reporter*, Sept. 5, 1974, 1–2).

8. In a letter written in 1932 to his cousin Edward Barnwell, Arthur Smith listed "some of the buildings I have designed for other architects." At the top of the list was the Atlanta City Hall. Others included the Henry Grady Hotel and the Mortgage Guarantee Building in Atlanta; the supreme court buildings of both Florida and North Carolina; Tubman High School and Houghton Grammar School in Augusta, Georgia; and several large hotels in Florida.

ROBERT G. STEPHENS TO ARTHUR WILLIAM SMITH
July 23, 1948.

Dear Arthur—

It is stimulating and refreshing to find that someone really thought of the 22nd of July and remembered it as the anniversary of the Battle of Atlanta. I have always carried the date in my mind and used to celebrate every year with a pilgrimage to the battlefields, ending up with a visit to the Cyclorama.[1] I could find no one interested and these journeys were always made alone. You could get into the cyclorama for ten cents and stay all day, if you wanted to and very rarely did you find anyone else there. I studied the great picture in such minuteness that I can to-day recall every detail of it and I can go into it and tell you just where the scene depicted is located on Atlanta's streets. I can now see the Hurt house in the distance with the figure of General Sherman sitting on a horse a little way from the old house and there is an ambulance wending its way up the hill across the fields toward the Hurt house and in it is the body of General McPherson, who has just been killed down on the left of the line. The Hurt house was located on what is now Cleburne Avenue and its exact location is where the Christian Church's Orphans Home is now located corner of Cleburne and Copenhill Avenues. Sherman is sitting on the side of a hill where now runs Copenhill Ave.

McPherson was killed in a little bunch of woods out on the extreme left of the Yankee lines where Hardee's corps attacked what was supposed to be an unexposed flank. McPherson was at the Hurt house talking to Sherman when he heard the heavy firing down to the extreme left and he mounted his horse and rode to the sound of the guns. He paused for a minute on the hill where the Murphy Junior High School is located and then rode down the hill into an ambuscade and was shot from his horse and killed instantly. The exact spot is now in the middle of the street which bears his name—McPherson Avenue—and located there is a cannon on a concrete base to mark the spot where he fell.

When I was a boy I took in some of the old breastworks, for I couldn't make the rounds on foot as I could later do in my automobile, and from year to year I about took all of them in. The Confederate lines ran from back of where Tech school is located now along a stretch paralleling North Avenue. They crossed Peachtree about where the Fox theatre is now and went on out to about where the Boulevard is now, running midway between Ponce de Leon and North Avenue. I remember once finding some minie balls in some of the breastworks right behind where the Knight apartments were afterwards located at Jackson street and North Avenue. The old works then ran along the crest of what is now Boulevard or a little east of it and where the Eggleston Memorial hospital is now located was a fort and from this point cannon fired across No-man's land, which lay between the Confederate lines and the Union lines which were on the top of the hill where Forrest road crosses Linwood Avenue. From Eggleston Memorial hill the lines ran south along Boulevard and through what is now Oakland cemetery on out to what is now Grant Park and Fort Walker in the park is an old fort site in the line of breastworks. The lines then went on down somewhere between Georgia Avenue and Glenn street to where the Pryor street school is located on a high hill between Pryor and Fortress streets, then on back north along ridges until they crossed Marietta street about State street and then on to back of where Tech school is to-day.

The Yankee lines were outside of the Confederate circle and, as they were closing in, they varied. You would find them at Battle Hill, Mozley Park, Fortified Hills, Druid Hills, and a big bunch of them in those woods that used to be right across North Avenue from where we lived on Linwood.

The 22nd of July used to be heralded in the papers and articles written, calling attention to the anniversary occurrence, but this last time I looked in vain for some mention of the day, but there was nothing as far as the papers we get here are concerned. I fear the old war has been eclipsed by the two World Wars and the threatened 3rd World War and will never be of the inter-

Arthur William Smith
(1881–1960) in his
Citadel uniform

est it used to be. We will just have to realize we are the rear guard of an old defeated civilization and stand at attention with the romance of the past on our left and the unknown of eternity on our right and dip our colors in salute to the March of Time.

Yours as ever,
Bob

1. A circular building in Grant Park in southwest Atlanta, the Cyclorama houses an immense canvas depicting the Battle of Atlanta. Painted in 1885–86 by William Wehmer and the American Panorama Company of Milwaukee, it was first displayed in Minneapolis and came to Atlanta in 1892.

Frances Maner Smith (1875–1939)

Archie Smith and Lizzie Smith in old age.
Courtesy of the Georgia Department of Archives and History

Arthur William Smith, top center; Robert G. Stephens (1881–1974), right, at University of Georgia class of 1902 reunion. Also pictured is David C. Barrow, left, Chancellor of the University of Georgia from 1906 to 1925.

Washington, Georgia

Sept. 23, 1949

Dear Arthur—

This looks like it is going to be a quiet morning, so maybe I can catch up a little in my letter writing. It is cool & nice this morning and the sun is shining bright and it is a beautiful day after a rainy, unpleasant day yesterday.

Your last letter came some weeks ago and as always I enjoyed hearing from you. You mentioned in it about the time I went up to Roswell and spent a week-end with you when you were there building some houses and asked if I remembered it. You know I do, for it is a pleasant memory tucked back in one of the drawers of my store house of "Happy Memories" and which I often pull out to live over and enjoy. If I am not mistaken it was the last of August 1904 that I went up to see you. I left Atlanta on the southern train from the old car shed and changed cars at Chamblee & bumped along to the old depot on this side the Chattahoochee River & got off there and caught a horsedrawn hack that carried me into the center of Roswell. I do not remember where I contacted you, but think you met me at the station and we rode in the hack together. I remember it was rainy & chilly and the hack had curtains that flapped dolefully as we rode across the River & up the hill into town. It was cold that night & you made up a fire in the old parlor and we spent a cozy evening around the old fire place. It is all engraved on my mind like a scene from the old plantation days "before the war." It *was* an old fashioned scene in an old fashioned day in an old fashioned era that is now gone to come no more. We are living in another world today, in another era, gradually and insidiously forced upon us and it looks like it is getting more complicated and more confused and nobody can read what the end will be. The cool weather and chill stayed the whole time I was at Roswell. I reckon it was one tail end of a coast storm. Now the old car shed is gone, the Roswell railroad from Chamblee is gone, the old depot is gone, the old horse drawn hack is gone, the old covered bridge is gone, Aunt Lizzie is gone—all the old fashioned things of that old era are "gone with the wind" to never come again. I am glad I knew them and saw them and lived a little while with them. My face is still turned toward the sunrise and I am not grieving for the things that are passed, am living happily in the present & going into the shadowy future with a manly heart and with no fear! . . .

Hope Miss Mary[1] is well. Give her my best regards.
With every good wish I am

As ever
Bob

1. Arthur Smith's wife, Mary Hatton Norvell Smith (1890–1981).

ROBERT G. STEPHENS TO ARTHUR WILLIAM SMITH
Washington, Georgia
August 16, 1951

Dear Arthur—

Your letter of August 5th came on time and I certainly was glad to hear from you and enjoyed every word of it. It brought back to mind pleasant times I had spent at the old place at Roswell and made me want to see the old place again, even if it has been modernized. I am sure it is wonderfully improved. I remember well the time I went up there the last of August 1904, just before I went off to fight in the Third Battle of Manassas. I left Atlanta on the afternoon of September 3, 1904 to go on that ever-to-be-remembered trip to Virginia. It liked to have killed me, but I am glad I had the experience, for it gave me an insight into War and made me a hater of war and a lover of peace. I was in Roswell the week before I left Manassas, I think. I remember it rained on me on the way up there via the railroad that ran from Chamblee and we had a fire and my impression of the visit is that I was there in the winter time. . . .

You mention August 5, 1923. I had forgotten the date, but I well remember spending the night with you, watching at the bed of your father. I was always so glad I could do that, for I was very fond of him and wanted to do something to show my regard for him and love for you. I never pass that place on Juniper street that I do not turn back the clock and look in on the scene of that night and give thanks for such friends. Twenty-eight years is a long time and they have slipped by before it can be realized. I was forty-two years old then and I thought I was very mature and that the sands of time were running low with me. Much water has gone over the mill since then and many changes have come into our lives, but the basic things are still the same.

As ever
Bob

Washington, Georgia

May 12, 1955

Dear Arthur—

It was lovely of you all to call me last night and tell me about your visit to Lucy and then for you to call her and tell her you had talked to me. You are always doing something nice for somebody and it is wonderful for you to be that way. I am glad you came to board at the Lucas Ranch and our paths crossed and then ran side by side for all these years. As the old toast is:

> "Here's to you and toward you,
> If I never had met you, I never would've knowed you!"

I received your letter before we went to Memphis and you were telling me about your visit to Valdosta and the running of the land lines of the old Riley place and it was most interesting. It is a "fur piece" from the old ante bellum plantation days down in Lowndes county to the hectic rush of this atomic age and it is hard to visualize the old plantation as you described it.[1] The "old order" has certainly passed away and we are living in an entirely different social order from what we were even when we moved to Washington. Our old place was alive then with cows, sheep, chickens, pigs, etc and you could get all the help you wanted from sun-up to dark and the fields were planted and we lived mostly on the place. It all stayed the same until the second year of the II World War and then the "old order" suddenly blew up right in our faces. The old farming system disappeared and the farm hands disappeared from the country places, farm houses were deserted and went vacant and to decay. From an agricultural county it all changed over night into timber and cattle. Our place now has no animals on it, no fields planted, the meadow is all in weeds and tares and nobody wants to work—it is all a place of memories. And I "feel like one who treads alone some banquet hall deserted."[2]

As ever

Bob

1. Today traffic thundering down Interstate 75 between Atlanta and Florida crosses over "the land lines of the old Riley place" as it passes southwest of the Valdosta airport, while a portion of the Riley land lies buried beneath the airport runway.

2. Another allusion to Thomas Moore's poem "Oft, in the stilly night." The poem concludes, "Whose lights are fled, / Whose garlands dead, / And all but he departed!"

ROSWELL

Viewing the town of Roswell as it appears today, it is difficult to realize that the colony was founded in a day which now seems so remote, even before the tracks of the retreating Cherokees had grown cold. Many of the houses which today we know, love and occupy as our homes, came into being as evidences of the culture of the older coastal cities which these settlers had undertaken to transplant to the wilderness.

It is this aspect of early life in Roswell which makes the town almost unique. These settlers, although they were truly pioneers living under most primitive conditions, brought a way of life with them which enabled them to live in a certain atmosphere of grace and charm until the outbreak of the Confederate war, and to continue to live in it with more or less success for a number of years thereafter, simply because they were overlooked by the outside world. . . .

Although my father moved from Roswell when I was a small child, yet I have had more or less constant contact with the town through all my life, and all the romance and picturesqueness of those early days is clear in my memory, either through stories told me, or through my own observation. . . .

Food was plentiful and abundant . . . and although money was not plentiful, still they enjoyed considerable ease and culture, although they were somewhat provincial, and apparently life went on without any great change until it was rudely interrupted by the outbreak of the Confederate War.

My father and Uncle William went to the Army, and the rest of the family "refugeed" to Valdosta for the duration. On his return from the service, my father met my mother Miss Gulielma Riley, who was also a refugee from Glynn County. They were married there, and returned to Roswell with the rest of the Smith family to make their home.

After the death of my grandfather and grandmother, the house was occupied by my aunt Helen, and Elizabeth Smith. The latter survived until 1915, having lived alone in the house for some eighteen years. . . .

112 East Harris Street
Savannah
Dec 22nd 1912

Dear Sister

We are kind of settled here for a while but do not know how long.

We had a place engaged to stay but after all arrangements were made to come and it was too late to change, the woman wrote that she had let some one else have the rooms. Mrs Newman is going to break up and there are other obstacles so we had to go to a hotel till we could find a place.

This place is quite promising except for the number of steps. I received your Christmas letter and another and you better continue to direct to Edwards care till further instructions.

Saturday no Friday night the 20th was the 48th anniversary of the evacuation of Savannah and the wonderful crossing of the river on the bridge made of flats. I crossed about dusk and the army was all night crossing. The Cadets and some Ga militia stayed at Hardeeville till the 23rd and then marched to Bamberg and took the cars for Augusta. On the evening of the 22nd Brother was ordered to some place on the Charleston and Savannah rail road and the last time I saw him was as he took the train 48 years ago this evening.

We have had several days of fine weather but today is drizzling and very uncomfortable and gloomy and feels as if it will be colder. . . .

ROBERT G. STEPHENS TO ARTHUR WILLIAM SMITH

January 14, 1956

Dear Arthur:

Our last letters crossed and I sent you a copy of the article about the Roswell library at the same time you sent me one.

Thank you for letting me read the letter your father wrote in 1912 about events in Savannah in 1864. He was just a boy soldier then from the G.M.I. and I reckon it all left a vivid impression on him. Now, tell me about his brother. That is new to me. When he says he was ordered to some place and "the last time I saw him was as he took the train 48 years ago this evening" what became of him? Was he killed or just numbered among those who never returned? I do not remember ever knowing your father had a brother.

Tell me about it. . . .

Afterword

We do not know what Arthur replied to Robert Stephens, nor do we know what our Uncle Arthur knew about his Uncle William's life or his death. Of his other ancestors we never heard mention. We regard Arthur as one of the kindest, most generous gentlemen we have ever known, but he was also somewhat reticent, and we never knew enough of his family's history to frame the questions that we would dearly love to ask today. The story that has been told in this book lay hidden in the letters and papers that were only recently found scattered throughout the Smith house.

Like Robert G. Stephens, we recall with some nostalgia our visits to Roswell. Along with our other two brothers, Thomas Fry and William Wirt Skinner, we experienced during our childhood a family ritual of Sunday afternoon drives to the Smith house, where our great-aunt Mary Norvell Smith and uncle Arthur Smith lived during the warmer months of the year.

The pilgrimage route from our home in Decatur, Georgia, to Roswell was a long, winding, two-lane blacktop road through country then largely untouched by developers. As children we played in the yard on those Sunday afternoons, pretending to ride the cast iron lions that still guard the end of the walkway to the back door of the Smith house while our parents visited with Arthur and Mary. Our reward for patiently enduring our stay was inevitably a six-ounce bottle of Coca-Cola, which Aunt Mary would cheerfully offer us, always wrapped in a paper napkin. We then would sit on the front porch in the big white Brumby rocking chairs while we smelled the aroma of the boxwood that grew all around; sometimes we would sit in the library, which was filled with many musty and worn leather-bound volumes from the eighteenth and nineteenth centuries. On occasion we had a southern fried chicken dinner with homemade biscuits in the dining room prepared by Mary and Arthur's devoted housekeeper, Mamie Cotton. But we were never allowed in the parlor of the Smith house, nor permitted to venture upstairs, and never did we set foot in the attic.

When Arthur William Smith died in 1960, the lineage of Archibald Smith reached its end. Our parents, James Lister Skinner Jr. and Josephine Fry Skinner, inherited the Smith house from our great-aunt Mary Norvell Smith when she passed away in 1981. In an effort to fulfill our father's promise to Arthur Smith to "take care of his ancestral home" and to preserve this historic home for future generations, our parents arranged the transfer of the Smith house to the city of Roswell.

Following our mother's death in 1986, it was determined that an inventory should be made of all the papers and documents in the house, and only then did the story of the Archibald Smith family's hardships and bereavement during the Civil War begin to unfold slowly before us. All of the letters to William Smith up to the time of November 5, 1864, were found in the attic apparently undisturbed, still tied in neat bundles at the bottom of the trunk that he had sent to Valdosta before Sherman arrived at Savannah. Other letters in this volume were found among the dozens of other trunks, boxes, and portable writing desks in the attic, stuck here and there between the pages of books, lying loose in drawers, or tucked away in wardrobes.

Also recovered from among the Archibald Smith papers during this time was the bulk of the manuscript autobiography of Henry Merrell, along with many of the supporting documents, letters, and the drawings he made depicting life in early Roswell. This remarkable memoir, edited by Dr. James L. Skinner III, was published in 1991 by the University of Georgia Press as *The Autobiography of Henry Merrell: Industrial Missionary to the South.*

The Burial of Latané *by William D. Washington. Engraving after a painting by William D. Washington. Eleanor S. Brockenbrough Library. The Museum of the Confederacy, Richmond, Virginia*

Today the Archibald Smith House, now called the Archibald Smith Plantation Home, is open to the public and serves as a teaching museum for local schools about life in nineteenth-century Georgia. On the grounds near the old corn crib still stands a three-hundred-year-old oak tree, the second oldest oak in the state of Georgia. From the base of the stone spring house below the garden terrace still emerges a trickle of cool clear water. Most of the original furnishings remain in place in the house, including Lizzie's piano and Archibald's plantation desk. And *The Burial of Latané* still hangs over the parlor fireplace, a silent reminder of what happened to this household during the darkest days this country has ever known.

Bibliography

Archival and Unpublished Genealogical works

Barrington King Papers. Georgia Department of Archives and History Microfilm 71/61 (AH 1232). By kind permission of Lois Simpson of Barrington Hall.

Camden County, Georgia. Deed Books F, L, and M. Woodbine, Georgia.

Chatham County, Georgia. *General Index to Wills, Estates, Administrations, Etc. in the Chatham County, Georgia, Courthouse, Savannah, Georgia.* WPA Project No. 165-34-6999, 1937.

Confederate Pensions and Records Department, Georgia. Alphabetical Card File. Georgia Department of Archives and History Microfilm, Drawer 253.

Georgia Historical Society. Laurel Grove Cemetery, General Index to Keeper's Record Book, 1832–1938. Savannah: Georgia Historical Society, n.d.

Habersham-Elliott Papers. Manuscript Collection No. 2510. Southern Historical Collection, University of North Carolina-Chapel Hill.

Hanleiter, Cornelius Redding. Hanleiter War Diary. Manuscript No. 109. Atlanta Historical Society.

Huxford, Folks, abs. "Genealogical Extracts from the Public Records of Camden County, Ga., Including Inscriptions from the Older Tombstones in the Town Cemetery." Typescript, Georgia Department of Archives and History, Atlanta, n.d.

King, Joseph N. "King Genealogy." Typescript, Georgia Department of Archives and History, Atlanta, 1959.

Merrill, Mrs. Arthur J., Evelyn Simpson, and Mrs. A. Taylor Heath. Typescript history of the King family and of Roswell, Georgia. Roswell: n.p., 1938.

National Archives. *Population Schedules of the United States, 1870.* Publications Microcopy No. 593. Roll 1166. North Carolina. Vol. 23 (450–834). Washington, D.C.: National Archives and Records Service, General Services Administration, 1965.

National Archives Microfilm Publications. *Compiled Service Records of Confederate Soldiers Who Served in Organizations from the State of Georgia.* Microcopy No. 266. Roll 141. Washington, D.C.: National Archives and Records Service, General Services Administration, 1959.

———. *Compiled Service Records of Confederate Soldiers Who Served in Organizations Raised Directly by the Confederate Government.* Microcopy No. 258. Rolls 116–21. Washington, D.C.: National Archives and Records Service, General Services Administration, 1960.

———. *Population Schedules of the Eighth Census of the United States, 1860.* Microcopy No. 653. Roll 117. Georgia. Vol 4 (1–543). Washington, D.C.: National Archives and Records Service, General Services Administration, 1967.

———. *Population Schedules of the Eighth Census of the United States, 1860.* Publications Microcopy No. 653. Roll 144. Georgia (Slave Schedules). Vol. 2 (1–272A). Washington, D.C.: National Archives and Records Service, General Services Administration, 1967.

———. *Population Schedules of the Seventh Census of the United States, 1850.* Microcopy No. 432. Roll 89. Georgia (Slave Schedules). Vol. 2. Washington, D.C.: National Archives and Records Service, General Services Administration, 1963.

Obituary Record of Yale University Deceased from June 1880 to June 1890. New Haven: n.p., 1890.

Rodgers, Robert L., comp. *Roster of the Battalion of the Georgia Military Institute Cadets in the Confederate Army Service in the Civil War from May 10, 1864, to May 20, 1865.* Atlanta: n.p., 1903.

Roswell Manufacturing Company. Meetings of the Stockholders of the Roswell Manufacturing Company, Roswell, Cobb County, Georgia, 1840–1900. DeKalb Historical Society Library, Decatur, Georgia.

St. Mary's Presbyterian Church Records, 1807–1918. Atlanta: Microfilm Division of Georgia Department of State, 1957.

Saint Marys Womans Club. "St. Marys, Camden County, Georgia, Oak Grove Cemetery Inscriptions." Typescript, St. Marys Library, 1953.

Smith Papers (AC 88–012). Georgia Department of Archives and History, Atlanta.

Stephens, Dan V. *Stephens Family Genealogies.* Fremont, Neb.: Hammond and Stephens, 1940.

Stiles, William Henry, Papers, 1749–1892. Manuscript Collection No. 229, Special Collections Department, Robert W. Woodruff Library, Emory University, Atlanta, Ga.

U.S. Naval War Records Department. *Official Records of the Union and Confederate Navies in the War of the Rebellion.* Series 1, vols. 3, 16. Washington, D.C.: U.S. Government Printing Office, 1903.

Varner Family Papers. Manuscripts Collection No. 1256, Georgia Historical Society, Savannah.

Williamson, William Wayne, Papers. Manuscript Collection No. 1280, Georgia Historical Society, Savannah.

Works Progress Administration of Georgia, Area Eight, Savannah, Georgia. "Annals of Savannah, 1850–1937: A Digest and Index of Newspaper Records of Events and Opinions." Vol. 15. Typescript, Georgia Historical Society, 1937.

Books and Articles

Allen, Catherine B. *The New Lottie Moon Story*. Nashville, Tenn.: Broadman Press, 1980.

Arnow, Isaac Flood. "History of St. Marys and Camden County." *Camden County Tribune*, April 20, 1951, 2; April 27, 2; May 4, 2; May 11, 2; May 18, 2.

Austin, J. P. *The Blue and the Gray: Sketches of a Portion of the Unwritten History of the Great American Civil War*. Atlanta: Frankling Printing and Publishing, 1899.

Avery, I. W. *The History of the State of Georgia from 1850 to 1881*. New York: Brown and Derby, 1881.

Bailey, Ronald H. *Battles for Atlanta: Sherman Moves East*. Alexandria, Va.: Time-Life Books, 1985.

Barnwell, Stephen B. *The Story of an American Family*. Marquette, Mich.: Stephen B. Barnwell, 1969.

Barrett, John G. *The Civil War in North Carolina*. Chapel Hill: University of North Carolina Press, 1963.

Bennett, Robert Berry. *Oak Grove Cemetery, Saint Marys, Georgia*. St. Marys, Ga.: n.p., 1983.

Black, Robert C. *The Railroads of the Confederacy*. Chapel Hill: University of North Carolina Press, 1952.

Boatner, Mark Mayo. *The Civil War Dictionary*. New York: David McKay, 1959.

Bohannon, Keith. "Cadets, Drillmasters, Draft Dodgers, and Soldiers: The Georgia Military Institute during the Civil War." *Georgia Historical Quarterly* 79 (Spring 1995): 5–29.

Bonner, James C. "Sherman at Milledgeville in 1864." *Journal of Southern History* 22 (1956): 273–91.

Brightwell, Juanita S. *Roster of the Confederate Soldiers of Georgia, 1861-1865*. Spartanburg, S.C.: The Reprint Co., 1982.

Bryan, T. Conn. *Confederate Georgia*. Athens: University of Georgia Press, 1953.

Buist, E. H. "John Elbert DuBose." In *Memorial Volume of the Semi-Centennial of the Theological Seminary at Columbia, South Carolina*, 263–64. Columbia: Presbyterian Publishing, 1884.

Candler, Allen D., ed. *Colonial Records of the State of Georgia*. Vol. 3. Atlanta: Franklin, 1905.

Capers, Major F. W. "G.M.I. Cadets in War Service." In *An Historical Sketch of the Georgia Military Institute, Marietta, Georgia*, by Robert L. Rodgers, 91–97. Atlanta, 1890. Reprint, Atlanta: Kimsey's Book Shop, 1956.

Carson, Charles C. "History of the Presbyterian Church of Valdosta." *Valdosta (Georgia) Times*, August 3, 1907, 12.

Carter, Samuel, III. *The Siege of Atlanta, 1864.* New York: St. Martin's, 1973.

Channing, Steven A. *Confederate Ordeal: The Southern Home Front.* Alexandria, Va.: Time-Life Books, 1984.

Chesnut, Mary Boykin. *A Diary From Dixie.* Ed. Ben Ames Williams. Cambridge: Harvard University Press, 1980.

Coleman, Kenneth, and Charles Stephen Gurr, eds. *Dictionary of Georgia Biography.* 2 vols. Athens: University of Georgia Press, 1983.

Conyngham, David Power. *Sherman's March through the South, with Sketches and Incidents of the Campaign.* New York: Sheldon & Co., 1865.

Cooper, Sarah Joyce King. *King and Allied Families.* Athens, Ga.: Agee Publishers, 1992.

Corley, Florence Fleming. *Confederate City: Augusta, Georgia, 1860–1865.* Columbia: University of South Carolina Press, 1960.

Coulter, E. Merton. *Travels in the Confederate States: A Bibliography.* Norman: University of Oklahoma Press, 1948.

Coulter, E. Merton, and Albert B. Saye, eds. *A List of Early Settlers of Georgia.* Athens: University of Georgia Press, 1949.

Coulter, E. Merton, and Wendell Holmes Stephenson, eds. *The Confederate States of America, 1861–1865.* Vol. 7 of *A History of the South.* Baton Rouge: Louisiana State University Press, 1950.

Coursey, W. Tony, and Kenneth H. Thomas, Jr., comps. *1860 Census of Georgia: Camden County.* Decatur, Ga.: n.p., 1985.

Cowles, Capt. Calvin D., comp. *The Official Military Atlas of the Civil War.* Washington, D.C.: Government Printing Office, 1891–95.

Cox, General Jacob D. *Sherman's March to the Sea.* New York, 1882. Reprint, New York: Da Capo Press, 1994.

Cozby, J. S. "Rev. George Whitfield Ladson." In *Memorial Volume of the Semi-Centennial of the Theological Seminary at Columbia, South Carolina,* 306–7. Columbia: Presbyterian Publishing House, 1884.

Crute, Joseph H., Jr. *Confederate Staff Officers, 1861-1865.* Powhatan, Va.: Derwent Books, 1982.

Davis, Burke. *Sherman's March.* New York: Vintage Books, 1988.

Davis, Jefferson. *The Rise and Fall of the Confederate Government.* 2 vols. New York: D. Appleton, 1881.

Doughtie, Beatrice Mackay. *The Mackeys and Allied Families.* Decatur, Ga.: Bowen Press, 1957.

"Dr. Robert G. Stephens." *Washington (Ga.) News Reporter,* September 5, 1974, 1–2.

Dyer, John P. *From Shiloh to San Juan: The Life of "Fightin' Joe" Wheeler.* Baton Rouge: Louisiana State University Press, 1961.

Eaton, Clement. *A History of the Southern Confederacy.* New York: Free Press, 1954.

Evans, Clement A., ed., *Confederate Military History*. 13 vols. Atlanta: Confederate Publishing Company, 1899.

Faust, Patricia L., ed. *Historical Times Illustrated Encyclopedia of the Civil War*. New York: Harper and Row, 1986.

Fielder, Herbert. *A Sketch of the Life and Times and Speeches of Joseph E. Brown*. Springfield, Mass.: Springfield Printing, 1883.

Foote, Shelby. *The Civil War: A Narrative*. 3 vols. New York: Random House, 1958, 1963, 1974.

Garrett, Franklin M. *Atlanta and Environs: A Chronicle of Its People and Events*. 4 vols. New York: Lewis Publishing, 1954–87.

Genealogical Committee of the Georgia Historical Society, comp. *The 1860 Census of Chatham County, Georgia*. Easley, S.C.: Southern Historical Press, 1980.

Georgia Historical Commission. *Georgia Civil War Historical Markers*. Atlanta: Georgia Historical Commission, 1964.

Griffin, Tharon. *The Descendents of James Griffin and Sarah Lodge*. Thomasville, Ga.: Craigmiles and Associates, 1993.

Henderson, Lilian, ed. *Roster of the Confederate Soldiers of Georgia, 1861–1865*. 6 vols. Hapeville, Ga.: Longino and Porter, 1960.

Henry, Robert Selph. *The Story of the Confederacy*. Indianapolis: Bobbs-Merrill, Charter Books, 1964.

Hill, Louise Biles. *Joseph E. Brown and the Confederacy*. Chapel Hill: University of North Carolina Press, 1939.

Historical Sketches of Old St. Marys. Compiled from the Files of the Southeast Georgian. St. Marys, Ga.: *Southeast Georgian*, 1909–11.

History of Lowndes County, Georgia: 1825–1941. Valdosta, Ga.: General James Jackson Chapter, Daughters of the American Revolution, 1942.

Hitchcock, Henry. *Marching with Sherman*. New Haven: Yale University Press, 1927.

Hitt, Michael D. *After the Left Flank: Military Operations in the Roswell Area after July 16, 1864, and the Journey of the Roswell Mill Employees*. Roswell: Michael D. Hitt, 1985.

———. *Charged with Treason: Ordeal of Four Hundred Mill Workers during Military Operations in Roswell, Georgia, 1864–1865*. Monroe, N.Y.: Library Research Associates, 1992.

Hoehling. A. A. *Last Train from Atlanta*. New York: Thomas Yoseloff, 1958.

Hughes, Nathaniel Cheairs, Jr. *General William J. Hardee: Old Reliable*. Baton Rouge: Louisiana State University Press, 1965.

Huxford, Folks. *Pioneers of Wiregrass, Georgia*. Waycross, Ga.: Herrin's, 1967.

———. *Pioneers of Wiregrass, Georgia, by Folks Huxford: A Finding List of the 3,000 Records in the Seven Volumes*. Clinch County, Ga.: n.p., 1983.

James, Edward T., ed. *Notable American Women, 1607-1950*. 3 vols. Cambridge: Harvard University Press, Belknap Press, 1971.

Johnson, Allen, and Dumas Malone, eds. *Dictionary of American Biography*. 20 vols. New York: Charles Scribner's Sons, 1928–36.

Jones, Archer. "Military Means, Political Ends." In *Why the Confederacy Lost,* ed. Gabor S. Borritt, 45–47. New York: Oxford University Press, 1992.

Jones, Charles C., Jr. *Historical Sketch of the Chatham Artillery during the Confederate Struggle for Independence*. Albany, N.Y.: Joel Munsell, 1867.

———. *The History of Georgia*. 2 vols. Boston: Houghton Mifflin and Co., 1883.

———. *The Siege of Savannah in December, 1864, and the Confederate Operations in Georgia and the Third Military District of South Carolina during General Sherman's March from Atlanta to the Sea*. Albany, N.Y.: Joel Munsell, 1874. Reprint, Jonesboro, Ga.: Freedom Hill Press, 1988.

Journal of the Congress of the Confederate States of America. 6 vols. Washington, D.C.: Government Printing Office, 1904–5.

Kennett, Lee. *Marching through Georgia: The Story of Soldiers and Civilians during Sherman's Campaign*. New York: Harper Collins, 1995.

King, William. "The Disputed Message." *Atlanta Daily Constitution*, June 5, 1879, 4.

Knight, Lucian Lamar. *Georgia's Landmarks, Memorials, and Legends*. 2 vols. Atlanta: Byrd Printing, 1913–14.

Lane, Mills, ed. *General Oglethorpe's Georgia: Colonial Letters, 1733-1734*. 2 vols. Savannah: Beehive Press, 1975.

———. *Marching through Georgia: William T. Sherman's Personal Narrative of His March through Georgia*. New York: Arno Press, 1978.

Lawrence, Alexander A. *A Present for Mr. Lincoln: The Story of Savannah from Secession to Sherman*. Macon, Ga.: Ardvian Press, n.d.

LeConte, Joseph. *'Ware Sherman,' A Journal of Three Months' Personal Experience in the Last Days of the Confederacy*. Berkeley: University of California Press, 1937.

Lee, F. D., and J. L. Agnew. *Historical Record of the City of Savannah*. Savannah: J. H. Estill, 1869.

Long, E. B., and Barbara Long. *The Civil War Day by Day: An Almanac, 1861–1865*. Garden City, N.Y.: Doubleday, 1971.

Martin, Clarece. *A Glimpse of the Past: The History of Bulloch Hall and Roswell, Georgia*. Roswell: Historic Roswell, 1973.

———. *A History of Roswell Presbyterian Church*. Dallas: Taylor Publishing, 1984.

Martin, Mary E. *Cobb County, Georgia, in 1860: A Transcription and Index of the Federal Population Census*. Marietta, Ga.: Mary E. Martin, 1987.

Martin, Mary E., and Sherman A. Martin, comps. *The People of Cobb County, Georgia, in 1870: An Index of the 1870 Census with Selected Abstracts and Annotations,*

Together with a List of 1860 Slave Owners and Slave Holders. Marietta, Ga.: Mary E. Martin, 1989.

McCall, Hugh. *The History of Georgia, Containing Brief Sketches of the Most Remarkable Events Up to the Present Day*. 1784. Reprint, Atlanta: Cherokee Publishing, 1969.

McGee, David H. "The Siege of Fort Pulaski: 'You Might As Well Bombard the Rocky Mountains.'" *Georgia Historical Quarterly* 79 (Spring 1995): 211–22.

Memoirs of Georgia, Containing Historical Accounts of the State's Civil, Military, Industrial, and Personal Interests and Personal Sketches of Many of its People. 2 vols. Atlanta: Southern Historical Association, 1895.

Miles, Jim. *To the Sea: A History and Tour Guide of Sherman's March*. Nashville, Tenn.: Rutledge Hill Press, 1989.

"Mr. Robert T. Myddelton Died Sunday." *Valdosta Daily Times*, December 2, 1912, 5.

Moore, Albert Burton. *Conscription and Conflict in the Confederacy*. 1924. Reprint, New York: Hillary House Publishers, 1963.

Myers, Robert Manson, ed. *The Children of Pride: A True Story of Georgia and the Civil War*. New Haven: Yale University Press, 1972.

Neagles, James C. *Confederate Research Sources: A Guide to Archive Collections*. Salt Lake City: Ancestry Publications, 1986.

Nevin, David. *The Civil War: Sherman's March*. Alexandria, Va.: Time-Life Books, 1986.

Nichols, George Ward. *The Story of the Great March*. New York: Harper and Brothers, 1866.

Otto, Rhea Cumming, comp. *1850 Census of Georgia (Camden County)*. Savannah: Rhea Cumming Otto, 1974.

———. *1850 Census of Georgia (Chatham County)*. Savannah: Rhea Cumming Otto, 1975.

———. *1850 Census of Georgia (Cobb County)*. Savannah: Rhea Cumming Otto, 1975.

Phillips, Ulrich Bonnell. *A History of Transportation in the Cotton Belt to 1860*. New York: Octagon Books, 1968.

Proctor, Madena Arnow. *Among Untrodden Ways: A Vignette of Delightful St. Marys*. St. Marys, Ga.: n.p., 1915.

Purse's Directory of the City of Savannah, Together with a Mercantile and Business Directory. Savannah, Ga.: Purse and Son, 1866.

Quintard, Charles Todd. *Doctor Quintard, Chaplain C.S.A. and Second Bishop of Tennessee, Being His Story of the War (1861–1865)*. Ed. the Rev. Arthur Howard Noll. Sewanee: University Press of Sewanee, Tennessee, 1905.

Reddick, Marguerite, comp., Eloise Bailey and Virginia Proctor, eds. *Camden's Challenge: A History of Camden County, Georgia*. Jacksonville, Fla.: Paramount Press for the Camden County Historical Commission, 1976.

Robertson, Lucille, ed. *Historical Sketches of Old St. Marys. Compiled from the Files of the* Southeast Georgian. St. Marys, Ga.: n.p., 1909.

Rodgers, Robert L. *An Historical Sketch of the Georgia Military Institute, Marietta, Georgia*. Atlanta, 1890. Reprint, Atlanta: Kimsey's Book Shop, 1956.

Scaife, William R. *The March to the Sea*. 2d ed. Saline, Mich.: McNaughton and Gunn, 1993.

Scott, Rev. E. C., comp. *Ministerial Directory of the Presbyterian Church, U.S., 1861–1941*. Austin, Tex.: Von Boeckmann-Jones, 1942.

Scruggs, C. P., comp. *Georgia Historical Markers*. Valdosta, Ga.: Bay Tree Grove Publishers, 1973.

Seymour, Ann Bishop, ed. *Cobb County Cemeteries*. Vol. 1. Marietta, Ga.: G. W. Publications for Northeast Cobb Genealogical Society, 1984.

Shadburn, Don L. *Cherokee Planters in Georgia, 1832–1838: Historical Essays on Eleven Counties in the Cherokee Nation of Georgia*. Roswell, Ga.: W. H. Wolfe Associates, 1990.

Shelton, Jane Twitty. *Pines and Pioneers: A History of Lowndes County, Georgia, 1825–1900*. Atlanta: Cherokee Publishing, 1976.

Sherman, William T. *Memoirs of General William T. Sherman*. 2d ed. 2 vols. New York: D. Appleton and Company, 1904.

Silva, James S. *Early Reminiscence of Camden County, Georgia. By an Old St. Marys Boy in His 82nd Year, 1914–1915*. Kingsland, Ga.: *Southeast Georgian*, 1975.

Sinclair, Arthur. *Two Years on the* Alabama. 3d ed. Boston: Lee and Shephard, 1896.

Skinner, James L., ed. *The Autobiography of Henry Merrell: Industrial Missionary to the South*. Athens: University of Georgia Press, 1991.

Southern Genealogists' Exchange Society. *1850 Florida Census: Nassau County*. Jacksonville, Fla.: Southern Genealogists' Exchange Society, 1974.

Spalding, Thomas. "Life of Oglethorpe." *Collections of the Georgia Historical Society* 1 (1840): 239–95.

Stevens, William Bacon. *A History of Georgia from Its First Discovery by Europeans to the Adoption of the Present Constitution in 1798*. 2 vols. Philadelphia: C. Sherman and Son, 1859.

Strayer, Larry M., and Richard A. Baumgartner, eds. *Echoes of Battle: The Atlanta Campaign*. Huntington, W.Va.: Blue Acorn Press, 1991.

Talmadge, Arthur White. *The Talmadge, Tallmadge, and Talmage Genealogy*. New York: Grafton Press, 1909.

Tancig, W. J., comp. *Confederate Military Land Units, 1861–1865*. South Brunswick, N.J.: Thomas Yoseloff, 1967.

Tankersley, Allen P. *College Life at Old Oglethorpe*. Athens: University of Georgia Press, 1951.

Temple, Sarah Blackwell Gober. *The First Hundred Years: A Short History of Cobb County, in Georgia*. Atlanta: Walter W. Brown Publishing, 1935.

Thomas, Emory M. *The Confederacy as a Revolutionary Experience*. Englewood Cliffs, N.J.: Prentice-Hall, 1971.

———. *The Confederate Nation, 1861–1865*. New York: Harper and Row, 1979.

Thomas, Susan Converse McKey, comp. "Some of the Confederate Soldiers of Sunset Hill Cemetery, Valdosta, Georgia." Typescript, South Georgia Regional Library, Valdosta, 1990.

Thompson, Shirley Joiner, comp. *The People of Camden County, Georgia: A Finding Index prior to 1850*. Kingsland, Ga.: *Southeast Georgian*, 1982.

———. *The People of East Florida during the Revolutionary War–War of 1812 Period*. Kingsland, Ga.: *Southeast Georgian*, 1982.

U. S. War Department. *The War of the Rebellion: A Compilation of the Official Records of the Union and Confederate Armies*. 70 vols. in 128. Series 1, vols. 14, 28, 31, 35, 38, 39, 44, 47, 52. Washington, D.C.: U.S. Government Printing Office, 1888–1901.

Vocelle, James T. *History of Camden County, Georgia*. Kingsland, Ga.: *Southeast Georgian*, 1967.

———. *Reminiscences of Old St. Marys*. St. Marys: St. Marys Publishing, 1913.

Walsh, Darlene, ed. *Roswell: A Pictorial History*. 2d ed. Roswell, Ga.: Roswell Historical Society, 1994.

Warner, Ezra J. *Generals in Blue*. Baton Rouge: Louisiana State University Press, 1964.

———. *Generals in Gray*. Baton Rouge: Louisiana State University Press, 1959.

Waters, Eleanor Tolliver, Betty White Lister, and Betty Park, abs. *Cobb County, Georgia, 1840 Census*. Marietta, Ga.: Cobb County Genealogical Society, 1989.

Wayne, General Henry C. "Military Reports." In *An Historical Sketch of the Georgia Military Institute, Marietta, Georgia* by Robert L. Rodgers, 92–96. Atlanta, 1890. Reprint, Atlanta: Kimsey's Book Shop, 1956.

White, George A. *Historical Collections of Georgia*. New York: Pudney and Russell, 1855.

———. *Statistics of the State of Georgia*. Savannah, Ga.: W. Thorne Williams, 1849.

Who Was Who in America: Historical Volume, 1607–1897. Chicago: A. N. Marquis, 1963.

Wilson, Charles Reagan, and William Ferris, eds. *Encyclopedia of Southern Culture*. Chapel Hill: University of North Carolina Press, 1989.

Wiley, Bell Irvin, and Hirst D. Milhollen. *Embattled Confederates: An Illustrated History of Southerners at War*. New York: Bonanza Books, 1964.

Wisenbaker, Thannie Smith. "First Impressions of Valdosta in 1863." Typescript, South Georgia Regional Library, Valdosta, n.d.

Yates, Bowling C. "History of the Georgia Military Institute, Marietta, Georgia, Including the Confederate Military Service of the Cadet Battalion." Typescript, Georgia Department of Archives and History, Atlanta.

Index

References to illustrations are printed in italic.

Adairsville, Ga., 45

Adams, Ellen S., 110, 114, 135

Adams, Theodore Dwight, 74, 79, 84, 86, 110, 114, 121

Adams family, 104

Alabama, C.S.S., xxxv, 66, 79

Albany, Ga., 7, 153, 218, 219, 222

Allatoona, Ga., 53

Alpharetta, Ga., xxxiii

American Missionary Association, 200

Anderson, Edward C., 66, 79

Anderson, Edward M., 66, 79

Anderson, Mrs. S. J., 91

Andersonville prison, xlv (n. 45), 47, 86, 92, 94, 114

Appenzell, Switzerland, xvi, 243

Appenzelle plantation (St. Marys, Ga.), xvi

Arkansas: manufacturing in, x, xxi; Pike County, xxiii, xxiv, xxxv, 8n; Camden, xxxv, 57, 103; residence of Merrell and Magill families, 47; postwar conditions in, 197–98

Arlington, Va. (Lee mansion), 83

Athens, Ga., 86

Atkinson, Rev. Joseph Mayo, 176, 177, 194, 196, 201, 203, 204; letter from, 188

Atlanta, Ga., xxxiii, 33, 50, 51, 54, 115, 120, 125, 141, 253, 263; as Sherman approached, xxxiv, xxxvi, 45–46, 48–49, 71, 74–75, 79, 84, 91, 92; battle of, xxxv, 89, 104, 108, 110, 256–58; fall of, 47, 110; Cyclorama, 256

Atlanta (battle of). *See* Atlanta, Ga.

Atlanta and West Point Railroad. *See* Railroads

Atlantic and Gulf Railroad. *See* Railroads

Augusta, Ga., 31, 73, 74, 104, 108, 110, 111, 150, 151, 153, 164, 165, 166, *167*, 171, 180

Austin family, 166, 171, 172

Autobiography of Henry Merrell, The (ed. Skinner), 269

Averasboro (battle of), xxxv, 162–63, *167*

Axson, Ellen Louise, 14

Axson, Mrs. Isaac Stockton, 176

Axson, Rev. Isaac Stockton Keith, 14, 176, 188

Bacon (soldier), 62, 76, 91, 97, 99, 110, 164, 169

Baker, Catherine Evelyn King, 23, 26, 74, 91, 120, 121, 122n, 221

Baker, Rev. William Elliott, 91, 120, 137

Baldwin family, 104

Baldwin Female Institute (Mary Baldwin College), 121

Ball's Ferry, Ga., 143

Baltimore, Md., 187, 250

Bamberg, S.C., 161, 162, *167*, 267

Barnsley, Mr. and Mrs. Godfrey, 113

Barnwell, Capt. Archibald Smith, xxxiii, 23–24, 30, 50, 54, 62, 66, 69, 76, 79, 81, 82, 83, 88, 91, 93, 95, 96, 97, 102, 103, 104, 108, 124, 132, 134, 135, 144, 148, 163, 164, 172, 175, 187

Barnwell, Charlotte Cuthbert, xxx, 33, 36, 50, 60, 62, 69–70, 77, 81, 102, 123, 140, 151, 164, 217

Barnwell, Edward (1785–1860), xxxvii (n. 2), 25n

Barnwell, Edward Williamson (1869–1951), 256n, 267

Barnwell, Eliza Ann (Leila), 36, 134, 136, 151

Barnwell, Eliza Zubly Smith, xxxvii (n. 2), xliii (n. 32), 25n

Barnwell, Elizabeth Osborn, 25n

Barnwell, Frances (Fanny) Morgandollar Riley, xxxiii, 54, 82, 87, 90, 91, 93, 102, 103, 109, 117, 123, 129, 132, 133, 134, 135, 139, 140, 170

Barnwell, Helen. *See* Geiger, Helen Barnwell

Barnwell, Dr. John Smith, 175

Barnwell, Thomas Osborn, 25, 27, 33, 66, 82, 114

Barnwell, Lt. Woodward, 36, 70, 76, 89, 103, 134, 151, 164, 175

Barnwell family, 160, 179, 181, 212

Barnwell's Light Battery, 24n, 70

Barrow, David C., *262*

Bayard, Florida, 17, 91, 109

Bayard, Nicholas J., 19n, 91

Beaufort, N.C., 162

Beaufort, S.C., xxxvii (n. 2), xlii (n. 25), 29n, 70, 210

Beaulieu (Savannah, Ga.), xxvi, *xxviii*, 87, 89, 93, 95, 96, 100, 135, 137, 144, 145, 152, *155*, 157, 164, 168

Beauregard, Gen. Pierre Gustave Toutant, xxvi, 117, 144, 145, 162

Beech Island, S.C., 210, 212

Benedict, David, 31

Bentonville (battle of), 163, *167*

Bessent, E. Julia, xxiv, xl (n. 14)

Bessent, John, Jr., xl (n. 14)

Bessent, Mary, xxiv

Bessent, Nanna, xxiv

Bessent, Ria (Maria), xxiv

Blackshear, Ga., 186

Blue Mud plantation (Savannah, Ga.), xxxvii (n. 2), 13n

Bob (slave/servant), 98

Bragg, Gen. Braxton, xxxi, 79, 81, 143

Branchville, S.C., 171

Brannon, Gen. John Milton, 186

British Museum, 237

Brockenbrough family, 200

Brooks, G.W., 165

Brown, Gov. Joseph E., xxix–xxx, xxxi, 27, 32, 36, 45, 77, 82, 86, 89, 94, 131, 142, 150

Brown, Larkin, 113

Brunswick (slave/servant), 91

Bryan County, Ga., 22

Bulloch, Irvine Stevens, xxxv

Bulloch, James Dunwody, xxxv

Bulloch, James Stephens, xvi

"Burial of Latané, The" (Washington), 200, 270

Burney, Isaac H., 97

Camden, Ark., 7, 200

Camden, S.C., *167*

Camden County, Ga., ix, xv, xxi, xxiii, xl (n. 13), 142

Camp, Elizabeth Hitchcock, 223, 224

Camp, George, 221

Camp, George Hull, 33n, 66, 75, 98, 104, 114, 121, 229, 236; letter from, 73

Camp, Hattie, 221

Camp, Jane Atwood, 32, 33, 40, 73, 97, 104

Camp, Lucretia Merrell, 67n, 74n

Camp, Mr. and Mrs. (John?), 221

Camp, Walter Bicker, 222, 223, 226, 229, 236

Campbell, Mrs. (Valdosta neighbor), 173

Capers, Francis Withers, xxxi, 9, 10, 17, 26, 46, 48, 57, 64, 88, 91, 96, 100, 136, 142–43, 144, 150, 158, 165, 174

Carmichael, Mrs. (hostess), 181

Cartersville, Ga., 112

Cassel, Lorena (Rena), 207n

Cassel, Thomas, 206

Cassville, Ga., xxxiv, 45

Cedar (Vickery) Creek, xvi

Central Railroad. *See* Railroads
Chambersburg, Pa., 112
Charleston, S.C., xxx, xliii (n. 30), 160, 162, 164, 166, *167*, 174, 180, 253
Charlotte (slave/servant), 114
Chatham Artillery. *See* Savannah, Ga.
Chatham County, Ga., xxxiv
Chattahoochee River, xv, xvi, 29, 226, 263
Chattanooga, Tenn., xxxi, xxxii
Cheraw, S.C., 162, *167*, 175
Cherokee Nation, xv
Cheves, Langdon, 62
Chickamauga (battle of), xxxiii, xxxvi
Cincinnati, O., 114
Citadel, 253
Clarinda. *See* Richardson, Clarinda
Clarke, Pvt. G. B., 8
Clay, Thomas Carolin, 15, 22, 37, 38, 70, 76, 152, 171, 174; letter from, 8
Clemens, Mary Read, xxvii, 91, 104,134
Clinch County, Ga., xxxii, xxxiii, 7, 12, 21
Cobb County, Ga., 175
Cold, David (slave/servant), xxxviii
Colquitt, Alfred Holt, 38
Columbia, S.C., 104, 120, 153, 162, *167*
Comfort, Rev. David, 176, 178; letter from, 177
Confederate States of America:
    conscription of soldiers, xxix, xxxiii–xxxiv; Congress, xxix, 77, 90n; currency, xxxiii; Department of the Trans–Mississippi, xxxv, 139; Department of South Carolina, Georgia, and Florida, 142
Coosawhatchie, S. C., 38
Cotton, Mamie, 269
Cozby, James Smith, 14, 37
"Crackers," 86, 94, 140
Crichton family, xxiv
Curtright Manufacturing Company, 66, 73, 75, 104
Cyclorama. *See* Atlanta, Ga.

Dalton, Ga., 41, 45
Daniell's Georgia Light Artillery, 76, 144
Darien, Ga., Bank of, xvi
Darling, Capt. Joseph, 166
Daugherty. *See* Dougherty, Mr.
Davis, Jefferson, xxv, 77, 89, 123, 129, 130, 133, 162, 223
Davis, Capt. John A., 166
Davis, Mr. (agent), 237
Davy (slave/servant), xxxviii
Dinah, 252
Dougherty, Mr. (recruiter), xxiii–xxiv, 9, 34, 89, 99, 172
Douglas, J. M., 165
Dow, Gen. Neal, 231
Downes, Miss (Valdosta visitor), 173
Dowse, Laura Philoclea, 14
DuBose, John Elbert, xxiv
DuBose family, 173
Duncan, William, 53, 79, 81, 108, 177, 184, 187, 194, 196, 201, 204, 208, 214, 238, 245; letters from, 183, 186
Duncan, Mrs. William, 184
Duncan and Johnston (factors), 53, 74, 79, 98
Dunwody, Charles Archibald Alexander, xxxvi, xlv (n. 44), 91, 229
Dunwody, Mrs. Ellen C., 229
Dunwody, Henry Macon, xxxvi
Dunwody, John, xvi, xxi
Dunwody, Rosa, xxxiv, 4
Durham Station, N.C., 163

Eatonton, Ga., 68
Eighteenth Battalion, Georgia Infantry, x, *248*
Elbert family, 170
Eldredge, Olney, 110, 114, 121
Eldredge family, 110
Elliott, Caroline (Carrie), xxvi
Elliott, George Herbert, 188
Elliott, Capt. George Parsons, 164
Elliott, John Gibbes Barnwell, 144, 145, 164

Elliott, John Mackay, 70, 129, 130, 135, 144, 148, 151, 154, 155, 166, 180, 185, 187–88, 206

Elliott, Leila, 181

Elliott, Margaret Cowper Mackay (Maggie), xxvi, xli (n. 18, 21), 14, 40, 79, 93, 96, 158, 161, 184, 200; letters from, 153, 180, 187, 206

Elliott, Mary Stiles. *See* Habersham, Mary Stiles Mackay Elliott

Elliott, Percival, 4, 152, 181, 184, 187–88

Elliott, Phoebe, 37, 152, 181, 184, 187–88

Elliott, Ralph Emms, 148, 154, 155–56, 180, 185

Elliott, Robert Habersham (Habby), 180

Elliott, Robert Mackay, 184

Elliott, Sidney Stiles (Siddie), xxvi, 108, 112

Elliott, Bishop Stephen, 184, 188; letter from, 182

Elliott, Gen. Stephen, 70, 162

Elliott, William Henry (Billy), xxv, xxvi

Elliott family, 37, 217–18

Evans, Clement A., 253

Eve, Joseph E., xxxvi, 34, 131

Ewell, Dr. James, 125

Fayetteville, N.C., 162, *167*, 175

First Alabama Cavalry (federal), 143

Florence, S.C., 162

Forrest, Gen. Nathan Bedford, 120, 130

Fort Jackson, Ga., 144

Fort McAllister, Ga. (Genesis Point), 8, 10, 17, 26, 144, *154*, 155

Fort Screven, Ga., xxv

Foster, Gen. John Gray, 17

Freedmen's Bureau, 236

Front Royal, Va., 108, 112

Garrard, Gen. Kenner, 46, 69n

Geiger, Dr. Charles Atwood, 15, 57, 66, 134–35

Geiger, Helen Barnwell, 15, 36, 50, 57, 66, 134–35, 136, 137

Genesis Point. *See* Fort McAllister, Ga.

George's Station, S.C., 162, *167*, 171, 174

Georgia, state of: agriculture, xx, xxxvi (n. 6); maps, *xxii, 52, 154;* early history, xxvi (n. 2); Civil War legislature, xxx, 7, 28, 33n, 37n, 150; taxes, 7; Home Guards (state militia), 71, 137, 142, 143, 144

Georgia Military Institute: cadets, x, xxix, xxx, 64, 114, 120, 130, 136; enrollment, xxix, xxxi; haven for sons of the wealthy, xxx; exemption of cadets, xxx, xxxi, 6, 9, 33; faculty, xxxi, 34; quality of education, xxxi, 34, 114, 131, 136; in Marietta, xxxi, 48, 49; problems with, xxxi–xxxii, 64, 119–20, 132–33, 136; tuition, xxxii; commissary, 26; engineer corps of the state, 33, 35; military engagements, 46; leave Marietta, 46, 48, 49, 51; in Midway, 46, 49, 51, 54, 103; in Milledgeville, 46, 49, 51, 97, 99, 100, 102, 104, 105, 106, 142, 150; in West Point, 46, 52, 53; at Gordon, 51, 142, 150; at the front, 72–73; libraries, 78; dormitories, 78; favorite of Gov. Joe E. Brown, 82; rations, 100, 105, 136; in Atlanta, 101, 103–4; casualties, 104, 105, 120, 143; regulations, 136; in Sherman's path, 141–42, *231*, 253; at Oconee Bridge, 142, 150–51, *154;* smallpox in camp, 149; in Savannah, *155*, 156, 158–59; in Augusta, 161, 165

Georgia Railroad. *See* Railroads

Georgia State Line Brigade, 144

Gettysburg (battle of), xxx, xxxvi

Givens, P. D.: letter from, 38

Glenn family, 187

Glynn County, Ga., xxxiii

Goldsboro, N.C., 163, *167*

Gordon, George Anderson, 4

Gordon, Ga., 47, 51, 150, *154*

Gordon, Gen. John B., 253
Gourdin's Station, S.C., 162, *167,* 174, 175
Grahamville, S.C., 50, 77, 81
Grant, Gen. Ulysses S., 84, 86
Green Pond, S.C., 164
Greensboro, N.C., 162, 175
Greensboro (Ga.) Female Academy, xx
Greenwood (New York City cemetery), 220
Griffin, Samuel (GMI cadet), 114, 119, 122, 131, 156
Griffin, Thomas Butler, 120n, 131
Griffith, Capt. (GMI commissary), 48, 51, 131
Guerard, A. G., 38

Habersham, Leila Elliott, 181
Habersham, Mary Stiles Mackay Elliott (later Huger), 37, 57, 96, 109, 148, 152, 155, 181, 218
Habersham family, 86
Hamilton, Miss (visitor), 104, 134–35
Hand, Catherine, xxxvi
Hand, Eliza Barrington King (later Bayard), xvi, 91
Hanleiter, Capt. Cornelius R., 148
Hanleiter, Lt. William R., 70
Hanna or Hannah (slave/servant), xxviii
Hanover County, Va., 200
Hardee, Mary Eliza, 26
Hardee, Gen. William J., x, xxxv, 89, 108, 142–46, 162–63, 166, *167,* 175, 209, 257
Hardeeville, S.C., 145, 146, 158, 161, 164, *167,* 267
Harden, Pvt. W. D., 8, 166
Hardy, Col., 156
Hardy, Dr. John G., 156
Harrison, Lt. George E., 124n, 168, 171
Harry (slave/servant), 11, 169, 170
Hartridge, Maj. Alfred L., 142–44, 154
Harvey, H. L., xxxi
Hatteras, Cape, 222
Heattie, 252

Heill, Lt., 175
Hill, J. A., 165
Hill, Mary Maxwell, 69
Hill, William H., 69
Hines, R. K., 166
Hinton family, 239
Hood, Gen. John Bell, 44n, 79, 86, 89, 90, 94, 108, 115, 117, 120, 141
Howard, Charles Wallace, 112
Howard, Ella Susan, 112
Howard, Jane, 112
Huger, Mary Stiles Elliott Mackay. *See* Habersham, Mary Stiles Elliott Mackay
Huger's Causeway, S.C., 146
Hutchinson's Island (Savannah, Ga.), 145, 146

Indian Springs, Ga., xxxi, 17
Isle of Hope (Savannah, Ga.), *xxvii,* 50, 62–63, 65, 69, 70, 71, 76, 84, 103, 123, 128, 132, 135, 137, 139, 148, 151, 152, *155*
Ivy Woolen Mills. *See* Roswell, Ga.

Jack (slave/servant), 4, 117, 125
Jacksonville, Fla., 180
Jersey Point plantation, xvi
John (slave/servant), 4
Johnson, Andrew, 236
Johnson, Dr. Charles, 188
Johnson, Capt. G. W.: letter from, 20
Johnston, Gen. Joseph E., xxxii, 44n, 45, 48, 53, 74, 79, 81, 86, 89, 91, 94, 141, 151, 162, 163, 177
Johnston, Mrs. (Raleigh benefactress), 205
Jonesboro, Ga., 108, 120
Joyner, Margaret, xxxvii (n. 2)

Kearsarge, U.S.S., xxxv
King, Barrington, xvi, xxi, xxxiii, xxxv, 40, 46, 47, 48, 62, 63, 79, 80, 90, 91, 104, 137, 200, 221; letters from, 53, 74, 97, 120, 152, 206

King, Col. Barrington Simrall, xxxv, 74, 120, 162

King, Bessie McCloud (Mrs. Barrington Simrall King), 120

King, Catherine Evelyn. *See* Baker, Catherine Evelyn King

King, Catherine Margaret Nephew (Mrs. Barrington King), 40, 49, 53, 75, 80, 83, 89, 90, 91, 104, 107, 121, 140, 152, 153, 200, 207; letter from, 221

King, Rev. Charles Barrington, 153

King, Clifford A., xxxv, 26

King, Eliza Barrington, xvi, 91

King, Florence Stillwell (Mrs. Ralph Browne King), xxvii, 23, 91, 104

King, Frances Price (Mrs. James Roswell King), 40, 91, 104, 113, 153

King, James Roswell, xxxv, 65, 81, 91, 113, 153

King, Joseph Henry, xxxv

King, Mary Read Clemens (Mrs. Tom King), xxvii, 91, 104, 134

King, Ralph Browne, xxxv, 23, 104

King, Roswell, xvi

King, Capt. Thomas Edward, xxxii–xxxiii, xxxv, xxxvi, xlii (n. 23), 93

King, William, 127, 133–34, 137

King's Bay, Ga., xvi

Kingston, Ga., xxxiii, xxxiv

Kingston, N.Y., 226

Kirby, Lt. Col. D.T., 143

Kirby Smith, Gen. Edmund, 75, 117

Kollock, Miss, 37

Kollock, Dr. Phineas, 38n, 111

Ladson, George Whitfield, 84

LaGrange, Ga., 252

Lake City, Fla., 20n, 24, 92

Lanesboro, N.C., 180

Law, Caroline Matilda, 14, 15

Law, Mary Louisa, 14

Law, Samuel Spry, 14

Law, Hon. William, 37

Lawrenceville, Ga., 53

Lebanon, Ga., x, xx

Lee, Gen. Robert E., xxx, 83–84, 86, 117, 162, 163, 167, 253

Leesburg, C.S.S., xxv

Lewis, Catherine Barrington Cook, xxxi

Lewis, John, xxxi, 74, 79

Lewis, Margaret, xxxi

Lewis, Robert Adams, xxxi, 74, 79

Lexington, Va., 91

Lincoln, Abraham, 117, 125, 163

Lincoln Hospital (Washington, D.C.), 184

Lineberger, Saloma, 118

Little Rock, Ark., 197

London, Eng., 227, 238–39

Londonderry, Ire., 226, 232–34

Long, Alexander, 125

Longstreet, Gen. James, 17, 29

Lookout Mountain (battle of), xxxvi

Low, Mary Cowper Stiles, xxvi

Lowndes County, Ga., xiv, xxxiii, 27, 33, 36, 54, 73, 265. *See also* Valdosta, Ga.

Lucas Ranch, 265

Luke, or Luck (slave/servant), 4, 11n, 114, 152

M., Capt., 8n, 15, 91, 95

Macdonald, Mr., 187

Mackay, Catherine, xxvi, 12, 25, 31, 37, 66, 89, 96, 99, 102, 138, 148, 159, 180, 217

Mackay, Elizabeth Anne, xli (n. 21), 37, 79, 81, 120

Mackay, Margaret Cowper. *See* Elliott, Margaret Cowper Mackay

Mackay, Sarah, xxvi, 12, 25, 60, 63, 70, 79, 81, 90, 96, 102, 138, 148, 159, 183, 188, 217–18; letter from, 184

Macon, Ga., 48, 49, 50, 51, 54, 66, 73, 90, 92, 104, 123, 129, 149, 153, 160

Maggiore, Lake, 243

Magill, Aurelia Isabella Bacon (Belle), 7, 47, 102, 139, 198; offers condolence to Smiths, 198

Magill, Charles Arthur, xiii, xxxv, 7, 49, 83, 102, 140, 148, 200, 239; offers advice to William, xxiii; offers condolence to Smiths, 197–98

Magill, Eliza, 209

Magill, Elizabeth Pye. *See* Merrell, Elizabeth Pye Magill

Magill, Elizabeth Zubly, 209

Magill, Helen Twining, 209

Magill, Helen Zubly (Auntie), xli (n. 27), 40, 47, 73, 98, 156, 185, 222, 242, 251; arrival in Roswell, xv; teaches Helen and Archie, xx, 213; writes letter for Archie, xxiii; travels with William, xxiv; describes Roswell fortifications, xxx; letters from, 39, 102; makes hats, 39–40; duties, 60, 235; gets letters about Roswell, 79, 113; her Valdosta room, 80, 87, 88, 91, 94; her inkstand, 85, 87, 94; describes Valdosta house, 103; requests feathers, 133; receives braid and palmetto, 139; her clock, 222; death, 252

Magill, Lt. John W.: recruiting duty, xxxiii–xxxiv; uses Smith home as headquarters, xxxiv; artillery duty, 30, 70, 76, 103, 137, 144, 164; furlough to Valdosta, 114, 125; courts Gulie Riley, 126, 128; illness, 148

Magill, Margaret Clay, 209

Magill, Matilda W., 209

Magill, Seagrove William, 37, 200; appears in Savannah, 180–81; letter from, 209; portrait, *210*

Magill, Sgt. William Alexander, 200, 209

Magnet (steamer), 226

Manassas (First battle of), xxxii, xxxv, xxxvi

Manassas ("Third" battle of), 264

Manget, Victor E., 67, 69, 72, 96, 165

Manget, Victor H., 34

Manigault, Capt. Joseph, 8n, 15, 91, 95

Maria, 252

Marietta, Ga., xxxi, xxxiii, 19, 33, 44, 46, 48, 49, 61, 63, 65, 72, 75, 120, 131, 175, 206, 207, 210

Marion, Niddy, 219

Martin, William Thompson, 29

Maryland (Early's invasion of), 84

Maryland Fund, 60

Mason, Annie, 190, 244

Mason, Martha, 244

Mason, Mary (daughter of Mary Ann), 217, 244

Mason, Mary Ann, 163, *195*, 203, 205, 215, 216, 229, 238; letters from, 189, 201, 208, 213, 215, 217, 224, 240, 244

Mason, Rebecca E., 206n, 217, 237, 241, 244, 246; letters from, 204, 216

Mason, Rev. Dr. Richard Sharp, 182, 183, 186, 187, 189, *193*, 201, 208, 214, 224, 225, 240, 244, 247, 250; letters from, 182, 185, 194, 203, 212, 238, 245, 246, 246, 247

Mason, Sally, 244

Mason, William, 190, 201, 208

Mason family, 199, 247, 250, 251

Maum ("Mauma" or "Mamma") Mannie (slave/servant), 50n, 152

Maxwell, Maj. J. A. (battalion of light artillery), 24n, 132, 134

McAlpine family, 229

McCall, Mr. L., 121

McClellan, Gen. George B., 110, 117, 125

McIntosh County, Ga., 97

McLaws, Gen. Lafayette, 91, 143–44

McPherson, Gen. James B., 112, 256, 257

McQueen, Anne Smith, xli (n. 18)

Memminger, Lt. Christopher A., 175

Merrell, Elizabeth Pye Magill (Aunt Bet, Ambet), xii, 47, 99, 139, 148, 217, 222, 224, 230, 244; arrival in Roswell, xv; marriage, xxi, xxxv, 200; travels with

Merrell, Elizabeth Pye Magill (*cont.*)
William, xxiv; in Camden, Ark., 7, 57,
209; trip to N.Y., Canada, and Europe,
200, 217, 219, 223, 229, 231, 233, 243;
sends photo of William, 216; sends
dress, 216; letters from, 219, 232, 238,
243; recalls William, 220, 234, 237; portrait, *233;* deafness, 242; displeasure
with Arthur Smith's name, 251
Merrell, Harriett Camp, 160, 222, 223
Merrell, Henry, xxiii, 47, 102, 230;
marriage, xi, xxv, 200; missions for
Confederacy, xv, 57, 139, 148, 197;
assistant at Roswell Manufacturing
Co., xxi; moves to Arkansas, xxi;
assisted by William xxi, xxiv; leads
tour of N.Y., Canada, and Europe,
200, 217, 218, 219, 220, 227, 229, 234,
238, 243; visit to Yankee relatives
disturbs Smiths, 200, 229, 236; prices
gravestone, 220; lends shirt to niece,
231; confronts Yankee general, 231;
portrait, *233;* sings hymn honoring
Willie, 239
Merrell, Lucretia, 67n, 74n
Methiglin, 106, 111
Midway, Ga., 48–49, 72, 103, 119, 131
Milledgeville, Ga.: site of Oglethorpe
University, xx, 46; state capitol, 46,
100, 103, 106, 150; duty station for GMI
cadets, 48, 51, 54, 65, 67–68, 97, 99,
100, 102, 105, 106, 131, 150, 159; threat
of attack upon, 66, 67–68, 86, 141, 142;
evacuation of, 93, 142, 150, *154;* mental
hospital, 126
Milledgeville and Gordon Railroad. *See*
Railroads
Millen, Ga., *154*
Miller, Mrs., 224
Minnie, Miss (wedding guest), 22
Minton, Axson, 74, 84, 104
Minton, Maj. John, 16n, 26, 74, 84, 207,
230

Minton, Mrs. John, 74, 84
Minton, Miss (daughter of John), 84
Minton family, 104, 122n, 230
Missionary Ridge (battle of), xxxvi
Mitchel and Smith (factors), 98
Mobile, Ala., 19
Montgomery, Ala., xxv
Montgomery (Savannah, Ga.), 30, 112,
148, *155*
Montreal, 226, 234
Moon, Charlotte (Lottie; governess to
Gulie Riley), 56
Morel, Miss (Savannah correspondent),
105
Morgan's Company, 30
Morris (slave/servant), 7n
Moses (slave/servant), xxviii, 11, 84, 86,
110, 252
Murdstone, Mr. (Dickens character), 134,
137
Myddelton, Robert T., 252

Nanny Sue (slave/servant), 11
Neufville, Edward F., 34, 101
Newbern, N.C., 162
Newnan, Ga., 94
New York City, 219–20
Niagara Falls, 223
Nicolson, Dr. (visitor), 29
Niter Bureau (Augusta, Ga.), 110
North Carolina Institute (Charlotte
Military Institute), xxxi
Nullification plantation, xxxvii (n. 2)

Ocean Pond, Fla. *See* Olustee, battle of
Ocean Pond, Ga. *See* Valdosta, Ga.
Oconee bridge (skirmish), 141–43, 151,
154, 158
"Oft in the Stilly Night" (Moore), 210,
265
Ogeechee River, Great , xxvi, 144, *155*
Ogeechee River, Little, xxvi, 11n, 144,
155

Oglethorpe, James Edward, xxxvi (n. 2)

Oglethorpe University, xx, xxiv, 46, 49, 57, 78

Old Fort plantation (Beaufort, S. C.), xxxvii (n. 2), xlii (n. 25), 220

Olustee, battle of (or Ocean Pond, Fla.), 16, 20n, 21, 24, 55

Owen, David Dale, xxiv

Parkertown. *See* Roswell, Ga.

Parsons, Elisha, 66, 96

Pease, Philander Pitkin, 79

Pennyworth Island (Savannah, Ga.), 145

Petersburg, Va., 84

Pocotaligo, S.C., 161, 166, *167,* 169

Polk, Gen. Leonidas, 44n

Porcher, Francis Peyre, 36, 117, 125

Postwar conditions in the South, 197–98, 209–10, 211–12, 229, 235–36

Pratt, Bayard Hand, xxxvi, 4

Pratt, Belle, 122n

Pratt, Catherine King, 79, 103, 110, 121, 212

Pratt, Charles Jones, xxxv–xxxvi, 207

Pratt, Henry Barrington, 4

Pratt, Horace A., xxxvi, 4

Pratt, Joanna Gildersleeve, 103

Pratt, Rev. Nathaniel Alpheus, xvi, 4, 74, 79, 97, 98, 103, 110, 113, 121, 140, 168 (n. 4), 177, 207, 209, 212

Pratt, Sarah Anna, 31n, 79, 97, 108, 110, 111, 122n, 124, 132

Pratt family, xxxvi, 104

Price, Gen. Sterling, 102

Prince (slave/servant), 114, 121

Proudfoot, Hugh W., 75, 97

Proudfoot family, 104, 122n

Pryor, James J., 62; letter from, 61

Quebec, 226, 233, 234

Quintard, Charles T., xxxvi

Quitman, Ga., 106

Railroads: Georgia, *xxii,* 44n, *52,* 86; Macon and Western, *xxii,* 44n, *52, 154;* Western and Atlantic, *xxii,* 44n, 45, *52;* Atlanta and West Point, *xxii,* 52, *52;* Milledgeville and Gordon, *xxii,* 92, 142, 150, *154;* Atlantic and Gulf, 8n, 11, *52, 155,* 171; Southwestern, 11, *52;* Central, 44n, 52, 54, 98, 142, 143, 151, *154, 155,* 156, 157n, 158, 159; Charleston and Savannah, 145, *155,* 267; Northeastern, 162, 174n

Rainwater, James A., 251

Raleigh, N.C., x, 175, 176, 187, 200, 225, 251; occupation of, 163, *167,* 203, 205; Peace Hospital, 163, 177, 179, 187, 189, 194, 203; City Cemetery, 241; Oakwood Cemetery, 242n

Read, Mary Talbot Locke, xxvii, 91, 104, 134

Rees, Miss (Roswell resident), xxxii

Resaca, Ga., 41, 45, 46

Richardson, Clarinda (slave/servant), 6, 13, 152, 252

Richardson, Maj. John M., xxxi, 34

Richmond, Va., 24, 120, 153

Riley, Elizabeth Ann Maner, xxxiii, 23, 49, 54–56, 57, 60, 89, 103, 108, 132, 252

Riley, Frances (Fanny) Morgandollar. *See* Barnwell, Frances

Riley, Gulielma English. *See* Smith, Gulielma English Riley

Riley, William M., 55

Riley family, 49, 89, 108, 114, 128, 159, 265

Ritchard, P., 174, 176

Robert (slave/servant), 200

Roché, Theophile, xlii (n. 27), 114, 134

Rock Mountain, 44

Roddey, Gen. Philip Dale, 94

Rome, Ga., 45

Rose Dew (Savannah, Ga.), xxvi, *xxviii,* 8, 10, 96, 100, 103, 123, 144, 145, 152, *155*

Roswell, Ga.: "colony," ix, xv, xvi, xx, xxxv; Roswell Manufacturing Company, xv–xvi, xxi, xxxii, xxxiii, xxxvi, xxxviii (n. 7), 46, 51, 53, 71, 74, 79, 91, 97, 98, 112, 115, 153; Primrose Cottage, xvi; "The Labyrinth," xvi; "The Castle," xvi; Presbyterian Church, xvi, xx, xxv, xxxvi, 7, 27, 30, 207, 254; agriculture, xvi, xx, xxxviii (n. 6); Great Oaks, xvi, xxxi, xxxvi, xliv, 79, 97; Barrington Hall, xvi, xxxii, xxxvi, 74, 91, 97, 122n; Mimosa (Dunwody) Hall, xvi, xxxvi, 91; economic classes, xx; defensive fortifications, xxx; Ivy Woolen Mills, xxxiii, 62, 74; diphtheria in, xxxiv, 4, 19; men in military service, xxxv–xxxvi; evacuation of, xxxvi, 45, 46, 49, 54, 73; destruction of the mills, xxxvi, 46, 51, 74, 97, 112, 113, 115n; occupation of, xxxvi, 46, 53, 62, 73, 74–75, 79, 83, 86, 99, 103, 110; Bulloch Hall, xxxvi, 122n; Roswell Battalion, xliii (n. 33); Holly Hill, xliv (n. 34), 74, 79, 91, 122n; treatment of founders' homes by citizens, 79, 113, 121, 122n, 140; deportation of millworkers, 112; Parkertown, 113; City Hall, 254; Roswell railroad, 263; life in 1904, 263; early life in, 266; library, 267. *See also* Smith Plantation Home

Roswell Guards. *See* Roswell, Ga.

Roswell Manufacturing Company. *See* Roswell, Ga.

Roswell Presbyterian Church. *See* Roswell, Ga.

Rountree, James, 202

Sackets Harbor, N.Y., 221, 229

Saguenay River, 226

Salkehatchee, S.C., 161, 166, *167*

Savannah, Ga., x, xi, *xxviii,* xxxiii, xxxvi, 6, 8, 14, 46, 50, 62, 101, 104, 105, 108–9, 111, 112, 114, 123, 133, 138, 143, 144, 151, 152, *154, 155, 167,* 180, 200, 209, 217–18; Savannah Volunteer Guards, x, xxv, xxxvi, 218; defensive positions, xxxviii, 11n, 141, *155;* defense of, 144–45; evacuation of, 145–46, *155,* 159–60, 163–64, 267. *See also* Beaulieu; Isle of Hope; Rose Dew; Whitemarsh Island

Savannah Volunteer Guards. *See* Savannah, Ga.

Scolds (or Scols) family, 61–62

Screven, Fort, xxv, xxvi

Screven, Gen. James, xxv

Screvens Ferry (Savannah, Ga.), xxxvii (n. 2), 145

Seagrave, Phoebe B., 114

Semmes, Adm. Raphael, 140

Servants. *See* Slaves

Setze, Dr. E. J., 17, 23, 26, 29

Seymour, Mrs. Horatio, 224

Sherman, R. E., 62

Sherman, Gen. William Tecumseh, ix, x, xi, xxxvi, 42n, 45, 46, 47, 75, 84, 89, 115, 118, 123, 125, 127, 133, 137, 141–46, 152, 162, 163, 171, 175, 253, 256, 269

Sherrod, Miss (occupant of Smith home), 63

Sherrod, Mrs. (occupant of Smith home), 85

Shreveport, La., 139

Signal Corps (CSA) x, xxvi, xxxiii, 7, 31, 38, 99, 100, 103, 105, 106, 114, 152, 176, 177, 187

Silvy or Silva (slave/servant), 252

Skinner, James Lister, Jr., 269

Skinner, James Lister, III, 269

Skinner, Josephine Norvell Fry, 269

Skinner, Thomas Fry, 268

Skinner, William Wirt, 268

Slaves ("servants"), xxxii, xxxviii; attempt to free, xxxvii (n. 4); wages paid, xxxvii (n. 4), 11 (n. 3). *See also* Bob; Brunswick; Charlotte; Cold,

David; Hanna; Harry; Jack; John; Luke; Maum Mannie; Morris; Moses; Nanny Sue; Prince; Richardson, Clarinda; Robert; Silvy; Tira

Slocum, Gen. Henry W., 162, 163

Smith, Anne Margaret Magill (mother), 30, 47, 54, 82, 183, 184, 190, 200, 201, 213, 238, 246; portraits, *xvii, 191, 234;* comments on Smith finances, xxi, xxxiii, 7; advice to William, xxi, 32; goes to Indian Springs, xxx; comments on military movements, xxx, xxxii, 13, 24, 29, 41, 49; religious faith, xxx, 4, 5, 10, 13, 14, 19–20, 28, 41, 65, 92, 93, 97, 101, 106, 114, 159, 170, 172, 173, 179–80, 242, 247; indecision about evacuation, xxxi, xxxii, 5, 13, 19–20, 27, 29, 32–33; concerns for Archie's military status, xxxi, xxxiv, 5–6, 7, 9, 10, 17, 26, 29, 31–32, 35, 46, 71, 88, 92–93, 106; preparing for evacuation, xxxii, xxxiv, 5, 13, 44; concerns about "unsafe" slaves, xxxii, 3–4, 13, 19, 106; relies on William's judgment, xxxii, 5, 7, 10, 13; concerns about food, xxxiii, 22, 25, 28, 29, 35, 41, 51, 57, 60, 65, 66, 128, 132, 135, 137, 151, 169; sends box of goods to William, xxxiv, 6; described by Archie, xxxix (n. 11); letters from, 3, 5, 6, 10, 17, 19, 23, 25, 26, 28, 31, 35, 41, 44, 47, 50, 57, 60, 64, 68, 71, 79, 92, 96, 101, 102, 105, 113, 118, 125, 128, 129, 135, 137, 159, 169, 172, 179, 196, 211, 219, 229, 237, 242, 247; concerns for Archie's health, 4, 6, 7, 10, 88, 96, 169, 173; concerns about servants, 4, 6, 11, 13, 114; costs and scarcities, 6–7, 23, 26, 29, 126, 128, 211; personal health, 7, 26, 30, 251; making clothes, 17, 23, 24, 65, 135, 138, 251; concerns for Helen's health, 19, 22, 23, 26, 29, 32, 35, 103, 130; describes a visitor, 29–30; comments on class, 32, 113; concerns for William, 35, 41, 46, 105, 106, 111, 114–15, 117, 123, 125, 128, 130, 132, 160, 169, 172, 179; concerns for family in Arkansas, 47, 57; concerns for Archie's safety, 57, 65, 92, 159–60; does kitchen work, 60, 235; concerns about Roswell, 66, 71, 113–14; concerns about family belongings, 79; mirror from Roswell, 83; fears Andersonville raid, 92, 114; looks for honey for Willie, 102, 105, 118, 125; needs a chair, 107, 111, 124; sends servant to William, 170; describes Willie, 196; asks for information about Willie's death, 196–97; angry with Yankee brother, 211; concerns for daughters' visit to the North, 229; mistakes Archie for Willie, 230; blindness, 251; death, 252

Smith, Archibald (1758–1830), xxxvii (n. 2)

Smith, Archibald (father) (1801–1886), xxi, xxii, xxvii, xxxi, xxxii, xxxiii, xxxv, xxxvii, xxxxviii (nn. 6, 7), 3, 5, 6, 9, 11, 11–12 (n. 3), 13, 19, 22, 29, 32, 39, 66, 83, 93, 108, 113, 120, 131, 213, 269; early days in Roswell, ix, xv, xvi, xx; attempts to liberate slaves, xvi, xxxvii (n. 4), 11–12 (n. 3); portraits, *xvii, 234;* advice to William, xxi, xxii, xxvii, xliv (n. 40); assesses Roswell fortifications, xxxi; leads removal to south Georgia, xxxii–xxxiii, xxxv, 3, 4, 5, 7, 9, 11–12, 13, 16, 19–21, 23, 27, 32–33, 47–49, 170; agricultural commentary, xxxviii (n. 6); finances, xxxviii (n. 7), 11, 64, 127, 173; characterized, xxxix (n. 11), 137; deafness, xxxix (n. 11), 251; religious faith, xxxix (n. 11), 21, 127, 236, 240; concerns for Archie's military status, 6, 29, 88; letters from, 12, 16, 21, 25, 126, 176, 235, 240; in Savannah, 12, 25; observations on troop movements, 16; provisions for soldiers, 20; concerns for Archie's health, 21; concerns for

Smith, Archibald (*cont.*)

Helen's health, 21; health, 25, 57, 60, 65, 72, 106, 114, 119, 125, 214; goes to Marietta, 32, 34; retrieves belongings from Roswell, 46, 54, 71, 79, 80–81; mends honey cannister, 106, 125; kills an ibis, 107, 109; tries to get shoes for Archie, 114, 126, 128; buys and breaks horse, 126–27, 170; resents William King, 127; tries to get corn, 128, 160; trip to Florida, 137, 139; Savannah property, 145; plants sugar cane, 173; concerns for Willie, 176, 177; purchases print of "Burial of Latané," 200; concerns for daughters' visiting Yankees, 200, 236; arrangements for monument, 212, 240, 244; describes family in 1880, 235–36; comments on postwar servants, 235–36; death, 252

Smith, Archibald, Jr (Archie, Sonny), x, xii, xxvii, 9, 11, 12, 14, 16, 23, 25–26, 32, 33, 36, 39, 47, 81, 101, 102, 128, 130, 148, 151, 153, 181, 198, 207, 223, 235, 242, 254, 267; portraits, *xix, 59, 260;* birth and early education, xx, 213, 251; sense of duty, xxix, xxxiv, 7, 49, 57, 61, 73, 77; concerns about the GMI, xxxi, 34, 61, 64, 78, 82, 109, 120, 131, 136; notes on Smith family history, xxxvii (n. 4), xxxix (n. 11); health, 4, 6, 7, 10, 11, 14, 21, 61, 68, 77, 88, 95, 96, 99, 101, 104, 114, 131, 159, 164, 165, 169, 173, 219, 239, 251; furloughs, 9–30 passim, 149, 161, 165, 166–69, 170, 173, 176, 181; characterized, 28, 66, 213, 250, 251; letters from, 33, 48, 51, 54, 61, 63, 67, 72, 77, 100, 119, 122, 130, 136, 149, 156, 158, 165, 267; hopes for Signal Corps, 34, 91, 94, 100, 106, 111, 114; participates in defense of Gordon, Ga., 46–47; duty as commissary sergeant for GMI, 48–52, 54, 64, 71, 88, 103, 117, 130, 136, 150–51; difficulties with cooking, clothes, 64, 65, 72, 97, 99, 106, 109, 119, 122, 128, 136, 158; participates in defense of Milledgeville, Ga., 67–68; participates in defense of Oconee Bridge, 142–43, 150; participates in defense of Savannah, 143, 153, 163–64; meets Willie near Savannah, 143–44, 158; recollections of GMI on Sherman's march, 150–51, 267; concerns for Willie, 158; in Augusta, 166, 169; plays violin, 222; visits Willie's grave, 250; goes to business college, 250; moves to LaGrange, Ga., 252, 266; death, 265.

Smith, Dr. Archibald, III, 251, 252

Smith, Arthur William, xii; birth, 251; marriage, 252–53; education, 253; describes Confederate veterans, 253; architecture, 254; portraits, *258, 262;* characterization, 265, 268; presentation at meeting, 266; residence in Smith home, 268; death, 269

Smith, Elizabeth Anne (Lizzie, Sister), xxiii, 11, 14, 32, 35, 36, 47, 90, 96, 98–99, 102, 112, 121, 122n, 129, 130, 139, 142, 185, 198, 251, 252, 263; writing, xi, 229, 238; arrival in Roswell, xv; portraits, *xviii, 228, 230, 261;* education, xx; making articles for sale, xxvii, 17, 21–22, 24, 109; observations on flowers, xxvii, 22, 32–33, 40, 81, 85, 90, 93–94, 109, 114, 117; concerns for Mother, xxx, 30, 88; plants roots, garden, xxxiv, 22, 95; musician, xxxv, 22, 31, 80, 270; reports kitchen fire, xlii (n. 27); letters from, 9, 21, 30, 80, 83, 88, 89, 93, 108, 115, 123, 217, 221, 222, 224, 226, 227, 237; concerns for Archie, 9, 30, 88; does not wish to leave Roswell, 13; requests flowers, palmetto, etc., 24, 39–40, 81, 82, 85, 90, 109; needs dental work, 66, 96, 98–99, 102; concerns about shipped piano, 73, 74,

76, 79, 80, 87, 88, 89, 91, 94; hatred of Yankees, 83–84, 115, 117, 118, 123–24, 223, 224; observations on military matters, 84, 89, 94, 108, 115, 117–18, 123–24; sends flower seeds to Willie, 85; sends hat to Willie, 89, 90, 94; observations on class, 94; religious faith, 94, 110, 227; knits gloves for Willie, 169; on trip to N.Y., Canada, Europe, 200, 219, 221–23, 226–27, 232, 233, 236, 237, 238; described, 213, 251; recalls Willie, 223, 226, 227, 237; death, 254, 266

Smith, Eliza Williamson, xxxvii (n. 2)

Smith, Eliza Zubly. *See* Barnwell, Eliza Zubly Smith

Smith, Frances Maner, 251, 252, *259*

Smith, Gulielma English Riley (Gulie), xxxiii, 47, 54–55, *58*, 89, 103, 108, 114, 118, 123, 126, 132, 133, 251, 252; reflects on life in Valdosta, 55–56

Smith, Gen. Gustavus W., 142, 144, 145, 165

Smith, Helen Zubly (Sissie, Zubly), xxv, 11, 24, 27, 30, 36, 39, 42, 47, 71, 90, 102, 108, 122n, 124, 129, 185, 219; writing, xi; portraits, xix, *228, 232;* birth and education, xx, 251; painting and observing flowers, xxiii, 40, *43*, 82, 139; makes articles for sale, xxvii, xxxiv, 17, 40, 83, 89–90, 94, 107–8, 124, 132; reports kitchen fire, xxvii–xxix; goes to Indian Springs, xxx; recovering from diphtheria, xxxiv, 19, 21, 22, 23, 25, 26, 27, 29, 32, 35, 41, 48, 50–51, 84–85, 103; distress over leaving Roswell, xxxiv, 44, 48, 50–51, 71, 80; letters from, 40, 82, 107, 111, 132, 138, 170, 213, 231; possible Savannah trip, 62–63, 64–65, 133, 134–35, 137, 138, 148; sickness and remedies, 72, 77, 106, 117, 125, 130; makes ink, 83, 91; distress over military situation, 92; needs dental work, 102;

orders chair for mother, 107, 111; raises pigeons, 107, 132–33; on trip to N.Y., Canada, and Europe, 200, 217, 219, 221, 231–32, 233; thanks to Rebecca Mason, 213; comments on Yankees, 231

Smith, John, xxxvi (n. 2)

Smith, John Joyner (Uncle S.), xxvii–xxviii, xxxvii (n. 2), 12, 23, 29, 47, 75, 83, 87, 93, 94, 98, 127, 153, 185, 187, 207, 212; home in Beaufort, S.C., xlii (n. 25), 28n

Smith, Margaret Joyner, xxxvii (n. 2)

Smith, Mary Norvell, xii, 254, 264, 269

Smith, William Seagrove (Willie), ix–x, xxx, xxxi, xxxii, xxxv, 13, 46, 103, 156, 183, 184, 186, 187, 209, 211, 212, 236, 254, 266; portrait, *ii, xviii;* at Oglethorpe University, v, xx; Arkansas textile manufacturing, x, xxi, xxiv, 35; as teacher, x, xxi–xxiii, 142; enlistment, x, xxv; duties in signal corps, x, xxvii, xxviii, 15, 87, 144, *154, 155,* 161–62, 164, *167,* 168, 171, 174, 175; evacuates Savannah with Hardee and moves through Carolinas, x, 145–46, *155,* 161–62, *167,* 168, 171, 174–75, 267; sends trunk, xi, 152, 168, 269; arrival in Roswell, xv; characterization of, xxi, xxii–xxiii, xxiv, xxv, 6, 22, 28, 177, 182, 194, 196, 197, 198, 203–4, 205, 206, 213, 214, 225, 242, 251, 338; letters from, xxi, xxiv, xxv, xxvi, 14, 36, 49, 62, 69, 76, 81, 86, 90, 95, 98, 100, 105, 111, 129, 133, 134, 148, 151, 157, 163, 164, 166, 171, 174, 175; observations of flora, etc., xvi, xxiv, xxxiv, 37, 70, 87, 99; plays flute, xxv; in camp, xxv, xxvi; military observations, xxvi, 81, 86, 158, 162, 163–64, 167, 171, 174, 175; gets palmetto, feathers, flowers, seeds, music for family, xxvii, xxxiv, 22, 24, 27, 35, 36, 39, 40, 76, 80, 81, 82, 87, 90, 91, 93, 94, 95, 97, 99, 109, 117, 124, 133, 135,

Smith, William Seagrove (*cont.*)
139, 152, 170; lacks clothes, xxxiv, 16,
23, 24, 89, 90, 94, 99, 133, 135, 138, 139,
139, 140, 168, 169, 186; microscope, 5,
152; groomsman at a wedding, 6, 14–15,
22; father seeks his advice, 13, 21; observations on class, 15, 36; pet dog, 26,
30; concerns for Archie, 36, 50, 77,
91, 95–96, 99, 101, 105, 111, 151, 157–
58, 164; rations, 37, 63, 99; requests
flowers, honey, 37, 96, 101, 102, 105,
107, 108, 111, 114, 118–19, 129; asked to
make flower frame, 40; furloughs with
and for family, 46, 62, 63, 64, 71, 80,
82, 85, 91, 117; concerns for home, 49,
86, 158, 167, 171, 174, 175, 190, 201,
204, 205, 214, 215; religious faith, 49,
98, 101, 174, 177, 179, 182, 187, 188–89,
190, 192, 194, 196, 198, 204, 214, 251;
health, illnesses, 101, 105, 106, 111,
114–15, 125, 129, 133, 166, 169, 171,
172, 174, 175, 176, 177, *178,* 182, 183,
185, 186, 187, 190, 194, 195, 201, 203,
205, 214; asked to get chair for mother,
107, 111, 124, 133; meets Archie near
Savannah, 143; endures constant
shelling, 144, *155,* 168; moves up to the
front in Georgia, *154,* 156–57; in Peace
Hospital, 163, 175n, 177, *178, 179,*
184n, 189, 194, 203; does own washing
and cooking, 164, 169, 170; throws
away rifle, 168; subject of search, 176,
177, 180, 184, 185; head papers, *178;*
loyalty oath, *179;* death, 188, 190, 194,
201, 204, 241; burial, 189, 192, 194,
200, 202, 202, 204; personal effects,
192, 196, 202, 208, 213, 225; monument
for, 199, 208, 212, 214, 215, 217, 220,
224–25, *226,* 229–30, 237, 237–38,
240–41, 244, 245, 246, 247, *248,* 249;
photograph sent, 216; remembered in
New York, Canada, and Europe,
221–22, 223, 226–27, 234, 237, 239, 240,
243

Smithfield, N.C., 162

Smith Plantation Home (Roswell, Ga.):
photographs of, *xi, xxix;* building of,
xvi; kitchen fire in 1863, xxvii–xxix, xlii
(n. 27); shed, xxviii; garrett, xxxii;
piano, xxxii, 29, 73, 74, *76,* 79, 80, 87,
88, 89, 91, 94, 270; plants and flowers
on the grounds, xxxiii, xxxiv, 22, 26,
29, 30–31, 35, 37, 40–41, 81, 131, 170,
242; condition of house following
evacuation, xxxvi, 74, 79, 97, 98, 112,
113, 121, 122n, 207, 229; storehouse,
xxxviii, xlii (n. 27); inherited by
Skinner family, 5, 269; letters and
papers, 6, 269; garden, 29, 32, 242;
greenhouse, 31, 106; furnishings
shipped to Valdosta, 46, 51, 71, 73,
74–75, *76,* 79, 82, 85, 86, 87, 90, 91,
94, 95; spring, 57, 235, 270; "The
Burial of Latané," 200, 270; reopened,
254, 264; parlor, 263, 270; present
condition, 270

Smith refugee home (Valdosta, Ga.), 16,
20, 23–24; flight to, 46, 50–51, 53; life
in, 47, 55–56, 57, 60, 64–66, 71–72,
79–80, 82–83, 85, 88–89, 93–95, 103,
106, 108–9, 128, 137, 160, 206, 269. *See
also* Valdosta, Ga.

Smith Wharf and Stores (Savannah, Ga.),
xxxvii (n. 2) 183

Soldier's Comfort (Riley home), 56

Staunton, Va., 74, 91, 98, 104, 137, 140,
152, 153

Steele, Gen. Frederick, 57

Stephens, Alexander H., 32, 36, 133, 253

Stephens, Linton, 33n, 37n

Stephens, Lucy Evans, 253, 265

Stephens, Dr. Robert Grier, 253–54, *262,*
268; letters from, 256, 263, 264, 265,
267

Sterling plantation (Glynn County, Ga.), xxxiii, 55
Stevens, Gen. Isaac Ingalls, 28n
Stevens, Thaddeus, 125
Stewart, Ann Eliza, 173; letter from, 208
Stewart family, 173
Stiles, Benjamin Edward, 108, 112, 114
Stiles, Elizabeth Anne Mackay, xli (n. 21), 37, 79, 81, 120
Stiles, Eliza Mackay, xxvi
Stiles, Eugene West, 78
Stiles, Joseph, 36n
Stiles, Katherine Clay, 108
Stiles, Mary Cowper, xxvi
Stiles, Robert Mackay, 99, 144, 145
Stiles, Sidney, xxvi, 108, 112
Stiles, William Henry (1810–65), 81
Stiles, William Henry (1834–78), xxvi, 81
St. Lawrence River, 226, 231, 233
St. Marys, Ga., x, xxiv; Presbyterian Church, xxi; Academy, xxi, xxiii; citizens, xxiv, xl (n. 13)
Stoneman, Gen. George (raid of), 89, 94
Stone Mountain, Ga., 44
Suwanee, Fla., 109, 114

Talmadge, Ga., 57, 65
Talmage, Ruth S., 68–69, 97, 101, 102
Talmage (or Talmadge) Samuel K., 46, 68, 97, 101
Tatnall, Miss, 37
Télémaque (Fénelon), 131, 163
Tennille, Ga., 154
Thomasville, Ga., 153, 163
Tira (slave/servant), 114, 121
Tobey, S. H., 165
Tobler family, 243
Tolverger, Madame (hostess), 243
Trans–Mississippi Department. See Confederate States of America

Tunnel Hill, Ga., 24
Turner's Ferry, Ga., 46
Tybee Island (Ga.), xxv, xxvi

University of Georgia, 252, 253, 262
Utica, N.Y., 200

Valdosta, Ga., 46, 47, 64, 76, 97, 98, 99, 104, 116, 220, 222, 265; haven for refugees, xxxiii, xxxv, 24, 46; Smiths contemplate going to, 3–4, 21, 23, 24, 27; soldiers en route to or from battle of Olustee, 16, 20; old Riley place, 55–56, 265; Ocean Pond, 108; Archie's route to, 167; Presbyterian Church, 177n. See also Smith refugee home
Vallandigham, Clement L., 117, 125
Van Dyke, Rev. Henry Jackson, 219
Vernonburg, Ga., 11n, 155
Vernon River (Ga.), xxxvi, 11n
Vicksburg (battle of), xxx, xxxv

Waldberg, Jacob, 3, 5, 169
Walker, George, 234
Waring, George Houston, 112
Washburn, Gen. Cadwallader C., 186
Washington, Ga., 220, 223
Washington, William D., 253, 265
Watertown, N.Y., 286, 313
Wayne, Gen. Henry C., 142–43, 154
Way's Station (near Savannah, Ga.), 8, 11, 37, 155
West, Charles N., 38
Western and Atlantic Railroad. See Railroads
West Point, Ga., 46, 52, 53, 61
Wheeler, Gen. Joseph, 68, 120, 142, 253
White, B. F., 166
White Bluff (Savannah, Ga.), 30, 111, 155

White House (Washington, D.C.), 83
Whitemarsh Island (Savannah, Ga.),
  89, 99, 103, 134, 135, *155*
Whites, the (couple), 69
Willis, Pvt.William, 12
Wilmington, N.C., 180
Wisenbaker, James, 57
Wood, Jason S., 74, 79

Woodrow, James, xxiv
Woodrow family, 104
Wright, Gen. Ambrose, 144, 145

Zubly, David, xxxvii (n. 2)
Zubly, Helen, xxxvii (n. 2)
Zubly, John Joachim, xxxvii (n. 2)
Zubly family, xvi